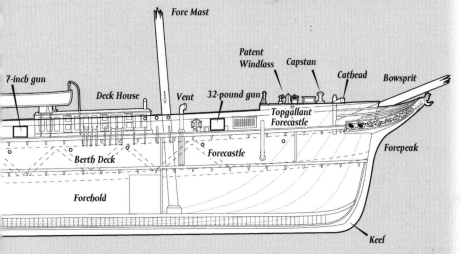

Fore Mast

Patent
Windlass

Capstan

Cathead

Bowsprit

7-inch gun

Deck House

Vent

32-pound gun

Topgallant
Forecastle

Forecastle

Berth Deck

Forehold

Forepeak

Keel

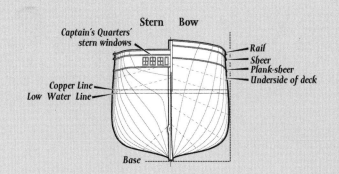

Stern   Bow

Captain's Quarters'
stern windows

Rail

Sheer

Plank-sheer

Underside of deck

Copper Line
Low Water Line

Base

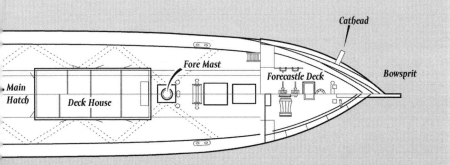

Cathead

Main
Hatch

Deck House

Fore Mast

Forecastle Deck

Bowsprit

SEA OF GRAY

SEA OF GRAY

The Around-the-World Odyssey of
the Confederate Raider *Shenandoah*

TOM CHAFFIN

Ⓗ Hill and Wang

A division of Farrar, Straus and Giroux

New York

Hill and Wang
A division of Farrar, Straus and Giroux
19 Union Square West, New York 10003

Grateful acknowledgment is made to the State Library of Victoria,
Melbourne, for permission to reprint the frontispiece image.

ISBN-13: 978-0-8090-9511-7
ISBN-10: 0-8090-9511-4

Designed by Jonathan D. Lippincott
Maps and endpapers designed by Joe LeMonnier

To my parents,
Martha Burch Chaffin and James Thomas Chaffin

In some unused lagoon, some nameless bay,
On sluggish, lonesome waters, anchor'd near the shore,
An old, dismasted, gray and batter'd ship, disabled, done,
After free voyages to all the seas of earth, haul'd up at last
and hawser'd tight,
Lies rusting, mouldering.

—Walt Whitman, "The Dismantled Ship"

Contents

Arctic Voyage of CSS *Shenandoah*

Bonded, burnt, or sunk:

A June 22–23
William Thompson
Euphrates
Milo
Sophia Thornton
Jireh Swift
Susan Abigail

B June 25–26
General Williams
Nimrod
William C. Nye
Catharine
General Pike
Isabella
Gypsey

C June 28
Waverly
Favorite
Brunswick
Hillman
Nassau
Isaac Howland
Martha
Covington
Congress
Nile
James Maury

ARCTIC
OCEAN

ALASKA

SIBERIA

Bering
Strait

Indian
Point

East
Cape

St.
Lawrence
Island

Cape Thaddeus

Cape Navarin

Cape Olyutorskiy

BERING SEA

Aleutian Islands

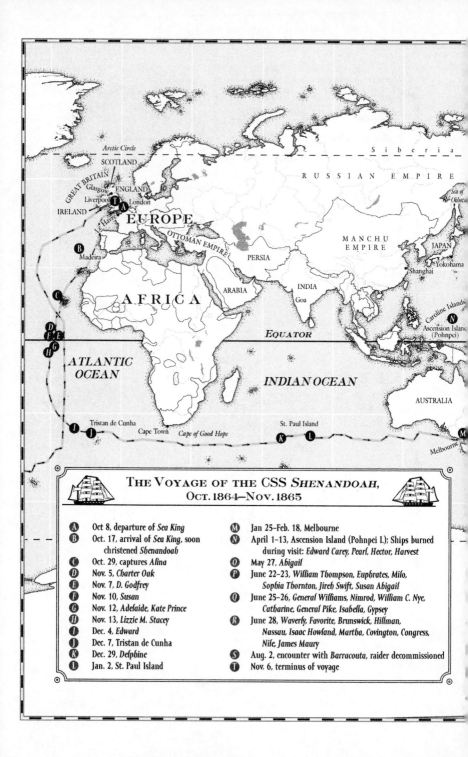

THE VOYAGE OF THE CSS *SHENANDOAH*, OCT. 1864–NOV. 1865

A Oct 8, departure of *Sea King*
B Oct. 17, arrival of *Sea King*, soon christened *Shenandoah*
C Oct. 29, captures *Alina*
D Nov. 5, *Charter Oak*
E Nov. 7, *D. Godfrey*
F Nov. 10, *Susan*
G Nov. 12, *Adelaide, Kate Prince*
H Nov. 13, *Lizzie M. Stacey*
I Dec. 4, *Edward*
J Dec. 7, Tristan de Cunha
K Dec. 29, *Delphine*
L Jan. 2, St. Paul Island

M Jan 25–Feb. 18, Melbourne
N April 1–13, Ascension Island (Pohnpei I.); Ships burned during visit: *Edward Carey, Pearl, Hector, Harvest*
O May 27, *Abigail*
P June 22–23, *William Thompson, Euphrates, Milo, Sophia Thornton, Jireh Swift, Susan Abigail*
Q June 25–26, *General Williams, Nimrod, William C. Nye, Catharine, General Pike, Isabella, Gypsey*
R June 28, *Waverly, Favorite, Brunswick, Hillman, Nassau, Isaac Howland, Martha, Covington, Congress, Nile, James Maury*
S Aug. 2, encounter with *Barracouta*, raider decommissioned
T Nov. 6, terminus of voyage

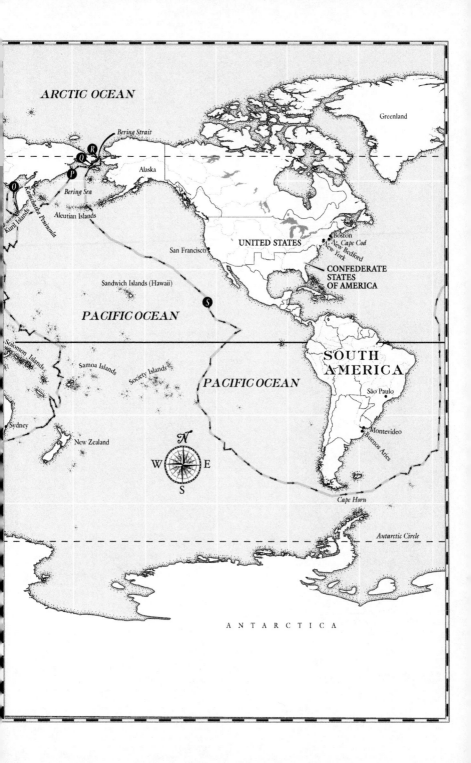

Sea of Gray

Of Ice Floes and Arctic Fires

It was just past 1:00 a.m., June 28, 1865, a few tilting spins of the earth beyond the year's longest day. And in the Bering Strait the hazy summer dawn breaking over the blue-white ice floes crowding its waters revealed a curious tableau: framed by the dark, distant, snow-crowned headlands to the east and west and, at a lower elevation, the two flat- and sheer-sided Diomede Islands tucked between those mainland heights, rose a forest of masts, sails, and rigging. Closer inspection revealed a listing three-masted whaleship. Moored to it by a web of radiating ropes bobbed five smaller vessels, the thirty-five-foot whaleboats that, on better days, the whaleship dispatched to harpoon the bowhead whales that brought white men to these remote climes. And, completing the scene, forming its outer perimeter, nine other whaling vessels swung at anchor in the eerily calm waters of this 37° F cloudless Arctic morning.

A day earlier the winds that often slice through this storied icy gut dividing North America and Asia had roiled those waters; swells had blown the *Brunswick*—the now-listing ship from New Bedford, Massachusetts—against one of the ice floes. During the summer these chunks of ice drift northward from

the Pacific to the Arctic through this fifty-mile-wide passage between Siberia's western and Alaska's eastern shores.

The collision stove a hole below the *Brunswick*'s waterline,
breaching the wooden planking and the copper-alloy sheathing
of her hull. Afterward the ship's officers and crew had done
their best to still the rush of seawater into the ship's holds. But
the ship's master, Alden T. Potter, knew that, with more than a
thousand miles of water between them and the nearest shipyard, he and his crew had little hope of repairing the vessel. In
the meantime, all he could do was what American captains had
always done in such situations: raise Old Glory upside down to
signal their distress to any ships that might sail by.

This being a busy passage in a busy whaling season, nine
other vessels, all flying the U.S. flag, soon lay anchored alongside the crippled *Brunswick*.

As the other whaling vessels answering the *Brunswick*'s distress
flag arrived, each vessel's master—as captains of commercial
ships are usually called—came aboard to survey the damage.
And each, in turn, concurred that the listing ship was a lost
cause. They also agreed with Captain Potter that his only re-
course was to fall back on the general custom under the circumstances: condemn the ship and auction off her cargo,
whaleboats, and whatever gear could be hauled off the vessel.
At the least, the *Brunswick*'s master could reduce some of the
losses to his ship's owner and insurers.

Decision made, they set to business and by the early morning of June 28 the auction had concluded. But as accounts
were being squared and sailors from the nine other whaling vessels were busy removing barrels and crates from the crippled
Brunswick, yet another ship hove into view, from the south.

Observing the ship's three masts and the plume of smoke rising from her, the whaling masters immediately concluded that she was an auxiliary steamer—so called because she was propelled by both wind and a steam-engine powered iron-screw propeller. Such vessels were rare, if not unknown, in these waters and, as the ship drew closer and they could see that she was flying a U.S. flag, speculation turned to her identity. Some thought the ship might belong to the Western Union Telegraph Expedition, yet another expression of America's ongoing commercial expansion, which continued even as the country was rent by civil war. That year the Expedition was conducting surveys for a cable to be stretched across the Bering Strait; the project sought to create a communications link—by way of Canada, Alaska, and Asia—between the United States and Europe.

Still others aboard the gathered whaleships speculated that the approaching steamship might be the Confederate raider that had, amid great controversy, stopped in Melbourne the previous winter. Over the past four years of war, the Confederates had dispatched at least twelve such cruisers into the world's oceans, charging them with destroying private, unarmed Union merchant, fishing, and whaling vessels. But the war was over. Weeks ago these sailors, when variously docked in San Francisco, Honolulu, and other ports, had read in newspapers that the war between the North and the South had ended nearly three months earlier. On April 9, Confederate general Robert E. Lee had surrendered the remnants of his Army of Northern Virginia to Union general Ulysses S. Grant at a place called Appomattox Courthouse, Virginia.

This latter fact dispelled much of the whalemen's anxiety. And who knew? Perhaps the approaching steamer could provide the *Brunswick*'s master and crew with passage out of this icy realm. Captain Jeremiah Ludlow of the *Isaac Howland*, one

of the whaling vessels gathered around the *Brunswick*, agreed
to carry Potter's request to the steamer. Dispatched in a whale-
boat, he soon stood on the steamer's deck. Ludlow failed to
learn the mystery ship's identity, and his reception by her officers had been a bit frosty. But they seemed to have expressed,
albeit in vague language, a willingness to provide passage for
Captain Potter and his men.

Later that day spirits aboard the *Brunswick* and the nine vessels grouped around her rose still higher. The men had spotted
a flotilla of five small boats, dispatched from the steamer, coming toward them. It seemed that the promised passage out of
the Bering Strait was about to be delivered. But, as the boats
came into clearer view, the sailors gathered on the decks of
the awaiting whaleships noticed that the approaching craft
carried uniformed Confederate navy officers. Moreover, almost
simultaneously, the whaling seamen heard a warning shot fired
in their direction from the steamer, and noticed that the Stars
and Stripes that had been waving over her foremast had been
hauled down. In its place rose the ensign of the Confederate
navy.

When the steamer had come within hailing range, one of the
Confederates shouted to the men gathered on the decks of the
ten whaling vessels: as of that moment, all of their ships and cargoes were prizes of the CSS *Shenandoah*. The Confederates ordered the more than three hundred men aboard the whaling
vessels—each carried a crew of up to thirty-five—to surrender
and come aboard the *Shenandoah* as prisoners of war. Failing
that, they could go down with their vessels, all of which the
Confederates threatened to destroy.

Alarm rippled across the decks of the whalers. Officers who
had assembled for the auction on the *Brunswick*'s decks rushed

back to their own vessels and began ordering their crews to weigh anchor and prepare to sail. Perhaps, they reasoned, if they could reach the nearby Siberian coast they would find diplomatic sanctuary inside Russian territory.

It was a futile hope. Unusually for this season and place, it was a windless day: no sailing vessels would be going anywhere quickly. And, in the end, the whaleships' masters aboard their unarmed vessels had little choice but to comply with the Confederates, who, that day and for the past few weeks, had stubbornly refused to believe the reports that had reached them of the war's end. Indeed, the master of the *William Thompson*, one of the captured whalers, recalled that a Confederate officer "exultantly stated that he did not believe Lee had surrendered."

As officers and men from the captured whalers began rowing to the *Shenandoah*, Confederate prize parties—small groups of seamen led by officers—commenced boarding the ten whaling vessels. Soon enough, the Confederates' plans became clear: two of the captured vessels, the *James Maury* and the *Nile*, would be "ransomed"—released after their masters had signed written promises stating that their vessels' owners would later pay the Confederate government a sum equal to the value of the vessels and their cargoes. Once the signatures were secured, those two vessels would be allowed to return to safe harbor in San Francisco.

The eight others would be burned to the waterline and sunk.

By 5:00 p.m. the prize parties from the *Shenandoah* were scurrying about all eight of the doomed vessels. In accordance with the Confederates' usual procedures, all crew members and living animals were removed from each ship. Likewise, all useful equipment, gunpowder, or stores were confiscated and taken back to the *Shenandoah*. Afterward, the parties searched the whaling vessels' holds for any available combustibles, including whale products, pitch, tar, and turpentine. These they spread throughout the vessels. Bulkheads, the upright walls compartmentalizing each vessel, were torn down and piled in cabins and forecastles; the bulkheads' destruction at once created fuel and improved draft for the fire to come. The Confederates then opened all the hatches and cut the rigging. With no wind, the sails hung limp and free. Finally, before leaving, the prize parties took fires from each of the eight ships' galley stoves and dispersed flames throughout the main decks and the holds.

A Confederate officer aboard the *Shenandoah* who witnessed the conflagration recalled "a scene never to be forgotten by any one who beheld it." As flames consumed them, the eight crewless vessels drifted like crazed, rudderless ghost ships amid the ice floes. "The red glare from the eight burning vessels shone far and wide over the drifting ice of those savage seas; the crackling of the fire as it made its devouring way through each doomed ship fell on the still air like upbraiding voices." Chaos reigned: "The sea was filled with boats driving hither and thither, with no hand to guide them, and with yards, sails, and cordage, remnants of the stupendous ruin there progressing. In the distance, but where the light fell strong and red upon them, bringing out into bold relief each spar and line, were the two ransomed vessels, the Noah's Arks that were to bear away the human life which in a few hours would be all that was left of the gallant whaling fleet."[1]

Sixteen years after General Robert E. Lee's troops stacked their muskets at Appomattox Courthouse, the Confederacy's president, Jefferson Davis, recalled the events of mid-1865 from a decidedly different perspective than that experienced by those aboard the *Shenandoah* and her fleet of captive whaleships amid the Bering Strait's ice floes.

In early April, as Union forces gathered outside Richmond, Virginia, the capital of the Confederacy, Davis—acting on advice from General Lee—had ordered the city's evacuation. By then, Lee's beleaguered Army of Northern Virginia, fleeing a Union advance, had marched west of Richmond, hoping to escape and fight another day. Davis and his cabinet, meanwhile, took a southwest train for Danville, Virginia. There Davis lingered long enough to issue a proclamation calling for continued resistance to Union forces. With Yankee troops hard on his heels, he then drifted farther and farther south: through Virginia's fields and leafy forests, into North Carolina, South Carolina, and eventually Georgia.

As Davis's scattered generals—Lee, Joseph Johnston, and Richard Taylor, among others—one after another, laid down their arms, the fifty-six-year-old president, deep into spring, still nourished stubborn hopes. If he could somehow link up with Southern troops still in the field, perhaps those in Texas under General Edmund Kirby Smith, he and his brethren in gray might reconstitute themselves as a guerrilla movement. And, if they could do that, who knew how long the Confederacy might be able to fight on? Perhaps long enough to exhaust a war-weary Northern public.

On May 10, Davis's luck, and with it his dreams, ran out: Union soldiers in Irwinville, Georgia, finally caught up with and arrested him. Three weeks later, General Smith's forces in Texas surrendered; and on June 23, the Cherokee chief and Confederate general Stand Watie, aware of Smith's surrender, accepted the inevitable. He galloped into the tiny Indian Territory hamlet of Fort Towson—in today's Oklahoma—and surrendered his battalion of Cherokee, Seminole, and Osage Indians to Union forces. The Confederacy had officially become a lost cause.

Even so, as former Confederate president Davis, now Union prisoner, recalled in his memoirs, one thought did bring him solace: "the Confederate flag no longer floated on land, but one gallant sailor still unfurled it on the Pacific"—"Captain Waddell, commanding the Shenandoah cruiser."

Then, en route to the Bering Sea, Waddell and his crew had been ignorant of the comfort their efforts lent their stateless president. Nor, for that matter, as they later claimed, did they know that, by then, they sailed without state or purpose. But just as war will have its heroes and its tragedies, so, inevitably, will it have its ironies. That the task of firing the final shot associated with that entire four-year ordeal of death and destruction fell to Waddell and the men of his *Shenandoah* was surely one of them.[2]

Boreal dawns, ice floes, and burning whaleships hardly belong to our usual mental repository of Civil War images. Such scenes evoke *Moby-Dick* more than they do *The Red Badge of Courage*. That the *Shenandoah* captured those ten whaling vessels in the Bering Strait more than two months after General Lee's surrender at Appomattox Courthouse adds only more incongruity. But on June 28, 1865, the obvious ironies, much like Davis's solace, meant nothing to the men gathered off this Arctic shore. For the whalemen and the owners of the destroyed ships, the consequences were tragic. For Waddell and his crew, oddly enough, heroism of a sort would soon be called for.

The *Shenandoah* began her life as the *Sea King*, a Scottish-built commercial steamer. Acquired by the Confederacy, she was, in October 1864, refitted as a man-of-war. Rechristened as the *Shenandoah*, she undertook a thirteen-month, 58,000-mile voyage, becoming the only Confederate vessel to circumnavigate the globe. During much of that tour, the sleek black 220-foot Confederate "commerce raider" dutifully followed orders, destroying thirty-two Union merchant and whaling vessels, and ransoming another six. The total value of the captured ships came to $1.4 million. During much of the final months of their cruise, however, the Confederates of the *Shenandoah* were on the run, their orders as meaningless as the strategy that once emboldened them, with captain and crew no better than pirates in the eyes of a victorious Union.

The origins of the *Shenandoah*'s destructive errand reach back to the beginnings of the Civil War, the earliest Union war strategy in that conflict, and the Confederacy's response to it. During the first few weeks of the war, the Union's chief general, Winfield Scott—resisting calls to answer Confederate belligerence with an invasion of Virginia—devised a strategy that, instead of emphasizing invasion, called for a slow strangling of the region's economic life. His strategy—soon derided by critics as the "Anaconda plan"—sought, simultaneously, to isolate the Confederacy's eleven states from one another and from the rest of the world. Scott called for Union gunboats to push down the Mississippi and other main rivers of the South, thus dividing and subdividing the region into increasingly isolated and vulnerable parts; he also called for a blockade by Union ships of the South's long coasts along the Atlantic Ocean and the Gulf of Mexico.

Pursuant to that strategy, President Lincoln, on April 19, 1861, proclaimed a Federal blockade of all Southern ports. The announcement heightened the sense of urgency among Southern war planners, but in truth the Confederates had already been anticipating a naval war. More aggressively than their Union counterparts, Confederate naval strategists had been planning for a war on the South's rivers, along its coasts, and on the world's oceans.

Enlightened strategists on both sides of the Mason-Dixon line knew of, and were inspired by, recent—and dramatic—advances in naval technology. As one historian has noted, if a contemporary of the sixteenth-century navigator Sir Francis Drake could have traveled ahead in time, he would have been entirely comfortable aboard a warship of the 1840s. But he would have been lost aboard one designed during the 1860s.[3] The French had shown the way. During the Crimean War, the French Navy, deploying slow-sailing, iron-sheathed barges, had devastated Russian defenses at Fort Constantine. On both sides of the Atlantic, the consensus among military planners quietly became that the future of naval warfare belonged to steam-powered ironclad ships armed with rifled, exploding-shell guns.

At the outset of the American Civil War, the United States, with its bustling industrial cities and factories, its navy, and its civilian merchant fleet, enjoyed obvious advantages over the largely agricultural South, which, for the most part, lacked such traditions. Though the South's wealth was built, in large part, on the export of cotton, the staple sailed from Southern ports in ships owned, in most cases, by merchants of the North and Great Britain.

Compared to the Confederacy, the United States, in both number of vessels and tonnage, boasted an impressive merchant fleet—second in size only to that of Great Britain. Moreover, the U.S. Navy possessed ninety ships. Even so, those advantages on paper concealed serious problems. At the Civil War's onset, of those ninety ships only forty were steamers. The others were in shipyards for repairs or still under construction. And nineteen vessels lay scattered at ports across the globe. Only six steamers sat in U.S. ports, ready to sail.[4]

To counter that shortage the U.S. Navy, through commercial brokers, began purchasing and chartering privately owned merchant ships. The sudden end of the North-South cotton trade, and the dangers of trying to run the Federal naval blockade, left scores of freight and passenger ships idle, and the U.S. Navy quickly began purchasing these vessels. In the first few months of the war, New York merchant George D. Morgan alone eventually added eighty-nine vessels to the Navy's fleet, prompting a public outcry against his 2.5 percent commission for each transaction. But, ranging from ferries to cargo ships, this magpie fleet offered no substitute for the steam-driven, ironclad, shallow-draft ships the war demanded.[5]

To make matters worse, President Lincoln selected as his Navy secretary Gideon Welles—a fifty-eight-year-old Connecticut-born former journalist and political appointee with scant background in naval matters. His only nautical background consisted of a four-year term in the 1840s as chief of the Navy's Bureau of Provisions and Clothing. Upon taking office, Welles, even as the administration prepared for war, showed no eagerness to supply the Navy with modern ships of war. Not until July of 1861—three months after the Confederate attack on Fort Sumter—did he get around to recommending to Congress the creation of a committee to consider the construction of ironclad vessels. And not until October—following Congress's eventual authorization to build such vessels—did the U.S. Navy order the construction of three ironclads.[6]

The Confederate navy chief was a different sort of man entirely. At the war's start, Stephen Mallory presided over a motley fleet of ten vessels armed with a total of fifteen mounted guns.[7] It had only one advantage: Mallory.

A vigorous exponent of naval modernization with broad expertise in maritime matters, Mallory, then in his early fifties, had grown up in Key West, where he spent much of his youth working in the islands' "wrecking"—oceanic salvage—industry. Afterward, he performed military service in the Second Seminole War (1835–39), and eventually became a popular politician among Florida Democrats. In 1850 he won a seat in the U.S. Senate, where, four years later, he became chairman of its Naval Affairs Committee.

In the U.S. Senate, Mallory became one of the era's most vigorous advocates of naval modernization. And, upon taking up his duties for the Confederacy, he brought that same spirit to the task of assembling his new nation's navy. In particular, he believed, the acquisition—whether by construction or purchase—of modern ironclad warships offered the Confederate navy its quickest means of gaining a rough parity with the U.S. Navy. In May 1861, two months before Welles thought even to convene a committee to consider the subject, Mallory flatly declared to the chairman of the Confederate Congress's Committee on Naval Affairs, "Inequality of numbers may be compensated by invulnerability; and thus not only does economy but naval success dictate the wisdom and expedience of fighting with iron against wood, without regard to first cost."[8]

But Mallory also knew that it would take time to build ironclads. He knew, too, that the Confederate search for merchant vessels that could be converted into ships of war would yield nothing like the Union's similar efforts. And so he turned to a strategy with a long pedigree in U.S. history: privateering, the commissioning and arming of private vessels to prey on the enemy's merchant fleet.

During the American Revolution and the War of 1812, privateers commissioned by the U.S. government had, by attacking the enemy's private merchant ships, increased the cost of war for their adversaries. Moreover, those attacks had been able to draw enemy military ships away from theaters of war as merchants clamored for protection.

Aware of that tradition, months before the Civil War erupted, Raphael Semmes—destined to play a major role in the Confederate navy—had proposed to a Confederate congressman the South's creation of "a well-organized system of private armed ships." Privateering, Semmes believed, appealed to Southern patriotism and to "private cupidity": "Even New England ships, and New England capital would be at your service, in abundance." From the Confederate navy, he vowed, "all that will be required . . . will be to put it under sufficient legal restraints, to prevent it from degenerating into piracy."[9]

Letters of marque—essentially, licenses issued by sovereign states to the captains of private ships authorizing the plunder of enemy merchant ships—exempted privateers from prosecution as pirates. Traditionally, the letters also allowed privateers to enter neutral ports with their prizes, which could be sold at considerable profit.

The difference between privateer and pirate was, literally, paper-thin; the legal force of a letter of marque made the difference. Even so, by the mid-nineteenth century privateering had fallen into disrepute among the world's major naval powers. In 1856 diplomats representing Great Britain, France, Prussia, Austria, Turkey, and Russia gathered in Paris and signed a treaty in which each agreed to forgo privateering—and otherwise not to grant right of entry to their ports by privateers representing enemies of signatories to the ban. The United States, however, declined to join the agreement. Although American naval officers shared the growing international disdain for the practice, the U.S. Navy, compared with that of other powers, possessed a fleet that was far from formidable. Its naval strategists were thus reluctant to abandon a practice that offered compelling advantages to underdog navies. As then secretary of state William M. Marcy told the Europeans, if his own nation abandoned privateering, "the dominion over the seas will be surrendered to those powers which have the means of keeping up large navies." By 1861, precisely because of the accuracy of that observation, Union strategists regretted not having signed the treaty.[10]

On April 24, 1861, days after the fall of Fort Sumter, Secretary of State Seward asked Charles Francis Adams, the U.S minister in Great Britain, to express the U.S. government's desire to enter into negotiations toward becoming a signatory to the 1856 Declaration of Paris. Too late. In separate replies, both the British and French governments responded that they welcomed the newfound U.S. interest in the accord. But they added that so far as they were concerned any resulting agreement would not affect their current, nominally neutral position regarding the conflict between the United States and the Confederacy. Simply put, both nations were disposed to granting Confederate privateers all rights traditionally accorded privateers.

But that disposition, as it turned out, was brief. On April 17, 1861, President Davis issued a proclamation offering "letters of marque and reprisal" to the owners of private vessels who were willing to hunt down and destroy enemy merchant ships. And on May 13, Great Britain—followed soon by other European powers—issued a proclamation of official neutrality in the conflict between the North and the South. Such pronouncements gave Confederate ships most of the rights accorded belligerents in time of war, including the right of Confederate naval ships and privateers to enter neutral ports. By the fall of 1861, however, long-standing Confederate hopes of military assistance from Great Britain abruptly peaked and, just as quickly, vanished. That November, Union captain Charles Wilkes seized two Confederate diplomats and their secretaries from the deck of the English mail steamer *Trent* in the Caribbean Sea. In the wake of the incident—a deep affront to official British pride—Confederate hopes of diplomatic recognition by and assistance from London surged. But just as quickly, conciliatory messages from Secretary of State Seward to British officials and the eventual release of the two Confederates resolved the controversy.

On January 31, 1862—underscoring its growing determination to avoid being drawn into the war—Queen Victoria's government greatly restricted access by Confederate ships to British ports, and altogether banned the entry of privateer prizes.

From the beginning, Stephen Mallory knew that his fleet's ultimate fate would not be shaped by privateers, nor by the ships left behind by the Union's mismanaged, hasty departure from the U.S. Navy yard in Norfolk, Virginia, nor by British diplomatic actions. From the start, he knew his main challenge was the task of building or buying new ships; for that purpose, he resolved, Confederate agents must go to Europe. The Confederate navy needed two types of vessels: to attack U.S. Navy warships blockading Southern ports, Mallory's navy needed advanced ironclad vessels; and, to augment its small, short-range fleet of privateers, the South also needed a fleet of commerce raiders—ships belonging to the Confederate navy that were devoted to destroying the private merchant fleet of the United States.

In all, the Confederacy commissioned twelve commerce raiders. Their importance to the South—if not strategically, then as boosters of morale and sources of propaganda—became increasingly important over time. For the first few years of the war, the Union blockade of the South's ports was largely ineffective. But by 1865, as U.S. Navy tactics improved, the Union cordon increasingly constricted shipping into and from those ports. That tightening, in turn, made Confederate efforts to attack the blockade, and to slip through it, increasingly futile. Adding to Rebel woes, the Union's capture of the inland Mississippi River port of Vicksburg in April 1863 effectively split the Confederacy into eastern and western sections, rendering Southern military actions on its rivers and coasts all the more futile. Discouraged by those naval setbacks and grimmer defeats in the land war, the Confederate public found succor in reading of triumphs in far-flung oceanic realms by such commerce raiders as the *Florida*, the *Alabama*—and, in time, the *Shenandoah*.[11]

Two

"A Good, Capital Ship in Every Respect"

James Dunwoody Bulloch, a formidable thirty-eight-year-old Georgia-born mariner, directed the Confederacy's operations in Europe from 10 Rumford Place, Liverpool, England. Bald but with a thick mustache and thicker muttonchop sideburns, Bulloch had hawkish features and an intense gaze that gave him away for what he was—an energetic aristocrat with an eye for details. Born into a distinguished Georgia family, as a young man he had served in the U.S. Navy, and afterward, for twenty years, on private merchant ships. Indeed, Bulloch's background in business and commercial trade, rare among naval officers, rendered him more valuable than other senior officers in the Confederate navy.

After his native Georgia seceded from the Union, Bulloch—beloved "Uncle Jimmy" to his nephew and future president Theodore Roosevelt—traveled to Montgomery, Alabama, the Confederacy's capital before it moved to Richmond, Virginia, to offer his services to navy secretary Stephen Mallory. And at their first meeting, on May 8, 1861, Mallory could not have been more direct: "It was thought to be of prime importance to get cruisers"—commerce raiders—"at sea as soon as possible, to harass the enemy's commerce, and to compel him to send his own ships-of-war in pursuit, which might otherwise be employed in blockading the Southern ports."

From the war's earliest months, Mallory had promoted a fleet of commerce raiders. Inexpensive and built for ocean speed, "with a battery of one or two accurate guns of long range, with an ability to keep the sea upon a long cruise and to engage or to avoid an enemy at will," such vessels could exploit the vulnerabilities under which cargo ships of the day still sailed.[1] In the 1860s, most of the world's marine commerce traveled on ships dependent on known wind and ocean currents for propulsion. That reliance meant that merchant fleets, though departing from various ports, traveled on well-known tracks and regularly converged and gathered in predictable locales in the world's oceans and along its coastlines, rendering these largely unarmed ships vulnerable to hit-and-run attacks by armed steam-powered cruisers. The fact that electronic communications at sea—telegraph, radio—had yet to be developed only compounded that vulnerability. Ironically, the U.S. Navy officer largely responsible, during the 1840s, for gathering and publishing that oceanic data—now turned against U.S. merchant ships—was none other Matthew Fontaine Maury, who by 1864 was a Confederate naval officer based in England, assisting in the procurement of oceangoing raiders.

Early in the war, Mallory began sending officers to Europe to purchase or build the ships he needed. During the course of the conflict, 104 Confederate naval officers found their way to Britain and the Continent, many charged with procuring ships, armaments, and other supplies. Such work often entailed constant movement from country to country and, as European neutrality hardened, cloak if not dagger.

There were contracts to negotiate, finished goods to inspect, officers to assign, crews to raise—and in a perfect world

Mallory would have created a clear-cut chain of command in Europe to coordinate these activities. But, instead, he tended to dispatch agents abroad who had no clear idea how they might work together. The result was mammoth waste and duplication of efforts, problems compounded by communication difficulties between Europe and Richmond, and even within Europe. Moreover, the inevitable indiscretions that came with having so many agents in the field increased their exposure by U.S. diplomats in Europe, as well as by European governments. The early neutrality of European governments toward the Confederacy had steadily evolved, from benign indifference to willful avoidance of any connection with what by the fall of 1863 seemed a doomed Southern cause.

From the start, Confederate hopes in Europe centered on two countries: Great Britain and France. The South, through its cotton trade, had long-standing ties with Britain, home to the world's most advanced shipyards. And France, which hoped to win control over Mexico, owed a debt of gratitude to the Confederacy for its quiet approval of that project. Commensurate with that diplomatic narrowing of the European field, by late 1863 three men, all of them former U.S. Navy officers, had emerged as the Confederate navy's chief European operatives—in France, Commodore Samuel Barron, and in England, Captain Matthew Maury and Commander James D. Bulloch.[2]

Barron reached Europe in October 1863 and was charged with taking command of a fleet of ten ships then being built in France and Great Britain. Eventually both countries, weighing consequences, blocked the release of those ships. Barron, who continued to hold the title of flag officer of the Confederate navy's European squadron, spent much of the rest of the war in

Paris recruiting officers for ships obtained by other Confederate agents in Britain—particularly those obtained by James Bulloch.

Of all the Confederate agents in Europe, none rivaled the eventual successes that Bulloch enjoyed. Of the eight major Confederate cruisers put to sea during the Civil War, all but two, the *Sumter* and the *Nashville*, were British-built. And of those built in Britain the three that most harmed America's commercial fleet—the *Florida*, the *Alabama*, and the *Shenandoah*—were put to sea by Bulloch.

Before dispatching Bulloch to England via Detroit and Montreal, and arming him with "wide discretionary power" to draw on deposited Confederate funds, Mallory, in a parting conversation, turned to diplomatic matters. He expected, he said, that Great Britain and other European powers would eventually extend various informal diplomatic courtesies to what, Mallory believed, the Europeans viewed as "the *de facto* Government at Montgomery." But, Mallory added, formal recognition of the Confederacy by those governments, if extended, would not come until the South had achieved "some substantial victories in the field." Commerce raiders held promise of yielding quick, if not decisive, evidence of Confederate prowess.

A raider's modus operandi was fairly simple. Upon spotting an enemy merchant ship, she would chase her down or draw her into closer range by flying false colors. The raider then fired a shot over the ship's bow, and, after her prey was brought to a halt, a party from the raider boarded the ship to collect papers and perhaps officers to be brought back to the Confederate ship's captain. The raider's captain would then determine whether the captured vessel and her cargo were the property of U.S. owners. If not, the ship was released. But if Yankee ownership was ascertained the ship's officers and crew, as well as any cargo and gear that might prove useful to the raider, would be confiscated. Then the ship was scuttled or set afire.

After her March 1862 launch, the *Florida*, over the next two years, captured and burned thirty-seven Union merchant ships in the east Atlantic before being captured off the coast of Brazil. The legendary *Alabama*, the second of the cruisers built for Bulloch in England, proved even more successful. Captained by Raphael Semmes and launched from Liverpool in late July of 1862, the ship, over the next twenty-three months—roaming as far as the Indian Ocean and the coast of Vietnam—captured more than sixty Union vessels. In June 1864, she was finally sunk off the coast of Cherbourg, France.

By early 1864, political, military, and diplomatic reversals, coupled with increasingly zealous surveillance by foreign and U.S. officials, had rendered it nearly impossible for Bulloch to commission the construction of any more warships in Europe. Bulloch, consequently, narrowed his overseas activities to the purchase of already constructed ships—and, at that, only ships of a commercial character. From the outset, British laws, designed to thwart British subjects and ships from contributing to foreign war efforts, demanded that Confederate agents exercise native cunning. Prior to sailing his ships from England, Bulloch registered each with a third-party, British owner. And only after being put to sea was the vessel, upon rendezvousing with a Confederate tender ship, armed and otherwise converted to a warship. At that point, title to the newly created man-of-war was transferred to the Confederate navy and the vessel was rechristened with a new name. Aware that a single conviction for having violated British law could end his entire mission, Bulloch, he recalled, made it "manifestly necessary to act with prudence and caution." No less aware of the stakes, U.S. diplomats and their hireling spies grew ever more aggressive in their surveillance.[3]

By mid-July, the *Alabama*'s destruction off France's Atlantic coast left Navy secretary Mallory determined to put another raider to sea as soon as possible, partly for strategic purposes but also to bolster the Confederacy's morale. As he wrote to Bulloch, "The loss of the *Alabama* was announced in the Federal papers with all the manifestations of joy which usually usher the news of great national victories, showing that the calculating enemy fully understood and appreciated the importance of her destruction. You must supply her place if possible."[4]

Ironically, however, the very success of the *Florida*, the *Alabama*, and other Confederate cruisers had added one more dilemma to those confronting Bulloch: toward what end would any new raiders be directed? Earlier cruisers, after all, had succeeded beyond the Confederates' wildest expectations. Writing to Mallory the previous February, Bulloch had reported, "There really seems nothing for our ships to do now upon the open sea." Even in the Pacific, passing mariners noticed a conspicuous absence of U.S. ships. As one correspondent wrote, "The master of a French ship reported not one American ship at the Guano Islands off Peru, where in 1863, seventy or eighty had waited impatiently for their profitable cargoes."[5]

By early spring, however, Mallory had a new target in mind. That March, in a letter to Bulloch, he proposed redeploying existing commerce raiders and acquiring new ones for a concerted assault on New England's globally dispersed fishing and whaling fleet. The *Alabama*, the *Florida*, and other raiders had already made sporadic attacks on New England's whaling vessels operating off the Azores and other Atlantic islands; likewise, there had been raids on fishing schooners off the New England coast. What Mallory now envisioned was something on a grander scale. By driving up operating costs and insurance rates for New England's fishing and whaling industries, he believed, the Confederate navy would render the region a powerful lobby in Washington devoted to ending the war. As he put it, "The simultaneous appearance of efficient cruisers on the New England coast and fishing banks, in the West Indies and South Atlantic, in the Pacific among the whalemen, and in the East Indies, would have a decided tendency to turn the trading mind of New England to thoughts of peace."[6]

The Confederate public and its leaders closely followed U.S. politics. And in recent months Southern hopes for an early peace had come to rest on the Democratic presidential campaign of retired Union general George B. McClellan. That summer, the general had been directing his campaign to a war-weary Union public; and, across the North and South, it was widely believed that, if victorious, McClellan would immediately sue for peace, perhaps even strike a deal with the South to allow it to peacefully reenter the Union with its system of slavery intact. By attacking New England's whaling industry, thereby inflicting economic losses on New England and the rest of the Union, Mallory believed, the Confederacy would drive voters to McClellan. By August, however, continuing Confederate setbacks, ongoing funding problems, and Bulloch's growing difficulties in acquiring ships led Mallory to refine his plans. Under the circumstances, his earlier idea of outfitting several cruisers to attack the New England fleet proved overly ambitious. Thus, in this more conservative version of his original strategy, two such ships would be fine. But instead of attacking fishing fleets in general, Mallory ordered Bulloch to focus attention on New England's Pacific whaling fleet.

Mallory's latest idea emerged during conversations with two Confederate naval officers—Commanders John Mercer Brooke and Robert R. Carter—both graduates of the U.S.

Naval Academy in Annapolis, Maryland, who had served aboard a U.S. Navy surveying expedition, conducted between 1853 and 1856, of the North Pacific Ocean. A broad scientific survey, the expedition had sailed as far north as the Bering Strait, and had taken both men, Bulloch later recalled, "over the routes and localities frequented by the whalers." In their conversations with Mallory, both officers recalled with awe the size of the New England fleet that "each summer, hunts the bowhead whale in the waters in and around the Bering Strait."

Mallory liked Brooke and Carter's proposal. And, like his earlier but now dismissed idea of an assault on New England's fishing fleet, Mallory liked the fact that this newer proposal entailed an attack on a vital industry of New England, spiritual home of American abolitionism and, for that reason, traditionally the South's fiercest ideological enemy. As he soon put it in a letter to Bulloch, "A blow at the whalemen is a blow at New England exclusively." But beyond that, such an attack—on a heretofore unprecedented scale—on New England's whaling fleet offered a chance to forcefully strike at a major U.S. industry, one that simultaneously played a vital role in American economic life and served as a training ground for the Union's mariners. As Mallory went on, "The enemy's distant whaling grounds have not been visited by us. His commerce constitutes one of his reliable sources of national wealth no less than one of his best schools for seamen."

It soon became clear, however, that only one ship could be fitted out. Fortunately, Commander John Mercer Brooke had one in mind. The previous fall, while he was in England, Brooke had joined Bulloch on a visit to the docks of Glasgow, Scotland.

There, both men had taken notice of a steamer named the *Sea King*, which seemed perfect for such a raiding expedition.

Bulloch later recalled the moment the two men spotted her: "In the course of our search we caught sight of a fine, composite, full-rigged ship, with something more than auxiliary steam-power, and all the necessary arrangements for disconnecting and lifting her screw. We were charmed with the ship, but could make only a very hasty and imperfect inspection of her, as she was in all the bustle of loading for her first foreign voyage. I took, however, a careful note of her"—including the fact that the ship was about to embark on a voyage to New Zealand that would take about ten months.

Now committed to attacking the whaling fleet, Mallory, in late September of 1864, dispatched the other of that strategy's co-authors, Commander Robert R. Carter, to Liverpool with a letter for Bulloch instructing him to purchase the *Sea King*. With the letter, Mallory also enclosed a memo from Commander Brooke providing a detailed itinerary for the proposed Arctic expedition.[7]

Carter reached Liverpool, and Bulloch, on September 28. As it happened, however, long before Carter's arrival Bulloch was already positioning himself to acquire the *Sea King*. The previous summer, acting on Mallory's earlier orders to find a ship to replace the *Alabama*, Bulloch had dispatched Richard Wright, a Liverpool shipping merchant more keen for profits than naturally sympathetic to the Confederacy, to search British ports for an auxiliary steamer. Coincidentally, Wright, in Glasgow, came across the same steamer—now returned from New Zealand—that had caught Bulloch and Carter's attention in the fall of 1863. As Bulloch later recalled: "He reported at once by telegraph and posted a letter the same day, advising me that the ship had just been discharged, was then entirely empty, and could thus be thoroughly inspected, but that she was already under partial engagement for another voyage, and if I wanted to secure her no time was to be lost."

Bulloch telegraphed back, instructing Wright to inspect the ship and, if all seemed in order, to purchase it. Inspection done, Wright did just that. And on September 16 Bulloch had the pleasure of writing to Mallory:

> I have now the satisfaction to inform you of the purchase of a fine composite ship, built for the Bombay trade, and just returned from her first voyage. She is 1,160 tons builder's measurement, classed A-1, for 14 years at Lloyd's; frames, beams etc., of iron, but planked from keel to gunwale with East Indian teak. She is full rigged as a ship, with rolling topsails, has plenty of accommodations for officers of all grades, and 'tween decks 7 feet 6 inches high with large air ports, having been fitted under Government inspection for the transport of troops.

Moreover, Bulloch proudly announced, "my broker has had her carefully examined by Lloyd's [of London] inspectors, who pronounced her a good capital ship in every respect."[8]

After Wright purchased the *Sea King*, Bulloch, aware that he was being watched, resolved to stay far away from the Confederacy's newest acquisition: "I knew that to set my foot upon her deck, or to be reported at any time within visual range of her, would be the immediate occasion of a consular report to Mr. [Charles Francis] Adams, which would be promptly forwarded to [British foreign minister] Earl Russell . . . and the hope of getting the ship to sea as a Confederate cruiser would be nipped in the bud." Indeed, "it was absolutely necessary to permit no one having the faintest odour of 'rebellion' about him to go near her." Beyond that, "she must be provided with an owner who would be willing to sell her again at an out-port, and who could be trusted to see that the essentials for her alleged voyage would be provided, and that all requirements of the law would be complied with."

From a distance, Bulloch began focusing on how to modify the steamer for her next cruise. Prior to her most recent voyage—leased to the British Army to transport troops to New Zealand to suppress a Maori rebellion—the vessel's berthing quarters had undergone modifications. Even so, she remained very much a merchant ship. Before commencing her run as a raider, the *Sea King* would need to be fitted for and armed with cannons, and her storage spaces reconfigured to create a magazine in which to store her ammunition. But Bulloch also knew that any modifications of the ship "not in harmony with her mercantile character . . . would cause inquiry." Such work would have to wait until the vessel was safely beyond England.[9] And though Liverpool was notoriously sympathetic to the Confederacy, merely having it moored there posed risks. Accordingly, after the purchase he ordered Wright to sail the *Sea King*, carrying a full load of coal, to London. The ruse was designed to bolster public declarations that the ship was embarking on a routine coal run to Bombay and a continuing voyage to other ports, the entire time at sea "not to exceed two years." To deflect surveillance, he instructed Wright, while en route to London, to make stops at other British ports—and so further the impression that the vessel was merely another cargo ship on a commercial venture.[10]

As Wright set about his busy voyage of appearances, Bulloch began purchasing arms and provisions for the ship's Arctic voyage. Simultaneously, he dispatched agents to find a suitable tender—a supply vessel that, loaded with those provisions, could rendezvous with the *Sea King* somewhere beyond British waters. There, beyond the legal reach of Crown officials, the cargo aboard the supply ship would transform the *Sea King* from a commercial vessel to a man-of-war. Bulloch eventually located the *Laurel*, a trim, iron-screw steamer then engaged in packet service between Ireland and Liverpool. And, after a brief run aboard the ship to observe her performance, he purchased the steamer and placed it in the hands of Henry Lafone, a Liverpool shipping agent sympathetic to the Confederacy who was already deeply enmeshed in blockade running.

Bulloch also needed Confederate naval officers for his Arctic cruise. His emerging plans called for them to gather in Liverpool, depart England aboard the tender ship *Laurel*, and only later be transferred to the *Sea King*. Once again, however, stepped-up British and U.S. surveillance of Confederate activities had to be circumvented. Following correspondence with Commodore Samuel Barron, Bulloch named Lieutenant William C. Whittle, Jr., as first lieutenant. And when Bulloch's first choice for captain proved unavailable, the commodore assigned command of the ship to Lieutenant James Iredell Waddell.

Waddell and his wife, Ann, were already living in Liverpool. Ordered there in the spring 1863, Waddell had arrived in England that May to take up service on one of two Confederate ironclads then under construction at the vast Birkenhead Ironworks, on the River Mersey, opposite Liverpool. But the vessels' seizure by British officials in October 1863 left Waddell without a ship to command and forced to follow the war from a distance. The carnage of the Battle of Gettysburg, amply photographed, had conveyed a sense of the tide turning against the

Confederacy, a sense not fully erased by its subsequent victory at the Battle of Chickamauga. With little else to do but read newspaper accounts of distant events, Waddell welcomed the order from Barron to begin making preparations to command what would be the Confederates' newest commerce raider. Bulloch then selected four other young lieutenants to join Whittle, and by early October all five lieutenants—as well as lower-ranking officers—had reached Liverpool.

Typical of the experiences of these newly appointed officers of the soon-to-be-launched raider were those of John T. Mason and Orris A. Browne, both midshipmen living in Abbeville, France. Upon receiving their orders, the two left for England. Arriving in Liverpool on Monday morning, October 3, they checked into the Adelphi Hotel, then went directly to Bulloch's office at 10 Rumford Place, where they met two other recruits who had recently arrived, Lieutenants Francis Chew and Dabney Scales. Bulloch welcomed the men and promised that they would soon be given funds for the purchase of uniforms and other necessities, but otherwise he provided only the vaguest outlines of the planned cruise. After telling the men to avoid his office thereafter, Bulloch said they should be ready to sail as early as the following Saturday. Beyond that, Mason recalled, "he simply told us that we were to live as quietly as possible."

That would be possible only after Mason and Browne had quitted the Adelphi. As Bulloch had told them, the hotel "was crowded with Yankee spies." Before the two officers checked out, Bulloch, aware that the presence of Confederate sailors in Liverpool was hardly a secret, had instructed them to "spread the report that we were going home." At the least, then, they could broadcast the diversionary story that they were about to sail for the Confederacy, perhaps to take up service along its coast.

The next morning, Mason and Browne, spreading the news that they were homeward-bound, checked out of the Adelphi Hotel and found new quarters in a nearby rooming house. There Waddell visited them and provided the funds promised by Bulloch—in Mason's case, thirty-five pounds. Soon they also met with First Lieutenant William C. Whittle, Jr., the ship's twenty-four-year-old executive officer. Orders were issued "to have our baggage ready by Friday & that our trunks were to be enclosed in wooden boxes in order to go aboard the ship as freight," Mason recalled. "Every thing was done with the utmost secrecy."

By early October, Captain Waddell had gathered what he considered to be a formidable group of officers for his ship. But he also needed a crew, and for the *Sea King* to be fully manned Waddell figured that in addition to his officers he would need about sixty seamen. The Foreign Enlistment Act, Britain's key law regulating its neutrality obligations, forbade the recruiting of those sailors on British soil. The Confederates' need of secrecy would require outright dissembling. Shipping in expectation of that straightforward coal run to Bombay, none of the prospective recruits would learn of the Confederates' plans until the *Laurel* and the *Sea King* made their rendezvous, far from British soil.

Then and only then would the cruise's purpose, commerce raiding, though not her ultimate destination, the Arctic, be revealed. Even the ship's senior officers were not to know, at least for now, where they were bound. To assist in winning enlistees for the crew, Bulloch and Waddell had persuaded a dozen or so men who had served on the *Alabama* to join the cruise. The hope was that these men, veterans of a widely celebrated raiding cruise would inspire seamen from both the *Laurel* and the *Sea King* to join the Confederates. On the assumption that not every sailor would accept the Confederates' invitation, plans called for the combined crews to exceed the sixty men that Waddell wanted.[11]

As Bulloch's plans evolved, he eventually settled on the Bay of Funchal on the Portuguese island of Madeira, off Africa's northwest coast, as the two ships' point of rendezvous. Twice before, Bulloch—with the *Alabama* and the *Fingal*, later the *Atlanta*—had used the nearby island of Terceira for the same purpose.

Under the pretense of organizing a routine run for a commercial ship, the shipping agent for the *Laurel* began advertising for a voyage to Havana. To perfect the ruse, "tickets were issued for the passengers under assumed names, so that the clerks in the office of the ship's agent would perceive that everything was going on in the ordinary course of their business." Similarly, shipping agent Henry Lafone was told in advance of the weight of the sealed boxes containing the armaments and stores that, eventually, would be loaded onto the ship. With such prior commitments from passengers and to cargo weight, Bulloch recalled, Lafone "had no difficulty in declining proposals from other sources without exciting suspicion." To command the *Laurel*, Bulloch called on Lieutenant John F. Ramsay of the Confederate navy; a British subject who prior to the war had served in the British merchant service and held a Board of Trade master's certificate, Ramsay would further throw off prying U.S. and British officials. After the *Laurel*'s rendezvous with the *Sea King*, plans called for him to sail on to Nassau, then to Charleston, where the *Laurel* would be placed into service as a blockade runner. Anticipating the *Laurel*'s run from Madeira to Nassau, Bulloch ordered Ramsay, once in Madeira, to take on as much coal as the ship could hold. To give Ramsay adequate time for coaling, the *Sea King*'s captain would be ordered to time his departure from London so that he would reach Madeira a day or two behind the *Laurel*.

By October 5, both ships—the *Laurel*, in Liverpool, and the *Sea King*, which by then was in London—were ready to sail. All Bulloch had to do now was await a telegram from London telling him that the *Sea King* had hoisted her anchor and steamed out to sea. Upon receiving that dispatch, he would order the *Laurel* to depart Liverpool and meet the *Sea King* in Madeira.[12]

THREE

Black Cruiser on a Thames Night

F ew, if any, other diners that Friday morning—October 7, 1864—took much notice of the plainly dressed young man as he took a seat at a lone table in the restaurant in Wood's Hotel, located in central London's High Holborn district. And for his purposes that was just fine. Acting on orders received the day before from Commander James Bulloch of the Confederate navy, the young man had, under an alias, taken a train to London. And, true to those same orders, that morning he entered the restaurant promptly at 11:00 a.m. Once seated, he placed his order. Then he deliberately pulled a napkin through a buttonhole on his coat and began reading the morning's paper.[1]

The news that greeted this young Confederate officer— though barely twenty-four years old, he had served on the CSS *Nashville*, the first Confederate ship to run the Union blockade and sail for England—was far from edifying. According to the *Times* of London, General Sherman's army now occupied Atlanta; the Union's general Philip H. Sheridan was chasing General Jubal Early down the Shenandoah Valley; and a long-planned Confederate scheme to free Southern captives from the Johnstown Island Federal prison on Lake Erie had quickly unraveled. Moreover, reflecting dimming Southern hopes for President Lincoln's defeat in his reelection bid next month, the *Times* reported that General John Frémont had abandoned plans to lead a splinter-party campaign for the White House that, weeks earlier, threatened to divide Republican voters.

Fortunately, this grim litany was soon disrupted. An older man entered the restaurant. Spotting the lone diner with a napkin pulled through his buttonhole and reading a paper, he walked over.

"Is this Mr. Brown," he asked, employing the prearranged nom de guerre.

As instructed, the officer answered yes. He then asked the older man if he was Richard Wright, the Liverpool merchant he had been ordered to meet. After Wright answered affirmatively, the two repaired to the officer's room.

There, able to speak more freely, the Confederate handed his visitor a letter of introduction. The letter conveyed the officer's rank and name—Lieutenant William Conway Whittle, Jr., Confederate States Navy—and identified him as the future executive officer, the second in command, of the ship that Wright, at great risk to himself, had just purchased for the Confederate navy.

Normally a cautious businessman, Wright, a month earlier, had abandoned his usual life on Liverpool's docks for a shadowy double life as a clandestine agent for the Confederate navy.[2] Wright had no particular sympathies for the Confederate cause. Money and a desire to ensure his family's financial security had brought him to this hotel room. His services had been enlisted by his son-in-law Charles Prioleau, of Fraser, Trenholm and Co., the trading house, with offices in Liverpool and Charleston, that served as the Confederacy's primary bank in England.

During the war's early months, James Bulloch and other Confederate agents had operated with relative openness in England and Scotland, purchasing ships and even contracting to have them built to be converted into cruisers for the Confederate navy. By October of 1863, however, much had changed. To the House of Commons and to Prime Minister Lord Henry John Temple Palmerston's Liberal government, the South increasingly looked like a lost cause. More particularly, Palmerston's foreign secretary, Lord John Russell, thanks to attentive pressures applied by Charles Francis Adams, the U.S. minister at the Court of St. James, had become increasingly responsive to American complaints of Confederate activities in Britain.

In the quest to gather intelligence on those activities, Adams had, in Thomas H. Dudley, the U.S. consul in Liverpool, a political appointee whose zealotry for the Union cause was matched only by his cunning in opposing slavery and the Confederacy.[3]

Dudley's posting in Liverpool proved fortuitous for the Union, for in providing men, arms, ships, and money for the Confederate cause, no other place in England rivaled this city of 440,000, with its five miles of docks and quays, and the shipyards across the River Mersey at nearby Birkenhead. Indeed, one contemporary reported that this city eventually flew more Confederate flags than Richmond. Building on long-standing business relationships, Liverpool's ties to the South remained strong throughout the war, British neutrality and the Union blockade of Southern ports notwithstanding. Its port served as an entrepôt for imported Southern cotton. And, supplying Rebel blockade runners, it exported manufactured goods coveted by the war-strapped Confederate home front.[4]

Liverpool's docks and countinghouses and Birkenhead's shipyards teemed with Confederate agents and Dudley's own force of cagey operatives. Those detectives, Dudley conceded to Secretary of State Adams, were far from "estimable men, but are the only persons we can get to engage in this business, which I am sure you will agree with me is not a very pleasant one."[5] From the war's outset, Dudley's detectives sought to find evidence of Rebel violations of Britain's Foreign Enlistment Act of 1819. This once obscure and, until the 1860s, vaguely defined law was the legal bulwark forbidding British citizens to sell arms and other military hardware to combatants in conflicts to which Britain was not a party.

British officials agreed that no one should be prosecuted for merely building a ship. It was when a British subject—or, for that matter, a non-British national residing in Britain—fitted out a ship for conflict by arming or otherwise modifying it for war that there was a violation of the Foreign Enlistment Act. More specifically, to violate the law such modifications must be made within Great Britain; they must be done for the purpose of sending the vessel into hostilities against a nation with which Britain was at peace; and, finally, it should be "clearly established . . . that the persons equipping etc. do so knowingly."[6]

As early as the autumn of 1863—the same season in which Bulloch first spotted the *Sea King* along Glasgow's docks—Dudley, traveling through Scotland on his own surveillance trip, had also noticed the vessel. What was more, Dudley immediately relayed to Minister Adams rumors of the ship's impending sale to the Confederates and plans to convert her into a commerce raider. And Adams in turn relayed those suspicions to Lord John Russell, informing the foreign minister that British subjects were assisting Confederate efforts to find a replacement for the recently sunk CSS *Alabama*. Back in Washington, Secretary of State William Seward, upon hearing the same report, warned

Russell that, given this advance notice, Britain would be held justly responsible for any losses that U.S. ships suffered as a consequence of Great Britain's failure to block the ship's departure.[7]

The reports that autumn from Dudley in Liverpool echoed similar intelligence that had reached Washington the previous spring. In an April 11 letter to Navy secretary Gideon Welles, Captain Napoleon Collins of the USS *Wachusett*, then in the Pacific, had reported that the captain of the American whaling vessel *Lydia* had been told by an English merchant in the village of Hobart Town in Van Diemen's Land, Tasmania, that the *Sea King* was being fitted out as a Confederate raider and her object was "to prey on the whalers in that sea."[8]

In actual practice, the Confederate secret was a sieve, and one of the ironies surrounding the raiding cruise was how easily it might have been thwarted before it even commenced. Dudley had identified the ship the Confederacy meant to convert, and both the U.S. minister in London and the secretary of state had put Britain's foreign secretary on notice. The cruise's intended mission had even become the stuff of whispers among the world's merchant marine. The best explanation for the Union's intelligence failure is also the simplest: knowledge is only as good as the ability to act on it for a certain effect. For their part, all the Confederate agents had to do was keep enough of their secret from enough people for enough time.

Aware of Washington's mounting scrutiny, Bulloch and his associates were at pains to ensure that U.S. agents would have no grounds for arguing that they had violated any part of Britain's Foreign Enlistment Act. That concern only steeled Bulloch's resolve that except for the ship's captain, none of those sailing aboard the *Sea King* should know her true mission. As far as the sailors aboard the steamer were concerned, she was headed out on a routine voyage—its first aim being the transport of a load of coal to Bombay. And, in accordance with

Bulloch's instructions, no Confederates had come near the *Sea King* since, weeks earlier, she had returned from her maiden voyage to New Zealand.

That evening, October 7, Whittle and Wright left Wood's Hotel and walked down Fleet Street to the Thames River. There, from a vista overlooking the East India Company dock, they stole a moment to gaze admiringly on the three-masted *Sea King*, freshly painted black for her imminent mission. Afterward, the two men repaired to a nearby pub. There they met Peter Corbett, a heavyset man wearing the blue uniform of a captain in Britain's merchant fleet. Corbett, the *Sea King*'s master, assured Wright and Whittle that everything was ready for the next morning's departure. Then the three men worked out the details. Wright would board the ship immediately and, as planned, debark at the English Channel port of Deal. Whittle would slip aboard the ship later that morning; to anyone who asked, he remained "George Brown," agent for the coal the ship was transporting to Bombay.

Whittle checked out of Wood's Hotel a few hours later. It was 3:00 a.m., Saturday morning, as he walked London's deserted streets back to the Thames. Standing amid the rows of warehouses and factor's offices that line the river, he gazed, once again, at the *Sea King*. Then, looking like any other late-arriving salt determined not to miss his ship, he crawled over her rail. Within the hour, mooring lines were run in and the sleek black ship disappeared downriver, into the dark.

On Saturday, October 8, hours after the *Sea King* had slipped down the Thames, the morning's light brought a letter to Charles Francis Adams from Thomas Dudley warning him of "a suspicious vessel called the Laurel at L'pool." Benjamin Moran, secretary of the U.S. legation, promptly suggested that Adams dispatch the USS *Niagara* to Liverpool. Two months earlier, having convinced British authorities that the CSS *Georgia*, in undergoing repairs and being sold to a private owner in Liverpool, was still a Confederate raider, Adams had managed to seize the ship. In the case of the *Laurel*, however, Adams, for reasons left unrecorded, disregarded Dudley's missive.[9]

Meanwhile, on the Confederate side of that morning's ledger of activities, hours after the *Sea King* sailed from London a telegram reached Liverpool alerting Bulloch to her departure. And Bulloch, in turn, notified Lieutenant John F. Ramsay—soon Captain Ramsay by virtue of his new position, if not rank, commanding the *Laurel*. Almost immediately Confederate officers were scouring Liverpool's waterfront, quietly gathering the ship's "passengers"—the officers and crew for Ramsay's own later blockade-running operations aboard the *Laurel*, and those who, if they agreed to sign on, would accompany the *Shenandoah* on her raiding activities. To hasten the *Laurel*'s departure, her cargo of armaments had already been loaded. All that remained to be done was to gather at Liverpool's Prince Albert Dock the twenty-three officers and others whom Bulloch had recruited. Once assembled, the men boarded the tug *Black Hawk*, which took them to the *Laurel*, waiting at anchor in the River Mersey. By daylight on the morning of October 9, a Sunday, the *Laurel*, after having her papers cleared for a trip to Havana, Cuba, and Matamoros, Mexico, weighed anchor and headed out to sea.[10]

On the evening of October 10, a telegram from Dudley reached the U.S. legation, reporting that the *Laurel* had, the day before, sailed from Liverpool. On board, according to Dudley, were the *Alabama*'s former commander, Raphael Semmes, eight other officers, and a crew of one hundred men. As legation secretary Benjamin Moran recalled in his journal, the news came "as a source of consternation to me." But Adams was out of town, Moran noted, and as he "left me no orders I could not act."

The following morning, with Adams still away, Moran sent a dispatch to Commodore Thomas T. Craven of the SS *Niagara*, then in the English Channel, alerting him to the *Laurel*'s departure and asking him to pass the report along to any other U.S. Navy commanders he might encounter. Drawing on details supplied by Dudley, Moran reported that the *Laurel* "has six 68-pounder guns in cases in her hold, with gun carriages ready for mounting." And he went on, "There is no doubt but this expedition has been fitted out for a piratical cruise against the United States, either in this or some other vessel. It is quite probable that there is some other vessel to which the men and guns are to be transferred."[11] Craven, upon receiving Moran's report, in turn alerted Captain Henry Walke of the USS *Sacramento*, then also cruising the English Channel.

On October 15, further word reached the U.S. legation. Minister Adams learned that the *Laurel*, the very same ship that had aroused Dudley's suspicions, had sailed to meet the *Sea King*.[12] Despite the accumulated evidence, and all the forewarnings, it seemed that another Confederate raider had been loosed on the oceans.

By late October, however, reports began drifting back to London that the *Sea King* had perished at sea. Sailors recently arrived in Liverpool aboard a British steamer, claiming to have been members of the *Sea King*'s crew, spread the story that the ship had sunk. Rumor had it that Captain Ramsay of the *Laurel*, ostensibly bound for Mexico, had rescued and subsequently deposited them at Tenerife, in the Canary Islands, where they had arranged passage to Liverpool.

Thomas H. Dudley, even on his best days, had a suspicious bent. So, in the weeks after the *Sea King*'s and *Laurel*'s disappearance into the Atlantic from their respective berths in London and Liverpool, he and his hireling agents began knocking on doors and prowling Liverpool's pubs and docks, searching for the sailors who claimed to have been rescued from the allegedly drowned *Sea King*. In time, Dudley found several seamen who confirmed his doubts about the raider's demise. These men, the consul learned, had not been pulled from any sinking ship. They had instead been taken to a desolate North Atlantic island and propositioned to join a Confederate commerce raider. When the men declined, Captain Ramsay of the *Laurel*, though eager to begin his blockade-running off the Confederate coast, made a detour from Las Desertas to Tenerife. After the holdouts agreed to sustain the fiction that they were survivors of the drowned *Sea King*, their return to Liverpool, along with Captain Corbett, was arranged. Meanwhile, as this latest display of Commander James Bulloch's maritime legerdemain unfolded, the *Shenandoah* had sailed unchallenged from Las Desertas. As Dudley talked to the returned seamen in Liverpool, he soon confirmed what he had suspected all along: the Confederates' newest commerce raider was still afloat and, by now, long gone.[13]

FOUR

Las Desertas

C ommander James Bulloch's orders to Captain James Waddell boiled down to this: After the *Laurel*'s cargo was loaded aboard the *Sea King*, the latter had been rechristened the CSS *Shenandoah*, a choice of name unexplained in any surviving documents. And after the two ships had gone their separate ways, Waddell was to sail toward Australia via the Cape of Good Hope. If he needed more coal, and being mindful of British neutrality obligations in that distant domain of the Queen's empire, Waddell could "touch" at Melbourne or Sydney. From there he would sail north up Australia's eastern coast, through New Zealand's whaling grounds, working his way through the broad Pacific, perhaps detouring along the way, to cruise for Yankee whaling vessels in that ocean's western islands or in its remote Sea of Okhotsk, tucked to the west of Siberia's Kamchatka Peninsula. For the cruise's final leg, and its operational heart, Waddell was to sail boldly into the Bering Sea to the Bering Strait, where, each summer, scores of New England whaling vessels gathered.

Beyond those general instructions, however, Bulloch offered Waddell little guidance. After Waddell had presumably decimated the whaling fleet, Bulloch counseled, "Your ship will probably be in want of repairs, and it may be necessary for you to decide what disposition could be advantageously made of her." One suggestion was that Waddell could drop south, toward the Marquises or another of the island groups off Central or South America's western coasts, where whaling fleets put in. There the Confederates could get the latest news on the war's development, and, thus enlightened, Waddell could decide on his next move. Bulloch's instructions thereafter descended into a fatalistic vagueness, the verbal perambulations of a commander far from certain of his side's eventual victory.

"You should at all times exercise a large discretion, and you would be perfectly justified in selling the ship and sending the crew to their homes," he counseled, before trailing off into various dispiriting suggestions: Waddell could do his best to try to find a European or South American port in which to anchor the steamer, admittedly an arduous proposition, given the Confederacy's diplomatic predicament. Or he could simply sell the ship—perhaps along South America's west coast or to "some adventurous speculators in the Eastern seas."

Pessimistic, necessarily imprecise, but also realistic, these directives were passed along to a captain whose crew would soon espy the same traits in him.

On the evening of October 14, the *Laurel* reached Funchal, on Madeira's southern coast. As expected, the *Sea King* was nowhere in sight. After dropping anchor, Captain Ramsay posted a lookout high in one of the ship's masts. To keep their mission a secret from the colony's Portuguese officials, diplomats posted to the port, and foreign visitors, he forbade both officers and crew to go ashore. As the ship bobbed at anchor in the harbor, the men could only gaze longingly on the colonial port's white, ornate limestone buildings and the palm- and eucalyptus-studded hills that rose behind them.

The *Laurel*'s recoaling commenced immediately upon her arrival. A day or two later, after the last chunk of coal had been shoveled aboard, a customs official asked Captain Ramsay why the steamer remained in port. Stalling for time, Ramsay answered that the *Laurel*'s engine needed repairs before sailing. Pressed for proof of the alleged malfunction, he produced a broken set of gears brought along for just such a situation. After examining the gears, the suspicious customs official took them ashore, vowing to have them repaired at a government workshop. Ramsay's story had bought the Confederates another day or two in port. But such prevarications could conceal the ship's secret for only so long. Where was the *Sea King*?

On the evening of October 17—the *Laurel*'s third day in the harbor—as moonlight dappled the Atlantic waters off Madeira, the ship's lookout spotted signal lights and the outline of a dark, ship-rigged vessel off the harbor's mouth. Beyond its generic usage, the term *ship*, when referring to sailing vessels, carries a specific meaning that is used to distinguish ships from barks. Ships possess a bowsprit and at least three square-rigged masts, each featuring lower, top, and topgallant members. Barks, by contrast, carry two square-rigged forward masts and a rear mast rigged fore and aft.

As the men gathered on the *Laurel*'s deck that night, all eyes fixed on the dim ship steaming across the horizon. But, just as quickly, the steamer turned south and disappeared. Then, soon enough, she reappeared from the same direction, only, after a few minutes, to disappear for the evening.

At daylight the following morning, the ship again appeared off Funchal. This time, however, signals were exchanged, conclusively establishing her as the *Sea King*. Ramsay immediately gave orders for the *Laurel*'s engine room to get up steam, and for a signal to be flashed to the port's captain, requesting that their papers be brought to the ship. But port officials were tied up by the arrival of a mail boat, and it was not until hours later, at 9:00 a.m., that the *Laurel*'s papers were delivered and the Confederates cleared to leave.

Before the Confederates left Liverpool, Bulloch had ordered Waddell to keep their mission a closely guarded secret from her prospective crew. The officers and seamen aboard the *Laurel*, whether Southern or British, were all pro-Confederate. But in agreeing to sail aboard the steamer, they were under the impression that they were bound for the Confederate coast to take up blockade running. It would be months before anyone besides Waddell knew that they were actually bound for the Arctic.

But, beyond that, even the essential fact that Waddell's officers and enlisted men would soon be engaged in commerce raiding remained a closely held secret. For now, the only officers aboard the *Laurel* besides Waddell privy to that basic information were Lieutenants William Whittle and John Grimball. And not until Waddell and his conspirators aboard the *Laurel* had met the *Sea King* did the men aboard the two ships learn the general purpose, if not the destination, of the cruise they were being asked to join. When and how that secret leaked is unclear; what is certain is that, prior to reaching Funchal, the crews of the *Laurel* and the *Sea King* learned just enough to be suspicious, but no more.[1]

As the *Laurel* caught up with the elegant black steamer, Captain Waddell instructed Captain Ramsay to signal the *Sea King* to fall behind, allowing the *Laurel* to take the lead. During the next few hours, Waddell, through his directions to Ramsay, guided the day's search for a hidden, natural anchorage for the transfer of armaments and other supplies between the two ships. As rumors aboard the *Laurel* hinted at the ultimate purpose of the ship shadowing her, the men gathered along her stern rail to appraise the handsome black steamer following in their wake.

Waddell's directions soon led them to a speck of land the Confederates called Las Desertas, presumably the island now called Deserta Grande, the largest of a trio of barely inhabited islands in the Madeira group. After a three-hour search along the island's coast, Captain Ramsay spotted a discreet and relatively shallow—18 fathoms, or 108 feet—cove beneath a high cliff on the island's lee. It seemed ideal for the morning's work. Soon enough, as Midshipman John Mason recalled, both ships were "anchored <u>close</u> under the cliff in water as smooth as glass."

The two ships were quickly lashed together. Leaving the *Sea King*, Lieutenant Whittle, fully abandoning his "George Brown" alias, climbed aboard the *Laurel* to report to Waddell. The Confederate officers on the *Laurel*, meanwhile, wasted no time in boarding the *Sea King* and, for the first time, inspecting up close this floating fortress of wood, iron, and hemp that would soon be their home. Midshipman Mason, by his own admission far from a seasoned mariner, nonetheless found himself overwhelmed by the high-masted ship anchored alongside the *Laurel* in the cove's tranquil waters. "I had not a word to say," he recalled, "but contented myself with looking on & listening to the remarks of others."

The adopted son of James Murray Mason, one of the Confederate diplomats posted to Great Britain, the young midshipman had attended the U.S. Naval Academy. He was slight, dark-haired, and handsome, and the thick beard that framed his face mostly underscored his youth. He was also earnest and learned—passionate about literature and all things French. But, beyond that, as Mason would demonstrate over the coming months, he was slow to accept character blemishes in those he admired, but once disillusioned, he revealed a brittle temperament.

After the outbreak of war in 1861 interrupted his studies at the academy, Mason fought at Manassas and later joined the Confederate navy, serving on the gunboat *Hampton*. As Mason inspected the *Sea King* that afternoon, the young midshipman spied a personal chance to advance: "She was a full rigged ship & as I looked at her three tall masts & her yards & rigging, I thought what a fine opportunity I would have of learning seamanship & made up my mind to make the most of it."[2]

Stem to stern, the *Sea King* stretched 220 feet and at her beam, her widest point, she reached 36 feet. With a depth of 20 feet 6 inches, she boasted a gross tonnage of 1,025. Topside, she possessed a sizable quarterdeck, her raised stern section, whose interior contained captain's quarters, a wardroom for high-ranking officers' dining and seven passenger cabins, soon converted by the Confederates to quarters for commissioned and other senior officers. A spacious deckhouse—a cabinlike structure on the midsection of the *Sea King*'s main deck—included the galley (the ship's kitchen) and twenty berths for petty officers. Divits on the main deck allowed for the suspension of most of the as many as five whale-boats that, over the next few months, would prove so essential to the Confederates' raiding. Beyond those features, the *Sea King*'s engineering gave her advantages over most ships of her day. As an auxiliary steamship she was propelled principally by the sails set from her three masts and, as needs arose, from coal-burning steam machinery. These dual-propulsion methods afforded the ship great range under sail, and dependable movement when needed for maneuvering in action or in narrow waters.

She employed Cunningham's Patent Self-Reefing Topsails. Still rare aboard ships of that day, this invention reduced the necessity of sending men aloft to close-reef—to reduce the amount of canvas exposed to the wind—on a ship's topsails. Instead of making dangerous, time-consuming climbs up the ship's mast, three men standing on deck each simply pulled on halyards, which—in much the same way cords open and close venetian blinds—reduced and furled each topsail and rolled it around to the desired mast position.

When steam power was needed, the ship's two boilers were fired up and the propeller was lowered and connected to the prop shaft. To reduce drag, when the ship's steam engine— capable of producing two hundred pounds of horsepower—was not in use, the raider's twin-bladed propeller could be hoisted out of the water. Beyond that, reinforcing the ship's modern novelty, her engine system had a telescoping smokestack that could be collapsed when the engine wasn't in use.

As an auxiliary steamer, the *Sea King* married the old technology of sail propulsion to two engineering advances that came of age during the first half of the nineteenth century: the steam engine and the screw propeller. Early steamships, many of which featured sails, had employed paddle wheels to propel them through the water. But while paddle wheels were adept on the world's rivers and in coastal areas, they proved to be unstable amid the currents and storms of the world's oceans. For that reason they were of dubious utility for international travel. Not until the development of a practical screw propeller, in the 1830s, was it possible to construct a truly stable steam-powered seagoing vessel. The brief era of auxiliary steamers had commenced.

The world's great navies, including those of Great Britain, France, Spain, and the United States, had built auxiliary steamers as early as the 1840s. But by the end of the Civil War era, ironclad ships propelled by steam had become the war vessel of choice. During the two decades in which auxiliary steamers flourished, there were fewer than two hundred built and, at any given time, no more than fifty in operation, and these almost exclusively within the world's great merchant fleets. They were used primarily on the long legs of interoceanic trade routes, in most cases to provide propulsion as the ships passed through the world's various doldrums—windless zones in which sails were of little use. By 1869, however, when the Suez Canal opened, reducing the distances involved in much international trade, the merchant auxiliary steamers had become artifacts of the past. Indeed, as that decade concluded and as steam engines improved and oil replaced coal, sails themselves became ever rarer features on the ships of the world's great navies and merchant fleets.

In the nautical nomenclatures of her day, the *Sea King*, in addition to being an auxiliary steamer, was also a composite ship. A skeleton of iron frames covered by six-inch teakwood planks held her together; copper sheathing protected her hull. The iron frame, lighter than those built solely of heavier wooden beams, increased the capacity of the ship's holds. It also increased the *Sea King*'s speed and structural stability. Indeed, the Glasgow shipbuilder Alexander Stephens, whose firm built the steamer, had been informed by the officers of the London trading house that commissioned her construction that they "wanted the fastest ship that can be got" for the purpose of being the first to bring "the season's tea to London."

Alexander Stephens & Sons hired the celebrated London marine architect William Rennie to design the ship. And by all

accounts the resultant *Sea King*—the first screw steamer to in-
corporate composite construction—more than met her patrons'
lofty expectations. Launched in August 1863, on Glasgow's
River Clyde, during her trial run off the Scottish coast, she
reached speeds of 12.25 knots, averaging 11.05 knots. On her
maiden voyage, the *Sea King* reached Auckland in seventy-four
days. From there she sailed to Sydney, and then to Shanghai in
twenty-three days. Carrying a cargo of Chinese tea, the new
steamer—spending en route five days at two coaling stations—
returned to the English port of Deal in seventy-nine days.
Those feats, closely monitored by James Bulloch and his colleagues in Liverpool, had rendered the *Sea King* a coveted tro-
phy for the Confederate fleet.[3]

As the Confederates gathered at Las Desertas walked the *Sea
King*'s mast-and-rigging-shadowed decks and wandered her rab-
bit warren of cabins and holds, most of what they saw and heard
left them dazzled. But they also found conditions that gave them
pause. As Charles E. Lining, the thirty-three-year-old prospective
surgeon for the Confederate's newest raider, recalled, "I found
her a splendid roomy looking ship, with a fine wardroom, but
nearly entirely void of furniture &c and the rooms were utterly
bare, mine, which was to be, having only in it a wash stand, no
bunk, no drawers, no nothing & most of the other rooms in the
same way. To make matters worse there were only <u>seven rooms</u>,
while we have ten commissioned officers."[4]

Executive Officer William Whittle, meanwhile, having spent
a week on the *Sea King* during the cruise from London, reminded Waddell of a problem of another, more serious, order.
The ship had reached Las Desertas with about forty men—far
fewer than they had hoped to have. That disappointing number

meant that once the Confederates disclosed their plans and began seeking men for their cruise they would, in all likelihood, be
forced to tender greater sums of money than anticipated to secure an adequately sized crew.

Another challenge made more difficult by the shortage of
men was the transfer of weapons, equipment, and provisions
from the *Laurel* to the *Sea King*. By naval tradition, officers
generally avoided shipboard physical labors. But the exigencies
of time and a scarcity of hands now dictated otherwise. The officers, as Midshipman Mason recalled, soon "took our coats &
vests off, rolled up our sleeves" and joined in the work, laboring
alongside the seamen.

Still more help came after Captain Waddell enlisted—actually,
impressed—a group of hapless Madeiran fishermen, who, eager
to sell their catches but also curious about the activities they had
stumbled upon, had edged their smack alongside the two ships.
Waddell, seizing a chance to provide the men working aboard
the two steamers with fresh food, bought the islanders' fish.
Typically, mariners of the day subsisted on a grim diet of salted
pork and beef and sea biscuits—oversized, flat, largely tasteless
crackers often mixed with gravy or water to produce a makeshift
soup. Given such bland rations, captains, eager to build ship
morale, welcomed the occasional opportunity to procure fresh
foods for their crews.

The men welcomed the fresh fish. But, as Mason recalled,
after making his purchases Waddell wasn't about to let the fishermen leave. "In order to keep them alongside the Ship for
fear they might go to Madeira & blow on us before it was
desirable," he hired them to help transfer cargo between the
two ships.

With tackles rigged aloft, soon enough heavy boxes were
swinging by ropes from one vessel to the other. "Gun carriages

and their fittings, ammunition, of powder shot and shell; stores of all kinds, all in boxes, were transferred from the Laurel to the Sea King," Whittle recalled. All of the men toiled until midnight—some even later. Then, as a guard-detail stood watch, most of them stole a few hours of sleep. They recommenced their labors at first light the next morning, and by 2:00 p.m. on October 19 the transfer of coal, armaments, and other provisions and equipment was complete.

All told, the job had taken a mere thirty-six hours. Its rushed, pell-mell character, however, left the *Sea King*'s deck a chaos of wooden crates whose contents would have to be unpacked. As Mason recalled, "There was no officer or man on board the ship who knew where any thing was stowed." But, as Waddell well knew, he could not afford to delay his departure any longer. Every hour spread the secret of his mission further; it was only a matter of time before there was a Union response. The remaining work, including cutting gunports for the ship and mounting her cannons, would therefore be done at sea.[5]

FIVE

"A Bucket of Sovereigns"

B efore commencing his cruise, Captain Waddell faced a final hurdle: enlisting a full complement of crewmen for the *Shenandoah*. Aside from the Confederate officers, the men aboard the *Laurel* consisted of the pool of seamen, most of them British, who had expressed a willingness to join a Confederate ship. But they had boarded the *Laurel* thinking they were bound for the other side of the Atlantic, to take up blockade-running along the Confederate coast. Because commerce raiding posed physical and legal dangers beyond those of conventional naval activities, Waddell knew that even without disclosing their Arctic destination, he would need help persuading men to ship on a raider. To make his case, he was counting on the open—and, he hoped, infectious—enthusiasm of the ten or so former crewmen from the CSS *Alabama*, the recently destroyed Confederate cruiser and celebrated legend among seamen of all nationalities.

The men aboard the *Sea King* were more numerous than those aboard the *Laurel*. But, unlike those aboard the *Laurel*, the seamen aboard the *Sea King* had never, so far as Waddell knew, expressed even nominal Confederate sympathies. They had sailed from London with no inkling that the voyage they had signed up for had anything to do with the Confederacy. Indeed, for all they knew they had shipped—signed shipping articles, a seaman's contract—for a standard voyage to Bombay and other ports, for a period of service not to exceed two years.

To skirt the demands of Britain's Foreign Enlistment Act, Bulloch had instructed Waddell to wait until the *Laurel* and the *Sea King* were well beyond British territory before disclosing his intention to launch a commerce raider. As a consequence, Waddell now faced the challenge of finding recruits among a group of men no doubt resentful that they had been brought to this forlorn island in the North Atlantic under false pretenses.

Waddell knew how many prospective recruits he had brought aboard the *Laurel*. And now he also knew that Captain Corbett had shipped a meager forty-five aboard the *Sea King*. Weeks earlier, Bulloch had ordered Corbett to seek out "only young, and as far as possible unmarried men, whose spirit of adventure and lack of home cares would . . . incline them to a roving cruise." And so, with that admonishment ringing in his ears, the time had now arrived for Waddell to learn what kind of men had in fact shipped.

Officers and men from both the *Laurel* and the *Sea King* were summoned to the *Sea King*'s weather deck. Moments later, Waddell appeared before them, standing on the ship's quarterdeck, the raised deck at the back of the ship reserved for officers. Now dressed in the gray uniform of a Confederate naval officer, his brand-new commission in hand, he looked down upon the assembled men and introduced himself. He told them that henceforth the *Sea King* sailed under a new commission and a new name—the Confederate States Ship *Shenandoah*—and otherwise "pictured to them a brilliant, dashing cruise, and asked them to join the service of the Confederate States and assist an oppressed and brave people in their resistance to a powerful and arrogant northern government." Beyond that, just as crew members on whaling vessels were enticed by "lays"—proportional shares of profits from the ship's hunt cashed out at the conclusion of their cruises—so commerce raiding held out the allure of shared monetary awards, issued on a sliding scale according to rank and based on the value of any ships that were destroyed. And if the ship could successfully be brought into a "prize port," a harbor that recognized the legality of the Confederates' commerce raiding, the rewards escalated. The problem, of course, was that outside their own blockaded coasts, few if any such ports existed—which, as a practical matter, meant that, in most cases, Confederate commerce raider commanders saw no option but to destroy their prizes on the high seas soon after their capture. And that necessity meant that Confederates on raiders, from officers on down, rarely if ever saw any prize money.

Oddly enough, a similar disappointment befell Union mariners serving in the U.S. Navy's often monotonous blockade service along the South's 3,800-mile coast stretching from Virginia to Texas. Like their Confederate counterparts, they had been promised a cut apportioned by rank of any spoils from captured prizes. In fact, many of the working-class and immigrant enlistees who comprised most of the U.S. Navy's lower ranks had been drawn into military service by precisely such promises of riches from captured prizes.

But like the Rebels, Union officers and seamen rarely received such payments. Until late in the war, when blockading tactics became more efficient, captures were rare: during the entire war, the blockade resulted in 1,419 seizures of Confederate ships; but in more than 7,500 instances, blockade runners managed to slip through the Union cordon; another 355 vessels were destroyed as they attempted to elude U.S. Navy blockaders. Beyond that, when the U.S. Navy did manage to get captured ships and cargo to port to be sold, the statutory shares of prize money paid each man who had served aboard the capturing ship, particularly seamen, proved disappointingly small.[1]

Even before the *Sea King* reached Madeira, her crew—their suspicions aroused by the otherwise sprightly ship's deliberate dawdling around Madeira—had begun to see through the subterfuge that they were transporting a load of coal to Bombay. In time, they suspected that the ship was enmeshed in some web of Confederate conspiracy. And by the time the steamer lay anchored off Las Desertas, that skepticism had hardened into absolute certainty and their resentment into naked anger.

As Captain Waddell stood on the steamer's quarterdeck, the deceived sailors leveled twelve days of accumulated rancor squarely at him. As young Midshipman Mason recalled, "Upon being informed of the true state of affairs, they became very indignant of the deception which had been unavoidably practiced upon them, and when asked if they would like to join the *Shenandoah*, they stubbornly declined our enticing offers of generous wages and liberal bounty."

Particularly frustrating to the Confederates was the fact that only half—or, according to some accounts, fewer than half—of the ten or so crew members from the late *Alabama* delivered on their promise to entice the other men to join the cruise, or even to ship on it themselves. Those *Alabama* men who did ship with the Confederates included Irvine S. Bulloch, the raider's eventual sailing master and the younger half brother of James Bulloch; master's mate John F. Minor; W. B. Smith, who became her paymaster; Englishman Henry Alcott, sailmaker aboard the *Alabama*, who accepted the same warrant aboard the *Shenandoah*; Boatswain George Harwood; and Matthew O'Brien, who became her chief engineer. Otherwise, as Midshipman Mason recalled, most of the *Alabama*'s men didn't care for the look of things, "got the devil into them," and defected "at the eleventh hour." Or, as Lieutenant Ramsay soon wrote to James Bulloch, in all his years at sea, "I never saw such a set of curs."[2]

Confronting the collective resistance, Waddell offered the men increasingly higher wages. One seaman recruited that day later recalled that Waddell had left Liverpool with the equivalent of $22,000 in British currency. To win recruits, Bulloch had, from the beginning, suggested offering monthly pay of £4, which was higher than the standard British sailor's pay. But when neither £4 plus a £10 bounty nor Waddell's eloquence stirred the men, he bid up the figure, eventually offering monthly pay of £7 and a £15 bounty to any able-bodied sailor willing to ship for a six-month enlistment. Eventually, to give their offers a more visible tangibility, "a bucket containing sovereigns was brought out on deck, and the officers took up handfuls to tempt the men." Beyond that, to set the right mood, acting sailing master, Irvine Bulloch, and First Lieutenant William Whittle provided generous rounds of libations.[3]

Captain Waddell eventually gave up on enlisting any more recruits that day. But Captain Corbett, determined to win a few more before he sailed from Las Desertas aboard the *Laurel* that afternoon, made one final attempt. He directed his final appeal to the men he had been brought out aboard the *Sea King*. But, as young lieutenant John Grimball recalled, the British merchant officer "might [as well] have spoken to the winds."

As the afternoon's shadows lengthened, the Confederates, even with the added inducements and the libations, had shipped only twenty-two out of fifty-five men, far short of the sixty that Waddell had hoped to have. And of those enlistees most had been willing to ship for only six months. The extent of the captain's difficulties was reflected in an odd ratio: the *Shenandoah*'s crew numbered twenty-four officers and twenty-two seamen.

Pondering such a small complement, the cautious Waddell began questioning the wisdom of even going to sea, a concern that he soon confided to Captain Corbett and the *Laurel*'s Captain Ramsay. As it turned out, both men shared Waddell's instincts, and both eventually advised him to adopt a cautionary course. Before heading into open sea, they counseled, sail to nearby Tenerife, anchor there, and send a message to James Bulloch asking him to dispatch more crew members.[4]

However prudent, the idea of steaming to Tenerife outraged the *Shenandoah*'s other officers. The wait there, they said, would only increase the steamer's exposure to interference by U.S. or even British ships. And, as the officers also reminded Waddell, Consul Dudley, Minister Charles Francis Adams, and other U.S. officials in Britain and elsewhere certainly knew by now that Bulloch had fitted out and sent to sea a new commerce raider. And over the past week their presence at Madeira had become an open secret. Indeed, a U.S. warship might be steaming toward them even as they debated the issue. What was more, Waddell's fellow officers voiced their disappointment that in seeking counsel the captain had turned to older, more cautious officers, men who were not even part of the *Shenandoah*'s crew. "Don't confer, sir, with parties who are not going with us" was Lieutenant Whittle's advice. "Call your young officers together and learn from their assurances what they can and will do."

At forty-one, James Waddell was more than two decades older than most of the cruiser's other officers. And at twenty-four even William Whittle was older than the ship's other four lieutenants: Francis Chew, John Grimball, Sidney Smith Lee, Jr., and Dabney Scales. Indeed, of the ship's entire roster of commissioned and non-commissioned officers, only Waddell and Lee had already experienced the venerable mariners' ritual of crossing the equator.

Bracing the *Shenandoah*'s youthful officer corps's zeal for both military adventure and the Confederate cause, all five—as did Waddell—came from prominent Protestant families of the South. Lieutenant Whittle's father, William C. Whittle, Sr., had a long career in the U.S. Navy dating back to the Seminole and Mexican Wars and had resigned the rank of commander in 1861, when he began his Confederate naval service. Lieutenant Grimball's father, John Berkley Grimball, was one of South Carolina's wealthiest planters and had enjoyed a long career as a state senator; at a state convention on secession in December 1860, he was among the majority of delegates who voted in favor of South Carolina's departure from the Union.

Even Sidney Smith Lee, Jr., the only one of the five young lieutenants who had held no U.S. Navy commission, hailed from a celebrated military family. During the late 1840s, his father had served as commandant of the Naval Academy at Annapolis; and, if that didn't make the point, his uncle was the Confederate general Robert E. Lee.

As was typical of his fellow officers, twenty-three-year-old Lieutenant Francis Chew's naval career had been inspired by a novel chronicling U.S. Navy Commodore Matthew Perry's 1853 expedition to Japan. The book was "profusely and beautifully illustrated," Chew recalled, and "my head was completely turned." Upon learning of his Confederate naval assignment, he recalled feeling as if all his boyhood dreams were about to come true: "I could hardly realize it, going to Europe, going to sea at last. What visions filled my imagination." Young midshipman John Mason, for his part, didn't need to reach back to the 1850s for his naval heroes. Among his personal belongings brought aboard the *Shenandoah* was a copy of Captain Raphael Semmes's memoir *The Cruise of the Alabama and the Sumter*, which had been published in London only months earlier.[5]

For Chew, and for Waddell's other young lieutenants, the prospect of sailing their newly commissioned commerce raider to Tenerife seemed a sad abdication of all those romantic visions. Confronting the young officers' protests, Waddell acceded to Whittle's request that he discuss the matter with them. He convened what Chew called a "council of officers."

Herman Melville, in *White-Jacket*, his fictionalized account of his own six months aboard a U.S. Navy man-of-war, observed that "a ship is a bit of terra firma cut off from the main; it is a state unto herself; and the ship's captain is its king." Those kingly powers notwithstanding, a ship tends to be either a smooth-running autocracy or an unhappy tyranny. Even so, despite the captain's absolute powers on paper, within the cultures of the day's Union and Confederate military services, such gatherings as those which Waddell held at Las Desertas—his oration before the prospective recruits as well as his later meeting with his lieutenants—were not without precedent.

No less an autocrat than Raphael Semmes of *Alabama* fame once indulged in such a democratic ritual. The incident took place in August 1862, on the island of Terceira, in the Azores. Semmes found himself confronting two shiploads of reluctant potential British recruits for the newly commissioned *Alabama*. "The *Alabama*," he recalled, "had brought out from the Mersey about sixty men, and the *Bahama*"—a tender—"had brought about thirty more." Gathering the sailors, Semmes spoke of the nobility of Confederate nationalism and promised them double normal seamen's wages, "lots of prize money," and generous liberties in exotic ports.

"In the end," he recalled, "I got eighty of these ninety men." But he vowed to never repeat such a gathering:

> The "public meeting". . . was the first, and last ever held on board the *Alabama*, and no other stump speech was ever made to the crew. When I wanted a man to do anything after this, I did not talk to him about "nationalities," or "liberties," or "double wages," but I gave him a rather sharp order, and if the order was not obeyed "double-quick," the delinquent found himself in limbo. Democracies may be very well for the land, but monarchies and pretty absolute monarchies at that, are the only successful governments for the sea.

Semmes's brief career as a saltwater democrat produced more recruits than did Waddell's similar venture in October 1864. It also apparently did no lasting damage to Semmes's command. In Waddell's case, however, both of his lapses into democracy on Las Desertas, soon repeated in other venues, boded ill for the tensile strength of his command. In the end, subordinate officers and crew came to welcome opportunities to argue against decisions that their captain—their "king"—had ostensibly already made.

At that council, Waddell confronted a youthful cadre of officers, lurching between the antithetical urges of their own inexperience and a romanticized call to the sea. He also confronted the fragile state of the Southern cause itself. These officers all read the same British newspapers, and they shared the same unspoken suspicion that an excess of caution might bespeak a faltering faith, and decisive action firm conviction.

All of the young officers voted to commence their cruise immediately; to compensate for the shortage of hands, Lieutenant Chew recalled, "the officers said unanimously that they would work with the men as long as it should be necessary." For his part, Lieutenant Whittle, the *Shenandoah*'s leanly handsome executive officer, used the meeting to establish a reputation for bold assertiveness. Soon he would ponder the possibility of commanding his own commerce raider.

Earlier in the war, Whittle had served for four months on the *Nashville*, the first Confederate ship to visit England. Upon the steamer's return, after being placed in command of the ship, he piloted her from Beaufort, North Carolina, on a daring sprint to sea, past two Union ships. Soon thereafter he was assigned to deliver plans for the construction of Confederate ironclads, from Richmond, Virginia, to Bulloch and other Confederate agents in England. Still later in the war, he was captured by Union forces outside New Orleans—only to escape under gunfire within twenty-four hours. At the time of his assignment to the *Shenandoah*, Whittle had been living in Paris, where he served on the staff of Commodore Samuel Barron and frequently acted as a courier carrying messages among senior Confederate officers in Europe.

At the council of officers, Whittle argued forcefully that going to Tenerife would likely prove foolhardy, reminding the officers of the recent history of the CSS *Rappahannock*. Eight months earlier, after docking at Calais for repairs, the raider was seized by French officials at the behest of U.S. diplomats. As

Whittle later recalled, "I never shall regret the advice I gave, which advice, I flatter myself[,] kept us at sea."[6]

Won over, or perhaps merely reassured, by the young men's bravado, Waddell gave orders to take to the open sea. There, he resolved, he would win from the ships they captured the recruits he had failed to get at Las Desertas. Bulloch's orders to Waddell, after all, had acknowledged the raider's likely difficulties in finding welcoming ports in which to refurbish her stores and equipment. Given that circumstance, Bulloch had advised, the *Shenandoah* would have to rely on an established practice of Confederate raiders: they would live off the sea. The cabins, holds, and decks of the ships they captured would supply what they needed. As Waddell recalled Bulloch's orders, "I had been directed to live off his [the enemies'] supplies, and I suppose inanimate as well as animate objects were embraced in those directions."

Earlier that day, Captain Corbett handed Waddell a bill of sale and title for the former *Sea King*, now the *Shenandoah*, and removed from the ship the register recording her pre-Confederate life. Waddell, however, also knew that to avoid running afoul of the Foreign Enlistment Act, the *Shenandoah* would have to forgo taking any prizes until Corbett had returned to England and canceled the *Sea King*'s formal registry. He was therefore eager to see Corbett on his way.[7]

At about 7:00 p.m., Captain Ramsay and the *Laurel*'s officers and crew, along with Captain Corbett and all the other seamen who had refused to ship and so were to be deposited at Tenerife, finally climbed over the *Shenandoah*'s side and into the *Laurel*. The two ships were unlashed; the local fishermen, no longer a threat to the conspiracy, were released to leave in their smack. As the *Laurel* steamed away, the Confederate navy's ensign, to cheers from the men aboard both ships, was unfurled over the *Shenandoah*. Like the Stainless Banner adopted as the Confederacy's national flag in 1863, the naval ensign featured the cross of St. George inside a canton set against a white field in its top left corner.

As the *Laurel* sank below the horizon that evening of October 19, and the *Shenandoah* completed her own final preparations for leaving Las Desertas, Captain Waddell faced a Pandora's sea chest of problems. There were, of course, all those boxes on the ship's decks that needed to be unpacked, organized, and stowed. Beyond that, the conversion of the *Sea King* into a man-of-war required modifications to the ship: gunports would have to be cut, and proper storage areas established for cargo and munitions. There was also the vexing matter of the size of the crew. The officers' earlier enthusiasm for taking to the open sea soon met a briefly immovable object. As the twenty-two crewmen attempted to hoist the *Shenandoah*'s anchor, they realized that they couldn't raise it from the cove's bottom. "The officers," Waddell recalled, "threw off their coats and assisted in lifting it to the bow." Finally, at 6:00 that evening, as the *Shenandoah* sailed from Las Desertas, Lieutenant Chew—free from the day's anchor toils—did his best to complete the job of effacing the words *Sea King* from the ship's stern.[8]

Six

Crossing the Royal Yards

C aptain James I. Waddell's triumphant announcement in his memoirs that, as of October 19, he and his crew "were now fairly afloat in a vessel of 1100 tons, English measurement, constructed for peaceful pursuits but metamorphosed into an armed cruiser" belied the true state of affairs.

At Las Desertas the men had loaded onto the ship six artillery pieces: two rifled Whitworth thirty-two-pounders and four 8-inch shell guns. Those six pieces lay impotent on the *Shenandoah*'s main deck, waiting to be fastened to their carriages and mounted. But first gunports needed to be cut into the ship's bulwark. Complicating matters, there was only one carpenter among the crew to direct the work. Until the *Shenandoah*'s broadsides brandished those six new armaments, her entire arsenal consisted of the two small twelve-pounder cannons that were standard for British merchant ships and the smattering of cutlasses, revolvers, and Enfield rifles distributed among the officers and crew at Las Desertas.

Adding to the crew's burdens, the barrels and crates that at Las Desertas had been crammed so haphazardly throughout the ship's decks, cabins, and holds still had to be properly stowed. And until order could be reduced from that chaos, movement aboard would remain difficult. Coal, for instance, filled much of the berth deck, the section just below the main deck normally used as the crew's sleeping quarters, and called the gun or 'tween deck on a man-of-war. Consequently, more than a few recruits spent their first few nights on the *Shenandoah* bivouacked on the main deck beneath the stars. And because coal also filled the forehold, which the ship's officers had intended to use as the *Shenandoah*'s magazine, much of the expedition's gunpowder was initially stored in Waddell's own starboard cabin in the ship's stern. ("Was it not a warm companion?" the captain later mused.) In truth, the presence of explosives in the ship's rear only heightened his anxieties about commanding what, for the moment, was largely an unarmed ship.

The Confederates organized into work details and fell to hammering, hauling, sawing, and lifting. As Waddell recalled, "All this service which is ordinarily done at a navy yard before a vessel is commissioned devolved upon us, out in midocean, without even a hope of successful defense or a friendly port to take shelter in, if attacked." That vulnerability to attack weighed heavily. "Every one perfectly understood that if we fell in with a United States steamer as we were then circumstanced, our race was run," Cornelius E. Hunt, one of the ship's young master's mates, recalled. A noncommissioned officer, the master's mate assisted in various sailing, navigational, and other operational tasks on the ship. Hunt—an intense young man who had served on the raiders *Georgia* and *Rappahannock*—was by turns arrogant and cunning; and he would later publish a lively if melodramatic account of the *Shenandoah*'s cruise.

As the ship's executive officer, Lieutenant William Whittle was in charge of her overall day-to-day operations. In assessing the raider's predicament he, like Hunt, found little to inspire confidence: "Never I suppose, did a ship go to sea so miserably prepared." That awareness haunted the raider's first days at sea like a bad hangover.[1]

The Confederate crew's paltry numbers and the labors required to fully convert the steamer into a man-of-war—all the while manning the engine room and sails—stretched officers and men to the breaking point. With barely enough hands to man the sails, the raider's officers during the cruise's early weeks found it necessary to rely largely on steam propulsion.

A small enclosure on the quarterdeck, the pilothouse, located at the ship's rear and close to her stern, served as command center. It enclosed the steamer's wheel room, home of the massive ship's wheel and the devices used to signal the desired speed and direction to the engineers in the engine room. Standing behind the wheel and gazing through windows toward the bow, the steersman controlled the ship's course. Just ahead of him, outside the wheel room, stood the binnacle, the stand for the ship's compass—it was left exposed to the elements lest any surrounding physical structures compromise its magnetic accuracy. Immediately behind the wheel room, the pilothouse also enclosed the ship's tiny chart room, where officers sat huddled at a small table, poring over the oceanic charts and navigational books housed in the room's cabinets and shelves.

Of course, all steaming operations relied on coal-heavers. In the ship's hot, cramped, barely ventilated engine room, they performed the nasty job of feeding coal into the furnaces that produced steam in the ship's two water-filled boilers. Alas, the three coal-heavers then in the crew were inadequate to fully man even one of the three watches needed when the vessel was steaming full-time.

Indeed, all in all, it required an engine-room crew of about eighteen men to fully operate a steamer the *Shenandoah*'s size. This "black gang," so called after the soot and oil that covered

these men, included the coal-heavers, but also, firemen (to supervise the boiler fires), oilers (to lubricate the engine, prefer-
ably with whale oil), and coal trimmers (to carry coal to the
furnaces and otherwise make sure that the coal, while stored
in the ship's hold and bunkers, remained balanced to ensure
smooth sailing). Several engineering officers supervised all of
these tasks. But short of hands during the Confererates' first
weeks at sea, the *Shenandoah*'s engine operated only during the
day—and often not even for the entire day.

At night the raider sailed on "short sails." By ordering the
sails reefed—furled to reduce the extent of canvas exposed to
wind—Captain Waddell reduced the chances of a squall's catching and dismasting the ship before his meager crew could take
in the canvas. But the prudence of shortened sails also reduced
the ship's speed and, in the minds of many of the *Shenandoah*'s
younger officers, simply delayed their first encounter with an
enemy ship.

No seamanship manual provided guidance in the unraveling
of a Gordian knot. But in deciding whether to go under full or
shortened sails, Captain Waddell confronted precisely such a
challenge during those first days aboard the *Shenandoah*. He
knew that the sooner they captured an enemy ship the sooner
they would relieve the shorthandedness that now imperiled the
cruise. But he also knew that if they hastened after a capture under full sails, that very shorthandedness might precipitate an accident that could sink, dismast, or otherwise damage the raider.
Even so, his caution invited criticism. Thus, during their first
weeks at sea, many of the raider's young officers came to see
Captain Waddell's penchant for sailing on short sails as evidence
of timidity, perhaps a lack of self-confidence or even ability.

More broadly, the officers quietly began to wonder whether
the captain's background had fitted him for command of a commerce cruiser—a vessel whose unorthodox mission demanded

resourcefulness, stealth, and courage. As Lieutenant Whittle put it, Captain Waddell was "accustomed, as a naval officer, to step on the deck of a man-of-war fully fitted and equipped at a navy-yard, where every facility aided to make everything perfect." Confronted with the *Shenandoah*, he "was naturally discomforted and appalled." In fact, Waddell's caution had come hard-earned, rashness in making past decisions having cost him dearly. In addition, he was still getting used to being called "Captain."

Early in the war Confederate navy secretary Stephen Mallory adopted a policy of allowing former commissioned officers in the U.S. Navy to enter the Confederate navy at the same rank. Thus, at forty-one Lieutenant James I. Waddell, CSN, remained by *rank* a lieutenant—a titular incongruity faced by most commanders of Confederate naval ships. Like them, however, Waddell, by virtue of his new position aboard the *Shenandoah*, was addressed by fellow officers in day-to-day exchanges as "Captain." And though he was a far more seasoned mariner than the steamer's other officers, and had witnessed hostile actions during the Mexican War and various incidents in China, he had never been in actual combat. In truth, little in his past, as his young officers had already surmised, had prepared him for his present role.

A broad-shouldered, mustachioed man whose aloofness bespoke a quiet intensity, Waddell seemed, upon first meeting, a model of military decorum and sobriety. A former student who recalled Waddell's brief turn as an instructor in navigation courses described him as handsome, a little over six feet in height, of fine physique, and weighing about two hundred pounds—a "splendid specimen of a manhood," "of noble bearing . . . gracious courtly . . . radiant with kindness." Only the slight limp with which he walked—the legacy of a youthful duel with a fellow midshipman concerning a young lady—betrayed his more impulsive propensities.

Born on July 13, 1824, in Pittsboro, North Carolina, Waddell won a U.S. Navy commission at age seventeen. In his memoirs, however, even Waddell offers no conclusive explanation for what, early on, turned his thoughts to the sea: "Perhaps the breezes of a loftier region sweeping over the red hills of old Orange [County] purified my heart." Whatever inland winds drove the young man to the sea, by the end of his teenage years he had enrolled at the U.S. Naval Academy.

The Civil War's commencement found Lieutenant Waddell, who by then had married Ann Sellman Inglehart, in Hong Kong aboard the docked *Saginaw*, a steamer in the U.S. Navy's East India squadron. As the first reports of war between the Union and the Confederacy reached Asia, he was ordered to board the U.S. sloop of war *John Adams* and return to the United States.

Waddell had hoped that war between his native South and the rest of the nation could be averted. But he had already concluded that if war came he would return to Dixie and join its war effort. So he welcomed the opportunity his orders presented. As Waddell boarded the *John Adams* for the return trip home, his plan, once back in the United States, was to resign his naval commission. However, that November, upon reaching the Caribbean island of St. Helena and learning of the war's first full action—the Battle of Bull Run—Waddell abruptly decided to simply walk off the *John Adams* and arrange his own transportation for the rest of the trip.

Waddell's rashness and his failure to anticipate its consequences, which prefigured decisions he would make aboard the *Shenandoah*, left him in a strange port with little, if any, money. Moreover, when he finally reached the United States he found himself unable to do what many other naval officers from the South were doing, formally resigning their U.S. Navy commissions and receiving all due back pay. In the wake of his abrupt departure at St. Helena, Waddell was informed by U.S. Navy secretary Gideon Welles that his name had been "stricken from the rolls" and that he had forfeited his pay.

In March 1862, Waddell received his commission as a lieutenant in the Confederate navy. A month later, on the eve of the capture of New Orleans by Union flag officer David Glasgow Farragut—indeed, even as Union ships were sailing up the channel below the city—Waddell participated in an evacuation of Confederate naval personnel, via steamboat, upstream to Vicksburg. Shortly thereafter, he and others realized that the withdrawal had left behind an almost complete Confederate ironclad in a New Orleans shipyard. Waddell volunteered to return with one other man in an open boat to destroy the ship. In a derring-do near encounter with arriving Union troops, Waddell and his partner barely managed to explode a charge of gunpowder, destroying the ship, before escaping with their lives.

In the wake of his New Orleans adventures, Waddell's superiors ordered him to Charleston. There, in anticipation of a siege of the city's harbor by Union ironclads, he was to direct efforts to destroy the invading ships. But the Union naval assault never materialized, and, in May 1863, Waddell was ordered to report to Flag Officer Samuel Barron in France. Upon reaching Paris that fall, Waddell met with Barron, who, on September 5, ordered him to Liverpool to report to Commander James Bulloch. After Waddell reached England, Bulloch, in orders penned on October 5, provided a sweeping description of his next mission: "You are about to proceed upon a cruise in the far-distant Pacific, into the seas and among the islands frequented by the great American whaling fleet, a source of abundant wealth to our enemies and a nursery for their seamen. It is hoped that you may be able to greatly damage and disperse that fleet, even if you do not succeed in utterly destroying it." Bulloch's orders, though specific in objective, also recognized the inevitable improvisational character of such a long voyage: "Considering the extent of ocean to be sailed over, the necessarily incomplete equipment of your ship at the beginning of the cruise, and your approaching isolation from the aid and comfort of your countrymen, a letter of specific instructions would be wholly superfluous."

Waddell possessed more than two decades of marine experience. But the open-ended nature of Bulloch's orders, and the legal questions that would likely attend all military decisions he made, presented him with a challenge wholly different from others he had faced. As Waddell himself acknowledged, "I had the compass to guide us as seamen, but my instructions made me a magistrate in a new field of duty, and where the law was not very clear even to lawyers." In addition to the books on navigation that soon lined the shelves of his *Shenandoah* stateroom, he carried works pertaining to international law, such as Robert Phillimore's commentaries on the law of nations, which in his leisure hours he read in earnest. But his new library notwithstanding, Captain Waddell would confront challenges during the coming days and weeks for which law books offered little guidance. Not only had the captain gone to sea in a ship whose preparedness was other than he would wish but his mandate and its legitimacy were far from straightforward.[2]

As the *Shenandoah* sailed south, toward the Cape of Good Hope, good weather held, and three days after they had sailed from Las Desertas any work that could be done was done: gunports were cut, bolt-holes drilled, the bulwark reinforced, cannons and carriages assembled, and cargo and stores properly stowed.

That accomplished, crew members began getting accustomed to their new quarters. Traditionally, on ships of that era, officers resided in the rear section of the vessel behind the foremast. Seamen found their quarters "before the mast"—in the forecastle, a houselike structure that rose from the main, or weather, deck near the bow; or in the berth deck, the next level beneath the weather deck—or, depending upon the ship and her circumstance, in both places. The level beneath the berth deck, the ship's lowest level, was given over to her various holds and storage areas and was not used for quarters.

The *Shenandoah* did have a berth deck, but she offered a slight variant on the traditional forecastle. Rather than in a freestanding structure on the weather deck, seamen not housed on the berth deck found quarters in the topgallant forecastle, an enclosure formed by a raised deck section close to the bow. Seamen constituted a broad group whose categories, taken from the merchant marine, included ordinary seamen (sailors with at least two years' experience), common seamen (those with less than two years at sea), landsmen (those with no sea experience), firemen second class, coal-heavers, and others.

As the *Shenandoah*'s cruise progressed and conditions grew crowded, the topgallant forecastle, besides quartering seamen, was also used as the ship's brig. Over time, the damp, narrow enclosure was used increasingly to hold, often in irons, captured seamen and crew members being punished for various infractions. Likewise, and sometimes simultaneously, it was used as a holding pen for livestock—goats, pigs, and the like—taken from prizes.

Petty officers, the low-ranking officers quartered in the twenty berths in the ship's deck house, held their temporary and tenuous positions at the pleasure of an appointing senior officer. Sharing the deck house with the ship's galley—her cooking area—petty officers included the master at arms (the ship's police officer), the cook, the yeoman (who oversaw the ship's stores and provisions), fireman first class, and a range of other specialized positions.

The ship's most comfortable quarters, however, were reserved for senior officers. At the top of the pecking order were the commissioned officers, who received their appointments from the Confederate Senate. Their ranks on the *Shenandoah* included the five young lieutenants serving under Lieutenant Commanding Waddell. In addition to those officers—called "line" or "sea officers"—other commissioned officers included various professionals, often recruited from civilian life, who met specific shipboard needs such as surgeon, assistant surgeon, paymaster, and chief engineer. Below them were the warrant officers, whose appointments came from the secretary of the Navy, and whose numbers included midshipman, boatswain, master's mate, and others.

Commissioned officers and some of the warrant officers found their commodious quarters aft, in the rearward section of the ship's weather deck—near the stern and under the raised quarterdeck, the highest of the steamer's principal decks. There, bathed in light from elegant stern windows, were found the captain's quarters. Just forward of the captain's cabins was the wardroom, a communal space for officers, illuminated by generous skylights, with seven separate cabins lining its length, each shared by senior officers.

In many ways, senior officers lived and worked in a separate sphere than that inhabited by petty officers and seamen. Emblematic of the difference in creature comforts of their different worlds, officers at the day's end retired to beds and cots in cabins. Seamen, by contrast, enjoyed little privacy and found their berths amid rows of cocoonlike hammocks strung from overhanging beams on the berth deck, and in uncomfortable wooden bunks built into the topgallant forecastle.

By military tradition, senior officers and seamen had few if any social interactions. Differences in class—and, as often as not, in language and culture—further divided them. Beyond that, the shipboard world in which petty officers and seamen lived, already confined by sea life, was further circumscribed by rules banning their presence in areas of the ship reserved for senior officers—the quarterdeck, officers' quarters, and wardroom. By naval tradition, only by invitation did even the ship's captain, who generally took meals in his own quarters, dine in the officers' wardroom.

And departing from arrangements on earlier vessels in which sailors met nature's call on the "head"—a toilet platform that extended from the base of the ship's bowsprit—the *Shenandoah* featured at least three water closets with state-of-the-art patent flush toilets, most of them aft, for the use of senior officers. Otherwise, crew members headed for a spare bucket or the side of the ship.

Once living quarters on the *Shenandoah* had been established, officers and crew settled into the normal routines of life at sea. Following man-of-war traditions, the days of most seamen on a Confederate raider began at daybreak, which, depending on the ship's location, might be as early as 4:30 a.m. Moving rapidly through the long, cavernous berth deck and the other quarters, the boatswain's mate, slapping hammocks and shouting orders to rise and shine as he passed, ordered the men to lash up and stow their hammocks and report to the weather deck.

The men generally took no more than ten minutes. Once on the upper deck, they stowed their rolled-up hammocks, performed their toiletries, and were assigned shipboard maintenance chores—everything from cleaning the deck with sand, water, and "holy stones" (heavy flat stones sometimes said to resemble family Bibles) to polishing "bright work" (the ship's various brass fixtures). Similarly, the ship's rigging demanded perpetual attention. While the raider's standing rigging (the cables that supported her spars) were of iron, her running rigging (by which sails were held in place and trimmed) were of rope. Throughout the cruise, the Confederates would use newer rope confiscated from prizes to replace older, damaged running rigging.

About an hour later, after an on-deck inspection, the boatswain piped the men to breakfast with his whistle. All meals were prepared in the galley in the deckhouse on the weather deck, where the ship's large range was located. In taking meals, sailors were divided into messes, usually groups of eight or so men with one man, in the rotating job of caterer, responsible for food preparation and delivery to the mess. Stewards served the officers a combination of standard fare from the galley and special dishes, often from livestock taken off prizes, prepared just for them. Depending upon rank, crew members took their meals in designated places in the ship—typically, the captain dined alone in his stateroom aft, commissioned officers ate in the wardroom between the rows of their cabins under the poop deck, petty officers ate in the deckhouse, and the crew gathered with their messes at trestle tables set on the berth deck and in the topgallant forecastle.

After breakfast the sailors attended to the day's duties and watches: assisting the ship's carpenter, boatswain, or other petty officers in their work, trimming sails, and engaging in various drills. To minimize distractions and skylarking, rules prohibited conversations, smoking, and singing while on duty; and whiskey among seamen was forbidden under any circumstances—except one. Given the restrictions under which they worked, these predominantly British seamen savored their twice daily cups of grog, a mixture of whiskey with water. Seamen were entitled to a gill of grog per day. The practice, which originated in the British navy, sought to control the consumption of whiskey on ships at sea. And though the U.S. Navy in 1862 had abolished grog rations, the custom continued to thrive on Confederate ships.

Depending on watch assignments, the men stopped for lunch at noon, completed the workday, and then had dinner. By 10:00 p.m. crew members, officers and seamen alike, unless assigned to later watches or duties, were expected to turn in.

Beyond those general rhythms, the ship's day was otherwise marked off into five 4-hour watches plus the two 2-hour dogwatches that passed during the dinner hours, with an officer of the deck in charge of each watch. By naval tradition, a ship's captain and executive officer, even if present on deck, issued most of their orders through the officer of the deck, who also recorded in the ship's deck log any changes in the weather, the ship's direction, ships or land sighted, steaming or sailing conditions and speed, and any other noteworthy developments during his watch.[3]

With the shortage of crew members during the cruise's early weeks, even the more daring Lieutenant Whittle worried about whether the Confederates had adequate numbers to attend to the ship's daily tasks. "Think of a ship of this size having only four men in a watch," he lamented. The steamer also lacked basic fixtures, such as washbasins, tables, and chairs. Moreover, by late October, as the *Shenandoah*'s southward course took the Confederates into tropical latitudes, heavy rains and violent squalls had begun to test the steamer's seaworthiness. "To our horror," Waddell recalled, "the decks leaked like sieves, and the seams of the hull were sufficiently open to admit a fine spray from a sea which had spent itself on her sides."

Even more worrying, as their work went forward the Confederates realized that they lacked functioning gun tackles for the ship's six new artillery pieces; no one, it seemed, had bothered to load the blocks, the pulleys in the rope-and-pulley assemblage by which cannons are pulled in and out of a ship's gunports. Without gun tackles to stabilize the artillery, when a cannon is fired aboard a ship its recoil can send it and its carriage careening to the vessel's far side. And because the carpenter could not improvise the requisite blocks, the *Shenandoah*'s six new cannons had, for the time being, to remain ornamental. Waddell would have to continue to sail largely unarmed, hoping that his first capture would supply not only additional crew but the missing blocks for his gun tackles.

Captain Waddell's concerns about the ship's state of readiness were further compounded by his long-standing reservations about seamen in general and their work ethic in particular. "Work is not congenial to Jack's nature. He is essentially a loafer," Waddell later wrote, expressing a common prejudice held by naval commanders. But though Waddell worried that his current crew might give potential recruits from captured ships a "bad impression," he remained confident that he would find new seamen. Each captured ship, he felt sure, was bound to have "one or more adventurous spirits . . . [who] would avail of the opportunity we would offer them in hope of prize money, and under the assurance of being well cared for." But his own musings belied this rosy expectation and presaged what was to come. If their blandishments failed to secure recruits, he noted, "We could rely on our men using rough arguments with those who were undecided."

Beyond useless cannons and a crew of less than certain commitment, Waddell also worried about another problem: how to find the Union whaleships they had been sent to sea to destroy.

Though Lieutenant Commander James Bulloch, back in Liverpool, had supplied Waddell with an impressive library of navigational books and charts, the captain still lacked the sort of charts he needed to successfully find Union whaling vessels. Bulloch's orders called for the *Shenandoah* to hunt whaling vessels in the Pacific, in eastern Siberia's Sea of Okhotsk, the Bering Sea, the Bering Strait, and the Arctic Ocean. But before he could do that, in yet another of the daunting ironies that bedeviled this cruise, he had to find one of those very same whaleships.

Unlike most vessels at sea, whalers sailed courses that were in many ways improvised, set by the vagaries of changing whale migrations. To keep up with such migratory shifts, whaling masters and mates participated in what was, essentially, an informal international network of exchanged information. All over the world, in ports and at sea, whaling masters held what they called "gams," sessions in which they visited one another's ships and exchanged the latest word on the whereabouts of whale pods, all the while carefully annotating their charts with the latest information. In a word, then, the charts that Waddell would need in order to pinpoint the Union's Western Arctic whaling fleet could not be bought; they would have to be captured from the whaling vessels.

On the eve of the *Laurel*'s departure from Liverpool, Bulloch had reminded Waddell that after taking command of the *Shenandoah* he should wait thirty days before taking any prizes. The delay would give Captain Corbett adequate time to reach England and cancel the *Sea King*'s English registry before the Confederates destroyed any ships—and thus, Bulloch hoped, preempt any accusations that they had violated the Foreign Enlistment Act.

But at sunrise on October 27, a week after the *Shenandoah* and the *Laurel* had parted company, the welcome call of "Sail ho!" from a lookout in the crow's nest resounded across the ship and Commander Bulloch's admonition regarding the registry's transfer was quickly forgotten. As it turned out, the deck officer on that day's morning watch was none other than James Bulloch's half brother, sailing master Irvine Bulloch, who, acting on Waddell's instructions, gave orders to ignore the earlier injunction and give chase.

It took several hours to stoke a coal fire in the boiler furnaces that was intense enough to produce sufficient steam to operate a steam engine. But, in anticipation of just such an opportunity, fires were already burning that morning. Bulloch relayed Waddell's orders to the pilot in the wheelhouse to signal the engineers in the engine room to open the valves on the engine, a signal typically sent in steamships through a succession of bell strikes indicating desired speed and direction. Steam rushed into the engine's two cylinders, thrusting its pistons forward and back, turning the crankshaft and spinning the raider's propeller, and soon sending the *Shenandoah* churning toward her quarry.

Exhilaration filled the raider. After months of preparations, the Confederates were savoring their first chance at the sort of glory that had made the *Alabama* a legend. And by noon a freshening wind rising from the northeast further stirred their excitement. It was a breeze of one to two knots—though the Confederates in their logbook did not designate it thus. Only decades later, after instrumentation could measure such phenomena, would mariners quantify wind speeds. During the *Shenandoah*'s era, mariners made do with the Beaufort Wind Force Scale—a continuum on which winds are ranked by force, not speed, on a scale of one to twelve. The system had been developed around 1805 by Admiral Francis Beaufort of the British

Navy. In 1838, it became a required component of daily British Navy logbook entries and soon thereafter in those of the U.S—and Confederate—navies. And, in the crisply poetic language of Admiral Beaufort's system, the "light breeze" moving the Confederates toward their prey that October afternoon rated a two, a condition in which "wind [is] felt on faces; leaves rustle; flags stir."

By 4:00 p.m., as the Confederates' pursuit of their quarry dragged through the day, Waddell had given orders for hands to go aloft into the ship's rigging to "cross"—fit sails upon—the ship's royal yards, her highest cross-masts, maximizing the ship's speed. As the *Shenandoah* steadily narrowed the gap between her and her prey, Lieutenant Bulloch called up to the lookout, "Can you make her out?"

"Aye, aye, sir. A square-rigged vessel. We appear to be raising"—gaining on—"her fast. I see her better now. A barque with long mastheads, and looks like an American."

"Very good," Bulloch answered. "Let me know when she shows her colors."

By then, Cornelius Hunt recalled, "from every part of the ship swarmed up the little company that composed her crew, and ensconced themselves in the rigging, and wherever there was a favorable point for observation, while spy-glasses passed from hand to hand, and opinions were anxiously interchanged as to what the stranger might prove to be."

An hour later, as the Confederates drew ever closer, they could make out a Union Jack flapping from the bark's peak. But the raider's officers remained undaunted; the flying of false colors, after all, was an old ruse used for centuries to both assist and defend against offensive actions by commerce raiders. When, for instance, Confederate forces seized the Gosport Naval Shipyard, in Norfolk, Virginia, in 1861 their booty included a large cache of foreign colors, which they promptly distributed among the ships of their navy. Indeed, most combatants in naval warfare up to the present have employed similar *ruses de guerre*—including, most recently, electronic versions of the old tricks.

As the *Shenandoah* drew closer to the bark, the Confederates, invoking the standard modus operandi of raiders, fired a blank cartridge over their quarry's bow. Immediately, the ship "hove to"—adjusted her sails to arrest her movement and reach a stationary position, a sail-trimming maneuver used in waters too deep for anchors. Afterward, a Confederate boarding party was dispatched to determine the ship's true national registry.

Typically, the officers of a Confederate boarding party making first contact with a suspected prize boarded the vessel, summoned the vessel's captain, interviewed him, and asked him to produce registry papers and other documents. If the raider's captain conclusively determined that the detained ship was not of U.S. registry, she was allowed to sail away unharmed. If, however, the Confederate officers determined that the vessel was, or might possibly be of U.S. registry, her captain and his mates—the officers on a merchant ship immediately below that of captain or master—were brought aboard the Confederate raider for further interviews and inspection of documents.

For the Confederates watching from the *Shenandoah*, their knowledge of such boarding-party protocols made them all the more eager to learn the consequences of their daylong chase. As ship's surgeon Charles E. Lining recalled, "We waited most anxiously on board to see whether her flag would come down or not, and were very much disappointed when we saw our boat shove off from her." The bark—the *Mogul*—was, as the Confederates had surmised, American-built. But an interview with her master and an inspection of the ship's papers convinced Waddell that she was, at that moment, sailing as an English cargo ship.[4]

The action taken by the *Mogul*'s original owner typified a popular Civil War–era trend among the owners of U.S. merchant and whaling vessels. Weary of rising marine-insurance costs and increasingly nervous about their vessels' vulnerabilities to Confederate raiding, a growing number of Northern shipowners sold their ships to foreign parties. Not until after the Civil War did U.S. laws allow shipowners to register their vessels, without selling them, under foreign "flags of convenience." The Civil War–era practice, meanwhile, of selling the vessels posed obvious problems for Confederate raiders. In many cases, Northern shipowners, reluctant to sell their vessels but determined to keep them at sea and eager to protect them from Confederate raiders, would arrange bogus sales to dummy foreign owners— replete with, for any Confederates encountered on the high seas, elaborate phony documents attesting to the alleged sale.

Officers in Confederate boarding parties were well aware of this ploy. Yet they also knew that they could, after the war, face criminal and civil charges for destruction of "neutrals" property. In the end, it was the judgment of a Confederate raider's senior officers that made the difference; after their interviews and inspection of documents, they rendered their final verdict on the waiting ship's fate. And having found the *Mogul* to be a duly registered British vessel, the Confederates reluctantly allowed the bark to sail away unharmed.[5]

SEVEN

King Neptune's Court

A t 1:00 p.m. the next day, October 28, the *Shenandoah*—having just passed latitude 18°58' N and longitude 26°10' W—spotted yet another set of sails floating just above the horizon. Following the previous day's disappointments, excitement ran high, particularly once, as surgeon Charles Lining recalled, "all the 'wise ones' on board pronounced her to be a Yankee." A daylong pursuit, however, left the matter in doubt. As darkness fell over the Atlantic, the Confederates hoped they could still find their potential prize come next morning.

The two vessels were running on the same course. But because the potential prize was on short sails all night and the *Shenandoah*, for once, wasn't, by the following morning, October 29, the Confederates had narrowed the distance between them and their quarry. With light winds stilling their forward progress, Waddell, just before twelve noon, deploying his technological advantage, issued instructions for the raider to get up steam. As the *Shenandoah*, hoisting an English flag, drew closer to her prey, the other ship, to the Confederates' delight, raised Old Glory. "I never saw greater excitement than was on board our ship," Lining recalled. "We had the first prize to the Shenandoah."

The Confederates immediately fired a shot over the ship's bow, she promptly hove to, and a boarding party led by Midshipman John Mason, Sailing Master Irvine Bulloch, and master's mate Cornelius Hunt was soon rowing toward the bark. As they pulled alongside their quarry an inevitable self-consciousness attended their approach. Midshipman Mason could not help but wonder about the impression the boarding party, out for the *Shenandoah*'s first capture, was about to make. Their boat, he lamented, "had no very neat appearance, all the men dressed differently, but the officers were O.K. for we had our uniforms, swords, sidearms &c. &c."

Once aboard the ship, the Confederate boarding party learned that the bark—the *Alina* of Searsport, Maine—was carrying a load of railroad iron from Newport, Wales, to Buenos Aires, Argentina. "On reaching the vessel," Hunt recalled, "we informed the Captain that his craft was a prize of the Confederate States of America, and ordered him to get his papers and proceed on board after our ship."

Complying, the *Alina*'s master, Captain Everett Staples, disappeared belowdecks for a few minutes, then returned topside with a tin box containing the ship's documents. Afterward, as ordered, Staples proceeded to the *Shenandoah* with the officers in the boarding party to meet with Waddell.

Captain Waddell talked with Staples and inspected his documents. Satisfied that the *Alina*'s destruction fell lawfully inside his raiding domain, Waddell then formally "condemned" the bark. During the next hour, the *Alina*'s other officers and crew, each carrying a sea bag containing his dunnage, were transferred to the *Shenandoah*. Hunt, meanwhile, accompanied the doomed ship's captain back to his bark for one last visit to gather clothing and other personal items—with the exception of sextants and other articles useful to, and consequently confiscated by, the Confederates.

A *Shenandoah* prize party soon began scouring the *Alina* for still more items. As the Confederates quickly learned, the bark was relatively new, had only recently left port, and thus carried a rich bounty of goods. In accordance with international law and Confederate naval regulations, strict guidelines—at least officially—governed the plundering of captured ships. Confederate policy, for example, forbade sailors to confiscate items for their own personal property. Sensitive to Northern barbs that Confederate commerce raiders were no better than pirates, the *Shenandoah*'s two senior officers, Waddell and Whittle, strove to enforce strictures against wholesale pilfering and kept copious records of all confiscations. And by some accounts they were successful. Three decades later, Midshipman John Mason claimed in a published article that the crew "made it a rule from the start that there should be no pillaging of the captured vessels. If we needed stores for the ship's use, we took them, but our sailors were never allowed to plunder on their own account."

But the diary of Surgeon Charles Lining, who participated in the raid on the *Alina*, offers a less blinkered depiction of an actual prize party at work. And, while he offers no inventory of which items, if any, were taken for private use, Lining does bear witness to "a scene of indiscriminate plundering" in which "every thing which could possibly be of any use was seized upon & put into the boats. I was looking out especially for the eatables, & got a very good store of canned meats &c &c. After all the useful things were disposed the spirit of plunder still prevailed, and Cabin doors were taken down, drawers from under bunks taken out, & sent on board. All furniture & crockery was removed." As the confiscating drew to a close, a scuttling party boarded and began making preparations to send the bark to the briny depths.

Throughout that day, Captain Staples of the *Alina* concealed his welling despair over his ship's imminent demise. But with his final visit to his doomed ship concluded, as he and Hunt made the short trip by rowboat from the *Alina* back to the *Shenandoah*, the old salt, by Hunt's recollection, could hold back no longer. "I tell you what, maty," he said. "I've a daughter at home that that craft yonder was named for, and it goes against me cursedly to see her destroyed."

To that lament, Hunt offered meager consolation. "Neither myself nor my brother officers have any disposition to do you a personal injury," he told Staples. "Our orders are to prey upon the commerce of the United States, and in carrying them out, private individuals have to suffer, as the widows and orphans of the South have done and are doing."

"I know it is only the fortune of war, and I must take my chances with the rest," Staples responded, "but it's d—d hard, and I only hope I shall have opportunity of returning your polite attentions before this muss is over, that's all."

As the two talked, the scuttling party, armed with augers, knocked a hole in the ship's bottom. "In the course of an hour," Hunt recalled, the party returned to the *Shenandoah*, "having performed their duty, and I stood leaning over the quarter railing, watching, with a curious heart-heaviness that none but a sailor can understand, to see the gallant old barque sink in[to] her ocean grave."

At about four o'clock the Confederates and their prisoners, all of whom were now aboard the *Shenandoah*, watched the stern of the *Alina* settle into the water, thus forcing her bow high into the air. It was, Hunt recalled, "the first time I ever saw a vessel sink at sea, and I confess it was some time ere I could fully recover from the unpleasant feelings the sight engendered." Lieutenant Whittle, for his part, offered a more mixed reaction to the *Alina*'s destruction. "The sight," he recalled, "was grand and awful."[1]

According to a later computation the total value of the *Alina* and her cargo was $95,000, a welcome windfall for the *Shenandoah*. Indeed, even the U.S. flag flown hours earlier at the bark's peak became Confederate property. The raider's crew also obtained various pieces of furniture, knives and forks, pitchers and washbasins, a spring mattress (for Waddell's cabin), and a chronometer, an expensive and highly reliable clock used for navigation. The *Shenandoah* apparently already had a working chronometer, but because of that instrument's fragility and importance for determining longitude, Waddell decided there could be no harm in having the *Alina*'s as a backup. Most critically, however, before the *Alina* sank into the Atlantic, the Rebels had rowed away with enough ropes and pulleys to fashion the gun tackles they needed to bring their six-gun battery to full strength.

Once aboard the *Shenandoah*, the *Alina*'s officers and crew grew nervous and fearful. Waddell, for his part, remained mindful of his need for more sailors. Twelve men—the captain, two mates, a steward, and eight hands—had been taken off the *Alina*. The captain and his mates, having signed paroles—sworn promises not to return to sea for the war's duration, or otherwise act against the Confederacy—were allowed to roam the *Shenandoah*'s decks freely. And though all of the *Alina*'s officers had declined to join the Confederates, they were assigned cabins off the *Shenandoah*'s wardroom, the space close to the stern that was otherwise used as the commissioned officers' mess. According to Hunt, the prize's officers were "treated with every consideration." As for the *Alina*'s eight crewmen, like her officers, they were also invited to ship with the Confederates. But when only one of them agreed to sign the shipping articles, the other eight were immediately taken to the topgallant forecastle and outfitted with single leg irons.

By the next day, however, minds had changed and Whittle could record, "Today to my great joy six of the eight, i.e. two frenchmen and four dutchmen shipped as seamen." Considering the math in the most flattering light, he exulted, "We now have fifty-three souls attached to the ship, of whom 24 are officers." In happy expectation, the executive officer predicted, "I trust that at this rate we may soon increase our crew from our prizes to sixty exclusive of the officers. This will make us eighty four all told." But, he added with reflexive defensiveness, "Even now we have enough to take care of her."

Not totally unburdened of thoughts concerning the Union prisoners confined in the topgallant forecastle, Whittle then penned a self-congratulatory diary note to himself: "My prisoners thank me for our kindness to them. What a contrast with the treatment of our noble veterans by their side." Whittle, like the other *Shenandoah* officers, was mindful of widely reported and, in fact, widespread incidents of Confederate prisoners—military and civilian—being held in irons in Union prisons and on Union ships. Engaged in a practice that called for the stalking of smaller, usually unarmed merchant ships, and often tricking those vessels through the ruse of flying false colors, Whittle was eager to have his and his ship's conduct perceived in the most favorable light. At the least, he wanted to dispel—if only for the sake of the law and posterity—any notion that coercion had played any role in their winning of recruits for the raider. After all, the shipping articles that enlistees signed fixing the terms of their service aboard the *Shenandoah* included a pledge that they were signing the document of their "own free will and accord."

Likewise, in his own *Shenandoah* memoirs, penned two decades later, Captain Waddell even implied that, in the end, it was the sheer kindness of the Confederates and the nobility of their struggle that persuaded the *Alina*'s men to ship. "Engaging in conversations with our men was but a prelude to an enlistment of their sympathies in our cause," he recalled. Unmentioned were the roles played by sheer ignorance, lack of fluency in English, and intimidation.

Hermann Wicke, a youth from Hanover, Germany, and a ship's boy aboard the *Alina*, became a coal-trimmer aboard the *Shenandoah*. His decision to ship had nothing to do with personal sympathies for the Confederacy. Immediately upon boarding the raider, the young sailor had been asked by Waddell to ship with the Confederates. "I was intimidated," Wicke recalled, "and not understanding English properly then, I replied yes to everything I was told and asked; I signed, being afraid that by not doing so I might lose my life."

Another German recruited from the *Alina*, however, required a bit more persuasion. F. C. Behucke, of Lebeck, initially refused Waddell's entreaty. "The master-at-arms was then called, who put me in irons and in [the] top-gallant forecastle, along with the sheep and hens, where I was kept from Saturday 3 p.m. until Sunday night 11 p.m." Thus enlightened, Behucke soon saw the wisdom of joining the Confederates.

Alina seaman William Bruce, a naturalized U.S. citizen, held out for ten days, during which time he was compelled to work as an assistant to the *Shenandoah*'s wardroom cook during the day; at night he was held in irons. Following repeated entreaties to ship, "I was called by the said Whittle aft, and he then said to me, 'Steward, you might as well join; it will be better for you'; and I thereupon, in consequence of being ironed every night, made [to] work during the day, and pushed about and

abused by the crew and officers, consented to join and sub-
scribed a document agreeing to serve as ward-room steward."[2]

In early November, with "glorious" weather prevailing and the
additional recruits from the *Alina* lightening their labors, the
officers and men of the *Shenandoah* had become a less irri-
table, more contented, lot. The men even welcomed the slash-
ing rainfalls that, on November 2, pounded the ship's decks.
"It rained in torrents and the officers & men availed themselves
of the fresh water to wash their clothes," Whittle recalled. Typically, on a man-of-war the washing of clothes was done with
saltwater and soap, a process that, with each successive wash,
leaves an accumulating residue of salt in the fabric—making it
increasingly stiff and uncomfortable and causing irritation to
the skin.

Indeed, the autumn shower, falling democratically on officers and enlisted men alike, seemed to level all the men into one
soggy brotherhood of equals. As the Confederates—"from the
Capt. down"—shared the day's rain-soaked washing rites, many
of them also filled their own personal water casks. In keeping
with Confederate navy regulations, each sailor aboard a raider
was entitled to one gallon of water per day from the ship's water supply, to be used for both drinking and washing. Any water
that could be gathered from a rainfall constituted a stroke of
good fortune, and a backup against drier days.

The *Shenandoah* possessed large tanks for collecting rain;
and her steam engine had equipment that could, from saltwater,
condense five hundred gallons of fresh water per day. But the
process used up twenty tons of coal, an expenditure that the
ship's officers were not always willing to make. Given that it was
not uncommon for ships to encounter days, even weeks, when

there was no rain, a cask filled by a good downpour was always welcome.

During those early days of November, the Confederates happily found themselves in the wake of sailing ships crossing the equator. Even better, for ships dependent on wind and ocean currents, a category that included most of the world's merchant fleets, these mid-Atlantic waters constituted a critical fork in the watery road of international commerce. Through them passed ships bound for, and sailing from, the Pacific along two of the world's great southern sea routes—westward via Cape Horn and eastward via the Cape of Good Hope. Given those circumstances, for a commerce raider sailing with the advantage of steam propulsion these waters offered rich possibilities.

On the afternoon of November 4—six days after the *Alina*'s capture—the *Shenandoah*'s lookout spotted a small sailing ship standing southwest. That night the Confederates managed to keep up with the ship, and the next morning, under steam in a dead calm, they gave chase. By 8:00 a.m., a Confederate boarding party had identified the vessel as the *Charter Oak*, a schooner from Boston bound, via Cape Horn, for San Francisco with a mixed cargo—including coal and furniture. The nine people brought aboard the raider that evening included the *Charter Oak*'s captain, his wife, her widowed sister, and her son. Waddell paroled the ship's captain; the two women and the boy were likewise freed, but without having to sign a parole. The *Charter Oak*'s other officers and men were, for the time being, placed in irons in the topgallant forecastle.

Like the *Shenandoah*'s first capture, the *Charter Oak* provided the Confederates with a welcome supply of goods—more furniture (sofas, small tables, and chairs), plus 600 pounds of canned lobster and various canned fruits and vegetables, including 2,000 pounds of canned tomatoes. Also discovered aboard the captured schooner was $200 in cash belonging to her captain. Waddell, however, in a gesture of Southern gallantry, promptly returned the money to the captain's wife "on condition she not give any part of it to her husband."

Late that afternoon, the Confederates torched the *Charter Oak*. To satisfy themselves that the flames completed the ship's destruction, the *Shenandoah* lingered for several hours. But Waddell also had strategic reasons for lingering. The burning ship, he believed, "would draw assistance," and for the *Shenandoah* yet another possible capture. However, when no rescue ships appeared Waddell issued orders for the raider to resume her southward course.

By custom, in the British, U.S., and Confederate navies, the first Sunday of each month on a man-of-war began with a general muster of the crew. And, as Herman Melville noted in *White-Jacket*, "this ceremony acquires its chief solemnity, and to a novice, is rendered even terrible, by the reading of the Articles of War." For a sailor, that document constituted a sort of Holy Writ in which his government codified the laws of conduct by which he was to comport himself and sternly stipulated the appropriate punishment—in most cases, death—for any violation.

Less serious, day-to-day shipboard offenses tended to be addressed by "the Captain's mast," a process in which infractions were adjudicated by the ship's captain, who, governed by naval regulations, assigned an appropriate punishment. While officially its namesake's purview, the captain's mast in actual practice tended to be administered by the ship's executive officer, who acted as the captain's eyes and ears in matters of crew discipline. More serious infractions, those requiring courts-martial and death sentences, came before the captain under the Articles of War. Capital offenses ranged from sleeping while on watch to insubordination and mutinous behavior.[3]

On November 6, when the *Shenandoah*'s crew first heard the Articles of War, few of the men—and even some of the officers—had yet to receive their uniforms. That fact, however, did nothing to diminish the reading's impact upon the assembled sailors. As Surgeon Lining recalled, "there was a great deal of punishing by death in it."

The next day, on the afternoon of November 7, the Confederates—at latitude 6°28' N, longitude 27°06' W—spotted and captured another bark, the *D. Godfrey*, of Boston, en route to Valparaiso, Chile. But although the vessel carried lumber and barrels of salted beef and pork, the Confederates declined any confiscations. As Waddell recalled, "The Shenandoah was full of provisions and room could not be found." All would be put to the torch. The Confederates later put the value of the ship and her cargo at $36,000.

As darkness fell over the mid-Atlantic, the *D. Godfrey* was set afire. "In fifteen minutes," Hunt recalled, "the flames were bursting through the skylight, and the work of destruction had begun." It made for an impressive scene. "Darkness had settled around us when the rigging and sails took fire, but every rope could be seen as distinctly as upon a painted canvas, as the flames made their way from the deck, and writhed upward like fiery serpents."

Standing on the *Shenandoah*'s deck, the *D. Godfrey*'s master grimly watched as the flames climbed his ship's sails, rigging, and spars. "That was a vessel which has done her duty well for forty years," he lamented. "She has faced old Boreas in every part of the world, in the service of her master, and after such a career, to be destroyed by men on a calm night, on this tropical sea, is too bad—too bad!"

Later that day, recording an inventory of their latest capture's human cargo, Whittle exulted, "Onboard of our prize there were ten souls, all told, viz. [a] Capt. & 2 mates, 6 seamen and a negro steward. To my great joy 5 seamen and the steward shipped—They are all good, young men and the darkey is the very man I want for ship's cook."

When entreating sailors to ship with them, Confederate naval officers pointed out the obvious rewards: sailor's pay and the freedom to move about the ship. Those advantages were contrasted with the bleaker alternatives, including no pay, nights and even days confined in irons, and possibly worse. The latter hint was usually enough. And in the case of the *Shenandoah* both Confederate and non-Confederate accounts agree that physical abuse of the sort that went beyond confinement in irons seemed to be the exception. In many, if not most, cases the Confederates simply found no need for such rough persuasion.

In a wartime letter to his father, Lieutenant Grimball recalled that most of the raider's prisoners were non-Americans with no pronounced loyalties to either side in the Civil War. "Initially, these captives generally refused to ship, but we kept them in irons so long that as is the case with all Sailors it makes but little difference to them what side of the fence they are on [. I]n preference to being in 'limbo' they joined the Shenandoah." Similarly, James Bulloch later recalled, with pro-Confederate exaggeration, that "the captured crews of American ships, expressed but little if any veneration for the 'old flag,' and did not appear to look upon the new arrangement of bunting at the peaks of the Confederate ships as a foreign invention. Many of the more intelligent of the officers, and not a few captains, expressed no animosity against the South."

Indeed, one historian later concluded that many prisoners from prizes captured by Confederate raiders even seemed, when enlisted to assist in their ships' destruction, "to take pleasure in knocking down bulkheads in order to ensure a good draught for the flames." But what Bulloch attributed to incipient pro-Confederate sympathies the historian attributes to simpler realities: the presence of great numbers of foreigners in the U.S. merchant marine who felt no loyalties one way or the other, and their desire to escape confinement by displays of sympathy to the Confederates.[4]

More to the point, fear and a simple desire to avoid physical punishment also played a large underlying and direct role in shipboard conversions to the Confederate cause. For as journals kept by officers aboard the *Shenandoah*—particularly that of Lieutenant William Whittle—make clear, physical abuse, part of the raider's standard repertory of punishment for shipboard infractions, played a part in coercing captured seamen reluctant to ship with the Confederates.

John Madden, a seaman from Boston captured aboard the *D. Godfrey*, was subjected to recruitment methods similar to those recounted by sailors aboard the *Alina*. When he first boarded the raider, he was told that if he didn't join the *Shenandoah* he would be put in irons and imprisoned in the coal hold. "Being sick at the time, and in order to avoid punishment, I consented to join her for six months." But several other men who shipped aboard the raider that same day were subjected to the harrowing physical punishment the Confederates called "tricing"—in which the subject's hands or thumbs were chained together around a beam over his head, so that his feet scarcely reached the deck. The ordeal caused excruciating pain, even more so in the case of recalcitrant offenders, for whom the chain was increasingly shortened, thereby raising them higher and higher. Though never officially adopted by the U.S. Navy, tricing had emerged on American ships after flogging was banned in 1850. On Confederate ships, however, most of which were commanded by former U.S Navy officers, the practice became a standard form of punishment for both prisoners and wayward crew members.

The Confederates "triced-up" up several *D. Godfrey* crew members. But, among those so abused, the case of the black steward John Williams stands out. Free African-American seamen had served on U.S. Navy ships since the early nineteenth century. After 1841, however, their numbers had been restricted to no more than 5 percent of the enlisted force. But after the Civil War commenced those numbers reached as high as 23 percent of the navy's total sailors. John Williams had numbered among those men.

Indeed, upon boarding the *Shenandoah* and being asked to ship aboard the raider, Williams cited his past U.S. Navy service as he declined the Confederates' initial entreaties. As Williams later recalled, Captain Waddell, the next day, came around and said, "I had better join the ship, as it would be better for me; that as colored people were the cause of the war, if I did not join it would go hard with me." For reasons Williams could not grasp, the captain "said he wanted to get all the colored persons he could."

"I offered to work, but refused to join," Williams recalled. Waddell countered with a threat to lock him in the coal hold for six months. The captain then followed his threat with an offer—"a month's advance (£6) which I refused, because I am a loyal citizen, and have served my time in the Navy of the United States." As Williams explained to Waddell, he had been aboard the steamer USS *Congress* when she was sunk by the Confederate ironclad CSS *Virginia*, in March 1862, and subsequently, until discharged by the Navy, aboard the frigate USS *Minnesota*.

Waddell thereafter forced Williams to work as a cook. But during the next few months the captain and Lieutenant Whittle continued their efforts to persuade him to ship. Each time, Williams later claimed, he refused, and received the same punishment: "I have been triced up by the thumbs seven times for upholding my country." Typically, he recalled, the tricing took place after the seaman's cooking shift had ended—often from 6:00 until 9:00 p.m. Unbowed, Williams never wavered in his refusal. On one occasion he even boasted to Whittle that if his former ship the *Minnesota* encountered the *Shenandoah* "she would blow this vessel out of the water."

During the coming months, Lieutenant Whittle's contempt for the cook, a defiant black man and a proud veteran of the U.S. Navy, and what he represented, came to burn with a white-hot intensity. In one instance, for example, when another sailor, George Flood, and Williams were brought before Whittle for fighting, the first lieutenant knew immediately how to adjudicate the case. "I justified Flood and triced up Williams. Here was a negro against a yankee. I had trouble in bringing him to his bearings but he finally came down."[5]

On the morning of November 9—two days after the *D. Godfrey*'s capture—the Confederates spotted yet another sailing ship, and she appeared to be an American vessel. A three-hour pursuit under sail, however, revealed her to be a Danish brig, the *Anna Jane*, bound for Rio de Janeiro. An officer was dispatched to the vessel and a deal was struck: in exchange for the

Alina's chronometer, and a barrel of beef and another of bread, the captain of the *Anna Jane* agreed to take on some of the *Shenandoah*'s prisoners and deposit them in Rio. Most of the Confederates welcomed their less crowded ship, but Whittle questioned the wisdom of the deal that his captain had struck: "I was opposed to the prisoners today being sent away as their release will certainly let all the yankees know that we are near."

On November 10, the Confederates captured the *Susan*, an ancient brigantine from Cardiff, Wales, bound for South America with a load of coal. Because the vessel had what appeared to be a paddle wheel on one side, the Confederates initially mistook it for a paddle-wheeled ocean steamer—a type of ship that by the 1860s, with the development of the screw propeller, had become a rare sight on the world's oceans. As Lining recalled, "She was one of the funniest looking craft I ever saw, very deeply laden with a wheel on the lea side[,] something like a steamboats', which turned as she moved through the water." In this case, however, the wheel was not for propulsion; its turning as the water passed over it powered a bilge pump necessary to keep the constantly leaking ship sufficiently free of water to maintain her course and stay afloat.

However decrepit, the *Susan* marked the Confederates' fourth prize and the first they had captured relying exclusively on sails for the *Shenandoah*'s propulsion. She and her cargo were valued at $5,436. After stripping the brigantine of all desired goods, recalled Whittle, "We scuttled her, and she went down bow first, her stern raising straight up into the air." Having by now become a connoisseur of the various ways in which ships slip beneath the waves, Whittle took due notice of how that afternoon's sinking departed from the phenomenon's usual physics: "It is rarely the case that a vessel will go down bow first, it is generally the reverse."

After boarding the *Shenandoah* that day, three Englishmen among the *Susan*'s crew shipped with the Confederates. The prize's crew also included four or five native or naturalized U.S. citizens, all of whom—"in preference to torture"—also decided to join the Confederates. However, most of the *Susan*'s total crew of approximately fifty men, excluding officers, were non-English speakers, Germans primarily. Because the *Shenandoah* was already crowded, the Confederates did little to encourage them to ship.

Two days later—just after midnight on November 12—the Rebels captured the *Kate Prince*, a large clipper ship from Cardiff bound for South America with a load of coal. Though the ship clearly had a U.S. owner and thus was fair game, Waddell, after talking to the ship's master and inspecting her documents, concluded that her cargo likely belonged to a British subject. In the parlance of commerce raiding, she was a neutral. Reverting to an occasional practice among Confederate commerce raiders, Waddell thus elected to ransom the vessel: allow her to continue her voyage unharmed in exchange for taking on the *Shenandoah*'s remaining prisoners. Her captain was, in turn, made to sign a bond for $40,000, to be paid to the Confederate government by the ship's owner after the war, presuming a Southern victory.

In gratitude to Waddell for sparing his ship, the *Kate Prince*'s master gave the Confederates two barrels of Irish potatoes. Such bonhomie notwithstanding, Surgeon Charles Lining considered Waddell's decision "a great mistake": "a ship worth so much money was ransomed for the sake of a cargo not worth seventeen thousand dollars at the most. Better to have burned her & let our government settle about the cargo afterwards."

Soon after daybreak that morning—November 12—after the *Kate Prince* had sailed away, the Confederates spotted the

Adelaide, a bark that, though flying Argentine colors, appeared to be of Yankee construction. Hours later, at about 12:00, Lining recalled, "Owing to her build &c. we hove her to & boarded her." The mystery of the ship's identity was hardly resolved when the *Shenandoah*'s boarding party met the *Adelaide*'s obviously American-born captain and inspected his documents. "These looked so suspicious that the boarding officer sent the Captain with his papers on board," Lining recalled. The ship, from Baltimore and bound for Rio de Janeiro, was carrying a load of flour. And, once aboard the *Shenandoah*, the *Adelaide*'s Virginia-born captain, James P. Williams, "did some tall swearing." Under oath, he told the Confederates that while his ship's owners lived in Buenos Aires, her cargo of flour belonged to a merchant in New York.

The Confederates, however, believed no part of Williams's story. "It was evident she had been put under the 'Buenos Ayrian' flag for some purpose, the only question was, was it a bona fide transfer," Lining noted. Later that day—still under oath—Williams finally admitted that, as the Confederates suspected, the ship's transfer to an Argentine owner was bogus. But another complication soon presented itself: "It appears that the Barque is the property of a Mr. Pendergrast of Baltimore Md, who is a good southerner, & who to save his property from the Yankees put this barque under the Buenos Ayrian flag[,] making a fictitious transfer of his vessel."

The Confederates knew of merchant Pendergrast by reputation, and considered him someone who "sympathized with our cause." Even so, Captain Williams's belated admission of that ownership enraged Waddell. The *Adelaide*'s master had, after all, lied under oath. Moreover, Pendergrast's professed Southern sympathies be damned: by carrying Yankee flour, he had proved himself a traitor to the Confederacy. The *Shenandoah*'s captain ordered a boarding party to begin preparing both the *Adelaide* and her cargo to be burned. Soon thereafter, however, while exploring the contents of a mailbag found aboard the brigantine, Lining found a letter that added yet another wrinkle to that day's mystery: a letter from a business associate of Pendergrast's which revealed that the bark's cargo of flour, like the ship itself, belonged to Pendergrast.

With that final piece of the puzzle in place, it suddenly occurred to the Confederates that Pendergrast, as a Southern sympathizer operating out of a Union port, had been playing his own version of the dodge performed by Northern shipowners who transferred ownership and registration of their vessels to avoid destruction by Confederate raiders. In a scheme the totality of which even the *Adelaide*'s master had, until that moment, been unaware, Pendergrast had made a bogus transfer of both his ship and her cargo to "shield them from the Yankee government."

Upon that realization, Waddell ordered a halt to the ship's destruction and the return of any goods already taken from her. "This was done," Lining recalled, "but it was found impossible to restore her to her original state. The Cabin was much knocked to pieces in making preparations to burn her—kerosene oil had been thrown over the deck—tar & oil had been poured upon the floor in the fore-hold to light her quickly—a good many articles taken from her had been lost, or destroyed, & other injury had been done."

The *Adelaide* remained seaworthy, but the Confederates were unable to repair all the damage they had done to the ship. Captain Waddell, however, did take one action to stem further difficulties for the ship's owner. When the *Adelaide* returned to Baltimore, he feared, Union port officials—noticing the damage to her and aware that she had been sailing waters shared by the raider the *Shenandoah*—might well deduce that she had been stopped by the raider but spared complete destruction due to her owner's Confederate sympathies. In that case, the Federal officials might well confiscate the ship and her cargo. To preempt such action, Waddell, ostensibly giving the ship a solid anti-Confederate pedigree, formally bonded the *Adelaide*'s cargo, thus providing her master with papers asserting that her owner owed the Rebels $24,000. But Waddell's paperwork also asserted that the ship herself had been spared because she had been sailing under a neutral flag—an assertion that in a legal incongruity also begged the question of why cargo on a neutral vessel had been thus bonded.

Beyond improvising such legal fictions, Lining recalled, "we could only write to Mr. P. appologising [*sic*] for our mistake."

The next day, Sunday, November 13, began at 10:00 a.m. with a general muster—with all the ship's officers assembled together for the first time in the brand-new gray uniforms that Commander James D. Bulloch had ordered made for the cruise. By all accounts, the men presented a smart appearance. The official Confederate naval officer uniform consisted of gray or white trousers, gray caps about four inches high with a patent-leather visor, and a long double-breasted gray coat with two rows of navy buttons running down its upper front. Rank was indicated by buttons (small, medium, or large), shoulder straps, cap insignias, and a band of gold strips around the jacket's lower sleeves, the top band of which was tied into a natty loop. Nevertheless, many Confederate naval officers resisted wearing the uniform. As one veteran later complained, "Who had ever heard of a gray sailor, no matter what nationality he served." Lieutenant Whittle, for one, concurred; recalling an assembly on the *Shenandoah*'s deck, he noted, "The men were all dressed in uniform and looked very well but gray will never stand the sea air. I have a suit which I never had on until I came onboard and now it looks as though I had been wearing it for a year." Reluctantly, Whittle found himself longing for—if only for its heartiness before the elements—his old U.S. Navy uniform: "Oh! no the old blue was the best, and I think the only color which will stand."[6]

Soon after the muster—at twelve noon that same day—the Confederates spotted, gave chase to, and soon captured yet another prize, the *Lizzie M. Stacey*, out of Boston and en route to the Sandwich Islands via the Cape of Good Hope. The Confederates put the value of the *Lizzie M. Stacey* and her cargo at $15,000. After stripping the schooner of desired goods and stores, they set her on fire at 6:30 p.m. Of the eight souls aboard the vessel, Waddell paroled her master and put his mate and six crewmen in irons.

But what most struck the Confederates about their latest prize was her speed. "She was new and fast," Waddell recalled. To that, Cornelius Hunt later added, "Had she been armed the *Lizzie M. Stacey* would certainly never have surrendered without a tussle, and with a favorable wind, I am inclined to believe she would have shown us a clean pair of heels." Indeed, Waddell and other officers even pondered duplicating the feat, accomplished by Raphael Semmes and other commanders during the war, of capturing Union merchant ships, converting them to raiders with new Confederate crews, and sending them off in search of more prizes. Raphael Semmes, for instance, while commanding the *Alabama*, had captured the merchant ship *Conrad*, then sent her out for raiding as the newly commissioned

CSS *Tuscaloosa*. The gambit held particular appeal for the young and ambitious Lieutenant Whittle, who, throughout the *Shenandoah*'s cruise, would pine for his own command. But though the *Lizzie M. Stacey* seemed ideal for such a conversion, the more cautious Waddell, citing "the scarcity of seamen," resisted the temptation.

As for further efforts to recruit men from their latest prize, the entreaties, threats, and tricings began the next morning. Of the six seamen, Charles Hopkins, an African-American, who had served as a steward aboard the *Lizzie M. Stacey*, became the first from that craft to ship with the *Shenandoah*, and the second black, after John Williams from the *D. Godfrey*, to be taken prisoner by the Confederates. Whittle promptly turned the "Baltimore darkey" over "to the tender mercies of the forward officer's mess." Following Hopkins, a Scotsman from the *Lizzie M. Stacey*, identified only as "Strachmen," became the second *Lizzie M. Stacey* crewman to ship. When none of the other four of the schooner's crew volunteered, however, Whittle ordered all of them to help shovel coal out of the berth deck—"supposing that they would prefer it to confinement."

The executive officer viewed this new assignment as a gesture of magnanimity, but he quickly learned that his perception was not universally shared. "Two of them who were yankees positively refused, but as I had given the order it must be obeyed," Whittle recalled. "I triced one fellow up, and the other said he would prefer to go to work to being similarly dealt with. The tricing up had a most wonderful effect—in two hours the man begged to be let down, as he desired to ship." Whittle had reason to be pleased: the gamble of not going to Tenerife, which he believed he had orchestrated, had paid off. In one month at

sea, the crew of the *Shenandoah* had doubled its original number. "We now have men enough to take care of the ship," Whittle concluded.

On November 15, with the raider now in the trades, the
Shenandoah marked her passage over the equator; and, like
sailors from time immemorial, the ship's officers and crew commemorated that transit with the traditional mock ritual of a
court presided over by "King Neptune." At 7:30 that evening,
as a wobbly trumpet fanfare announced his arrival, a crewman
costumed as the fabled sea king, carrying a giant harpoon and
accompanied by others disguised as his royal retinue, climbed
over the ship's bow. A line of sailors soon queued up for audi-
ences with the briny monarch. One by one, as the men came before him, King Neptune posed questions to each of the ship's
crew and officers who had never before crossed the equator—
which, in this case, was all but a handful of those aboard.
Depending on the individual sailor's answer to the king's question—which could be as simple as "Where are you from?"—the
supplicant might get a dousing of water, an unwelcome shave,
or worse, a mouth-washing with a gruesome mixture of grease,
soap, and other ingredients.

Of the ship's officers, only Waddell and Lieutenant Sidney
Smith Lee, Jr., had crossed the equator before. Thus, tallying
the ship's entire roster of officers and men, King Neptune
had a long line of supplicants. Even Executive Officer William
Whittle was not exempted from the rites, and stripped down to
his undershirt for the ritual shave accorded by the sea god. "The
shaving soap they used on me," he recalled, "was a most wonderful mixture of soap, grease, molasses and stewed apples."[7]

EIGHT

Breezing Up

evities like King Neptune's visit relieved the daily grimness of shipboard life, but they also underscored the growing necessity of such releases. By mid-November the esprit de corps of the *Shenandoah*'s first days had given way to the harsher realities of life at sea. Weeks earlier, both officers and seamen had exuberantly worked shoulder to shoulder to get the steamer to sea. But, though necessity still compelled officers to occasionally roll up their sleeves and work up a sweat with the rest of the crew, the cruise's early élan soon gave way to the hardships of damp, confined conditions, chronic manpower shortages, and a hardening of the ship's formal chain of command. Lieutenant John Grimball recalled that the officers "had long since given up hauling on ropes." Instead, "they now walked the Quarter Deck with kid gloves[,] the remains of some of their Paris purchases."

As officers and crew interacted on the ship's decks and in her cramped cabins and quarters, informal alliances and feuds developed. Occasionally, tensions flared into fisticuffs. More often, they manifested themselves as sullen brooding, meanspirited gossip, and acts of pettiness. In November, for instance, Surgeon Charles Lining, upon inspecting an injury suffered by ship's carpenter John O'Brien, adjudged it insufficiently severe to place him on the ship's sick list—a coveted spot that exempted the listee from shipboard duties until he recovered. Lining's decision irritated O'Brien. Compounding his sins, the surgeon, when he saw the carpenter in the days ahead, failed to inquire about his health. Later, when Lining requested some painting supplies from O'Brien, the carpenter claimed he could not find them. "He has taken a great dislike to me," Lining noted in his journal. "The fact is that he has been a politician in some Navy Yard in the U.S. & accustomed to have all about him do just as he wanted them to do, and now as he can't get that he thinks he must growl." The two men never came to blows, but a stony silence soon grew between them.

By mid-November—as the *Shenandoah* had passed south of the equator and King Neptune climbed aboard the raider's decks—the Confederates' numbers had swelled to sixty-two men—thirty-nine seamen and twenty-three officers. During the coming months, polyglot enlistees from various Indian Ocean and Pacific cultures would swell their ranks still more. But already, with the recent recruits from the *Alina*, *Charter Oak*, *D. Godfrey*, *Susan*, *Kate Prince*, and *Lizzie M. Stacey*, this steamer, with her increasingly multicultural crew, showed signs of becoming a Tower of Babel. Chew noted that the cruiser carried crewmen from the "Confederacy, U. States, England, France, Holland, Denmark, Sweden, Norway, Russia, East India, Africa, Ireland, Scotland, Wales. What a medley!"

"With such a mixture of nationalities," Lieutenant Whittle recalled, "the most rigid discipline had to be, and was, maintained, and the happiness of all was promoted by prompt punishment of all offenders. This, of course, devolved on me." As the ship's executive officer, Whittle's duties included a wide range of day-to-day responsibilities, from navigation to supervising the daily watches. Herman Melville recalled the burdens placed on a man-of-war's executive officer: "By the captain he is held responsible for every thing; by that magnate, indeed, he is supposed to be omnipresent; down in the hold, and up aloft, at one and the same time."

As for Whittle, he took a heartfelt pride in the *Shenandoah*'s steaming and sailing capabilities. Recounting the capture of the *Susan*, the first prize the raider overtook exclusively under sails, Whittle wrote in his journal on November 10, "Today we tacked ship three times and each time the ship went round beautifully—I never saw a vessel work better. With even our few men we can tack her very easily." His pride, however, did not rob him of the occasional common touch. Still later that day, he supervised, and eventually joined, the shipboard routine of "holystoning" the ship's decks.[1]

To Whittle, successful ship-handling required a disciplined crew, and this discipline, in turn, depended upon the resolute supervision of the men by the ship's officers. Key to that supervision, he believed, was his own willingness to punish acts of insubordination and other violations of ship regulations. And, by all accounts, the twenty-four-year-old Annapolis graduate relished that role.

On November 24, for instance, after two seamen who had engaged in a fistfight were reported to him, Whittle—based on his own account of the incident—seemed to take pride in devising a penalty that reflected his judgment of each man's culpability. "It now became my painful duty to punish them, which I did in a novel way, by putting them in single irons each one embracing the other, around an iron stancheon. The first impulse on their part was to laugh at the joke, but they soon concluded that it was all on one side, and send [*sic*] me word 'please to let them down.' I did so after they had been long enough their [*sic*] to make an example of them."

In a similar spirit three days later, when the executive officer caught Thomas Hall, another crewman, engaged in some "piece of scandalous behavior" (unspecified in Whittle's diary), he was more than prepared when the first tricing failed to evoke the proper spirit of contrition: "He was afterwards very abusive and I gagged him and triced him up higher." Even after Hall's second tricing, however, Whittle had no expectation that he had completed the intended rehabilitation: "This punishment will I think last Hall for a few days at the end of which time I think he will try his hand again—when, if I repeat the dose with a gradual increase he will be made as good a man as any to be found."

Whittle's diary also teems with solemn expressions of devotion—toward the pieties of his Episcopalian faith, the Confederacy, and, most poignantly and frequently, toward his sweetheart, Pattie, back in Virginia. "My love for her is as singular as it is pure," he vowed. "I never saw her but on one single occasion, and still my love for [her] is such as I never experienced for any person before." Indeed, brutality and piety threaded Whittle's hours and days into a seamless mesh. Confronting a French sailor accused of insubordination one Sunday, Whittle bound and gagged the offender. And when the seaman proved still unrepentant, Whittle recalled, he triced him up: "He was very determined not to be subdued, but I brought him down by tricing him a little higher each time—and when I took him down he was like a Lamb." The executive officer then spent the remainder of that Sabbath in more tranquil devotions: "I have spent the day in reading the [Sunday] service and rereading some of my letters from my own Pattie."[2]

As the *Shenandoah*'s disciplinarian, Whittle's feats of rough justice, comporting with naval traditions, projected a patriarchal, Old Testament–style zeal to provide moral uplift for those he commanded. "Discipline is more necessary to the happiness of men than any thing else," he wrote in his journal. "By discipline I do not mean tyranny but a thorough governing—You must thoroughly examine all reports, give the accused the advantage of any doubt, but finding him guilty punish him well— Let the man see that you are ruled by Justice, and he is ruled by you." From Whittle's perspective, most of his discipline cases originated with men not from merchant vessels but from those who had served on U.S. Navy ships. But because the men who serve on military ships are, when accused of violating rules, subject to sterner consequences than merchant sailors, so punishing them, Whittle believed, required more rigorous measures. "Nearly all old man-of-wars men try these experiments and if not punished will go on—but if they are met properly they behave beautifully," he concluded.

By Whittle's reckoning, no one—himself included—was exempt from his scrutiny. That November, while attempting, not for the first time, to quit smoking, he depicted the effort in his diary as a test of his moral character. Then and there, he resolved to stop both chewing and smoking tobacco. Using an ironic choice of metaphor given the cause for which he was fighting, he pledged to "do my best to break the chains of slavery to a habit which has done me so much damage—I may not have the power to quit it, but I am going to make all the effort that I am capable of—God give me strength."

Even as Whittle spread his gospel of chains, bruised wrists, and holystoned decks, yet another shipboard drama was playing out in and across the *Shenandoah*'s cabins, holds, and decks. From the start, Captain James Waddell had seemed to many of the Confederates an aloof figure. By late November, however, as the forty-one-year-old Waddell settled into his first command, this man, who once had seemed merely a distant, possibly shy, officer had begun to show signs of becoming a full-fledged autocrat. In ways large and small, he increasingly irritated officers and crew. In November, he issued his first written order—a dress code—to the ship's officers, a dictate that to many of them seemed gratuitous, even silly. "'Orders' are all the order of the day," Lining complained, "& the Captain has promulgated his first. Among others was one requiring all officers, when they go out of the ward room to wear their uniforms—black & blue pants are allowed—nothing but grey coats or jackets. No slouch hats to be worn. This last rather knocked [off] my <u>broad brimmed</u> [hat], & compels me to wear my cap. I drew some flannel from the ship & went to tailoring, to make myself a coat jacket to wear in these tropics."

Further grating on the crew members was what many perceived as the captain's excessive penchant for sailing under short sails. To them, the practice increasingly denoted a commander fearful of engaging the wind and, ultimately, his enemy's ships. "A splendid breeze, & we are going faster now than we have ever done before under sail," Lining observed in mid-November. "But we find, that whenever <u>night</u> comes on, and she is going her nine or ten knots, the skipper begins to get uneasy, can't sleep, gets fidgety, & then takes in sail."

As each man on the ship took the other's measure, one fact became increasingly clear: they were bound together for the long haul. Weeks earlier, Lining had predicted that the cruise would be a "short one"—over within months of their leaving Las Desertas. In his November 19 journal entry, however, resigning himself to a far longer outing, the surgeon concluded,

"Before we get through with this cruise, we will be counting, not by months, but by years."

By late November the *Shenandoah*'s southward course had put her off Brazil's long Atlantic coast. There, hurried by the trade winds, the Confederates scudded along at a brisk nine to ten knots. Because they had now reached the path of American ships sailing from New York via Cape Horn to San Francisco, Waddell had high hopes for more captures. But although they spotted many ships—and on the twenty-sixth gave chase to what turned out to be an English vessel—none of them proved to be American.

In the early hours of December 4, the *Shenandoah*, by then having bent to an eastward course, toward the Cape of Good Hope, encountered what appeared by the cut of her sails and her rig to be an American-built whaling vessel. "She looked Yankeeish," Lining observed. As the Confederates, giving chase, pulled closer to their quarry, the ship raised the flag of the newly formed republic of Italy and hove to. Hoping the Italian colors were a ruse, the Confederates raised an American flag. And, just before 5:30 a.m., they dispatched a boarding party led by Sailing Master Irvine Bulloch to the *Dea del Mare*, from Genoa.

Even if the ship the Confederates were now boarding turned out to be what she seemed to be—an unarmed Italian merchant ship—merely boarding her and conversing with her officers entailed a risk. All manner of vessels filled these Atlantic shipping lanes—including U.S. Navy men-of-war, which by now were certainly on the lookout for the *Shenandoah*. The Italian vessel, once released, might easily communicate, directly or indirectly, the raider's presence to any nearby enemy ships.

To reduce the odds of that eventuality, surgeon Lining recalled, the Confederate boarding party, using a sartorial deceit, removed "their Caps and grey suits, & were dressed as much as possible in blue." But sailing master Bulloch, who led the party, after interviewing the ship's master and poring over her papers, reached the expected conclusion. "It turned out as we feared," Cornelius Hunt recalled. "She was American built, but had been sold to the Italians to keep her out of the hands of enterprising gentlemen in our line of business." The Confederates could only hope that their disguises had fooled the Italians.[3]

Later that morning, the Confederates spotted another possible prize. But as they approached the craft they began to suspect that she might be a Union gunboat and decided to go no closer. Still later that morning—at 10:45—the Confederates made out, faintly in the cloudy distance, what turned out to be Inaccessible Island, of the remote Tristan de Cunha Island group, roughly midway between South America and Africa—1,400 miles to the south of her nearest neighbor, the island of St. Helena, and 1,700 miles west of Cape Town, the closest major port. As all the officers were aware, the island group was adjacent to a rich whaling ground, and its main and namesake island, Tristan de Cunha, served as a popular stopover for whaling vessels. As early as December 2, Whittle had expressed hopes that the *Shenandoah* might stop there, catching any Yankee whaling vessels that might be in port. By noon the cruiser stood some forty miles northwest of Tristan de Cunha, and though Waddell claimed sympathy with officers eager to make a stop at the island, the day's faint winds, their dwindling coal supply, and his growing reluctance to use the steam engine, led him to decide against it.

Continuing on their westward course, the Confederates, at 5:00 that afternoon, spotted yet another possible prize. This time, however, appearances did not deceive: as the *Shenandoah* drew nearer, the bark raised Old Glory. Indeed, when a Confederate boarding party reached the already hove-to bark, it found the whaling vessel's crew already in the process of "cutting out"—cutting up and hoisting aboard—a right whale they had just taken.[4]

The bark's master, Charles Worth, and her papers quickly established that the Confederates had just captured the *Edward*, an American whaling vessel from New Bedford, Massachusetts. Because the longevity and peripatetic character of a whaling vessel's voyages demanded that she leave her home port prepared for far longer cruises—often lasting years—than merchant vessels, Waddell counted on the *Edward* to supply the Confederates with far more bountiful provisions than those offered by other prizes. But because it was already late in the day, he decided to wait for morning to begin transferring cargo from the *Edward* to the *Shenandoah*.

In the end, the Confederates spent two days hauling booty from the *Edward*. A later assessment put the value of the vessel and her cargo at $20,000—a modest amount compared with that of other prizes. But, measured against the *Shenandoah*'s needs that season, the bark constituted a gold mine: 50 barrels of beef, 49 barrels of pork, 46 barrels of flour, 6,000 pounds of ship biscuits, 1,200 pounds of soap, 600 pounds of coffee, 400 pounds of butter, other foodstuffs, and a wealth of rope, canvas, and blocks. "We have more than enough provisions to last us our cruize [*sic*]," Whittle exclaimed. The Confederates also gained three brand-new whaleboats to replace two decrepit boats the *Shenandoah* had been carrying. For many of the raider's southern officers in command of this cruise, the moment also marked their first visceral encounter with the very enterprise they had been dispatched to attack. Seizing that opportunity, Hunt recalled, "a number of our officers went off to see what a whaler was like, and inspect the blubber which had been cut from the sea-monster which was still moored alongside."

Upon capturing the *Edward*, the Confederates brought her captain, his three mates, and twenty-two sailors to the raider. Although they paroled the captain, fearing a possible uprising they confined in irons the mates and the rest of the vessel's crew. Of the bark's twenty-two captured seamen, most of whom were Portuguese, none consented to ship with the Confederates. The *Edward*'s crew, Whittle self-servingly complained, "are so cowardly that you could not induce them to ship." The specifics of Whittle's inducements that day to the Portuguese sailors are unknown, but his judgment of them—in light of his subsequent and documented methods of persuasion—rings hollow.

The *Edward*'s confined crew members, along with the three prisoners from the *Lizzie M. Stacey*, brought the *Shenandoah*'s prison population to twenty-nine. That number, in Whittle's estimation, was "entirely too large to permit them to run about the deck—more particularly as we have captured the majority of our crew." The executive officer knew, after all, not to place excessive faith in conversions won by tricing up captured sailors.

On the afternoon of December 6, the Confederates set fire to the *Edward*. "I have rarely seen any thing which is more beautifully grand than a ship burning at sea," Whittle exclaimed. Captain Waddell, presumably, also enjoyed the fire. But by now he was preoccupied with another matter: the mutinous dangers posed by all those foreign seamen crowding his ship. Before he took any more prizes, and found himself with more captives, he needed to find a place to deposit his prisoners. Reversing his earlier instructions, he now gave orders for the *Shenandoah* to drop south, toward the still nearby island of Tristan de Cunha.

The next morning that tiny British colony's northwest shore was in sight. Upon spotting an English flag, the Confederates hove to. The island, the cone of an extinct volcano, rises dramatically from the sea. Its edges are green-fringed with forests, and its higher elevations lost in fog and clouds. Waddell and several other Confederates rowed toward the settlement of Falmouth Bay in the boats confiscated from the *Edward*. Joining them were the prisoners, dunnage in hand. Meanwhile, the Confederates still aboard the *Shenandoah* bartered with visiting islanders, who accepted flour taken from the *Edward* in exchange for fresh milk, eggs, chickens, and meat. Hours later, when Waddell and company had returned, he recounted the deal he had struck ashore: in exchange for six weeks of rations to feed the prisoners deposited on Tristan de Cunha, the island's governor had agreed to allow them to wait on the island until a passing ship took them away.

That same afternoon, December 7, the Confederates concluded their brief visit to Tristan de Cunha and resumed their eastern passage around Africa's southern tip. "It is a great relief to get clear of prisoners," Whittle acknowledged. But he and others regretted that they had left twenty-eight men at Tristan de Cunha. As master's mate Cornelius Hunt lamented, "they might have to remain for many weary months, ere a passing ship would take them off."

Even so, putting the best possible spin on the situation, Hunt also noted that, at least for now, the former prisoners "had the free range of a charming island, where reigned perennial summer; besides, there were a number of the gentle sex in want of mates, I learned, and where there are pretty women so circumstanced, there can sailors be happy."[5]

But the Confederates need not have worried. Three weeks after the *Shenandoah*'s departure, the marooned men left the island on a passing ship—the USS *Iroquois*, a U.S. Navy steamer hunting for the Confederate cruiser. During the entire war, the U.S. Navy concentrated most of its ships off the South's coast, maintaining the naval blockade and interdicting blockade runners. Even so, ships were dispatched to hunt for Confederate raiders, and, like other men-of-war, the *Iroquois* had been churning the broad Atlantic—calling at ports from Le Havre to Rio, and from Dover to Madeira—on a peripatetic and mostly luckless hunt for Confederate cruisers. In his search the *Iroquois*'s captain, Christopher Raymond Perry Rodgers, like other Union commanders, was often guided by orders from U.S. Navy secretary Gideon Welles but just as frequently by the latest tip that flitted his way from a newspaper or a passing ship.

Captain Rodgers had been in Montevideo, Uruguay, when on December 12 he first learned of the *Shenandoah*'s attacks on Union merchant ships off Brazil's coast. Assuming that the Confederate ship would eventually land at Cape Town, Rodgers, the following morning, sailed for Africa's southern coast. En route, he would stop, on the twenty-eighth, at Tristan de Cunha—long enough to discover and pick up the stranded sailors. Upon reaching Cape Town on January 9, 1865, Rodgers found no Confederates. But before leaving the port he wrote to Gideon Welles, alerting him to the *Shenandoah*'s latest predations and his own next course of action.

Thanks to Charles Francis Adams, Thomas Dudley, and other U.S. diplomats in Great Britain, Welles had learned months earlier that the *Shenandoah*—then still the *Sea King*—had slipped away from England. But not until early to mid-January did reports of the Confederate raider's destructive passage through the Atlantic begin reaching Welles. When they did arrive, they came late, weeks after the captures they described, and, for the most part, provided only vague and often erroneous conjectures about the cruiser's movements. Rodgers's report from Cape Town was no exception: "I have . . . no knowledge of the movements of the *Shenandoah* since she left Tristan de Cunha, but I believe that she has gone to the East Indies. Thither, therefore, I shall follow her with all dispatch." Equally unhelpful, William H. Clark, captain of the U.S. Navy's *Onward*—just back from her own Atlantic cruise in search of the *Shenandoah*—wrote to Welles from Montevideo, on February 14, relaying a report he'd heard that the Confederate cruiser had been sunk off one of the islands of the South Atlantic.

In the wake of Rodgers's report, Welles ordered the USS *Wachusett*, then docked in Boston, to sail to the East Indies and join the *Iroquois* in her hunt for the *Shenandoah*. But the vastness of the globe's oceans and the *Shenandoah*'s advantages of disguise, surprise, and maneuverability rendered the Union hunt a thankless, if not a fool's, errand. Beyond that, by the early months of 1865, General Sherman was wrapping up his March to the Sea and the Confederacy stood in general collapse. Union naval strategists were increasingly focusing on priorities closer to home and to the war's denouement.[6]

As Union ships steamed for the East Indies, the *Shenandoah* was bound for Australia, a fact that Waddell had not revealed to the raider's officers but, oddly, had elected to share with the governor of Tristan de Cunha. In his orders to Waddell, Commander

James D. Bulloch had suggested, "It would be well to touch off Melbourne, and if coal is to be had take on board as much as you can well carry, or, if there is lack of coal at Melbourne, proceed to Sydney, New South Wales, for the same purpose." But Waddell, typical of men-of-war commanders in all navies, had still not shared his superior's medium- or long-range orders for the cruise with any of his own subordinate officers, including First Lieutenant William C. Whittle, Jr.

Taking advantage of that day's sturdy westerlies, Waddell—on December 7, 1864, the day the *Shenandoah* left Tristan de Cunha—instructed Whittle to order the crew to hoist the propeller from the water and, for now, place the ship under sail. The next day, however, as the Confederates inspected the propeller, they noticed a crack running across a brass band on the engine's coupling. In view of the fact, Whittle recalled, that "our propeller is to us our life we stopped all work to have it fixed." Though the propeller was out of the water, its usual sternward position when not in use rendered it, for purposes of repairs, largely inaccessible. "To get the propeller up so that it could be worked at was now the trouble," Whittle recalled. "To do this we had to take the top off of our Pilot House." Only after the pilothouse's roof had been pried off did they discover "that the brass bearing of the couppling was cracked. It is an old break and has been done for a long time." By Whittle's account, had the Confederates not found the crack when they did, "it might have proved fatal to us."

The Confederates eventually fashioned a temporary repair for the engine, but Waddell knew they needed to find a shipyard with a good mechanical shop to properly fix the band. The closest would be found in Cape Town. But, after pondering his options, and knowing that he was heavily dependent on his sails, Waddell elected to drop southward—well below Cape

Town—and catch the strong west winds that parallel latitude 40° south—in sailor's argot, "the roaring forties." In that windswept realm, he would try to reach, via the Indian Ocean, the city of Melbourne and its shipyard. Five weeks away, Melbourne was far. But as a marine entrepôt linking a gold-mining region with the world at large, it had the appeal of teeming with precisely the sort of single young men from all over the world that Waddell needed to round out a full complement of seamen. And the repair of the ship's engine, he decided, would provide the perfect pretext to prolong the steamer's stay in that British port long enough to recruit those young men.

Buffeted by the roaring forties, the raider crossed the Greenwich Meridian on December 11, and on the sixteenth rounded the Cape of Good Hope—beating by two weeks Bulloch's orders to Waddell that he try, by New Year's Day, to pass Africa's southern tip. By late December, as the Confederates brushed against Antarctica's frosty climes, the strong winds of earlier weeks had grown into frightening squalls of snow and hail.

In the language of ships at sea, in which what landlubbers call big waves are called "seas," those seas that rush onto a ship's deck are said to be "shipped"—as in "We shipped some heavy seas." Moreover, vessels vary remarkably in their ability to shed excess water and, according to their tendency to do just that, they are labeled either a "dry ship" or a "wet ship." By that December, the *Shenandoah*'s officers had by common consent—particularly as they plowed deeper into the roaring forties—reached a firm decision on that matter. As Whittle put it on December 15, "She is decidedly a wet ship."

On the morning of December 25—at latitude 42°57' S, longitude 53°25' E—a harrowing gale shook the raider. In the

close-reefed diction of ship deck logs, Lieutenant Dabney
Scales, the watch officer on duty, captured the storm's arrival
and detailed the countermeasures taken to keep the raider afloat
and on course: "From 4 to 8. Fresh gales from S.W.; very heavy
sea running; shipped several seas; 5:30 wind increasing, close-
reefed Main Topsail; 5:30 battened down hatches." But those
succinct lines betray none of the wind-, sea-, and rain-driven
human dramas that also animated the morning. Surgeon Lining, for instance, recorded, "We shipped such a sea that it came
up nearly to the rail, washed one man, 'West' [over] the lee rail
into the sea, but fortunately the next sea washed him back
again. Several men were swimming on deck." As high waters
threatened to flood the weather deck, " 'Whittle' knocked out
the lee port aft"—the most rearward gunport on the main
deck—"& hollered for all hands to come on deck."

Later that day, the wardroom officers settled down for a
Christmas feast prepared, in large part, from provisions captured from prizes. "Cook & Steward tired themselves and gave
us a first rate dinner," Lining exulted. "Who would think that a
ship which had not dropped an anchor for sixty seven days
could have for dinner goose, fresh pork, nice corned beef, fresh
potatoes &c. Mince pie &c. &c." As the officers were savoring
their repast's bounty, however, a wave crashed over the ship's
starboard quarter, sending a torrent of seawater belowdecks.
"We were boxing about," Hunt recalled, "at the mercy of old
Neptune's irate temper, drenched with water the greater part of
the time, and generally and profoundly miserable."[7]

The surging seas that rattled the Confederates' Christmas dinner only compounded discords that were already roiling crew
morale aboard the raider. Most particularly, Lieutenant Whittle,
puzzled by Captain Waddell's behavior, increasingly wondered

why his relationship with the captain had become so strained. As he pondered that question, he recalled an incident from months earlier.

Captain Waddell's wife, Ann, had left Liverpool to return to her home in Maryland on October 8—the same day that her husband and his fellow Confederates left Liverpool aboard the *Laurel*. As the couple packed for their travels in the days leading up to their separate departures, Ann Waddell had stolen a few private moments with Lieutenant Whittle to exact a promise from him. "She begged me," Whittle recalled, "to keep out of all quarrels on the cruise."

At that moment, the first lieutenant, charmed by Mrs. Waddell, had agreed to the promise without giving it much thought. But as the weeks aboard the *Shenandoah* passed, Whittle had been pondering it more and more. Beyond the duel from which his captain still limped, what other events in her husband's past had compelled Ann Waddell to exact such a pledge from his executive officer?

In ways tangible and intangible, short- and long-range, the success of a cruise depended upon a smooth working relationship between a ship's captain and his executive officer. Commander Raphael Semmes, for instance, enjoyed a famously hand-in-glove rapport with Lieutenant John McIntosh Kell, Semmes's executive officer on both the *Sumter* and the *Alabama*. Early on in the *Shenandoah*'s cruise, however, clear signs emerged that Waddell and Whittle were not to enjoy such a symbiotic rapport. From the outset, the two had differed over matters such as the proposed detour from Las Desertas to Tenerife, sail-trimming, and the bonding of the *Kate Prince*. To some extent, such differences issued from a generation gap. Waddell had completed his studies at Annapolis before an 1851 reorganization, deepening and lengthening the academic program, created the institution attended by most of his younger officers. From his perspective, however, "practical seamanship cannot be learned from books." Put another way, if the younger officers saw in the captain's actions an excess of caution, Waddell tended to see those younger men as, for the most part, untested sailors.

Though no visible rifts had opened between the two men, by mid-December differences in style, temperament, and generation had created wearing frictions—particularly as Waddell increasingly interfered with the executive officer's day-to-day orders to subordinates.

On December 13, Whittle learned that an order he had issued that day to the boatswain to trim a sail had, hours later and without his knowledge, been countermanded by Waddell. Following similar incidents, Whittle had not protested to the captain about such meddling in his orders. But this time, in the first lieutenant's mind, the captain had crossed a certain line. "Now he has the power to give any order he chooses," Whittle complained, "but he should do it through me—if my orders are to be changed in this way in trifling matters, I may as well take a watch and give him the Executive duties." Three days later, the rift between the two officers widened still further, after Waddell—once again without consulting Whittle—decided that he wanted two of the ship's commissioned officers, Lieutenants Dabney Scales and Francis Chew, removed from the supervision of their respective watches.

In the days leading to this order, the steamer's rudder had produced increasingly foreboding noises—disturbing the sleep of the captain and other crew members and generally sounding as if it were about to be wrenched off. As the grinding noise grew louder and louder, Waddell became increasingly concerned—and irritated. Surgeon Lining quoted the captain as confiding to him that he "would give $5000 had he not taken command of this ship, so much is he worried & bothered." Anticipating stormy weather and knowing that Scales and Chew were scheduled for that night's watches, Waddell told Whittle that he lacked confidence in their "seamanship." It was then that Waddell ordered the executive officer to replace the two officers.

By that December, according to most accounts, Lieutenant Scales had earned a reputation for sound seamanship. But, in fairness to Captain Waddell, the hapless twenty-three-year-old Chew also had established himself as a jinx, if not something worse. Three days before Waddell's order to remove the lieutenant from his watch, Lining noted, "Chew is a most unfortunate fellow; if any thing happens it is sure to be in his room." In Chew's cabin that day, a slop tub—a vessel for wastewater from his wash basin—"capsized," Lining recalled, "making a perfect wreck" of his quarters. When the surgeon went topside to tell Chew of the accident, he found him airing the contents of his sea trunk. But before Lining could report the news, a gust of wind overturned the trunk, sending Chew's cherished letters and other documents over the ship's rail. Two days later, Lining noted, as the raider listed in heavy seas, deck officer Chew "made a slide to leeward & nearly went overboard"—losing, in the process, his officer's cap.

Whittle later came to share aspects of Waddell's assessment of Chew. But at the time of the incident he considered both Chew and Scales to be competent sailors. At that point, what most concerned Whittle was the propriety of Waddell's order removing the two officers from their watches. Whittle implemented the order but considered it a grave mistake. In removing two commissioned officers from their duties, he believed, Waddell had overstepped the legal bounds of his command. Both officers, after all, as he soon reminded Waddell, had been so "appointed by the President of the Confederate States, 'by and with the advice and consent of the Senate.'" Beyond that, Whittle asked—pointing out that both Scales and Chew, like Waddell, held commissions as lieutenants—"what right he had to say that Mr. Chew was not to be trusted with the deck when the wording of Mr. Chew's commission was identically the same as his own." Compounding his alleged transgressions, Waddell had even ordered Chew replaced by master's mate John F. Minor, one of the *Alabama* crewmen who had shipped aboard the *Shenandoah* at Las Desertas.

Mostly, though, Whittle regretted the ill will created by the incident. Chew soon submitted an application to resign from the Navy and leave the ship at the next port. And Waddell, upon learning of the application, promptly accepted it. Only after Whittle persuaded the captain to restore Chew to his watch did the insulted lieutenant agree to withdraw the application. Waddell eventually, though grudgingly, restored both men to their watches—with the understanding that under dangerous conditions a more experienced officer would join each of them on the quarterdeck.

That action, however, hardly concluded the crisis. Nor did it bolster Whittle's confidence in Waddell's command. "I know that everything like an esprit de corps will be destroyed by such arbitrary and unwarrantable acts of authority," Whittle noted in his journal. On December 17, with Chew restored to his post, an exhausted Whittle made a confession to the captain: "I told him my promise to his little wife, and said that I had kept it as long as I could." Having thus unburdened himself, Whittle stoically hoped for the best.

But if the episode had undermined Whittle's respect for the captain, it also—as Lining's secondhand account of the same Whittle-Waddell exchange makes clear—apparently damaged Waddell's faith in his own command: "Whittle told me something of his conversation with the Captain yesterday & how the Captain had said that all his old friends had deserted him, & that every body had turned against him. How childish & foolish that is, for if he would only act rightly we would all be with him."

Moreover, the fact that the captain's self-doubts, as revealed in his exchange with Whittle, were noted in a secondhand account is doubly damning. On a ship at sea, everyone is removed by one degree of separation, few secrets remain secret for long, and in Lieutenant Whittle, Waddell had an executive officer who could not be trusted to retain confidences.[8]

By December 29, the squalls that had tormented the Confederates in their passage through the roaring forties had given way to calmer winds. "It was blowing fresh and we were under easy canvas," Lieutenant Chew recalled. At about 3:30 p.m. that afternoon, the *Shenandoah*'s lookout espied what was initially believed to be a French ship. But when the Confederates raised a Union Jack over their peak, they were delighted when the approaching vessel responded by hoisting Old Glory. Soon enough, a party of Confederates were boarding the American bark *Delphine* of Bangor, Maine—out from London in ballast, and sailing for Akyab, Burma, to pick up a cargo of rice. The Confederates later placed the value of the *Delphine* and her scant cargo at $25,000.

At 10:15 that evening, Lining recalled, "we saw the fire break out fore & aft, & in a short time she was wrapped in flames." Never had he seen a fire burn so quickly. Soon enough, it occurred to one of the onlookers savoring the spectacle that the boat party responsible for the evening's pyrotechnics had failed to return to the *Shenandoah*. Had the men, for some reason, failed to get out of the doomed ship? Had their boat capsized as they were leaving the *Delphine*? Or, as Lining cynically speculated, had the boat's crew simply been "drunk & could not pull" back to the *Shenandoah*? Their fears, as the surgeon recalled, were soon put to rest: "About 11:15 p.m. much to our delight, we saw her coming off & soon had the pleasure of getting them safely on board."

According to Lieutenant Whittle's journal entry for that day, the *Delphine*'s crew included the captain, two mates, and twelve seamen. Of those crewmen, six—including a steward—immediately shipped with the Confederates; the other six were placed in irons. The captain and his mates signed their paroles and were set free.

The most conspicuous newcomer from the *Delphine*, however, was Lillias Lervene Nichols, the wife of the ship's captain, William Green Nichols. As he recalled it, Waddell's acquaintance with Mrs. Nichols began with an intended deception. As the Confederates initially boarded the *Delphine*, Waddell recalled, Captain Nichols pleaded with him to spare the bark, owing to his spouse's failing health. A skeptical Waddell ordered Surgeon Lining to examine her. Afterward, Lining assured Waddell that no harm would result from the woman's transfer between ships. Then a chair was prepared and a whip fitted to the main yard to lift her, her young son Phineas, and her maid aboard the *Shenandoah*.

Captain Waddell invited all of them—Mrs. Nichols, her husband, their young son, and her maid—to visit his cabin. Mrs. Nichols had already heard that the Confederates were contemplating a stop at nearby St. Paul's Island, and, as the family was leaving his cabin, Waddell later recalled, "Mrs. Nichols asked in a stentorian voice if I was captain, what I intended to do with them, and where would they be landed."

"'On, St. Paul, madam, if you like,'" he joked.

"'Oh, no, never. I would rather remain with you.'"

"I was surprised to see in the sick lady," Waddell recalled, "a tall, finely proportioned woman of twenty-six years, in robust health, evidently possessing a will and a voice of her own."

If Waddell harbored any resentments from Lillias Nichols's apparent effort to deceive him, they quickly evaporated. Indeed, by her own account Lillias Nichols became something of a confidante to Captain Waddell—a young woman with whom he felt comfortable sharing his longings to see, once again, his own wife, who awaited him in Maryland. In time, she and her entire family became a welcome fixture aboard the raider. Officers and crew took particular pleasure in watching the boy Phineas—by now "Phinizy" to the Confederates—running back and forth across the raider's deck as he played with two goats taken from the *Delphine*.

When January 1 rolled around, the *Shenandoah* had been in commission for two months and eleven days. To celebrate the arrival of 1865, the wardroom officers invited the Nichols family to join them for a New Year's dinner. Not only that, Whittle recalled, "we hoisted the Confederate flag & kept it up all day to welcome the new year." Since leaving Las Desertas, Waddell later noted, the raider had already destroyed or ransomed property valued at more than the cost of the ship. But those conquests only nourished the Confederates' appetite for more prizes. The following day, the ship's lookout spotted the South Indian Ocean islands of Amsterdam and St. Paul—a long-standing stopover for passing whaleships and sealers, roughly midway between Africa and Australia, at latitude 38°39' S, longitude 77°30' E.

In calling at the island, Waddell hoped to surprise any un-suspecting whaling vessels in port. He also wanted to stop to "regulate"—reset—the ship's chronometer from a fixed and es-tablished geographic position.

Once off St. Paul, Waddell ordered the *Shenandoah* to hove to. Placing Lieutenant Grimball in command of one of the whaleboats, he ordered a party to go ashore and visit the is-land's tiny French colony and destroy the property of any Yan-kees who might be in port. Except for the handful of men who had gone ashore at Tristan de Cunha, most of the cruiser's sea-weary souls had not set foot on land since leaving Las Desertas. Thus, as Grimball picked the men who would row ashore, he had no shortage of enthusiastic volunteers.

In the end, only officers were selected; the others would have to watch and wait to learn the visit's outcome. The shore party, however, found no whaleships in port. But, using the fishing gear they had brought along, they were able to bring back a load of fresh fish. Fresh or salted, fish, owing to the dif-ficulties of preserving it, constituted a rare treat aboard ships of that era. The Confederates also purchased eggs, a few chickens, and—to lighten spirits on the raider—a pet penguin around whose neck someone promptly secured "a rag resembling a shawl."[9]

The *Shenandoah* left St. Paul on the afternoon of January 2. As they departed, most of the ship's officers assumed that Captain Waddell intended to sail for Cape Leeuwin, on Australia's southwestern tip, where the Indian and Southern oceans meet. The idea held wide appeal among the ship's young warriors. Most New England whaling vessels bound for the Bering Sea's whaling grounds doubled Cape Horn, then sailed north toward the western Arctic. Some, however, got there by sailing around the Cape of Good Hope and then heading north. Of those, many lingered at Cape Leeuwin in hopes of killing a right whale. But in the weeks after the *Shenandoah*'s stop at St. Paul it slowly became clear that her aloof commander, if he had ever truly considered that destination, had abandoned any thoughts of venturing to Cape Leeuwin.

Waddell had yet to reveal to anyone aboard the *Shenandoah* his intention of stopping at Melbourne. Even so, rumors had begun circulating through the ship that, as Midshipman Mason put it, the Confederates were "on our way I suppose to Australia." As late as January 13, Waddell, however, had made no formal declaration of the raider's destination to his officers. They would learn it only through inference. On that day, Waddell ordered Lieutenant Francis Chew to find the bearings for Cape Otway, near Melbourne. "From this I suppose we are bound for Melbourne, near that cape," Chew, writing in his journal, concluded. "I have heard whispered about the ship that the Capt. would touch at some port in Australia; it is now confirmed."

By January 16, the *Shenandoah* had reached a position of latitude 39°57' S, longitude 119°38' W. Just before twelve noon that day, further exasperating the officers who favored cruising along Australia's southwestern coast, Waddell, frustrated by a calm that had slowed the raider, gave orders to get up steam and head more landward. He apparently intended to shape a faster, more direct course toward Melbourne, a course that, to Surgeon Lining, seemed "a useless & extravagant expenditure of coal, I think, when we may not be able to get any elsewhere."

Whatever reasons propelled Waddell to bypass Cape Leeuwin and sail directly for Melbourne, his course had clearly distanced the *Shenandoah* from the whaling vessels that, if found there, would have broken the tedium of the Confederates' January transit across the Indian Ocean. For just as the capture of enemy prizes constituted the sine qua non of a raider, so for the sailors did those captures make the difference between days of quotidian toil and the promise of glory and plunder. Master's mate Cornelius Hunt spoke for every Confederate crew member when he recalled:

> On a cruiser, one constantly alternates between a life of stirring excitement and absolute stupidity.
> When in pursuit of a prize, all is life and animation. The rigging is filled with eager, excited faces, spy-glasses pass from hand to hand, orders are hurriedly given and instantly obeyed, and until the capture is effected, and the ship disposed of, there is little rest for anyone. Then follows, perhaps, weeks of idleness, with nothing to break the tedious monotony. The watches turn out and in, yawning, the lookouts mount aloft, and sleepily throw a glance over the broad expanse of water,—at seven bells, the master comes up with this sextant, to "take the sun," and work out the position of the ship, with his logarithms—in the forecastle, tough yarns are spun by solemn visaged old sea-dogs, and at night perhaps a violin or banjo furnishes entertainment for a little knot; but with every expedient that can be resorted to, and the working of the ship, a light labor with so many hands to assist in it, the time drags wearily, and if one has not the resource of some mental occupation, it falls in the course of time just short of unendurable.

In the early hours of January 17, the cry of "Sail ho!" and the sight of a large ship with double topsails darkening the horizon lifted the Confederates' lassitude. A boarding party, led by Francis Chew, soon determined that the *Nimrod*, though Yankee-built and, once upon a time, Yankee-owned, had been lawfully transferred to a British owner. More disappointment came later that day. After bidding the *Nimrod* goodbye, the Confederates learned that the valve to the air pump on the *Shenandoah*'s steam engine had broken. They hove to, let the steam go down, triced up the propeller, and stopped for the evening to make repairs.

At 5:00 a.m. the following morning—January 18—the ship's chief engineer, Matthew O'Brien, completed the repairs. But he had further bad news: the propeller had again broken. Fresh from his triumph with the engine's air valve, O'Brien now prepared, once again, to repair the ship's propeller. As he did so, Waddell gave the order to take advantage of the fresh breezes that were beginning to rise. By night, sailing under reefed topsails, the Confederates soon found their eastward course toward Australia buffeted by gale-force winds.[10]

During late January, as the raider's destination became increasingly clear to all aboard, Lieutenant Whittle—acting on the pride felt by all executive officers before an extended port visit—began sprucing up the raider. Work details busied themselves with tasks ranging from repainting the ship's black hull to holystoning her berth deck, still black from the coal dust that had recently covered it.

Anticipating landfall, Waddell found time to write a long letter updating Commodore Samuel Barron on the cruise. He also composed an addendum to the parole document that the prisoners who were still aboard the raider had signed earlier. To the usual promise exacted from signatories not to, upon their release, take up arms against the Confederates, the captain added another—that they swear not to reveal any information that might endanger the *Shenandoah*. When the document was placed before Captain Nichols, he—weary of life aboard the raider and eager to be done with it—readily signed it. Mrs. Nichols, however, reacted with disdain. As Lining caught the moment, "When it came Mrs. N's turn, she let loose with her tongue, pitching directly into her husband for telling her to sign it & say nothing, by telling him that she did not intend to hold her tongue, nor did she consider herself bound by what she was going to sign, that she would talk, for at least they could not stop her tongue."

In the end—as eager as her husband to leave the ship—Mrs. Nichols signed the document. Afterward, she sarcastically asked if the Confederates had anything for her young son Phineas to sign. "No, Madame," Lieutenant Sidney Smith Lee, Jr., answered. "We are much more afraid of you than we are of him." Standing quietly nearby, Lining later recalled, "She went out in a towering rage."

At least one soul aboard that floating mass of iron, wood, rope, and canvas felt no enthusiasm for the approaching port-of-call. "As long as we have to go to port, I do not care how soon we get there, but I had much rather not go at all," Lieutenant Whittle confided to his diary. At least, he consoled himself, he would be able to learn the outcome of the previous November's electoral contest between President Lincoln and his Democratic opponent, retired Union general George B. McClellan. Because McClellan, if elected, was widely expected to immediately sue for peace, Whittle gave himself free rein to fantasize that the *Shenandoah*'s arrival in Melbourne would be greeted with the welcome news that the long war between the North and the South had already ended.

Mostly, however, Whittle, along with other officers aboard the *Shenandoah*, considered Waddell's planned Melbourne stop to be strategically foolhardy. "I think that our cruise will be greatly injured by it," he confided to his journal on January 22. Without mentioning recoaling, the winning of new recruits, or any other possible objectives of the stopover, Waddell, in alluding to his desire to put in at Melbourne as opposed to some other port, had mentioned only that he hoped to post letters aboard a mail steamer that he had learned was due to leave there on January 26. Waddell's stated reason merely perplexed and annoyed many of the *Shenandoah*'s officers.

Nothing, they complained, promised to more loudly broadcast their presence and movements than a stop in Melbourne precisely when a mail ship was scheduled to leave that port. As Whittle put it, "from that place there are little vessels carrying regular mails to different fishing depots, at which the yankee whalers congregate, and as soon as they hear that we are in the neighborhood they will all run into port, and we will catch very few."

On January 25, steaming on an easterly course from Cape Leeuwin across the Southern Ocean, the Confederates spotted Cape Otway along Australia's southeastern coast, quickly followed by the opening to Port Phillip Bay, and—once inside that estuary—Hobson's Bay. As the raider steamed deeper into the bay and found no awaiting Union ships, the Confederates' anxieties gave way to a feeling of relief, even of celebration. As they approached the docks of Sandridge, Melbourne's port, a harbor pilot was taken aboard to guide the ship into a berth. And, Lining recalled, word quickly spread of their arrival, creating an "immense sensation." The news-starved Confederates were grateful when "steamboats came off to meet us, throwing papers on board," but otherwise they could only marvel at the numerous boats that circled them, "filled with persons [eager] to see a 'Confederate.'"

From conversations with the harbor pilot and from the Melbourne newspapers tossed aboard the steamer, the Confederates devoured the latest war news—even though "latest" in this case meant news from the previous fall that had just reached Melbourne a week before the *Shenandoah*'s arrival. As they read the papers, the Confederates found meager solace in reports that Federal forces were again stalled in their ongoing efforts to capture the Confederate capital at Richmond. Most of the warfront news, after all, was singularly discouraging. They learned of the seizure by the U.S. Navy the previous fall of the Confederate raider CSS *Florida* at Bahia, Brazil. Another report noted that, after capturing Atlanta, General William Tecumseh Sherman's army was again on the march—though it remained unclear whether his forces intended to capture Savannah and Charleston on the Atlantic coast, or to drop still farther south through Georgia to liberate the notorious Confederate prison camp at Andersonville. Equally dispiriting, the *Shenandoah*'s crew learned that President Lincoln had handily defeated General McClellan—thus scotching for now the mariners' hopes for any peace to celebrate.

But, however disconcerting that news, "joy predominated" that afternoon aboard the *Shenandoah*. For most of these tars, the approaching landfall—in the balmy January climes of the Australian summer—would mark their first step on dry land in three months.

Captain Waddell broadly shared their enthusiasm. But he was also too keenly aware of the presence of English and American authorities ashore—authorities who would take a dim view of his arrival in this British colony—to be without apprehension.[11]

NINE

"A Decidedly *Recherché* Affair"

At 6:45 on Wednesday, January 25, 1865—ninety days out of Madeira—the CSS *Shenandoah* anchored in Port Phillip Bay, by the borough of Sandridge, four miles southwest of Melbourne. Due to the steamer's draft, security concerns, and perhaps a shortage of piers, she dropped her anchors in the harbor, a short distance from Sandridge's docks. Crowds already gathering ashore and on the decks of the ships and boats surrounding the Confederates gawked at them. Amid the bustle, a customhouse boat edged alongside the raider. These government officials, Lining recalled, were "accustomed only to see merchantmen, & wanted to treat us as such" rather than as a man-of-war. And though Waddell refused the customs agents' request to board, in an incident that Lining fails to specify in his journal, the captain "permitted a step in that direction." Foreshadowing later difficulties, that alleged lack of firmness was bound to haunt the Confederates. Lining, for one, foresaw it: "I know the consequences will be rather humiliating to us."

Fifteen minutes after dropping their anchors, Waddell dispatched Lieutenant John Grimball to make the four-mile trip to Government House bearing a letter to Sir Charles Darling, governor of the state of Victoria:

Sir:

I have the honor to announce to your Excellency the arrival of the Confederate States steamer Shenandoah, under my command, in Port Phillip, this afternoon, and I have also to communicate that the steamer's machinery requires repairs, and that I am in want of coals. I desire your Excellency to grant permission for me to make the necessary repairs, to take in a [load] of coals, to enable me to get to sea as quickly as possible. I desire also your Excellency's permission to land my prisoners. I shall observe the neutrality.

I have the honor to be your obedient servant.

James I. Waddell

Early the next morning, the *Shenandoah*'s paymaster, William Breedlove Smith, came ashore in one of the raider's boats carrying a bulging letter bag. If Waddell posted a letter from Melbourne to Commander James Bulloch, it has since gone missing. We do know, however, that the letter bag carried off the *Shenandoah* that morning contained a letter from Waddell to Commodore Samuel Barron, in Paris. And enclosed with that brief letter was a lengthy report for Navy secretary Stephen Mallory, updating him on the raider's activities since leaving Las Desertas. In spirit, the report to Mallory was more buoyant than the communiqué sent to Bulloch three months earlier. Picking up where that earlier letter had left off, Waddell's latest dispatch told of how, before leaving that island, he had called a meeting of the ship's officers to discuss how best to proceed in their, at that time, "feebly manned ship." And with satisfaction Waddell now reported how "the sentiments expressed on that occasion justified my taking the sea, and the sequel sustains that decision as fully as the officers have redeemed their promises."

He told Mallory of the hard work that had converted the *Shenandoah* from an ill-supplied, hastily loaded, merchant ship into a smooth-running, well-stowed man-of-war. He also told how the raider's first few captures had allowed the Confederates to overcome their initial deficits in crew numbers and various material needs. After detailing the raider's activities and announcing that "God has been very merciful and kind unto us," Waddell anticipated their being "detained here a few days, making some repairs and coaling, and will then proceed on my cruise." And, in the report's final sentence—overlooking the general languor that weighed on many of the officers—Waddell put a stoically bright face on general conditions: "We are all well and cheerful, but anxious for an honorable settlement of our national difficulties."

Few wartime letters from *Shenandoah*'s crew members survive. But doubtless many of the men aboard the raider who dispatched correspondences that morning did so at least partly to dispel false impressions left by earlier newspaper reports that they had, months earlier, perished at sea. Lieutenant John Grimball did just that in a lengthy letter to his father that recounted the raider's first four months at sea. "In regard to our future movements the success of our cruise requires me to be silent," he wrote. "But as 'the past can never be recalled,' and will sooner or later be made public, I consider myself at perfect liberty to give you an account of myself up to this time." Left unreported was what, even then, was unfolding around the Confederate ship.

Spurred by newspaper reports of the raider's arrival, crowds larger than the previous day's began gathering onshore and in boats that crowded around the raider. The Queen's Australian subjects had first learned of the *Shenandoah* earlier that month when local newspapers reported her launch. And although the Confederates' very presence in port repudiated the subsequent stories of the raider's demise, the crowds assumed the accuracy of at least one element of those gloomy reports: that the doomed raider was captained by the famous Raphael Semmes, commander of the late *Alabama*. Thus, Lieutenant Francis Chew recalled, many of those who clustered on the docks to gawk at the *Shenandoah* during her first few days in port were eager not only to see with their own eyes that the raider was still very much afloat but also to catch a glimpse of the late *Alabama*'s dashing commander: "If we were asked once where was Semmes we were asked five hundred times, and it was difficult to make them believe that he was not onboard."

Many of the curiosity-seekers wanted to board the raider. But Waddell—still awaiting the governor's permission to remain in Victoria—refused most requests. He made exceptions for two British maritime officers, whose subsequent accounts of their visits—though filtered through the biases of Her Majesty's officers—offer glimpses of life aboard the raider as she reached Australia. Captain Henry King, a British naval agent serving aboard the merchantman *Bombay*, then in port, noted that the *Shenandoah*'s crew seemed to be "almost entirely" composed of English and Irish seamen. "The ship appeared to be in good order," he reported. "Her officers are a gentlemanly set of men, in a uniform of gray and gold; but from the paucity of her crew at present, she cannot be very efficient for fighting purposes."

Captain Charles B. Payne, a former Royal Navy commander who visited the raider, painted a still less flattering portrait of the raider's condition: "The state of the vessel on deck, aloft, and in the engine room, I think both slovenly and dirty, and does not reflect any credit upon her officers," Payne reported. "There appears to me to be about forty to fifty men on board, slouchy, dirty, and undisciplined. I noticed also a great number of officers, and could not help remarking that the number appeared out of all proportion to the few men I saw on board."[1]

That same morning, January 26, Melbourne's U.S. consul William Blanchard arrived at his office to find a clutch of unexpected visitors. They were none other than William Nichols, the former master of the *Delphine*, his wife, Lillias Lervene Nichols, their young son Phineas, and their maid—along with the late merchantship's two mates and six crew members. Captain Nichols informed the consul that they had been released from the *Shenandoah* after her arrival the previous afternoon, and that all of them had been aboard the raider since their ship's capture the previous December. Captain Nichols then told Blanchard about the parole documents they had signed only three days earlier, in which they had promised not to disclose any information that might lead to injury to or the capture of the steamer, or otherwise damage "the so-called Confederate cause."

Already infuriated that the *Shenandoah* had been allowed to land—and remain—in the harbor, Consul Blanchard was delighted to find the former prisoners in his office. He immediately began taking depositions. Captain Nichols, while talking to the consul, made nominal efforts to honor the terms of his parole; though he discussed the raider, he declined to speak about her armaments and other military components. But the other former prisoners, particularly Mrs. Nichols, felt no such constraints. During the next few hours, all of them contributed to a thoroughgoing description of the cruiser and their experiences on board. The men who had been confined in irons until they had relented to ship with the Confederates offered the most dramatic testimony.

Even before concluding that day's interviews, Blanchard, aware that the mail steamer was departing that day, penned a letter to the U.S. minister in London, Charles Francis Adams. Drawing on all that he had heard that morning, Blanchard gave Adams a vivid description of the ship, including an inventory of her armaments. He also recounted that, according to the depositions he had just taken, the Confederate ship was leaky and generally in poor condition; her officers, he wrote, believed it was unsafe to fire a broadside, fearing the ship could not take the strain of having all of her guns on one side fired simultaneously.

According to the prisoners, the ship's crew—officers and seamen alike—now consisted of seventy-nine men. And, lest there be any confusion over the vessel's British origins, Blanchard told Adams that the former prisoners had described how several letters of the ship's original name, *Sea King*, could still be made out on her stern; and that the ship also carried forks, spoons, water buckets, and other items inscribed with her original name. Blanchard promised to soon have photographs made and sent to Adams documenting the British merchantman origins of this Confederate raider. Hoping to prod more immediate action than Adams could offer, Blanchard sent a copy of the letter to the U.S. consul in Hong Kong, along with a note asking if the consul might persuade the U.S. Navy to dispatch a Federal cruiser to take on the *Shenandoah*.

At 3:30 that afternoon, even as Blanchard was taking depositions from the *Shenandoah*'s former prisoners a dispatch reached him from James G. Francis, Victoria's commissioner of trade and customs. The letter stated that the *Shenandoah*'s captain had applied for permission to land "certain prisoners" at Sandridge. But before acting on the request Francis wanted to know if Consul Blanchard would be prepared to "take care and provide for them."

With those "certain prisoners" already seated in Blanchard's office, Commissioner Francis's letter had been overtaken by actual events. Even so, the consul found the letter useful, in that, from his perspective it vindicated an argument that was already forming in his mind. Then and there, Blanchard dashed off a letter to Victoria's governor, Charles Darling. Recounting his conversations that morning with the former *Shenandoah* prisoners, Blanchard noted that they had seen clear evidence that the raider was the former British merchant ship *Sea King*. Given that origin, the raider's subsequent activities, and the fact that the ship had never entered a Confederate port "for the purpose of naturalization," he concluded that she thus lacked, for legal purposes, any true national origin. For that reason, he further decided, the vessel was not entitled to privileges accorded belligerent ships in neutral ports. The U.S. consul then asked Governor Darling to order the raider seized for "piratical acts."[2]

Also on the morning of January 26, Governor Charles Darling was meeting with his executive council to determine what should be done with the Confederate ship that had found her way to their port. The end result of a two-hour discussion, Darling's decision that morning granted Waddell all that he had asked for. The governor instructed trade and customs commissioner Francis to direct a letter to the Confederate commander according him permission to land his prisoners and to resupply, recoal, and repair the *Shenandoah*. Reflecting the government's nervousness about the situation, however, Francis's eventual letter to Waddell also stipulated that the captain should promptly provide the government with a more detailed account of his specific needs, "in order that Sir C. Darling may be enabled to judge of the time which it may be necessary for the vessel under your command to remain in the port." The governor had no interest in extending an open-ended invitation to his Confederate visitors.

That same afternoon of January 26, at about 2:00 p.m., Waddell received Commissioner Francis's letter granting the *Shenandoah* permission to remain in port for repairs and coaling. By then the crush of onlookers around the ship had become so great that, Francis's letter in hand, Waddell opened the ship to all who wanted to come aboard. "They went every where," Lining recalled, "poked into every thing, & even while at dinner we had difficulty in keeping them out of the ward room." Moreover, the surgeon noted, "Several very pleasant gentlemen came off, but a great deal also of Riff-Raff." Lieutenant Whittle, his passion for order affronted by the commotion, felt equally put upon. "I never saw anything like the rush; the anxiety to see the ship & crew—The[y] look at us with apparent surprise that we have not tails."

Soon after anchoring in Port Phillip Bay, the Confederates began making preparations to send the ship into dry dock for repairs on her propeller coupling. And, even as the *Shenandoah* swung at anchor, they began summoning engineers, carpenters, and caulkers aboard to see to various maintenance chores. Pitch and sawdust soon covered the ship's decks. Even so, "We have been flooded with visitors," Midshipman Mason recalled. "Two or three tug boats & any number of little sail boats have been plying all day, ladies, gentlemen, men, women & children of all sorts & description; it was enough to set any one crazy." For the ship's young officers, however, nothing engaged their attentions more than the young women among their visitors. As each steam tug edged alongside the raider, Lieutenant Chew recalled, "We would look out for pretty faces & if found we stood near the gangway so as to take them in charge. If they were particularly agreeable we took them aft & to the cabin & requested the pleasure of a glass of wine with them."

In Melbourne, as throughout the British Empire, America's Civil War sparked robust debates. Nurturing pro-Union sentiments, British subjects tended to oppose slavery—a disposition reinforced by the presence of many free American blacks who worked in Victoria's gold fields. Reflecting such sympathies, a stage production of Harriet Beecher Stowe's *Uncle Tom's Cabin* ranked as the most popular American play in the colony.

Even so, the Confederacy enjoyed—in Melbourne as in Liverpool—a robust acclaim among a wide range of classes. In part, such expressions reflected the same underdog sympathies that bolstered the Confederacy's popularity in England, particularly during the Civil War's early years, when many genuinely believed that the South might prove victorious. In Victoria, however, such sympathies gained still more momentum from local memories of an 1854 rebellion against the British Crown by miners in Ballarat, the gold-mining district north of Melbourne. The colonial government quickly suppressed the Eureka Stockade revolt. But, eleven years later, the miners' failed campaign for more democratic rights remained for many in Victoria a cherished episode in which they saw parallels to the Confederacy's own uphill fight against the more powerful Union.

Unlike Sydney and other major Australian cities, Melbourne, founded in 1835, had been established not as a penal colony but as an enclave of free white, Anglo-Saxon settlers from Van Diemen's Land—today's Tasmania. Located on the banks of the Yarra River, which flows into Port Phillip Bay, Melboure grew steadily during its first few years, gathering a population of ten thousand by 1840. However, the discovery of gold to its north in the summer of 1851 altered the city's fate. Miners from Van Diemen's Land, China, Europe, and North America poured into central Victoria's mining region. In the process,

Melbourne became a supply base and entrepôt for the boom, and by 1860 the city's population had swelled to 123,000. As the boom faded and Melbourne lost some of the trappings of its more frenzied days, it nonetheless developed an established gentry nourished by its continuing links to mining and commerce.

Though its rowdier days had passed, Melbourne still teemed with exactly the sort of men that Captain Waddell had hoped to recruit from the *Sea King* at Las Desertas: young single men with a lust for adventure and money. And, by 1865 the surface gold had disappeared and the mining industry increasingly belonged to impresarios with the capital to dig deep into the earth. Against that background, the share of the potential prizes that a cruiser could win seemed to offer a tantalizing lure for disaffected young miners at loose ends; as one miner who later joined the *Shenandoah* put it, "The pay is nothing to boast of, but there is a chance of making a good deal in the shape of prize money."

Further bolstering the Confederates' hopes, many of those who had flocked to Australia during the gold frenzy were Americans. And many of those Americans, for one reason or another, supported the Confederacy. While in Melbourne, the *Shenandoah*'s men encountered many American expatriates who were eager to quietly assist them. A native of Virginia who owned one of Victoria's largest gold claims, for instance, deployed several tugboats to assist the raider—a donation that, according to Mason, saved the Confederates "several thousands dollars."[3]

After Captain Waddell opened the *Shenandoah* to visitors, she became the focus of increasingly larger crowds. They gawked at the steamer from points around the harbor, as well as from the decks of other ships in the bay. "Shilling to the steamer," read signs advertising rides to the raider. Soon it seemed that the entire city was scrambling to board the *Shenandoah*. On Sunday, January 29—a day on which more than seven thousand people eventually jammed the Melbourne–Sandridge rail line—the crowds began arriving by 9:00 a.m. and kept coming until 5:00 p.m. "At one time, there was scarcely standing room on the decks," Lining recalled. "People were on the sails, in the tops, & two steamboats loaded with passengers were alongside, but were obliged to be sent off for want of room to stand." By the next day, however, the caulkers, carpenters, and mechanics had returned to their work and visitors were banned.

But by then, another problem dogged the Confederates: even as they were beginning to confront the legally nettlesome problem of local men openly seeking to join the raider, the Confederates were having trouble keeping the men they already had. "We had application after application to join the ship, but gave the same reply," Whittle noted on January 28. In all cases, he—and other *Shenandoah* officers—claimed, the Confederates answered such requests with a firm "No." Conversely, several Confederate seamen who were allowed to go ashore on Sunday had not returned by that following Monday morning. Whittle had even heard that "the [U.S.] Consul is now said to have some of our men, at boarding houses defraying all their expenses." Indeed, as it turned out Blanchard was doing just that and more; in addition to paying lodging costs, he was also providing the men with a substitute income. "I did this," he wrote to Secretary of State Seward, "with the view of liberating the men, of reducing her crew, which was mostly made up of such impressed men, and of obtaining information that the men I then had would not give on account of their parole." As Blanchard increasingly discovered, many of the raider's former prisoners—at least until financial inducements were offered—had been inclined to at least partially honor the vow of silence concerning details about the *Shenandoah* that Waddell had exacted from each of them before issuing their paroles.

During the *Shenandoah's* stay in Melbourne, shipboard responsibilities generally kept Whittle and Waddell aboard the raider. Other officers and crew members, however, were subject to fewer constraints. Typically, on Confederate ships, shore leave was granted successively to watches—or to sections constituting one-fourth or one-sixth of the vessel's total complement.

As a consequence, local street life was soon enlivened by the Confederates' presence. In the gray-and-gold dress uniforms that they invariably wore ashore, the ship's officers soon discovered that their costumes exuded charms they had lacked in the damp, salt-sprayed air of the open sea. Quite simply, the raider's officers became the toast of Melbourne. Beyond native, and naive, sympathies for their cause, the sheer notoriety of the Confederates drew attention. They were, after all, the only representatives of the Confederate cause to find their way to Australia's shores. Adding to the mystique, the *Shenandoah* quickly became known as a "Phoenix-like" reincarnation of the renowned CSS *Alabama*, and after the early reports that her captain was none other than the *Alabama's* Captain Raphael Semmes were dispelled, Captain Waddell was simply celebrated as "the *successor* to Captain Semmes."

Not that the raider's other officers lacked for attention—they were presented with open passes for the decade-old Sandridge–Melbourne rail line. Honorary memberships in Melbourne's best clubs were bestowed. Five celebrations were held in their honor "in such rapid succession that the memory of one was lost in another." A special evening performance of *Othello* was staged in tribute to the Confederates, and during intermission the house band performed "Dixie," eliciting both cheers and hisses from the audience.

On January 27, the *Shenandoah*'s officers toured Victoria's new Parliament buildings, then under construction. Captain Waddell and two fellow officers also observed deliberations in Victoria's Legislative Assembly, sparking a commotion among members of the House and in the public gallery. That same day, a group of *Shenandoah* officers received a tour of the headquarters of the city's exclusive Melbourne Club. And, on January 31, the club hosted a formal dinner in their honor—an affair that, in the end, only Captain Waddell, Paymaster William Breedlove Smith, Lieutenants Smith, Lee, and Scales, and Midshipman Mason were able to attend. The news that the gentlemen of the prestigious Melbourne Club had acknowledged the Confederates raised some eyebrows about town. The Melbourne *Age* fumed

> that the soft-headed flunkeys who are recognised as the leaders of the Melbourne Club are capable of any misdemeanor against common sense and good taste, there can be no doubt. Many of them, however, are Government officials, and it cannot be permitted that they should commit a breach of the neutrality enjoined by her Majesty without being called to account . . . Success to the Confederate cause will, of course, be drunk in gin cocktails, which the gentlemanly pirates are said to be skilled in brewing.

But, in the end, the sumptuous, wine-sodden repast—served by liveried stewards and attended by some sixty of Melbourne's most prominent citizens—proved a splendid affair. Club members offered only two toasts that evening—the first was to the Queen, and the second, to the Confederates' great surprise, "to the Capt. & officers of the 'Shenandoah.'" Even more startling, the club members "gave three cheers—a thing which they said they had never done before, as it was forbidden by the rules of the club." At around eleven o'clock, when dinner broke up, the gentlemen repaired to the smoking and billiard rooms. And, toward midnight, when the Confederates finally left—too late for them to make the last train back to Sandridge—Waddell gave them all permission to remain ashore for the evening. Afterward, Mason recalled, the officers went on a "bit of a lark" before eventually finding rooms that morning at the Albion Hotel.[4]

A week later—on the evening of February 9—Grimball, Lining, Bulloch, and Smith took a train to the town of Ballarat, forty miles north of Melbourne, as honored guests of two prominent American-born magnates in the gold-mining region. The four Confederates arrived late that evening and joined several prominent local gentlemen for dinner at Craig's Royal Hotel. The next day, after touring several mines, the Confederates returned to Craig's, where they were honored with a lavish gala, the Buccaneer's Ball, that was a dazzling success.

"It was," Cornelius Hunt recalled, "a decidedly *recherché* affair." The ball began at 10:00 p.m. and stretched to 4:00 a.m., by which time, Lining recalled, "I had nearly danced my feet off." And, as Hunt further remembered, "Many a grey uniform lost its gilt buttons that night, but we saw them again ere we bade a final adieu to Australia, suspended from watchguards suspended from the necks of bright-eyed women."

Other attentions, however, the Confederates found less welcome. On January 29, Midshipman Mason and Lieutenant Scales—both Episcopalians—found their way to a Sunday service in a little Church of England chapel behind Parliament House. Once inside, however, they were discomfited by glares from congregants who "stared at us with gaping mouthes [*sic*] & starting [*sic*] eyes, as if they were astonished most *amazingly* to see two of the 'Piratical gentlemen' from the 'Shenandoah' in the house of God—perhaps they thought we came there by mistake, thinking it was a billiard saloon or something of that sort."

In another incident, Cornelius Hunt recalled, after a handful of the *Shenandoah*'s officers had gathered for dinner at one of their favorite spots, the American-owned Scott's Hotel, one of the Queen's local subjects "invited himself to join us." Hunt recounted that, once seated, the guest "forthwith commenced a tirade upon rebels and the Southern Confederacy, making use of such language as gentlemen seldom submit to in silence." Fred J. McNulty, the ship's Irish-born assistant surgeon, threw the first blow, and, as others joined the fracas, glasses and decanters were soon flying and knives drawn.

For Midshipman Mason, such encounters resulted from what he viewed as the Confederates' lack of discretion in recruiting the ship's petty officers—many of whom were foreign-born. "I fear we will not carry away the same reputation we brought with us," he wrote. "The fact of the matter is we have too many good for nothing fellows that we were compelled to make officers for want of others & the consequence is they go on shore in uniform[,] get drunk[,] raise a row, & disgrace the ship [and] the uniform."

Soon after receiving permission to remain in port, Captain
Waddell contracted with the local marine-engineering firm of
Langland Brothers & Co. to make all necessary repairs to the
ship. As that work proceeded, however, the *Shenandoah*'s officers discovered that their ship needed more repairs than they
had anticipated. A diver who inspected the raider's hull found
that her bracings—the wooden supports that held the iron apparatus by which the propeller was lifted out of the water—had
rotted away. It was also discovered that the castings, the stern
bearings for the ship's propeller shaft, were gone.

In short, the *Shenandoah*'s condition was a far cry from
what any self-respecting sailor would call seaworthy. A subsequent report by the Langland Brothers firm stated that to replace the linings on the outer stern it would be "absolutely
necessary" to move the ship, for at least ten days, into the government's patent slip—its dry dock. To that end, on Saturday
morning, February 4, a tug towed the *Shenandoah* the two
and a half miles' distance, southwest across Hobson's Bay, to
Williamstown. There a gang of stevedores began the time-
consuming process of loading the raider's contents onto
lighters—shallow-draft boats. Not until February 9 was she hoisted
onto the cradle on which she was rolled, on rails, into the dry
dock.

Though government-owned, the Williamstown dry dock
was leased to the Langland Brothers firm whose engineers were
expected to tend to the *Shenandoah*. Colonial officials assumed
that this arrangement would ensure that the Confederates complied with all British neutrality laws. Day-to-day activities, however, soon breached that barrier. "Every facility was afforded to
us by the officials and people of Melbourne, to make our repairs
and to procure our supplies; indeed, everything we wanted,"

one seaman recounted. According to the same sailor, an "English government engineer" who came aboard several times each day supervised much of the work. Though helpful to the Confederates, it was hardly an arrangement likely to go unnoticed for long by Victoria's officials—nor by U.S. consul William Blanchard.[5]

TEN

"The Old Sea Dogs Chuckled"

So far, so good. During their first week in Melbourne, the Confederates had encountered no U.S. Navy ships, and the local U.S. consul's protests over their presence had been rebuffed. Moreover, they had won acclaim from much of the local population, and their repairs and replenishing of coal and provisions were proceeding apace. Even so, the Confederates knew that local admiration for their cause remained far from unanimous. Throughout Melbourne, despite abundant expressions of pro-Confederate feelings, Old Glory waved over many of the area's homes and businesses. The Confederates even claimed that a "friendly source" had warned them of a plot to destroy the steamer by means of a "torpedo"—a bomb— placed alongside the ship. Waddell issued orders that at least three guards be posted aboard the ship at all times.

At night, master's mate Cornelius Hunt recalled, "if a boat was discovered in our vicinity, she was hailed three times, and then if a satisfactory answer was not received, our orders were preemptory to fire into her."

The Confederate sentries fired on no ships. But a ship swinging at anchor not far away in the harbor and flying Old Glory certainly caught their attention. And, as it turned out, crewmembers aboard that neighboring ship more than reciprocated the attention. Indeed, since the raider's arrival in Hobson's Bay on January 25, several men aboard the *Mustang*, a visiting merchant bark out of New York City, had kept a constant watch on the Confederates.

The 315-ton *Mustang* had reached Melbourne a month earlier, on December 26. And her master, W. Q. Sears, and his crew, fervent Union supporters, were outraged by the raider's presence in the Queen's ostensibly neutral waters. Thus, in the days after the Confederates' arrival, the *Mustang* could be found "lying near the *Shenandoah* and flying the American colors in defiance" of the "pirate ship."

According to accounts provided by *Mustang* crewmembers the following summer to San Francisco's *Daily Alta Californian*, those displays of contempt in Hobson's Bay soon hardened into plans for more conclusive action: "While the *Mustang* was lying near the pirate, Captain Sears of the former vessel, and five other Americans formed a plan to give the skulking freebooter a slight surprise. A torpedo was manufactured, with 250 pounds of gunpowder, and rigged with a revolver cocked, and so placed as to insure [*sic*] an explosion on the pulling of a line attached to the trigger." More to the point, the men recalled, they made sure that the bomb "was of sufficient capacity to blow a large hole in the bottom of the Anglo-Confederate pirate craft" and "break her back."

Under cover of darkness, a sabotage party soon approached the steamer. Lest they be overheard by the sentries posted aboard the *Shenandoah*, the men rowed quietly. Edging alongside the raider, they put their bomb in place. Then, eager to place themselves at a safe distance from the steamer, they quietly rowed away.

According to the *Daily Alta Californian*, however, all the

saboteurs' cunning could not overcome a stroke of bad luck—for, in the end, the torpedo failed to explode. "The swinging of the *Mustang*, unfortunately broke the chain by which it was held, just in time to prevent the blow-out coming off as per arrangement, and the attempt was reluctantly abandoned."

Apparently neither then nor later did the Confederates learn of their close call with the *Mustang*'s torpedo. References to the scheme surface in no *Shenandoah* documents. Remembering the sentries posted aboard the raider to thwart just such sabotage, Cornelius Hunt later recalled that vessels of seemingly "doubtful character" often passed in the dark. But all, when hailed, scurried away. Even so, fears of a torpedo attack remained sufficiently strong to prompt Captain Waddell, on January 31, to request police protection for the *Shenandoah*. Nine days later, Melbourne's police chief, Thomas Lyttleton, promised that the *Shenandoah*, still enjoying the governor's goodwill, would be accorded "particular attention."

Still other troubles were brewing for the Confederates. In several instances a handful of the *Shenandoah*'s petty officers overstayed their shore leaves and, in a few cases, had to be forcibly brought back to the steamer.

More serious difficulties for the raider were about to come from U.S. consul William Blanchard's office. The passengers from the late *Delphine* were not the last of his visitors with incriminating stories to tell. Since the *Shenandoah* anchored in Melbourne, Blanchard had continued to receive a steady stream of former prisoners from the steamer. All told, more than a dozen crew and passengers of the *Delphine*, the *D. Godfrey*, the *Alina*, the *Susan*, and the *Lizzie M. Stacey* darkened Blanchard's door. In some cases Blanchard heard from former detainees who had signed paroles before leaving the raider. But he also heard from men who had languished in irons, or who had shipped with the Confederates, or both.

Still building his case against the Confederates, the U.S. consul took an affidavit of each sailor's story. But what Blanchard took as proof of Confederate violations of British neutrality laws, Waddell viewed as evidence of illegal encouragement of military desertions by the United States government. To Richard C. Standish, commissioner of police, Waddell—citing instances of men who had signed lawful shipping documents only to jump ship in Melbourne—complained that Blanchard and local Union sympathizers had prompted the men to desert their lawful military duties with bribes of $100 a man. Based on those claims, Waddell, on February 1, asked Standish to arrest the errant crewmen and return them to the *Shenandoah*. Standish, however, demurred: "The law," he answered, "does not enable me to issue such instructions to the police." The commissioner's response frustrated Waddell. Equally important, the government's decision offered a powerful inducement for any other Confederate seamen who, entertaining second thoughts about the cruise, were pondering desertion.

By February 7, Governor Darling's patience with the Confederates' presence had worn thin. That day, Commissioner James G. Francis sent Waddell a letter reminding him that the *Shenandoah* had now been in port for twelve days and asking when he planned to sail. Francis also reiterated that Great Britain had traditionally promoted strict compliance with its neutrality obligations, making it clear that a stiffening of resolve was in the air. The Williamstown dry dock into which the raider was to be pulled was privately owned. Even so, Francis reminded

Waddell, British neutrality obligations explicitly prohibited any governmental assistance to the Confederates, even on private property—indeed, "the use of appliances, the property of the government, cannot be granted, nor any assistance rendered by it, directly or indirectly, toward effecting the repairs of the Shenandoah."

Waddell, answering the letter that same day, responded that a series of recent gales had interrupted the Confederates' unloading of their ship in order to get it onto the dry dock. He hoped, weather permitting, that task would be accomplished by the end of the day. But it wasn't until February 9 that the *Shenandoah* was out of the water, and when, five days later, she remained in dry dock, Commissioner Francis sent another letter to Waddell, this time asking him whether he could now "state definitely when the Shenandoah will be in a position to proceed to sea."[1]

Behind Commissioner Francis stood Victoria's governor Charles Darling, and hectoring both was U.S. consul William Blanchard. Indeed, in this erstwhile diplomat, the *Shenandoah*'s commander had an antagonist every bit as tenacious as Blanchard's counterpart in Liverpool, Thomas H. Dudley. Blanchard, like Dudley, had impeccable antislavery credentials. Prior to the war, he had served as editor of the *National Era*, an abolitionist newspaper published in Washington, D.C. And if Blanchard needed any further reason to fuel his zeal to end the *Shenandoah*'s cruise, he soon found one.

Among the more recent *Shenandoah* detainees to arrive in Blanchard's office was John Williams, the black sailor taken from the *D. Godfrey* and coerced into shipping with the Confederates. There are no records showing how long, after the

Shenandoah reached Melbourne, Williams had been contemplating his escape. It is clear, however, that in the weeks since November 8, when he was taken aboard the raider, his relations with her officers had deteriorated. On January 12, after allegedly catching Williams stealing shirts from the wardroom, Whittle gave instructions to "discontinue his rations of grog until further orders and trice him up when he is not at work." Docked in Sandridge a week later, according to the ship's log, Deck Officer Lieutenant Sidney Smith Lee, on January 29, "put Williams in double irons & gagged him for drunkenness & disorderly conduct." Regardless of the truthfulness of the accusations, this much is certain: unlike others from the *Shenandoah* who had appeared in Consul Blanchard's office, Williams had made a bona fide escape. In a measure of Waddell's feeling about the black seaman, Williams had been accorded no shore leave to overstay.

So one morning, seizing upon a moment of Confederate inattention during his regular workday as a cook, Williams slipped off the raider, swam to shore, and found his way to the U.S. Consulate. Once in Blanchard's office, Williams told his gut-wrenching story of being coerced through brutal tricings into working for but, he swore, not joining the Confederates. The story followed an arc by now familiar to Blanchard. But what really caught the consul's attention was Williams's recounting of more recent events. The men for whom he cooked aboard the raider, Williams said, now included fifteen or twenty recent Confederate recruits brought aboard in Melbourne. If true, here was clear evidence of a breach of neutrality obligations.

Soon thereafter, still more evidence against the Confederates reached Blanchard as eight other *Shenandoah* escapees arrived at his door. On February 14, for instance, German seaman F. C. Behucke Herman Wicke—formerly of the *Alina*, captured in late October—provided particularly useful testimony.

After John Williams's escape from the raider days earlier, Wicke said cooking responsibilities aboard the ship had fallen upon a new enlistee—a local man known as Charley, who was recently recruited in Melbourne. Echoing a claim made by Williams, Wicke told of how the recent enlistees were being hidden in the ship's topgallant forecastle.

Blanchard's earlier complaints about the *Shenandoah*'s presence in Australia had rested upon broad principles of diplomatic law. He now dashed off a new chain of letters, each escalating in urgency, to Governor Darling. The letters, Blanchard hoped, attested to the sort of specific instances of wrongdoing that no self-respecting royal official could ignore.

Darling quickly turned the matter over to the local police. They, in turn, assigned a detective to look into Blanchard's latest charges. Within two days, a report vindicated the U.S consul's accusations. Arrest warrants were issued against Charley and the others who, according to Blanchard's affidavits, had been locally recruited by the Confederates. The warrants charged the recruits with violating the Foreign Enlistment Act and the Queen's Neutrality Proclamation of May 1861.

On February 13, Police Superintendent Thomas Lyttleton and two constables approached the dry-docked *Shenandoah* in Williamstown to execute the warrants. But Lieutenant John Grimball, who in Waddell's absence had been left in charge of the ship, refused to allow a search of the vessel.

Lyttleton returned the following morning. But Waddell, who was now back on the ship, also refused the search. The captain later claimed that he informed the police that he had enlisted no recruits in Melbourne but, more significant, that diplomatic immunity—"the well known doctrine that a vessel of war is part of the territory of the country to which she belongs"—precluded any search of the ship by colonial officials. He offered, instead, to order two of his own petty officers—the "police of the Shenandoah, viz., the master-at-arms and his posse"—to search the ship. Lyttleton declined the offer.

Upon learning of the Confederates' refusal to allow the search, Governor Darling ordered the suspension of Commissioner Francis's permission for the ship to remain in port for repairs and provisions. Beyond that, Francis telegraphed Police Inspector Beavers of the Williamstown station, ordering him to proceed at once to the government shipyard with all the police he could muster. Once there—unless Waddell agreed to have his ship searched—Beavers was to end all work by British subjects. And, aware that repairs on the by now coaled and otherwise resupplied ship were virtually complete, Commissioner Francis also ordered Beavers to prevent the raider from setting sail.[2]

At 5:30 p.m. that same day, February 14, Beavers and a contingent of some two hundred policemen, soon joined by fifty soldiers, arrived at the Williamstown patent slip. Immediately ending all work on the ship, the officials took control of the dry dock and the wharves on either side of it. Surgeon Lining, recounting the incident in his diary, captured the shared sense of outrage among the *Shenandoah*'s officers: "I don't know that I ever felt more humiliated in all my life as when I saw policemen on each side of the ship, with guns in their hands, keeping guard over us, while we lay perfectly helpless on the slip unable to work, or to make the slightest resistance."

Still later that afternoon, a letter arrived for Waddell from Commissioner Francis, stating that if the Confederates agreed to the long requested search of their ship the cordon of police and soldiers would be withdrawn, the shipyard reopened, and the workers allowed to resume their repairs to the steamer. As he had done at Las Desertas when another crisis had imperiled his command, Waddell called a council of his officers.

This time, however, he confined the council to Lining and just three of his lieutenants—Whittle, Lee, and Grimball. Owing to his ongoing doubts about Lieutenants Francis Chew and Dabney Scales, Waddell excluded both men from the conference. Those attending reaffirmed their opposition to any search of the ship. As a formality, at Lining's suggestion Waddell ordered Lieutenant Grimball and the master-at-arms to replicate the Confederates' earlier search of the ship for the men sought by the police. Afterward, Waddell appointed Lining to draft a letter to Francis "denying that the men were on board, but refusing any search" by British authorities. Lining wrote the letter, read it aloud, and incorporated changes suggested by Waddell and the officers of that evening's council. In the end, the letter couched their predicament in the grand language of international law.

> According to all the laws of nations, the deck of a vessel of war is considered to represent the majesty of the country whose flag she flies, and she is free from all executions except for crimes actually committed on shore, when a demand must be made for the delivery of such person and the execution of the warrant performed by the police of the ship.

Waddell dispatched the letter to Commissioner Francis and, that evening, ordered all the *Shenandoah*'s officers and crew to begin securing the ship against boarding. By Waddell's own admission, the latter constituted a dubious command. "Of course, if any attack was made," he later wrote, "the attacking party would have knocked away the props and the vessel would have fallen from the slip and been rendered a hopeless ruin." The impasse, and the policemen surrounding the *Shenandoah*, remained when the sun rose the following morning.

During the night of the fourteenth, however, the final touches on the steam engine's repair had been made and the engine parts hoisted into place. With the raider now ready to sail, Waddell, painfully aware of his fragile, if not indefensible, circumstances, resolved to force the issue of the ship's release. On February 15, he wrote yet another letter. Bypassing Commissioner Francis, he now addressed his concerns directly to Governor Darling. Laying down an ultimatum, Waddell called the police action at Williamstown a de facto seizure of his ship and asked if the royal governor intended it as such: "The course which I proposed to pursue in case his Excellency was aware of the seizure, was to regard officers and men as prisoners of the British Government, to haul down the [Confederate] flag, and proceed with my command to London by the next mail boat." To increase pressure on the governor, Waddell sent Lieutenant Grimball to Darling's residence with orders not to return without an answer.

With a stroke of his pen, Waddell had raised the stakes for Victoria's government and, by implication, for Great Britain. Up to now, however awkwardly, Governor Darling had managed to steer a middle course between Waddell and U.S consul Blanchard's competing demands. But now, with the Confederates vowing to abandon their ship, Waddell had raised the ante, threatening to cast Governor Darling as the protagonist in an international diplomatic imbroglio similar to that which had erupted after American naval captain Charles Wilkes seized the British mail steamer *Trent* in November 1861.

For weeks now, Darling and his colleagues had sought permission to board the Confederate raider. But now Waddell was offering, in effect, *to give him the entire ship*. In his diary, Midshipman Mason deftly captured the dilemma ensnaring the governor. Darling, he noted, faced "the predicament of the man who drew the Elephant in the lottery." Indeed, so confident was Waddell of his gambit's eventual success that, even before hearing Darling's response, he ordered his men to prepare the raider to leave the dry dock and hired the tug *Black Eagle*, instructing its captain to be prepared to tow the *Shenandoah* back toward Sandridge.

By then, Governor Darling had grown weary of the stand-off. Moreover, he was eager to defuse a potentially explosive situation—explosive politically and perhaps even literally. Indeed, the Melbourne *Argus* speculated that the governor's dispatch of police to the Williamstown dry dock was in fact an effort to pre-empt a conspiracy to sabotage the raider, presumably the one orchestrated aboard the *Mustang*. Accordingly, Darling, via his usual proxy, Commissioner Francis, dispatched a letter to Williamstown ordering the workers there back to work. The letter, which reached the shipyard at 2:30 that afternoon, lifted Francis's earlier orders to block the *Shenandoah*'s departure. Lieutenant Francis Chew, though mistaking diplomatic for military cunning, savored the Confederates' triumph: "We were masters of the situation; they were at the mercy of our guns."

At high tide that day, or around 5:30 p.m., the *Black Eagle* towed the *Shenandoah* off the Williamstown dry dock and returned her to Sandridge, where once again the steamer soon swung at anchor. The following day and the next, lighters and other vessels came alongside and loaded the ship's provisions, which included a fresh supply of 250 tons of coal.

At daybreak on Sunday morning, February 18, Captain Waddell ordered steam gotten up and all hands on deck. After twenty-three full days in Melbourne, the Confederates were finally getting under way. With the sweet notes of the boatswain's pipe, the sound of sailors scurrying to and fro on the freshly holystoned decks, and the clanking of the windlass hauling up the anchors, the ship suddenly breathed new life. At eight o'clock, when full light gave the harbor a gold shimmer, the Confederates began steaming out to sea. As a precaution against any pro-Union saboteurs afloat or onshore, Waddell had ordered all guns loaded and prepared to fire. By 11:45 a.m., after they had passed out of Hobson's Bay and back into deep water without a weapon being fired, officers and crew breathed easier. After all, as Lining recalled, "Large bets had been offered that our ship would never pass through the heads." But not until an hour later, when the pilot boat came by for their pilot, did the Confederates believe for certain that they had ended their Melbourne adventure unscathed.[3]

According to Cornelius Hunt, once the *Shenandoah* passed the head of Hobson's Bay, thus reentering international waters, the Confederates learned, to their astonishment, that a group of stowaways, having eluded all their professed efforts to keep unauthorized people off the steamer, had found their way aboard.

> Fourteen of the number crept out of the bowsprit, which was of iron and hollow, where they had come very near ending their existence by suffocation; twenty more turned out of some water-tanks which were dry; another detachment was unearthed from the lower hold, and at last the whole number of stowaways were mustered forward, and word was passed to the Captain to learn his pleasure concerning them.

According to Hunt, Captain Waddell, confronting this scene, "without any circumlocution demanded of our new recruits to what country they belonged and for what purpose they were there."

> The old sea-dogs chuckled, rolled over their tobacco, hitched up their trousers, and with one accord, protested that they were natives of the Southern Confederacy, and had come on board thus surreptitiously for the purpose of joining us.

All told, according to Whittle, forty-two stowaways appeared on the steamer's deck that day. In his memoirs, Waddell—though professing to have been surprised by the stowaways—nonetheless made it clear that he welcomed their appearance. Moreover, he called the recruits a fair trade for those who, he said, had "deserted" the ship at Sandridge: "We had received thirty-four young American seamen and eight others of different nationalities in exchange for our Irish Americans, sixteen Germans and a Negro, who had deserted in Hobson's Bay, under a promise of $100 cash from the American consul."

Oddly, after devoting in his memoirs thousands of words to his purported efforts in Melbourne to uphold all relevant neutrality obligations, Waddell devoted a single sentence to the stowaways' deception in boarding the *Shenandoah*: "These men had smuggled themselves on board the ship the night before we left Hobson's Bay." The shrugged shoulders of that sentence's see-no-evil, passive construction, however, offers a broad hint as to just who bore ultimate responsibility for the recruits' illegal boarding of the raider.

On January 25, soon after arriving in Port Phillip Bay, Captain Waddell closed his first letter to Governor Darling with a declaration: "I shall observe the neutrality." And neither while in Melbourne nor later did Waddell or any of the other officers acknowledge that they had attempted to recruit additional crew members.

But, then again, such lofty pledges came from officers who, to lure enemy ships toward them, routinely engaged in the deception of flying foreign flags. And from the moment their anchors plunged into the waters of Port Phillip it seemed obvious that the Confederates were intent on doing more in Melbourne than simply repairing, reprovisioning, and recoaling their ship. As was obvious even to casual visitors aboard the raider, the Confederates needed more crew members to round out a full complement, and Melbourne, in all likelihood, would be their last opportunity to win such enlistees before they reached what Waddell alone knew was the steamer's ultimate destination: the Arctic's whaling grounds.

The *Shenandoah*'s past history made it clear that her officers were not committed to observing the spirit or substance of Britain's Foreign Enlistment Act and other neutrality laws. At most, Waddell sought to project an *appearance* of observing the letter of those laws. For diplomats, colonial officials, and other observers in Melbourne, the only question was how tissue-thin that appearance would become.

Unbeknownst to the raider's officers, Waddell's resolve to get to Melbourne likely issued less from his desire to meet a mail steamer than from his appointment to meet a supply ship. Apparently amending his original October 5 orders to Waddell, Commander James Bulloch had secretly dispatched the tender *John Fraser* from Liverpool to Melbourne bearing a load of coal for the *Shenandoah*. The practice was hardly without precedent. Throughout the *Alabama*'s career, Bulloch had dispatched a similar tender, the bark *Agrippina*, to various points around the world to recoal and resupply that raider.

In one of the two versions of his memoirs, Waddell makes brief mention of the *John Fraser*, only to dismiss the notion, current even during the *Shenandoah*'s stay in Melbourne, that the collier "was supposed to be my consort, but there was no truth for the suspicion." That denial, however, of breaching yet another British neutrality obligation—of a piece with Waddell's denial of recruiting seamen in Melbourne—carries all the sincerity of the cat caught with the canary in its mouth.

More forthcoming testimony would later come from William Temple, a British seaman who served on the *Shenandoah* for her entire cruise: "Before we left Melbourne we were coaled by the ship John Fraser, from Liverpool, which I have since learned was sent out with coal expressly for us." One of several large merchant sailing ships owned since before the war by Fraser, Trenholm, and Co., the *John Fraser* was placed under the British flag in July 1861 in order to avoid capture by the first United States warship she might encounter.

In Melbourne, Waddell recalled, the *Shenandoah* was "taken to the coal ship *John Fraser*, which vessel had recently arrived from Cardiff with coal and of the kind I wanted." More specifically, as he later noted, the Welsh coal, invaluable to a ship with a vested interest in preserving the element of surprise, "makes a white vapor which could not be seen two hundred yards off." As for the fortuitous, almost simultaneous arrival of the two ships in Melbourne, Waddell in his memoirs coyly attributed the timing to "coincidence"—even as he allowed, "She arrived in very excellent time to supply my want, and I purchased of her 250 tons of coal."[4]

In Waddell's defense against charges that while in Melbourne he failed to uphold Great Britain's neutrality obligations, in fairness it should also be noted that his first responsibility as a commander was to advance the cause of the Confederacy, not to uphold Britain's laws or its fealty to promises made under international treaties. "The Shenandoah's people were not the custodians of British law," Waddell later wrote. "The British authorities are the proper custodians of British law; with them alone it rests to take care that no breach of neutrality does take place in the event of an armed steamer of a belligerent power entering their ports and harbors."

Beyond that, Consul Blanchard's indignation at the *Shenandoah*'s activities contained an element of hypocrisy. During the Civil War, the U.S. Navy routinely violated the neutrality of various foreign ports—including those of Gibraltar, Brazil, and Ireland; it assaulted Confederate ships in foreign waters; and, like Waddell, it also recruited nationals of other countries in neutral ports. Seamen, for instance, for the USS *Kearsarge*, which ultimately sank the CSS *Alabama*, had been recruited in Ireland. Similarly, by encouraging—and even providing cash to encourage—desertions from a legally recognized navy in a neutral port, Blanchard violated long-standing international laws.

But, beyond matters of law, there was the issue of Waddell's personal effectiveness. For all his cunning, the captain's behavior was often politically ham-fisted. He seemed unmindful of the political advantages that accrue from personal relationships—a curious lapse for a Southerner, given the role of such dynamics in his region's politics. Two days after the *Shenandoah* anchored at Sandridge, for instance, Waddell apparently had an appointment at Melbourne's Government House to meet Victoria's governor Charles Darling. But when he—along with Grimball, Scales, and Lining, all decked out in their finest uniforms and dress swords—arrived promptly at 12:30 and found the governor not yet in his office, the captain, leaving his card, departed in a huff. Minutes later, as the officers were riding off, they passed the governor in his carriage, returning to his office.

Waddell, however, stubbornly resisted returning. As Lining recalled the captain's vainglory: "It was then too late to turn back—an hour had been appointed, the Gov. was not there, & it would not have become our position to have kicked our heels in his waiting room." Perhaps so. But, then again, the Confederates might have had an easier time in Melbourne had their captain enjoyed a personal relationship with Victoria's governor. At the least, he might have dealt directly with Darling rather than with his subaltern, James G. Francis. Instead, Waddell apparently never met Victoria's governor. Even so, despite such lapses the *Shenandoah*'s captain had managed to repair his ship and replenish her with additional crew and provisions. But his windy indifference to the currents of manners and politics would continue to bedevil his course.[5]

ELEVEN

"Doubtful Shoals"

S oon after nightfall on Sunday, February 18, the day the Confederates left Hobson's Bay, the *Shenandoah* reached Bass Strait, the waters between Australia's southern shore and Van Diemen's Land. The seas were calm that evening, the skies clear. Captain Waddell, after the uncertainties of the past few weeks, stood on his poop deck and found a moment for reflection amid the moonlight-splattered waters that spread before him, a moment which, recalled years later, inspired him to quote a few lines from Edgar Allan Poe's poem "The Bells":

> *The stars that oversprinkle*
> *All the heavens, seem to twinkle*
> *With a crystalline delight*

The next day the *Shenandoah* left the Bass Strait, and by dusk two days later, February 21, the Confederates had finally lost sight of land. As they rounded Australia's southeastern coast, then steamed northeastward, John Blacker, one of the so-called stowaways recruited in Melbourne, greatly assisted their navigation. Soon made Captain Waddell's clerk, Blacker, an

Irishman, was a former sea captain himself and, as it turned out, an old hand at sailing these waters.

But Blacker's knowledge of the shoals, rocks, and islands of Australia's coast could not save the *Shenandoah* from other forces that were about to ruffle her cruise, including a debilitating loss of shipboard morale resulting from Captain Waddell's increasingly erratic behavior. During the Confederates' three weeks in Melbourne, a sense among the crew of confronting a common menace had allowed them to transcend many of the tensions that had roiled the voyage's first three months. But, once in the relative safety of the open sea, with fresh provisions and an augmented crew, the old tensions revived, including those between Captain Waddell and his commissioned officers. On February 23, five days after the *Shenandoah* had left Hobson's Bay, Lieutenant Whittle complained of Waddell, "I do not know half the time what is being done in the ship, as he gives orders which should either eminate [*sic*] from or pass threw [*sic*] me. This way of doing business does not suit me."

Bypassing Whittle in the chain of command, Waddell not only undermined his executive officer's authority; he also assured that only the captain, on any given day, possessed a broad perspective of the ship's immediate course. Officers acting on Waddell's instructions could only speculate about the role each of his individual orders played, if at all, in his sailing plans. Moreover, Waddell's own memoirs shed but faint light on his thinking during this leg of the raider's cruise.

Upon leaving the Bass Strait, Waddell contemplated several gambits intended to capture a few more American whaling vessels before the raider reached her ultimate destination, of which he alone on the ship was aware: the Arctic. He might round

New Zealand's northern tip and drop down its eastern coast to hunt for the whaling vessels that came into ports there for provisions. Or he might try his luck on the whaling grounds off Norfolk and Lord Howe Islands, about 450 miles northeast of Sydney.

But, even as Waddell contemplated his various gambits, he knew that he was racing against time. No doubt warnings of the Confederates' presence in these waters had already gone out from Melbourne. And he was also racing against the arrival of March 1, the traditional departure date for the whaling vessels that stopped along New Zealand's eastern coast for supplies. And from the start nature had thwarted the *Shenandoah*'s race. On February 20, the raider's second day out of Melbourne, as the Confederates approached Cape Howe, Australia's most southeasterly point, strong headwinds from the north slowed their progress. Two days later, when favorable winds finally rose, these proved too light to allow them to make up for the time already lost. In late February, when they reached a position north of New Zealand and were preparing to sail south down its eastern coast, yet another wind—this one from the southeast—thwarted their forward passage.

Shipboard circumstances were more encouraging. At 10:00 a.m. on Sunday, February 26, Lieutenant Whittle called the entire crew on deck for an inspection, a general muster, and, for the benefit of the new men, a reading of the Articles of War. "We now muster stronger than ever before," he exulted. "We have now onboard ninety six men, and we feel that we can take care of the ship in all weather."

Moreover, the crew now had more room for their daily routines. During the Confederates' first months at sea, the removal of the coal that once covered much of their berth deck had created more sleeping space. Beyond that, the coal's removal gave them room on the berth deck to install a new galley, acquired in Melbourne and capable of preparing meals for the expanded crew. And that, in turn, gave the raider's officers, after leaving Australia, the perfect excuse to make a long desired modification—the removal of what Whittle called "a great nuisance," the ship's deck house. "We have had all the time," he recalled, "a most unsightly and useless house on our Spar deck forward and it has always looked very unlike a man-of-war." Thus, once at sea, the Confederates delighted in removing the old deckhouse and cutting a stovepipe hole for the new belowdeck galley.

Twenty-three of the Melbourne men had shipped as seamen, assigned to assist the ship's daily operations. Early in the cruise, Lieutenant Whittle had imagined how he would man each of the raider's four mast departments (foretop, maintop, mizzen, and main). Each department would, in turn, be divided into aft and starboard watches, and from those he would assign daily duty watches. With the twenty-three new seamen, a number that more than replaced the sailors lost in Melbourne, Whittle now brought the number in each mast department halfway up to what he considered the ideal complement. Moreover, he assigned seven of the new men to the ship's engineering department, most to serve as firemen.

Of the new enlistees, ten others were made petty officers, thus doubling the number aboard, to help supervise the enlarged complement of seamen. The new petty officers created a greater distribution of authority in the ship's lower ranks and gave the ship a better ratio of commissioned officers to crew. More generally, the raider's commissioned officers hoped that the expanded workforce would improve shipboard morale, and that high-ranking officers would no longer be compelled to participate in labors normally performed by seamen.

Whittle took particular satisfaction in organizing five of the new men into the nucleus of a marine guard. The Confederate Congress, in March 1861, had passed legislation creating for its navy a corps of Confederate States Marines. That same legislation had also adopted for these new marines the rules and regulations that the U.S. Congress had enacted when, in 1852, it formally established the U.S. Marines. By a tradition reaching back to the creation of the British Royal Marines in 1664, marines were regarded more as warriors afloat than as sailors. In their early years, marines had two chief roles: to serve as sharpshooters perched in the masts and rigging of men-of-war, and to serve as police aboard those same ships. By 1861, advances in armaments had cast marines out of the rigging of the world's ships. They now manned more formidable guns and cannons on the ships' decks. But their role as shipboard police persisted, and it was in that latter role that Executive Officer Whittle envisioned his marine guard performing their main service aboard the *Shenandoah*.

This new detail needed to be well trained, but it also needed to project an aura of authority. Whittle thus welcomed the fortuitous coincidence that a tailor numbered among the raider's new recruits from Melbourne; he promptly ordered a set of uniforms for his brand-new guard.[1]

By February 28, the *Shenandoah* had reached latitude 32°21' S, longitude 169°17' E—a position some five hundred miles northwest of New Zealand and about six hundred miles east of Lord Howe Island. Waddell made no formal announcement, but the *Shenandoah*'s other officers had deduced that he, to their chagrin, was deferring any immediate plans for raiding. To Surgeon Lining, what particularly grated, aside from the missed opportunities for more prizes, was the captain's apparent inability to adhere to a singular course of action: "How I do wish some people could stick to one thing at a time & not be as vacillating as the wind, he ought to have caught several prizes before now, particularly if we had gone to Lord Howe's Island, which would not have been out of our way."

Though tight-lipped about this period, in his memoirs Waddell acknowledges that delays in leaving Melbourne and in sailing up Australia's eastern coast had shortened the raider's odds of catching any whaling vessels off Australia's or New Zealand's coasts, or off Lord Howe and Norfolk Islands. He assumed that word of the *Shenandoah*'s presence in Melbourne had by then reached Sydney, and thus all the whaling grounds anywhere near that port. By necessity, the Confederates were thus forced to follow their now fleeing quarry. As Waddell put it, "It was very certain that the birds had taken shelter, and I would probably find them further north."

By March 1, Waddell had settled into a northerly course between New Caledonia and Fiji. In the end, though, instead of whaling vessels in those seas, what the Confederates found was four days of heavy storms. "In twenty-three years of service," Waddell recalled, "I had never seen such a succession of violent squalls. The vessel was enveloped in a salt mist and knocked by every angry sea." Soon caught in a typhoon, Waddell, fearing the raider might be run aground on nearby islands, close-reefed the ship's fore- and topsails, and ordered the ship to lie to for two days.

March 5 proved especially brutal. "A heavy sea came rolling in forward, striking the ship a terrible blow, making her tremble in every part," Lieutenant Chew recalled. Waves flooded the main deck, filling it with water beyond the meager capacity of the scuppers at the deck's edges to drain it. Moreover, the water's sheer volume—tons of it trapped between the bulwarks surrounding the deck—shifted violently as the storm rocked the ship, threatening to capsize it.

Compounding these woes, the storm soon tore one of the raider's twelve-pounder cannons from its carriage and lashings. Suddenly the Confederates faced the chilling prospect of a half ton of iron caroming about in the waters trapped on the rolling and pitching deck. Somewhere in those dark waters lurked an iron tube whose weight and force could maim or kill a man, or, if it broke through the deck, sink the entire ship. In a display of authentic physical courage, Lieutenant Whittle and several other men, braving high winds and convulsively shifting waters at least up to their waists, rushed into the flood and knocked gunports open to allow the water to drain from the deck. Then, passing ropes about the cannon, they managed to secure it, "thus," Chew recorded, "disposing of quite a terrible customer."

By March 9, after being battered by four days of driving gales and rain, the raider reached latitude 26°25' S, longitude 173°46' E—a position in calmer seas some five hundred miles southeast of New Caledonia. "How pleasant is a moderate breeze and smooth sea after having been tossed about by the tempest!" Chew confided to his diary. But good weather could not quell a growing restlessness among the *Shenandoah*'s officers and crew. The men longed for something, anything, to happen—a stop at one of the tropical islands they passed each day, perhaps, or the capture of another whaleship. Waddell, Chew complained, was missing chances to do both. He recorded his lament on March 10, as the *Shenandoah* sailed past the Norfolk and Howe's island chains. Echoing charges made by one of the ship's junior officers, who claimed to have served seven years on a whaling vessel, Chew groused that had they touched at the two chains, "five or six captures at least would have been made." "The Capt. passed them unceremoniously, appearing to consider them unworthy of notice." In all likelihood, Chew's source was Waddell's new clerk, John Blacker. For Chew and other men aboard the raider, the adventure of their first few months at sea had given way to a growing sense of ennui and, at the edges, malcontent.

That same day, Waddell, frustrated by the northerly winds blowing against them, ordered the propeller lowered into the water. Since February 19, the raider had been exclusively under canvas, and the men welcomed the increased speed. "We are all glad to know that we are rapidly approaching the whaling grounds," Chew wrote, "even at the expense of burning coal; a very valuable article—and its value is enhanced by the knowledge that we will not be able to get any more."

Over the next few days, basking in freshening trade winds and clear skies, Chew and other officers found time after dinner to linger in the ship's gangway, smoking, talking, and singing, and to relax in the wardroom over conversation and games of chess. But by March 17 the rains had returned. As the raider's officers, when off duty, huddled in the wardroom for an ongoing chess tournament, those on topside duty did their best to keep the *Shenandoah* on course and—albeit futilely—to keep themselves dry.

The disagreeable weather exacerbated the crew's irritation with Waddell. Like others, Midshipman Mason blamed the captain for the fact that, since leaving Melbourne a month earlier, they had found no whaling vessels: "Here we have been cruising around in the most outlandish places, not going nearer than three or four hundred miles to any of the numerous islands that dot this part of the Pacific ocean; indeed I believe we have found a portion of the world that no mortals ever explored." More specifically, Mason attributed their failure to find new prizes to Waddell's decision to make the long—and, to Mason's mind, unnecessary—layover at Melbourne. Not only had the captain forgone possible prizes to be had in the whaling ground around New Zealand but his decisions had harmed the ship.

Mason recounted in his diary that the *Shenandoah*'s engineer, Matthew O'Brien, upon realizing the damaged condition of the ship's engine during their passage through the Indian Ocean, had urged Waddell not to run it "unless absolutely necessary" until they could reach a port for repairs. Like other crew members, Mason still believed that the *John Fraser*'s presence at Melbourne had been a lucky coincidence. And, while he knew that the steamer needed repairs, provisions, and coal, he also continued to believe that Waddell had rushed the cruiser to Melbourne mainly to reach the mail steamer before her scheduled departure. And that, in Mason's mind, had led the captain to imprudently order the engineer to "run the machine." By Mason's lights, Waddell had won his race to reach the mail steamer, but he had compounded the damage to the engine— thus necessitating the raider's time-consuming removal to the dry dock. And that delay, he was convinced, now prevented the Confederates from catching the whaling vessels they had hoped to find in the South Pacific.[2]

On March 14, the *Shenandoah* reached latitude 15°33' S, longitude 174°7' E—a position about three hundred miles northwest of Fiji Island. That morning, Lieutenant Francis Chew had the forenoon watch, the 8:00 a.m. to noon shift—and shared it with an unusually loquacious Captain Waddell. The captain, Chew recalled, expressed his frustration at not being able to catch "the New Zealand fleet" of whaling vessels in the waters to their south. Even so, Waddell still hoped that they might yet find some of those vessels on their cruising grounds off several nearby archipelagoes—the Solomon, Fiji, Gilbert, Caroline, and Ellice island groups. But Waddell made it clear that his thoughts were already roaming beyond those possibilities. "There is," he said, stunning Chew, "another fleet of whalers called the Polar fleet whose cruising ground is in high northern latitudes." The captain told Chew that, as soon as the Confederates' searching of the South Pacific's islands was complete, "he will go to the North Pacific to look after the Polar fleet."

Never before had Waddell shared the objectives of this cruise with anyone on the ship. "Now there is the programme; now let us see how it is carried out," a stupefied Chew confided to his diary—and promptly told others on the ship. To receive such a revelation from a captain whose behavior, only months earlier, had led Chew to consider resigning from the navy was a true marvel. After all, such unguarded gregariousness in no way reflected Waddell's general interactions with the officers and crew. Indeed, during the weeks after leaving Australia the captain's isolation seemed to deepen—an estrangement highlighted by his growing remove from Executive Officer William Whittle. Eight days after the *Shenandoah* had left Hobson's Bay, Whittle noted in his journal, "There is a dark cloud which overhangs us and she is not the happy ship she might be." The captain, Whittle reported, was "still in the dumps." Unaware of Waddell's chats with Chew, Whittle noted, "There is not an officer to whom he speaks on duty except his clerk."

Two days later, Whittle reported, "W's dumps continue. I am entirely at a loss to understand this man, who I once thought I knew." Beyond his own anguish, Whittle feared the ramifications of the captain's behavior on the other men aboard the raider: "I am fearful that his conduct to me will not go unnoticed by the crew, upon whom it could have no other than a bad effect. I trust it will; for I consider it is more incumbent on the captain's 1st Lt. to keep upon good terms than every one else . . . The Captain now not only does not speak to me privately but does not <u>even speak</u> to me officially."

The next day found an increasingly exasperated executive officer indulging in his perennial daydream of the *Shenandoah*'s capture of a swift ship that could be fitted out as a new raider under his command—"a fast bark of about 400 tons with double topsail yards and I would make application to take charge of her . . . Oh how I would glory in such a chance." Whittle even composed a list of prospective officers for his new raider: "Lee, Scales & Bulloch are all applicants for any vessel that I am placed in." At the collision point of his frustrations and daydreams lurked darker, even mutinous, meditations. "In fact," the disaffected young first lieutenant mused, "I could take any of them as all would like to go."

By mid-March, however, the relationship between the captain and his executive officer showed signs of a thaw—a development aided no doubt by Waddell's promise that Whittle would receive his desired independent command with the next prize suitable for conversion into a raider.

As the relationship between the two men grew if not warm, at least less frosty, Waddell increasingly confided in Whittle. In most cases, the captain's confidences took the form of dispiriting complaints on one of two topics: the conditions under which he worked, including the caliber of his officers, and his own real or imagined physical ailments. On March 15, Waddell's two obsessions coalesced in a single grievance concerning watch officer Lieutenant Dabney Scales. Because Waddell did not trust the young officer's seamanship, he felt compelled to remain on deck whenever Scales was on watch. And those hours, combined with the time he normally lingered on the quarter deck, had made his feet horribly sore. That condition—coupled with not getting enough sleep—was, Waddell said, taking a toll on his overall health. By Whittle's recounting of the episode, the captain "felt himself breaking."

From Whittle's perspective, the captain grossly underestimated Scales and his other officers: "He has not sufficient confidence in the ability of his officers—in which he is wrong, for I never saw a better set, and one[s] who learned so rapidly." But more than that, Whittle believed, Waddell exalted his own role on the ship to the point of being "a perfect martyr": "He was so blue & melancholy that I pitied him, and told him that he was very mistaken as to S's qualifications and that I considered his [Waddell's] being on deck unnecessary." Privately, Whittle dismissed the captain's complaints as so much whining. "I never saw any man feel it necessary to remain on deck so much," he wrote. "He complains of never getting sleep enough, and really it seems to me that he gets more sleep than any man in the ship." Having heard enough, Whittle demonstrated that he, too, knew a thing or two about playing the martyr, and finally told Waddell that he would lift some of those claimed burdens.

> I volunteered to keep all Scales' watches with him in addition to my duties as Executive officer, which God knows are far more trying than those of any man I ever saw. My legitimate duties keep me on deck from seven in the morning until 8 at night, and then to keep one of *three* watches, (for Jack Grimball is sick), is very trying, & will tell on me, but if one is to break down it had better be me than him—and I shall stand it as long as I can walk.[3]

Even so, beyond whatever appetite for self-glorification drove Whittle that day, the ship—on that rainy, sweltering Ides of March in the South Pacific—did face navigational perils, real and imagined, that would challenge the most seasoned mariner. "Surrounded as we are by rocks, islands and doubtful shoals the navigation is intricate," Whittle noted. More than that, the men suffered from the widespread fear among European and American sailors, a fear rooted in documented incidents of that era but also inflamed by hyperbole, that the Pacific islands teemed with cannibals. "If by misfortune we should run ashore and be wrecked we would probably be thrown on the Fijis or New Hebrides, and we might be eaten by cannibals," Whittle wrote. His imagination, fortunately, also provided him with resources against such a fate. "I am decided that in such a case I would cover myself all over with coal tar, curl my hair and I might pass as an uneatable negro."

As March waned, Waddell's relations with the other Confederates showed no improvement. And the past few weeks' rains, conspiring with the tropics' steadily rising temperatures, had swollen the number of officers and crew on the ship's sick list. In winds so light that the *Shenandoah* commenced steaming again, the raider's fit officers also knew that they now lay in the direct path of whaleships sailing between the Navigators and Caroline island groups. At least initially, however, no whaling vessels darkened the lonesome line of sea and sky that encircled the Confederates. "I often take a glass and sweep the horizon but to no purpose," Chew lamented on March 23. "Nothing breaks the monotony of sea & sky."

At 8:00 that evening, aware that they lay some twenty miles from Drummond Island, better known as Tabiteuea, a popular stopover in the Gilberts for whaling vessels, Waddell gave orders to let the steam go down and for the ship to lay to for the night. With the officers and men now aware that they would head toward the island in the morning, the raider was suddenly abuzz with anticipation. The captain, Lining reported, "expects to take at least <u>seven whalers</u>."

Soon after first light the next morning, when the Confederates began steaming again, the cry of "Land ho!" sounded from the masthead. Within an hour the excited crew had spotted "a long line of trees rising above the water." And by 9:30 the raider lay within six or seven miles of Drummond. The Confederates, studying the low-lying island's dense forests from the raider's deck with glasses, noticed three islanders in an outrigger canoe paddling toward them. The men, Chew recalled, were small of stature, with dark complexion and thick, shaggy black hair, and "as naked as a new born babe . . . not unlike our Indians." Lining's description of the men was less charitable: "They were a horrid looking set of devils, more like monkeys, than men." Once alongside the *Shenandoah*, however, the islanders declined to come aboard.

Chew, observing that reluctance, speculated that "probably this is the first steamer they ever saw." In all likelihood, however, the *Shenandoah* was not the first large ship or the first steamer that the natives had seen. And, assuming the islanders had seen such vessels, they had good reason to distrust the white men who sailed on them. Those mariners included whalemen who sometimes lured men away, never to return to their home island or, worse, the notorious "blackbirders"—labor recruiters who during the latter half of the nineteenth century plied the South Pacific's waters. Recruiting labor principally for the sugarcane and other plantations of Fiji, Samoa, New Caledonia, and Australia's Queensland, blackbirders by 1865 were becoming known for using all kinds of unscrupulous methods, even posing as priests, to lure island natives aboard their ships to serve for years in harsh conditions on plantations before their potential return to their home islands.

At least one member of the *Shenandoah*'s crew spoke the islanders' tongue—Kiribati, a language of the Micronesian geographic area—and, as he interpreted, the Confederates fell into conversation with the boatmen, who soon conveyed unwelcome news: there were no whalers at Drummond, and it had been a long time since any had called at the island. The news came as a crushing disappointment to the Confederates; "all our visions of Seven on fire were dissipated," Lining recalled.

Waddell, "disgusted" by this latest letdown, immediately ordered the ship's officers to make all sails and stand to the northwest. By Chew's account, not until the next day—March 25—when the rains returned did the Confederates' shared frustration stemming from their anticlimactic call at the island fully sink in. "Disappointment in not finding any yankees at Drummond island remains pictured on every countenance," Chew recalled. "Where have they hid themselves is the universal question; some of the officers say that they entertain doubts of the existence of a whaling fleet in these apparently deserted regions."

Equally oppressive, Chew recalled, was the men's disappointment that they had been unable to land on Drummond "in order to examine the island & see man in a complete state of nature."

This equally shared by all; for myself I would have been highly delighted with a stroll beneath the waving cocoanut trees. And again I might have been able to procure some shells for Sister. I heard her once express a wish to have a collection of Ocean shell; I have never forgotten it & should I be fortunate enough, while here in the Pacific, to go onshore I will make these my first care.

That same day, March 25, they crossed the equator for the second time in four months, and Lining could not resist contrasting that crossing with their last: "Difference in feelings, apathy having taken the place of enthusiasm & the feeling of pride in the ship—All I care for now is to have the cruise over, & a chance of once more getting out of her." Lieutenant Chew's mood was no less despondent. "We continue our weary, solitary way to the N & W, still no sail," he lamented. "We sail along slowly, over a quiet almost glassy sea. Can a place seem more out of the world than where we now are?"

Three days of squalls gave way, on March 29, to cloudy skies, and just before sunset that afternoon the Confederates spotted a sail against the northern horizon. As the raider's excited officers and crew, craning for a better view, gathered on the main deck, the *Shenandoah* set a course to cut off the vessel. Soon enough, the Confederates had forced their quarry to heave to with a blank cartridge fired from a twelve-pounder and a boarding party had been dispatched.

The excitement aboard the raider, however, soon collapsed. The ship proved to be the *Pfeil*, a schooner from the Sandwich Islands—Hawaii—out on a trading expedition. But, before saying goodbye to the Confederates, the schooner's Dutch captain did share some tantalizing intelligence: at nearby Strong's Island—today's Kosare Island—which he had recently visited, he had found no ships. But about three weeks earlier he had seen three U.S. whaling vessels at Ascension—today's Pohnpei or Ponape—Island, which lay a day's sail away.

The next morning Waddell set a course toward Ascension

Island. But, despite the intelligence by the *Pfeil*'s captain that no ships had been spotted at Strong's Island, Waddell insisted on having a look. The most easterly of the Caroline Islands, Strong's was another favored stopover for whaleships in this equatorial realm. By 3:00 that afternoon, the *Shenandoah* was approaching the island's northern end. But, after coming within five miles of Strong's, and sailing around to its principal anchorage and spotting no sails, Waddell resumed their course toward Ascension.

The following morning, clear skies, strong northeastern breezes, and calm seas greeted the Confederates. At 9:30 they came within fifteen miles of McAskill—today's Pingelap—Island, another speck of land in the Carolines often used by whaling vessels for stopovers. But, preoccupied with Ascension and the American ships reputed to be there, Waddell made no effort to inspect McAskill. Instead, the Confederates spent the entire day sailing toward Ascension. By 9:00 that evening, Waddell was convinced that the raider lay within fifteen miles of that destination—perhaps even within viewing distance of the island, though it was too dark to say. The order was given to haul on the halyards of the Cunningham's Patent Self-Reefing canvas and furl the topsails for the evening. The Confederates would lie to for the night, and by morning's light they would take their first steps on dry land since leaving Melbourne six weeks earlier.[4]

TWELVE

Ascension Island

A t daybreak, April 1, 1865, the Confederates began steaming toward Ascension Island. A stubborn morning rain, however, prevented them from seeing land. But when the sky cleared they found themselves gazing upon the jungle-covered ridges that rose above the mangrove-limned beaches and coral reefs that fringed the island. As they approached one of the island's principal anchorages, Lohd or Lea Harbor—today's Pohnahtik, Lohd Pah Harbor—on the island's southeastern shore, they could see four sailing craft: two ship-rigged whaling vessels, and two whaling barks. And though the Confederates assumed these were British vessels, certainly they were worth a closer look.

As they steamed closer to Ascension, the Confederates spotted a whaleboat rowing toward them. Two miles from the island, they stopped to allow it to come alongside. Moments later, a scruffy-looking Englishman was scrambling up the raider's companion ladder. Once on deck, he introduced himself as Thomas Harrocke, a resident of Ascension who often served as a harbor pilot and a general intermediary with the island's natives. Mistakenly believing the raider to be a British vessel on a mapmaking expedition, a common enterprise in the Pacific during that era, he had come to offer his services. "We had the English flag up and he supposed us to be the English surveying ship," Whittle recalled.

Harrocke soon disappeared into the captain's stateroom to confer with Waddell and Whittle. There the officers told Harrocke that their ship was not British. Presumably the Confederates were out of uniform, or, if they were wearing them, their nationality didn't register with this man who was so removed in time and place that he had only the vaguest grasp of the vagaries of Western politics and wars. In any case, the *Shenandoah*'s officers told Harrocke that he had just boarded a U.S. Navy man-of-war. They then hired him to pilot them into the harbor for $30, but under threat of being shot to death if the ship foundered on the barrier reef that encircled the island. "The harbor was most too confining for a vessel of the Shenandoah's length, and there were a few known dangers below the surface of the water," Waddell remembered.

A shaken Harrocke soon appeared on the raider's poop deck, nervously calling out instructions to the helmsman as he guided the steamer into the harbor. Though, according to Chew "frightened out of his wits," Harrocke was also starved for conversation in his native language. So, beneath the clanking of the ship's steam engine, he soon fell into conversation with the officers gathered around him. Looking up at the scene from a lower deck, master's mate Cornelius Hunt was struck by the contrast between the disheveled creature giving directions and the Confederate naval officers clustered about him. "I could scarcely conceive a more degraded looking object," he later recalled. "He had adopted perforce, no doubt, the habits of the Islanders; his body was tattooed with all manner of fantastic designs, and he spoke his mother tongue with hesitation and difficulty."

The officers gathered around Harrocke learned that he was originally from Yorkshire. A former convict, he had been shipped to one of Britain's penal colonies in this part of the world. Afterward, having gone back to sea, he was shipwrecked on Ascension. Harrocke had been on the island for ten years, during which time he had married a native woman who bore him two children.

Harrocke typified the sort of Occidental mariners of that era who found their way to these climes. Ascension islanders belonged to what today is known as Micronesia. But ever since the 1830s, when merchant and whaling vessels began making occasional stops there, small groups of white men could be found at any given time living on this island—better known by its indigenous names, Ponape or Pohnpei, and as part of the Federated States of Micronesia. Most of these interlopers were fugitives from Britain's Australian penal colonies, seamen who had deserted their ships, or shipwreck survivors. Once on the island, they cast their lot with the natives, marrying and supporting themselves as beachcombers, gathering the tortoise shells that, by the 1830s, were attracting trading schooners. In many cases, like Harrocke's, these whites acted as middlemen in negotiations with the island's native chiefs and visiting European and American mariners.

After securing the *Shenandoah*'s anchorage, Captain Waddell, despite a lashing rain falling across the harbor, was determined to ascertain the nationality of the four vessels they had spotted. Shouting above the downpour, he ordered four boats lowered into the water. Each carried two officers and sailors armed with sidearms and revolvers. As the boats edged away from the raider, one of the *Shenandoah*'s gunners fired a blank cartridge, the steamer's Union Jack was lowered, and the Confederate flag was hoisted in its place. Observing these events with growing puzzlement, Harrocke turned to the deck officer and asked why the cartridge had been fired, where the four boats were going, and what was the identity of the flag that now flew over the steamer.

Informed that the banner belonged to the Confederate States of America and that Lohd Harbor's newest arrivals planned to burn the four vessels, be they American, anchored there, Harrocke, by Hunt's recollection, expressed dismay. "Well, you and the Yankees must settle that business to suit yourselves," he said. "If I had known what you were up to, maybe I should not have piloted you in, for I don't like to see a bonfire made of a good ship."

An hour after the boarding parties had left the *Shenandoah*, the leaders of the four details—Lieutenants Chew, Lee, Grimball, and Scales—sent word back to Waddell that, despite initial impressions, none of the whaling vessels was British. All four, they reported, were American. When the boarding parties reached them, however, one of the vessels may have been flying the flag of the Kingdom of Hawaii; accounts vary. In any case, the Confederates declared the vessels American and captured all of them. The boarding officers soon returned to the *Shenandoah* with documents and the captain's mates from the four vessels. But the Confederates had found no captains. All four, Waddell soon learned, had gone ashore for the day to visit a Protestant mission in the village of Rohnkiti, on the island's southwestern shore.

Christian missionaries, many of them New England Congregationalists, had been hunting converts in these Pacific Islands

since the early nineteenth century. By 1852, having firmly established themselves in Hawaii, and alarmed by reports of moral
depravity among both natives and non-natives elsewhere in the
Pacific, they began looking south, toward other islands, for converts. By the mid-1850s, they had begun their first mission on
Ascension.

Waddell could meet the four whaling masters later. In the
meantime, he made a preliminary inspection of the captured
vessels' documents and interviewed the mates brought to the
Shenandoah. After provisionally concluding that the ships were
American-owned, he ordered all of the mates placed in irons.

The 130 seamen aboard the four vessels—the majority of whom
were Kanakas, natives of Hawaii—would be accorded different
treatment. By the 1840s, as Yankee seamen on American whaling vessels declined in numbers, Pacific-bound New England
whaling masters, after leaving Massachusetts, stopped in the
Azores to pick up Portuguese crewmen. Depending upon
the route a ship took, other seamen might be picked up on the
coast of West Africa or on South America's west coast, where
Peruvian and Chilean hands could often be shipped. If once in
the Pacific still other hands were required, the vessels' crews
would be rounded out with natives of various Polynesian cultures: Samoa, the Marquesas, Tahiti, New Zealand, and Hawaii.
Of those, Hawaiians were considered by far the best seamen of
the Pacific, and by the 1850s more than six hundred Kanakas—
acquired through bonds posted with the Kingdom of Hawaii's
royal monopoly on their marine services—were serving aboard
the world's whaling vessels.

The predominantly Kanakas crews of the four whaling vessels captured at Ascension were officially declared prisoners. But

because of their Hawaiian origins and their presumed indifference in Union-versus-Confederate matters, Waddell adjudged
these unarmed men no threat to the raider. No doubt their cu-
mulative numbers also influenced his decision. He ordered
them placed ashore and allowed to remain free.[1]

That same day, Waddell sent word back to the boarding parties
to begin transporting spoils from the four vessels. At 5:00 that
afternoon, even as this work commenced, the Confederates
aboard the *Shenandoah* spotted a small rowboat entering the
harbor. As it approached the shore, its passengers spotted the
Confederate flag flying over the *Shenandoah*. "For a moment,"
Cornelius Hunt recalled, "they rested on their oars as though
undetermined what to do, and then put about and pulled
toward the shore; but escape was not so easy." Before the
boat's occupants, the four missing captains, had time to make
their next move, Waddell dispatched a boat toward them carrying armed men. Not long afterward, as the captains boarded the
Shenandoah their grim countenances grew more leaden as they
walked past the piles of goods and stores on the raider's deck
that had already been taken, and were still arriving, from their
vessels.

Two of the whaleships in the harbor were ship-rigged vessels,
the *Edward Cary* of San Francisco and the *Hector* of New Bedford. The other two were barks, the *Pearl* of New London,
Connecticut, and the *Harvest* of Honolulu, Hawaii. On boarding the *Shenandoah*, the captains of the four vessels met with
Waddell. None of the four, Waddell recalled, offered "good reason why their vessels should not be confiscated and themselves
held as prisoners." The *Harvest*'s captain, however, insisted that
his vessel was not a U.S. ship. Though the vessel had once flown

Old Glory, John Eldridge, her master, assured Waddell that she had been sold to a new owner in Hawaii and should thus be spared. But, after the master allegedly failed to produce a bill of sale satisfactory to the Confederates, Waddell ordered the bark torched along with the other three vessels.

Epidemics of smallpox and influenza during the 1850s had reduced Ascension's population from ten thousand to fewer than five thousand. And the remaining islanders were scattered across 130 square miles of mountains, lagoons, forests, and shoreline. Even so, Ascension's population vastly outnumbered the *Shenandoah*'s crew. Moreover, Waddell and the other crew members were also aware—through first-person accounts of the island by such authors as James F. O'Connell and by seamen's lore—of what seemed to be the islanders' fearsome warrior traditions. These, after all, were a people for whom toughness ranked as a singular indicator of one's morality. The tattoos that covered Harrocke, and which the *Shenandoah*'s men found both appalling and fascinating, bore vivid witness to the value these people—both men and women—placed on the ability to endure pain.

As a later historian of the island put it, "The courage to withstand the month-long ordeal of having elaborate patterns etched into the skin with an ink-dipped rake made of thorns or sharpened animal bones attested to the worth of an individual. No man or woman was considered eligible for marriage without the proper marking of the body. Men had their arms and legs tattooed; women, in addition to these areas, had their buttocks, thighs, and genital regions marked." In addition, males on the island submitted to a rite of passage that required the castration of the left testicle.

Each of Ascension's five tribes was ruled by a single chief—or "king," as the Confederates called the sovereign. Pondering the *Shenandoah*'s vulnerabilities as the raider lay anchored in Lohd Harbor, Waddell concluded that it would be prudent to invite the chief who ruled the chiefdom encompassing Lohd Harbor to visit the *Shenandoah*. To deliver the invitation, on the Confederates' second day at Ascension Waddell dispatched a detail of six armed men led by Cornelius Hunt, with the Englishman Harrocke acting as their interpreter.

Hunt's party set off in the captain's personal gig for a nearby beach where the king often held forth inside a tiny bamboo hut. But as the men rowed ashore through the surf they confronted, by Hunt's recollection, what surely ranks among the more unlikely scenes of hostile military action in the annals of the Civil War:

> A crowd of natives rushed down to meet us, armed with stones, which they hurl almost with the precision of a rifle-ball, and swords manufactured from sharks' teeth, the edges of which are dipped in a subtle poison that leaves certain death in any wounds they inflict. The appearance of this heathenish multitude was anything but conciliatory.

Harrocke stepped in and, defusing the situation, explained to the islanders the detail's purpose. Even so, the king was not to be found. He was, the natives explained, at a festival taking place inland, at a tribal gathering place. Two or three of the natives agreed to take Hunt to the festival. So, as Hunt recalled, "leaving my men in the boat and accompanied by the interpreter, I set forth for the first time in my life to pay a visit to royalty."

After a steep hike into the island's upland interior, the party arrived at the festival venue. "It was a rude, extensive building, built of bamboo, with a high peaked roof and eaves which extended nearly to the ground," Hunt recalled. Inside, about three hundred people were gathered. At the center of the gathering sat the king himself—"naked with the exception of a tappa made of grass, worn about his waist, and smeared from head to foot with cocoanut oil." Like most of his followers, Hunt noted, the king's earlobe had been pierced with a gaping hole that was used to carry a "huge misshapen tobacco pipe."

As Harrocke translated, Hunt relayed the captain's invitation. The king in due time accepted the entreaty. After giving himself "a fresh coating of cocoanut oil," the sovereign— eventually joined by everyone else at the festival—set off with Hunt and Harrocke back to the shore, where the Confederates awaited the shore party's return. There Hunt, Harrocke, the king, and four of his aides joined the original detail of Confederates in the gig and shoved off for the *Shenandoah*. Behind them followed a flotilla of canoes, from fifty to a hundred according to various accounts, each carrying up to five of the king's subjects.

When the royal retinue reached the raider, it found Waddell and his officers suitably decked out in their gray dress uniforms with the gold-striped trims. Waddell, pressing his advantage, had already decided to treat this occasion as a state visit and accord the monarch all courtesies due any head of state. Thus, after climbing up the steamer's companion ladder, the chief— "the Nahnwarki," by title—and the attendants who accompanied him were, after stepping onto the gangway, officially received by Captain Waddell and First Lieutenant Whittle. "I wish I had a photograph of him," Lining wrote that day. "He is almost 5 ft. 8 in., dark complexion, not at all an intelligent countenance, hair black & of moderate length, with a circlet of beads around his head, & a collar around his neck. The lobes of both ears were bored & stretched to such an extent as to easily admit one's finger, & and in one of them he had a clay pipe introduced & kept in place by a half turn. A broad belt was around his waist, which with the clout finished his costume." The king's attendants, Lining recalled, were dressed in much the same manner, and all of them were so "sloshed down well" with coconut oil that "whenever they leaned up against any place they left a mark." As Francis Chew noted, "How their bodies glistened in the rays of the sun!"

As the scores of islanders who had followed the king gathered around the *Shenandoah* in their canoes, the king and his party repaired to the captain's cabin with Whittle and Harrocke. There, pipes were lit and Waddell offered his guest a drink—a glass of Schiedan schnapps, by his account. And, as Harrocke interpreted, Waddell began explaining the purpose of the *Shenandoah*'s visit; as usual, he presented the Confederate cause as a matter of a heroic, besieged people resisting predatory invaders. "It was explained to him," Waddell recalled, "that the vessels in port belonged to our enemies who had been fighting us for years, killing our people, outraging our country-women, and desolating our homes, and that we were ordered to capture and destroy their vessels whenever and wherever found, and that if the laws of his Majesty would not be violated, the vessels in port would be confiscated."

Based on their first impressions of these captured vessels' contents, Waddell added, there seemed to be little aboard them that would be of use to the *Shenandoah*. He then proposed a deal: if the king would guarantee the *Shenandoah*'s safety while in the harbor and post guards onshore to protect her, the Confederates would allow his people, once Waddell's men were done with the whaling vessels, to scavenge all four ships for any-thing they wished to take. In addition—to arm the guards and as a gesture of friendship—Waddell would deliver to the king twenty-two muskets and some ammunition already taken from the *Harvest*. The muskets, however, constituted a dubious gift. The *Harvest*'s master had intended to use them for trading with Pacific islanders. But, as Waddell later admitted, the weapons were old, in poor condition, and appeared "very dangerous." And if he ever found himself facing one of the rickety firearms given to the king, "I would have preferred the muzzle to the chamber as far as danger is concerned."

Unaware of the muskets' condition, the king readily agreed to Waddell's offer. But the sovereign also asked that the four vessels be torched inside the harbor so that his people might be allowed to strip the metal off their hulls' bottoms. "This was of course readily acceded to by us as it obviated the necessity of our taking them out to apply the torch," Whittle recalled. Still later, the king would select the specific spots in the harbor where the vessels would be destroyed.

"The pipe and schnapps having fulfilled their office," as Waddell later put it, an easy conviviality now enveloped the cap-tain and the king. To seal the day's bargain, Waddell presented the king with a ceremonial sword taken from the *Lizzie M. Stacey*.

After the talks, the king accepted an invitation to tour the raider. By the day's end, Whittle recalled, the *Shenandoah*'s of-ficers and their guest had become "best friends" and the king left the ship "declaring that we all had his hearty welcome." Afterward, the king's hosts rowed him back to shore in the captain's gig—his subjects, once again, trailing behind in their flotilla of canoes. Later that day, Waddell sent off to the king the promised muskets and ammunition, as well as two boxes of tobacco. Returning the Confederates' ostensible goodwill, the king, during the *Shenandoah*'s stay on the island, "sent on board fruit and fish several times and visited us daily."

When Waddell, reciprocating protocol, visited the sovereign's coastal home, he presented the Nahnwarki with a silk scarf. The king, in turn, presented Waddell with a "belt for the shoulders," a sash woven by a local craftsman of native coconut fibers and wool from a visiting whaleship. Waddell treasured the sash. "The belt is peculiar, exhibiting skills in the art of weaving and taste in blending colors," he recounted. His affection for it, however, was not entirely aesthetic. Following four years of fruitless Confederate efforts to win diplomatic recognition from the world's governments, Waddell wrote years later, the garment is "preserved as a memento of the only sovereign who was fearless enough to extend hospitality to a struggling people and to sympathize with a just cause."[2]

On April 3—the raider's third day on Ascension—as Waddell granted shore leave to many of his men, others continued ransacking the four prizes. Because at least three of the vessels were returning from successful whaling expeditions, their decks and holds teemed with the harvests of their hunts. Between the *Edward Cary* and the *Hector* alone, the Confederates found five hundred barrels of whale oil. They also found various harpoons, whale lines, and other equipment. But because the Confederates were not in the whaling business the boarding parties found relatively few stores and items that seemed to be of value to the *Shenandoah*.

Afterward, the island's natives were, as promised, invited to come aboard the four condemned craft and take anything that they wanted. "All day long they swarmed over the vessels, like driver ants upon a dead carcase," master's mate Cornelius Hunt noted. "Canoes were constantly passing to and fro, laden with ship's bread, tobacco, bits of iron, harpoons . . . and all sorts of odds and ends, until they were fairly surfeited with plundering." Captain Waddell likewise marveled at the islanders' industriousness. "Every movable plank, spar and bulkhead was soon taken on shore for flooring purposes," he recalled. "The sails were removed from the yards and the sailrooms for tents and to be converted into suitable sails for their canoes." Waddell was later told that the copper from the vessels' bottoms would be pounded into breastplates for the island's warriors and used for trade with neighboring tribes.

Initially, the Confederates found themselves disappointed with their own haul from the four ships. Even so, when they returned to the *Shenandoah* and began inventorying their plunder, they realized that they had hardly come up empty-handed. From the four ships the Confederates gathered eight chronometers, two sextants, and five or six quadrants. They also seized valuable items intended as trade goods, including scores of muskets and ammunitions and two dozen U.S. infantry coats and pants. The latter, Waddell concluded, seemed ideal for the expanded version of the ship's marine guard that he and Whittle hoped to enlist.

And beyond the plunder officially taken from the four ships were the items, mostly small souvenirs, claimed by individual officers as their own personal property in defiance of standard rules and procedures. Lieutenant Chew, for instance, left the *Pearl* with several seashells, a whale's tooth, and a spear. Giving new meaning to the term literary prize, he also took a copy of Adolphe Thiers's *History of the French Revolution*.

———

But of all the items confiscated that day, what Waddell most cherished was a group of charts depicting the whaling grounds to their north. James Bulloch, in outfitting the *Shenandoah*, had supplied the captain with a wide array of specialized ocean maps. Even so, the raider had sailed without the sort of charts that Waddell knew would be essential to the cruise's ultimate purpose of Arctic raiding. Typically, such charts—actually, freshly annotated copies of older charts—were by necessity compiled at sea aboard whaling vessels and, Waddell noted, "show every track they make where they have been most successful in taking whales." The ephemeral nature of the charts dictated that they be acquired close in time and space to the whaling grounds to which Waddell had been dispatched.

Armed with precisely such charts, once daunting nautical vistas suddenly seemed to Waddell wide open. "With such charts in my possession," he recalled, "I not only held a key to the navigation of all the Pacific Islands, the Okhotsk and Bering Seas, and the Arctic Ocean, but the most probable localities for finding the great Arctic whaling fleet of New England."

Once the *Shenandoah* had anchored at Ascension, her officers knew that, in the job of stripping their four new prizes of plunder and transferring the spoils to the steamer, they faced formidable work. But that was hardly the only task facing the crew. They also needed to clear space for the foodstuffs that were about to come aboard: goods from the prizes, gifts from the king, and provisions purchased on the island. To do that, the coal now piled in the ship's forehold would have to be transferred to the main hold and the coal bunkers. And before the ship sailed again, Waddell also remained determined to have some repainting done and the running rigging overhauled.

Even so, both Waddell and Whittle knew that the crew needed a respite from the demands of life at sea, and that Ascension presented a good, and safe, opportunity for such a break. As Whittle put it, "We have much work to do—but we could not have a better time or place." On Ascension, unlike in Melbourne, no U.S. consuls or British officials skulked around the steamer. And Captain Waddell enjoyed the goodwill of the local chief, whose armed guards stood sentry day and night over the raider.

The officers of the Confederates' four prizes languished in irons aboard the *Shenandoah*. And the 130 seamen from those vessels—confirming Waddell's judgment that they represented no threat to the raider—had quietly melted into Ascension's population of fellow Pacific islanders. "They went off amongst the natives," Mason observed, "by whom they were kindly treated & when on shore I saw several of them in the huts, sitting quietly with the women & mending their clothes, apparently tolerably well satisfied."

In short, for Waddell and the *Shenandoah*'s other officers, this island seemed free of any group that would wish to, or could, do them harm. Or, as Whittle wrote in parsing Ascension's geopolitics, "This is an island under none but local authority, and protection with no civilization and everything is under our guns."

Equally reassuring to the officers, the island also lacked bars in which crew members might tarry and be drawn into fisticuffs with locals. For that matter, it even lacked liquor; the island's closest cousin was sakau, Ascension's libation of choice—a mildly narcotic drink fashioned with extracts from a pepper shrub root containing naturally occurring depressants. And because of the island's remote location, Waddell also had little reason to worry about possible crew desertions.

For those reasons, and because he felt the need to bolster his flagging popularity, Waddell could afford to be more generous in allotting shore liberties here than he had been in Australia. Indeed, on April 9, Lining recalled, the captain was particularly generous: "All our men were allowed to go on shore on liberty."

Escaping the ship's confinement and the ceaseless rolling and pitching of life at sea constituted a welcome relief. Unbound from the dismal regularity of watches, Lieutenant Whittle's irons and tricings, and other shipboard tedium, the sailors savored the sweetness of idle time and the freedom to roam at will—even if some of their recreations proved, as an entry in Lining's diary attests, woefully familiar: "Having nothing to do again today, Grimball, Bulloch & I took a whale boat & went sailing." Most of the men, however, reveled in cavorting in Ascension's abundant forests, creeks, and inlets. After months of saltwater baths at sea, Francis Chew, for instance, enjoyed "the grand luxury" of a bracing dip in a secluded, shade-tree–sheltered swimming hole in a creek in the island's interior. "We were in the water about two hours, and such a swim I have not had since leaving Missouri," he exclaimed.

If the sailors sought a permanent reminder of their time on Ascension, they could barter for a sample of the island's defining art—a tattoo, or "pricking," as it was also called. "Many officers went on shore," Whittle noted, "and all had some thing pricked in their arms." Surgeon Lining and Lieutenant Chew both numbered among the raider's officers who eagerly acquired the island's ne plus ultra souvenir. Describing the process of having a bracelet "pricked" onto his wrist by an elderly island woman, Chew recalled that she inscribed the image using a makeshift wooden apparatus that consisted of "four or five wooden needles secured at the end of a stick," which she dipped into a black dye derived from some sort of nut. The process, he recalled, was not for the faint of heart. "The operation is very paining, and while smarting under it I somewhat regretted having commenced."

Crew members also inevitably found their way to Nan Madol, a complex of medieval ruins, four miles up the coast from where the *Shenandoah* lay anchored. The island's Saudeleur Dynasty built the structures during the eleventh or twelfth century. For the Confederates, Nan Madol, even then a celebrated site, presented a staggering archaeological spectacle—a sprawling collection of mysterious stone-walled enclosures behind which sat still more enclosures and the remains of even more perplexing temples and other buildings. Often called "the Venice of the Pacific," Nan Madol spread over ninety-two artificial islands, surrounded by lagoons and laced with a labyrinth of man-made canals, and occupied a one-fifth-square-mile area. Nan Madol, in turn, belonged to a much larger surrounding area of ruins stretching over eleven square miles.

Although Lieutenant Chew found the ruins "indeed wonderful," he was at a loss "to say what they were or by whom built; the natives know nothing of them." But he was willing to hazard a guess about who *hadn't* constructed them. Because the horizontally stacked columns of basalt that composed most of the ruins lacked "mortar of some sort," he knew that "no civilized man" could have built them. Even so, he found them impressive, noting, "It must have been done years ago when the island was more populous before the people became degenerated."[3]

After months at sea, the crew no doubt gave the island's women their avid attention, if not a conspicuous place in their diaries.

The Confederates who authored the *Shenandoah*'s extant diaries, memoirs, and letters hailed from a conservative Christian culture. Given those origins, and the fact that many of them were married or had sweethearts waiting for them, one would assume that, even if they had slept with the native women, they would have been unlikely to record accounts of doing so. Even so, in at least one passage, a Confederate officer's description of the women of Ascension, however racist, bespeaks a familiarity, an affection, even a tenderness, that belies the usual Puritanical sensibility these men usually brought to sexual matters. "Generally speaking," Lieutenant Francis Chew wrote in his diary, "they are ugly but they have the most beautiful, jet black hair and the most symmetrical limbs, small delicate feet & hands. Almost all I saw . . . would have been a fine model for a painter & sculptor."

Fleeting couplings between those women and visiting sailors had long played a role in the island's transactions with the outside world, particularly with visiting whaling vessels. The logs and diaries of other European and North American vessels that visited Ascension teem with accounts of the island's native men exchanging the sexual favors of their wives, mothers, sisters, and daughters for a few plugs of tobacco. Discovering, upon the *Shenandoah*'s arrival at Ascension, several native women apparently in the paid company of sailors aboard the whaleships already at anchor, Midshipman John T. Mason reacted with such outrage, and apparent embarrassment, that he could not bring himself to express his distaste in his native language. Instead, in his diary he recorded his jeremiad in his schoolboy French, which translated, comments:

In terms of virtue, there is none. It is a great honor to be the mistress of a white man. The young girls since the age of eight are all equally mischievous. One must say that it is this way for the entire island, it is their religion. Upon arriving on the whale-boat, I found thirty or so women who were entertaining themselves on the decks of the whalers. These were the mistresses of crew-members, each sailor had his <u>woman</u>. The captains and the officers of these ships always chose the daughters of the king or chiefs.

This sexual trafficking, however, also constituted an illicit trade by which the island's less exhalted men bypassed the usual monopoly on trade exercised by the island's five chiefs. Sometimes items such as cloth, mirrors, hairbrushes, and trinkets were exchanged. But usually tobacco constituted the medium of exchange, if only because it was a commodity that could be discreetly passed along from the sailors to the women to their men. Beyond that, tobacco represented a commodity that the men could accumulate without drawing attention from the chieftains.

While the memoirists from the *Shenandoah* make no mention of their own purchases of sexual favors from the island's women, their accounts do contain ample references to those women. They also noted, as Midshipman Mason attested, that "one has no need of money here for [with] a little tobacco or a coloured handkerchief such as the old negroes wear on their heads at home one can get any thing he wants." Eager to curry favor with the men, and aware that the things they wanted ashore could not be bought with money, Waddell sent each man off with a quantity of tobacco. As Hunt recalled, before taking shore leave each sailor "was furnished with a small quantity of tobacco, the standing medium at Ascension, and I dare say they enjoyed themselves."

A contemporary reproduction of unknown origin of the *Shenandoah* in ice, apparently derived from an oil painting. (Courtesy of the Naval Historical Center)

Based on an 1874 watercolor by Benjamin Russell, this lithograph depicts the raider off Siberia's coast with prizes. Vessels are (left to right): *Susan Abigail*, *Euphrates* (burning in distance), *Shenandoah* (with smokestack), *Jireh Swift* and *William Thompson* (both burning in distance), *Sophia Thornton*, and *Milo*. Note the prisoners crowded onto the deck of the *Milo*, spared to transport them to San Francisco. (FDR Library)

A rare photograph of the *Shenandoah*, taken while in dry dock for repairs in Melbourne, Australia (U.S. Navy Historical Center)

Lieutenant Commander James Iredell Waddell, captain of the *Shenandoah* (*left*), and First Lieutenant William Conway Whittle, Jr., her executive officer (*below*). Graduates of the U.S. Navy Academy at Annapolis, Maryland, the *Shenandoah*'s two most senior officers had a contentious relationship. (U.S. Navy Historical Center and South Carolina Confederate Relic Room and Museum)

A cartoon satirizing Confederate President Jefferson Davis's capture by Union troops on May 10, 1865, while on the lam in Georgia and disguised as a woman. Captain Waddell, still in the Pacific, had yet to commence the most destructive phase of his commerce-raiding. (New York Public Library)

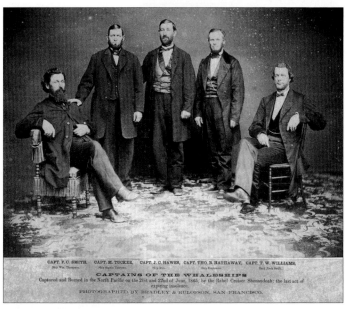

Captains of whaleships destroyed in the Arctic by the *Shenandoah* (New Bedford Whaling Museum)

Jefferson Davis, president of the Confederacy (*left*), and Robert E. Lee, general of the Army of Northern Virginia (*below*). On April 9, General Lee surrendered his army at Appomattox Courthouse, Virginia—for all practical purposes ending the Civil War. Davis, however, urged continued resistance, and while imprisoned took solace in the *Shenandoah*'s ongoing cruise. (Library of Congress)

Confederate Navy Secretary Stephen Mallory. A former U.S. senator from Florida and—as opposed to his Union counterpart, Gideon Wells—well versed in naval affairs, Mallory encouraged the use of commerce raiders against the enemy's civilian ships. (From *History of the Confederate Navy*, J. Thomas Scharf)

Commander Matthew Fontaine Maury, CSN. Known as "the pathfinder of the seas," Maury advocated for the *Shenandoah*'s cruise, providing essential books and charts. (From *History of the Confederate Navy*, J. Thomas Scharf)

Commander James Dunwoody Bulloch, CSN, was the Confederacy's key European operative. Thirty-eight years old when he arrived in Liverpool, he remained there for the rest of his life. (From *History of the Confederate Navy*, J. Thomas Scharf)

A rare Civil War–era photo of the River Mersey and the port city of Liverpool, the Confederacy's British base for blockade-running and commerce-raiding operations (National Museums Liverpool, Merseyside Maritime Museum)

Charles Francis Adams, U.S. Minister to Great Britain, son of former president John Quincy Adams, and father of future author Henry Adams. Minister Adams spent much of the war urging, usually unsuccessfully, Prime Minister Lord Palmerston's government to enforce Britain's neutrality obligations. (Adams National Historical Park)

Thomas H. Dudley, U.S. Consul in Liverpool. Confederate Navy Commander James Bulloch's nemesis in Liverpool, the consul's zealotry for the Union cause was matched only by his cunning in attempting to thwart Confederate activities in Britain. (American Philosophical Society)

Midshipman John Thomson Mason of the *Shenandoah*. As his diary kept aboard the raider attests, his romantic notions of life at sea did not survive the cruise. (South Carolina Confederate Relic Room and Museum)

Missouri native Lieutenant Francis Chew of the *Shenandoah* was twenty-three years old when the raider commenced her voyage. (Museum of the Confederacy)

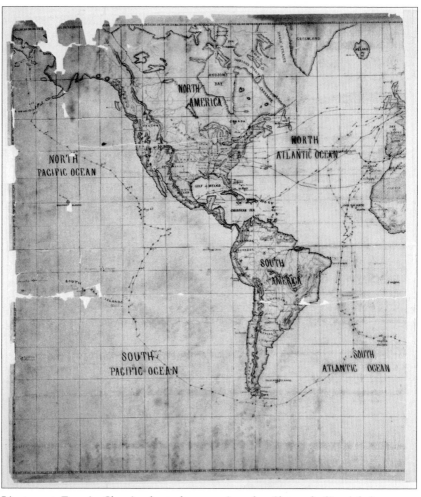

Lieutenant Francis Chew's chart documenting the *Shenandoah*'s global voyage.
(Southern Historical Collection, University of North Carolina at Chapel Hill)

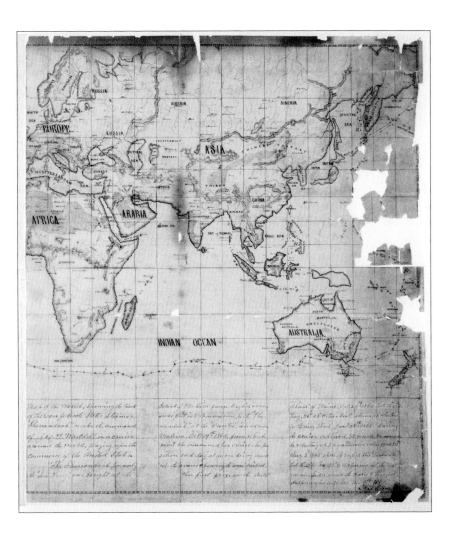

Taken at Leamington Spa, England, in autumn 1865, this image depicts assistant surgeon Edwin G. Booth, captured at Mobile Bay (seated), and, standing (left to right), former acting master Irvine S. Bulloch of the CSS *Shenandoah*; assistant surgeon Bennett G. Green, affiliation unknown; First Lieutenant William H. Murdaugh of the CSS *Hampton*; and Surgeon—and diarist—Charles Lining of the *Shenandoah*. (U.S. Navy Historical Center)

Master's Mate Cornelius Hunt of the *Shenandoah*, who in 1867 published one of the first accounts of the commerce raider's cruise. (U.S. Navy Historical Center)

On January 26, 1865, a day after the *Shenandoah* arrived in Melbourne, Australia—ostensibly only for repairs, supplies, and coaling—Captain Waddell threw the steamer open to visitors. (State Library of Victoria, Melbourne)

The "Buccaneer's Ball," depicted here, was staged to honor the *Shenandoah*'s officers and took place on February 1, 1865, at Craig's Royal Hotel in the gold-mining town of Ballarat, forty miles north of Melbourne. (State Library of Victoria, Melbourne)

In this cartoon from *Melbourne Punch*, Victoria's trade and customs commissioner, James G. Francis (center), lectures Captain Waddell (right) as he apprehends an Australian man (left) known as Charlie the Cook, who had been recruited by the Confederates to ship aboard the *Shenandoah* in defiance of British laws banning enlistments of British subjects. By February 18, 1865, when the raider ended her three-week visit to Melbourne, simmering legal tensions created by her visit had come to a boil, threatening to create an international diplomatic imbroglio. (*Melbourne Punch*)

A 1985 stamp issued by the Federated State of Micronesia commemorated the Confederates' visit in April 1865 to what they called Ascension Island—better known as Pohnpei and Ponape. (Collection of Rev. Tom Smith, S.J.)

This engraving from the *Illustrated London News* depicts the *Shenandoah*'s return to England on November 6, 1865. (Manuscript, Archives and Rare Book Library, Emory University)

A December 9, 1865, *Harper's Weekly* cartoon depicts Captain Waddell as Rip Van Winkle. Published a month after the *Shenandoah*'s return to England, the cartoon lampoons Waddell's professed ignorance of the Civil War's end. (Manuscript, Archives and Rare Book Library, Emory University)

A poster advertises a March 1866 auction of the *Shenandoah* by Thomas Dudley, the U.S. consul in Liverpool. Upon anchoring the steamer in Liverpool's harbor, Waddell immediately surrendered her to British officials. Days later, after releasing her crew, British officials turned over the ship to U.S. officials. (Library of Virginia)

On the evening of April 3, Lieutenant Sidney Smith Lee, Jr., acting on Captain Waddell's orders, set fire to the *Pearl*. The following day, Waddell ordered John Grimball to burn the *Edward Cary*, and Francis Chew to destroy the *Hector*. Because the fourth whaleship, the *Harvest*, contained provisions that awaited transfer to the *Shenandoah*, the Confederates postponed her destruction.

The next day, details led by Grimball and Chew lifted the anchors of the *Edward Cary* and the *Hector* and allowed them to drift onto a shoal a safe distance from shore. During the next three days the eventual conflagrations, intensified by five hundred barrels of whale oil, created sublime spectacles. "What a destruction of property, obtained by so much toil and hardships!" Lieutenant Chew lamented. Indeed, that young officer's firing of the *Hector* nearly cost him his life. The close call occurred as Chew was stoking flames below the main deck in the ship's cabins and saloons, all of which were paneled with boards of flammable white pine: "I remained longer than was prudent, had I been much longer in finding the exit I believe I would have fallen from suffocation."

Finally—on the morning of April 10—the last remaining whaleship, the *Harvest*, was hauled alongside the *Shenandoah*. During the next few hours, quantities of grain, salt, beef, pork, molasses, and other provisions were transferred from the *Harvest* to the Confederate steamer. The transfer also included harpoon lines and four or five new sails. All in all, Chew estimated, after assessing the total haul gathered at Ascension, "we now have rations of every thing allowed for about eleven months; of bread, however, we have enough for over two years." That evening, their plunder complete, the Confederates, delivering the coup de grâce of their incendiary cycle at Ascension, set the *Harvest* afire.

In the hours before the *Shenandoah* sailed from Ascension, on April 13, the officers from the four whaling vessels were paroled and released. All the prizes' sailors, who had been free but officially remained prisoners, were also formally paroled. Before leaving, the *Shenandoah*'s officers, for the final time, made their usual appeal for men to ship aboard the raider. Since their arrival, they had managed to recruit ten sailors from the four captured whalers. Among the recruits were two American sailors from the *Harvest*—James Welch and Joseph Stevenson, a free black man. In the end, however, the Confederates, that day, recruited only one more man on Ascension, bringing their total from the island to eleven. "The prisoners," Hunt recalled, "seemed to prefer being left on shore to accompanying us on our long and uncertain voyage."

Before sailing from Ascension, the Confederates presented their former prisoners with an array of the *Shenandoah*'s stores, weapons, and ammunition, and two whaleboats—all confiscated from the whaling seamen's former vessels. Doubtless the *Shenandoah*'s officers suffered guilty consciences and anxieties over the legal consequences of, once again, paroling prisoners so far from home. But the presence of the Congregationalist mission on the island assuaged some of those concerns. Making the erroneous assumption that Ohioan Albert Sturges, the mission's chief, was a New Englander, the Confederates reveled in the mistaken irony that the sailors were being left with a clergyman from the very region whose reforming zeal and abolitionism had rendered its whaling fleet such an appealing target for the *Shenandoah*. As Hunt sarcastically asserted, the pastor "hailed from the goodly Commonwealth of Massachusetts, so it was fair to presume that the morals of our discomfited foes would be well cared for during their stay in his diocese."

After getting up steam at first light on April 13, the *Shenan-*

doah, at 7:30 a.m., weighed anchor and—with Thomas Harrocke, once again, piloting—eased out of Lohd Harbor and back into the Pacific. Before letting their steam go down and putting the raider back under canvas on a northwesterly course, the Confederates discharged Harrocke. This time, however, instead of being scared out of his wits, the tattooed Englishman returned to the island with a gift from the Confederates—in what Lining recalled as "a nice whale boat and his pay."

Months later, the *Kamehameha V* sailed from Hawaii, specifically to pick up the approximately 130 Kanakas, other Pacific islanders, and New Englanders left behind by the *Shenandoah*. Several mariners from the four ships burned by the raider, however, elected to remain on the island. Among them was John Eldridge, master of the *Harvest*, who soon began working as a boat pilot around Ascension, started a family there, and whose descendants still live on the island.[4]

Thirteen

Pacific Spring

U pon leaving Ascension on April 13, 1865, the Confederates steamed out of Lohd Harbor up to the island's northern shore. There, picking up northeast
trade winds, lifting the steamer's propeller, and ordering all sails
set, Captain Waddell pointed the *Shenandoah*'s prow toward
a northwesterly course. The next day proved delightful. With
steady winds and the ship still under canvas, Lieutenant Whittle
could not have been happier with her performance: "She is like
a duck in the water, steers beautifully, and under short sail has
averaged about 9 knots. This is splendid, and I consider that she
is now in better trim & order than she has ever been." Indeed,
that day an astounding 210 miles of foam slipped across the
raider's bow.

Reflecting her sprucing-up at Ascension, the ship's performance
seemed but one more manifestation of the cosmic good cheer
that the island had bestowed upon the Confederates. Beyond
replenishing their provisions and spirits, their thirteen days on
the island had rolled by like some idyll from one of the romantic novels devoured by the raider's young officers to combat the

monotony of life at sea. As the men savored their memories, the sojourn seemed like a two-week dreamscape in which the daily toils of life at sea had been redeemed for a world of endless, tobacco-fueled shore leaves featuring sylvan swimming holes, readily available young women, sakau highs, beckoning tropical landscapes, and the freedom to roam at will like so many Lord Byrons in gray. Swelling their romantic imaginations still further, Ascension had even offered the Confederates the fantastical Jules Verne–like ruins of a lost civilization.

But, like all dreams, the idyll at Ascension proved vulnerable to ever-encroaching realities. On their first day on the island, even as the Confederates celebrated their capture of the four whaling vessels, such intrusions had begun to seep through, darkly staining the pastels of their tropical tableau. That afternoon—April 1—as the raider's boarding parties rifled among the vessels' documents, they came across newspapers from the past fall that telegraphed ill tidings for the South's war effort. One story detailed Union general William Tecumseh Sherman's "march to the sea" that fall and his capture of Atlanta and Savannah. Another reported Confederate general John Bell Hood's defeat in December, at Nashville. More recently, one story reported that January's Union capture of the Confederates' coastal redoubt Fort Fisher, which, if true, guaranteed Federal control of the port at Wilmington, North Carolina.

The *Shenandoah*'s officers looked mightily for distractions from the reports. Even better, they sought reasons to dismiss them. Whittle's first diary entry on the news—written on the day the raider reached Ascension—devoted only three sentences to them, concluding, "All this, if true, is very bad." After the distraction of the king's first visit to the raider and, the next day, with so many men and officers on shore leave, the officers remaining aboard the *Shenandoah* found themselves left with little else to contemplate. "Most of the day was spent in digesting the news," Whittle conceded.

If, as the reports indicated, the entire state of Georgia now lay under General Sherman's control, Whittle had little trouble envisioning their adversaries' next move. Charleston was "open for an attack in the rear, which will, I fear ensure its fall," the executive officer reflected in his journal. Worse, he added, Sherman's victories in Georgia and his defeat of General Hood in Tennessee augured a route for the Confederacy's land forces. "This shows that we are weak and will I fear cause an evacuation of the ground gained." As for the reported Union capture of Wilmington: "This if true, closes our last port of Wilmington and closes all doors to the world." Summing up the doleful reports, Whittle allowed, "If they all be true, it is terrible." But, like other *Shenandoah* officers, he still looked for reasons to discredit them. And, for Whittle, the fact that they had appeared in San Francisco newspapers furnished just such a reason: "Much allowance is to be made for this news coming via California, which it is well known is very unreliable."

Midshipman Mason was so disturbed by the reports that he refused to actually read the newspapers. Not until two weeks later, when the Confederates were again at sea, could he bring himself even to acknowledge them in his diary. And, when he did, he simply dismissed them because of their sheer awfulness: "I cannot believe all these reports[,] for that reason I did not look at the papers, nor read any of the 'official' reports. May it be all a falsehood." In his next sentence, Mason's attentions plunged into the warm tropical waters that blessed that day's sailing: "The weather is still warm here, the thermometer varying from 80 to 85 & 90; for we are in Lat. 12°, with the sun nearly in the zenith, we have a fine breeze however which makes it quite pleasant on deck."

By mid-April the Confederates were far west of the International Date Line and gliding through the Pacific's equatorial waters, with no way of knowing how rapidly events on their native shores had barreled beyond their worst fears. During their first day at sea after leaving Ascension—April 14—thousands of miles to their east a crazed actor had entered a theater in Washington, D.C., and mortally wounded the president of the United States. Moreover, twelve days before President Lincoln's death, Southern forces under General Robert E. Lee—fleeing an anticipated Union assault—had abandoned the Confederate capital of Richmond. Even more baleful to the *Shenandoah*'s cause, seven days after Lee's retreat—and a mere five days before Lincoln's death—General Lee, at a place called Appomattox Court House, Virginia, had surrendered his Army of Northern Virginia to Union general Ulysses S. Grant. That day, General Lee told Grant that he possessed no civil authority to offer a surrender on behalf of the Confederate nation. Even so, most citizens on both sides of the Mason-Dixon line had construed his surrender as ending the long war between North and South.

The previous October, when Waddell first stepped aboard the *Sea King* as she lay anchored off Las Desertas, he knew of the Confederacy's faltering military fortunes. He also knew that throughout the war, diplomats of the Confederacy, the United States, Great Britain, France, and other nations had been engaged in an intense colloquy about the legality of commerce raiding. Thus, from the moment that he first set foot on the steamer's quarterdeck, he knew that, as the captain of a military ship preying on unarmed merchant ships, he sailed in legally murky waters. But what he didn't know, couldn't know, was that because of that document signed at Appomattox Courthouse, those waters had suddenly become infinitely murkier, much more a sea of gray than he could have imagined.

That mid-April, as the raider plowed through the South Pacific, Captain Waddell was pondering other plans besides attacking whaling craft in the Arctic. Detouring from their course toward that chillier destination, he longed to spend a few days cruising in the westward tropical tracks plied by Asia-bound U.S. merchant ships.

Blown by the trade winds that ruffle the Pacific's water between 17° and 20° north latitude, the tall Yankee clippers that departed from San Francisco and other West Coast ports found inside those parallels a brisk course toward Shanghai, Hong Kong, and other Asian ports. Waddell knew that even on her best days and under both sail and steam, the *Shenandoah*, though technically a clipper herself, could rarely match these sleek Yankee clippers for speed. With their astonishing displays of canvas and stealth, these ships were triumphs of marine architecture and could routinely cover more than 350 miles in a single day. More than that, the captains of these clippers were hired to push the sailing capabilities of their ships. Toward that end, they carried abundant replacement spars and sails, anticipating in their speedy passages precisely the sort of mishaps that the conservative Waddell, commander of a military vessel, sought so much to avoid.

But, then again, the *Shenandoah*'s captain also knew that the element of surprise and the maneuverability of steam power gave his ship her own advantages. Moreover, he had good reasons to tarry in these waters: he did not want to reach the Arctic too quickly.

Waddell had long planned to spend time cruising the waters of Siberia's Sea of Okhotsk, west of the Kamchatka Peninsula, before reaching the Bering Sea and the Bering Strait. He wanted to give the spring thaw time to clear those waters of ice. He also knew that dense fogs prevailed in the Sea of Okhotsk during May and, consequently, wanted to avoid reaching that inland ocean before June 1.

The splendid weather and steady winds that greeted the *Shenandoah* as she departed Ascension Island on April 13 held over the coming days. Sailing under only topsails for much of the time, the Confederates covered 1,133 miles during their first six days out from the island. Balmy breezes and a benign sun interrupted by occasional showers rendered their days a welcome respite from recent travails; at night, the Confederates gazed upon a sea of moonlight-flecked whitecaps. "Never in our various experience of sea life had any of us seen such or more charming weather than we now enjoyed," Waddell recalled.

By April 17, the Confederates found themselves at latitude 17°35' N, longitude 150°27' E, a position squarely across the tracks of the clippers they hoped to capture. Up to now, all of the raider's captures had been through happenstance. Now, for the first time, the cruiser would be engaging in her namesake activity and the Confederates thrilled at the prospect of capturing a Yankee clipper.

During the next few days, the raider roamed back and forth in the waters between today's Wake Island and Saipan, covering as few as ten miles in a single day. Each day, however, passed with no sign of any prizes. Though frustrating, the lull in prize-taking and the persistence of calm weather did provide the ship's officers with ample opportunities to conduct musters and drills and to tend to the cruiser's maintenance. "I hope soon to have the rigging in good order as we may very soon have a gale," wrote Executive Officer William Whittle, who knew that the "noble NE trade" filling their sails would soon give way to more fearsome weather.

"The ship now looks very well alow and aloft," Chew recalled. "The decks begin to resemble those of a man-of-war for the first time. We have never been able to get them in good order on account of transferring so much coal, and also on account of not having sand"—for holystoning decks—"important article having been forgotten at Melbourne; we left Ascension with a good supply and we have used it freely."

Pride in the *Shenandoah*'s rejuvenated appearance notwithstanding, the Confederates, as they lucklessly cruised for clippers, suffered a return of the restlessness that had dogged them in the Indian Ocean the previous fall. "Nothing of interest occurs, the drill routine is repeated from day to day with dreadful monotony," Chew complained. "This cruising without seeing sails is any thing but pleasant." Compounding frustrations, the Confederates' zigzagging hunt in search of the clippers was diverting them from their primary northern course.

To stave off boredom, officers caught up on their reading. Chew read, for the second time, Germaine de Staël's romantic novel *Corrine, or Italy* and began Rousseau's *Confessions.* He even found time before each morning's breakfast for a session in Jean Louis Fasquelle's then popular *French Course, or a New Method for Learning to Read, Write, and Speak the French Language.*

Midshipman Mason finished a work entitled *Les marines de la France et de l'Angleterre,* and began Charles Dickens's *Martin Chuzzlewit.* "I don't think much of the first chapter, but intend to wade through at all hazards," he noted. But, in the end, no book could stave off Mason's acute homesickness. The midshipman had begun this cruise with idealistic ambitions of polishing his seamanship. But, increasingly weary of life at sea and of the war, he found himself fantasizing about an end to both. "What a blessed thing it would be! and how pleasant it would be to steam into a Confederate port in the 'Shenandoah.' But I am building 'des chateaux en Espaigne' & must come down to the sterner reality of life again."

By April 23—by then at latitude 18° N—Waddell, unbeknownst to his crew, had concluded that he'd had enough of these empty waters; he was ready to again head north. As the *Shenandoah* resumed her track toward the Arctic, the Confederates experienced bouts of rain and heavy seas. But even after the northeast trades gave way to crisp southeastern breezes, the days remained pleasant, even invigorating. "The weather is getting delightfully cool," Chew noted on April 29. But it did not last. By the next day, the gentle southeastern breezes had given way to fiercer winds, and the raider, on her steady northern course, found herself in the path of doggedly accruing monsoon storms rolling up from the southeast.

For Lieutenant William Whittle, that morning commenced routinely. With light "baffling airs"—variable winds—the spruced-up *Shenandoah* was gliding at a brisk twelve knots on her northward course. But, as the hours passed, freshening squalls rose from the southwest. More ominously, Whittle noticed a sure harbinger of bad weather: the falling mercury column on the ship's barometer. "We prepared for it," he recalled, "by furling the Mizzen Topsail & close reefing the fore & mainsails."

That day "the wind has blown from most every point on the compass," Mason observed. Moreover, he recalled, the raider was twice taken aback—a predicament in which an unexpected shift in wind direction pushes a ship's sails against her masts. Always perilous, it's a situation that risks snapping a ship's masts. And, once dismasted, a sailing vessel becomes hostage to the merciless vagaries of winds and waves. Other crew members, meanwhile, Mason noted, "availed themselves of the rain, the first we have had since leaving Ascension," to savor "the most exquisite luxury" of washing their by now stiff, skin-irritating clothes in fresh water.

Despite the day's sound and fury, however, by evening all seemed calm. Whittle ordered the ship placed under full topsails for the night. Before retiring that evening, he found time to put an optimistic stamp on the situation in his diary: "I trust we are not going to have a gale."

The first lieutenant was wrong. The next morning, May Day, found the Confederates in the very storm that Whittle had hoped to avoid. "I was woke this morning by the rolling of the ship and the seas striking against the ship's side," Chew recounted. That morning's gale soon abated, and the following morning brought similarly tranquil airs. But that same day, foreshadowing what lay ahead, Whittle, studying the skies, spotted "what I have heard was never seen north of the 'Line' i.e. a large albatross." Ominously, he also noticed on the sea increasing quantities of driftwood, "which looked like a portion of a wreck."

Equally disturbing, five days later Whittle noted that the terms of three more of the men who had enlisted for six months had expired that day, and none had elected to reship. "This makes twelve who are only awaiting an opportunity to get clear. These are, thank goodness the last 'six months men,' and I am heartily glad of it. These taken from our 104 leave 92 souls all told belonging to the ship."

The Confederates' northern course during those early days of May brought them intervals of calm. They enjoyed bracingly cool days and cooler nights, all the while buffeted by pleasing variable winds from both the north and the south. After dallying in tropical climes for so many weeks, the raider's crew, as degree by degree they passed into the northern Pacific, welcomed the cooler temperatures. As Whittle, on May 5, confided to his journal: "The weather, effected as it is by the wind from the snow clad cliffs of Japan is very chilly—but it is bracing and we are men being by gradual transition prepared for the intense cold before us—Going as we do, from extreme warm to extreme cold weather & back must make us suffer but what care we, in such a cause." Sustaining that same chilly stoicism the following day, Whittle added, "The weather is quite cold, our time passes monotonously, but their [*sic*] are so many of us, and all so cheerful that we manage to drive a good deal of care away."

The next day, May 6, temperatures fell into the twenties, the first seriously cold weather the Confederates had experienced since the previous year's Christmas in the roaring forties. On his forenoon watch—8:00 a.m. to 12:00 p.m.—Francis Chew donned an overcoat and thick gloves, "and by dint of walking the deck managed to keep up the circulation; but when I ceased moving about, the piercing wind seemed to penetrate me."

With each passing day, these chilling northern Pacific gales seemed to be gathering with the inexorable fury of a Beethoven symphony. Each day the ship's successive deck officers, frequently joined by Captain Waddell, stood in rain gear on the *Shenandoah*'s storm-tossed quarterdeck and declaimed orders to crewmen aloft and on deck. Shorten this sail and furl that one, they variously instructed, all the while quietly listening for the ominous creaking of wood and rippling of canvas that warn of too much wind filling a ship's billowed sails. Captain Waddell, characteristically tight-lipped with his officers, had yet to acknowledge that he had abandoned his quest for a clipper and set a course for Siberian waters. Even so, as Chew watched the captain silently pace the quarterdeck on the forenoon watch of May 9, the lieutenant felt sure that that quest by now lay safely behind the raider's stern. "We are heading to the northward, bound, I suppose, to the Okotch [*sic*] Sea," Chew concluded. "We have been for some days past in the northern route of China traders, not a single sail has been seen. I think the Capt. is disgusted and is going up to the cruising ground of the whalers."

At 8:30 a.m. the next day, when Chew returned to the quarterdeck, the sky had calmed. But "there was an ugly, cross sea running." The lieutenant had seen such waters often enough to know that they signaled an approaching gale. If he needed further evidence, the sky soon armored itself with "a heavy, threatening appearance." To the north, thick piles of fog and cloud stacked themselves against the horizon. Captain Waddell soon joined Chew on the quarterdeck, and, during the next few hours, ever freshening and shifting winds rushed over the *Shenandoah*, violently rocking her masts and hull like some oversized baby crib.

Soon enough, a full-bore squall enveloped the Confederates. A thick mist fell over them—obscuring their vision—quickly followed by heavy rains. Within minutes the temperature dropped from 46° to 39°. "Never have I seen a gale come up so suddenly & blow with such terrific force," Chew recalled. "Had there been much sail on the ship it would have been impossible to have reduced it in time and the ship would have been greatly damaged if not lost." The gale's first blast broadsided the cruiser. So powerful was the gust, Chew surmised, that had the ship's topgallant sails been on, the raider would surely have gone over on its side and begun taking on water—"spars, sails, & other debris would have told the mournful story of 'foundered at sea.'" And this storm, by Chew's account, had only begun to feel its powers.

> By eleven o'clock it blew with awful violence and the sea, dark, gloomy and mournful, was like a boiling chaldron [*sic*], the waves running mountains, high foaming, hissing in mad fury, running impatient to engulf the ship. Ah! what a grand, what a sublime, what an awful scene! The roaring of the waves, the morning of the blast as it swept by with such awful force, and the creaking & groaning of the ship in every part, as she rushed headlong into the abyss or was thrown high in air by the waves; she seemed an insignificant toy in this wild strife of the elements. The waves were constantly breaking over us, flooding the decks fore & aft.

"At 3:00 p.m.," Chew recalled, "when the fury of the blast had enveloped us, the ship was 'low to' "—down in the trough of a giant wave, and—"in coming up a tremendous wave struck the ship and came pouring over her." Only later did Chew realize that one of the "much dreaded revolving hurricanes"—a cyclone—had hit the cruiser. In such storms, he noted, "the wind blows in circles round a common centre, the whole body moving along at the same time."

The following day brought a brief respite. But two days later, May 13, saw a gale so severe that its winds reduced one sail to windblown shreds. Boatswain George Harwood immediately began overseeing the replacement of the canvas; from prizes, the raider had obtained a ready supply of extra sails. But before that new sail could be raised, the vestiges of the old one, now whipping violently in the gale, would have to be gathered and cut away from the yard.

The deck officer ordered the maintop men aloft into the teeth of the storm. Slowly, cautiously, the sailors began climbing the mast as it rose and plunged with the ship as she rode up and down one behemoth wave after another. Each upward step by the men increased the dizzying arc of their swaying through the chaos of wind and rain. As the raider slipped into the trough of a wave, the crewmen, clutching spars and lines for their lives, found themselves barely above the raging sea. The next moment, as the ship righted herself, they found themselves skyward-bound. Soon reaching the main topsail yard and gripping the spar for dear life, they began inching their way outward, slowly cutting out the shreds of the former sail. By the day's end, and without loss of life, the new sail had been put in place.

But the *Shenandoah* was hardly out of the gale. The new sail was barely in place before another giant wave rolled over the cruiser, drenching everyone topside. The dunking was so complete that crewmen had to knock out ports in the ship's bulwarks in order to drain the water that covered the deck. Minutes later, however, yet another wave flooded the deck. So violent was this wave, Hunt recalled, that it carried away one man—"who, strange to relate, was the next moment dashed on board again by another sea, terribly frightened but otherwise uninjured."

The storm persisted for another twelve hours. And when it passed the Confederates found themselves afloat on a calm sea under a clear sky. Crowding that sky were thousands of right-whale birds, a species, Hunt noted, "always found in the vicinity of the marine monster bearing that cognomen." The *Shenandoah*'s men had been at sea for seven months, yet only now were they approaching the whaling grounds that lay at the incendiary core of James Bulloch's original orders.[1]

FOURTEEN

Sea of Okhotsk

By May 18, 1865—having now reached latitude 46°29' N, longitude 155°52' E—the Confederates' northerly course had put them due east of Russia's Kuril Islands and south of Siberia's Kamchatka Peninsula. The gales that had bedeviled the *Shenandoah* had been left far behind to their south. Even so, as Lieutenant Francis Chew recalled, "most disagreeable weather" still prevailed. Subfreezing temperatures tormented deck watches, and fog and rain enveloped the raider. The damp cold even reached deep into the interior of the unheated ship.

Two days later, snow began falling through the morning fog—the first snow the Confederates had seen in months. "Chests and clothes-bags were ransacked for woolen underclothing, and heavy pea-jackets and overcoats were in requisition throughout the entire ship's company," Cornelius Hunt recalled. Adding to the novelty, birds, identified by Chew as robins and sparrows, appeared around the ship—a sure sign, the men hoped, that they were close to land. Sure enough, when the snow ceased at 9:00 a.m. and the skies cleared, they spotted, about forty miles off their port bow, Onekotan Island. It sat at the northern end of the Kurils island chain, which is strewn north to south between the Kamchatka Peninsula and Japan.

After weeks afloat on a trackless ocean, the Confederates reveled in espying any land. More particularly, they knew that somewhere north of that day's position in these forlorn waters, between the Kurils and the Kamchatka Peninsula, they would find the Amphitrite Strait—today's Kuril Strait—the gateway to the Sea of Okhotsk.

For the rest of the day, the Confederates sailed north, but stiff southwest winds hampered their progress. And by the time they had come within forty miles of the strait's entrance, night had fallen and fog again concealed the waters around them. Unwilling to risk entering the strait under those conditions, Captain Waddell ordered the ship laid to for the evening. And when the officers repaired to the wardroom that night, a surprise greeted them. Traditionally, the only stoves on men-of-war were in the galley, for cooking. Only merchant ships had them elsewhere, to provide heat. But that evening, when the officers entered the wardroom, they encountered the warmth of a glowing coal fire. The *Sea King*'s stove, originally packed away, had been installed earlier that day on Captain Waddell's orders.

At first light the next day, May 21, as the *Shenandoah* steamed into the Kuril Strait, the Confederates got a closer look at Onekotan Island, off their port beam. To Lieutenant Chew the island's high, snowclad volcanic peaks, glistening in the morning sun, seemed beautiful. But as the raider plowed deeper into the strait and came closer to the island, the lieutenant recorded, it "appeared the most desolate and uninviting piece of terra firma I have ever seen."

At noon the raider concluded her passage through the Kuril Strait. As the Confederates entered the Sea of Okhotsk, a frigid southwest wind began stinging their cheeks. Captain Waddell had long been wary of this cold, foggy realm; his preference had been to reach the Sea of Okhotsk after June 1, when he could have been reasonably certain of avoiding extremes of cold, fog, wind, and ice. The unsuccessful cruise for Yankee clippers in more southerly waters meant that Waddell now found himself entering this desolate Siberian sea almost two weeks earlier than he would have liked.

Earlier in the day, during a lull in the wind, the *Shenandoah*'s propeller had been lowered into the water and the ship commenced steaming. But now, as the southwest winds picked up, the captain ordered Lieutenant Chew, that morning's deck officer, to clew up the raider's square sails. And though the ship was still under steam and four miles from the nearest shore, Waddell, revealing what Lining recalled as his "skittishness" about these waters, ordered the lieutenant to rush his work. "Make haste, Mr. Chew," he barked. "I don't want to go on shore here." Ironically, it was Waddell's own strategy that necessitated hugging the shore.

Captain Waddell knew that whaling vessels in the Sea of Okhotsk tended to hunt not in the sea's center but along its edges. Thus, he told Chew, he intended to set a course that traced the sea's entire coastal margin. From the Kuril Strait, Waddell began his circuit by steaming north along Kamchatka's western shore. Beginning this latest chapter of their voyage, the Confederates, during their first three days in the Sea of Okhotsk, confronted the expected fog and rain, and temperatures just below freezing. But, for the most part, the sea's winds remained moderate and neither ice nor gales fell across their path.

The officers, meanwhile, when not on their watches, continued to enjoy their wardroom, with its recently installed stove. "It is quite small," Chew wrote, "but efficient for the size of the apartment. What a difference in every respect. Dry, warm quarters. One can read or write with some care and comfort. Now the greater part of my time is devoted to reading. I have four hours watch in the morning after which I am free." Having completed, for the second time, *Corrine, or Italy*, Chew was now well into the second volume of the four-volume edition of Adolphe Thiers's *History of the French Revolution*, which he had taken from one of the vessels captured at Ascension Island.

All seemed relatively calm. But beyond the stable weather and the wardroom's airs of literary repose, the Confederates, even when not voicing their fears, remained mindful that they were far from home and in alien and dangerous circumstances. Cornelius Hunt recalled, "I do not suppose there were half a dozen men on board, who, of their own accord, would have selected that cruising ground, not withstanding the inducements it offered; but our orders were to proceed thither, and nothing short of the probable destruction of the ship would have been regarded as an adequate excuse for not carrying them into effect."

The Confederates continued their northern course during the next three days. And on the morning of May 27 they spotted what Captain Waddell had hoped to avoid by not reaching this remote arm of the North Pacific until June. At 10:00 a.m. during his forenoon watch, Chew spotted a large ice floe off the ship's port beam. Reinforcing their fears of the insidious interplay between fog and ice in these waters, no crewmen had seen the ice until the raider almost collided with it.

A crewman sent aloft with glasses to investigate soon reported that the ice floe appeared to be of limited size and posed no immediate threat to the raider. But before he came down something else also caught his attention, and he shouted, "Sail ho!" Though the cry raised the crew's hopes of making their first Arctic capture, it soon proved to be a false alarm.

However, later that afternoon—at 2:00 p.m. on May 27—another cry of "Sail ho!" heralded the real thing. Waddell ordered a Russian ensign hoisted and began the chase. But, unfortunately, a large ice field lay between the Confederates and their prey. As the lookout continued to scan the ice and the sea before them, the raider's other crewmen and officers rushed to the *Shenandoah*'s rails to make out the scene as best they could.

The *Shenandoah* and the fleeing bark were running on parallel lines on either side of the floe, and by the time the two reached the ice's northern extremities the distance separating the vessels had narrowed to a few hundred yards. As both reached the ice field's limits and entered open water, the Confederates realized that the whaleship, which was flying the U.S. flag, had turned and was now headed straight toward them. The *Shenandoah*'s crew—suddenly within hailing distance of the vessel and hauling down their Russian flag and raising their Confederate ensign—barely had time to fire their blank cartridge before ordering their quarry to heave to and prepare to be boarded.

The bark proved to be the *Abigail*, of New Bedford, Massachusetts. The vessel had been at sea for three years. Most recently, she had sailed from Yokohama, Japan. Upon spotting the raider, with her Russian Navy ensign flapping in the wind, the whaleship's master had mistaken the *Shenandoah* for a Russian man-of-war. Twice each year, the Russian Navy sent out such ships to provision Russian whalers in the Sea of Okhotsk. In sailing toward the supposed Russian ship, the *Abigail*'s captain, Ebenezer Nye, was hoping for a gam with the ship's officers—a chance to compare notes and charts pertaining to these waters. While Russians were old hands in the Sea of Okhotsk, American whaling vessels had not ventured there until the mid-1840s.

Taken in by the *Shenandoah*'s ruse, Nye realized his blunder only after the raider's boarding party was standing on the deck of his bark. According to Cornelius Hunt, when Nye was told by a Confederate officer that he and his vessel were now prisoners of the CSS *Shenandoah*, he appeared befuddled. "The skipper looked at him for a moment, scratched his head, laid in a fresh chew of tobacco, and then remarked as coolly as if giving the order to heave up his anchor, 'Well, I s'pose I'm taken! but who on earth would have thought of seeing one of your Southern privateers up here in the Ochotsk [*sic*] Sea. I have heard of some of the pranks you fellows have been playing, but I supposed *I* was out of your reach.'"

Nye's Confederate interlocutor offered a ready rejoinder to the Yankee captain's lament: "Why the fact of the business is, Captain, we have entered into a treaty offensive and defensive with the whales, and are up here by special agreement to disperse their mortal enemies." According to a later newspaper account of the exchange, however, the New England sea captain was far from stoically good-humored during his exchange with the Confederates, declaring to Waddell, "You have not ruined me yet; I have ten thousand dollars at home, and before I left I lent it to the government to help fight such fellows as you."

Lying to alongside the *Abigail*, the Confederates spent two days transferring men and cargo. To Hunt, the bark's crew possessed the same admirable nonchalance as their captain: "They were of similar timber to their commander, and one of them remarked as he came over the side, that 'he had not expected to take steam home, and to tell the truth he had just as lief trust to sail,' but they accepted their change of fortune with general good humor, and even single irons and confinement in the top-gallant forecastle did not seem to materially depress their spirits."

All in all, the Confederates transferred thirty-six men as prisoners from the *Abigail* to the *Shenandoah*. Among those, several elected to ship with the Confederates. And of those recruits one—the first—quickly stood out: the *Abigail*'s second mate, Thomas Manning. A native of Baltimore, with avowed Southern sympathies, Manning, Hunt recalled, won the Confederates' attention with extravagant promises made "not only to cast in his lot with us, but to pilot the *Shenandoah* to the spot where the whaling fleet, which contained more than one vessel upon which he had served, was pursuing its bold, laborious calling."

Waddell, accepting Manning's offer, soon accorded him the rank of corporal. The *Shenandoah*'s other officers, however, had reservations about the turncoat Manning. Hunt called him "the most disreputable of men," but even he had to admire the zeal that Manning brought to his Rebel conversion. "He did nothing by halves, but set resolutely to work to induce as many as possible of his shipmates to follow his example, and several of them did so, not knowing, however, that he intended to conduct us to the ships that contained the friends and acquaintances with whom they had grown up from boyhood. Had they been aware of it, I do not believe a man of them would have enlisted under our flag."

Meanwhile, led by Captain Nye, those who resisted all recruiting inducements sought in vain to be landed by the *Shenandoah* on the shores of the Sea of Okhotsk. There, they imagined, they would find and join a ship from the Russian whaling fleet.[1]

That day, May 27, deep into the night and through much of the next day, a prize crew led by Lieutenant Dabney Scales stripped the *Abigail* of provisions and equipment. The whaleship, having just sent home a substantial amount of whale oil and cash, had only twenty barrels of whale oil on board. Nonetheless, she yielded an interesting haul that included purchases made during the ship's recent stop in Yokohama. In spring 1865, the mania for things Japanese unleashed twelve years earlier by U.S. Navy Admiral Matthew C. Perry's forced opening of Japan to Western trade remained in full bloom. And just as Occidental artists ranging from Claude Monet to Vincent van Gogh would fall under that spell, so the Confederates that day eagerly hauled away from the *Abigail* an exquisite cache of up to thirty silk dresses, beautifully crafted wooden boxes, and other souvenirs of Japan purchased there by the captain and other officers. The ship's holds also contained large quantities of potatoes, four or five hogs, a large supply of salt, seven boxes of tobacco, and boxes of canned meats. From the haul, Captain Waddell even managed to acquire a stove for his own quarters.

Of all the goods plundered, however, a cache of some twenty-five barrels of brandy, rum, and whiskey proved most noteworthy. Labeled for use "in case of sickness," the casks had been the personal property of Captain Nye. Typical of whaling captains who supplement their regular pay with side businesses, Nye had been selling the whiskey to his officers and crew. He had also planned to trade liquor for furs among various indigenous Arctic peoples.

The *Shenandoah*'s officers initially welcomed the whiskey. As Mason recalled, it "came in very well as we were much in want of 'grog.'" But even before the barrels came aboard the raider they proved a problem. The first prize party sent to the *Abigail* to bring over the barrels failed to resist the temptation to sample their contents. When that first party failed to return, a second prize party rowed over to the bark, but its members, too, soon fell into a similar revelry. Afterward, a third prize party yielded to the same temptation. "In brief," Cornelius Hunt recalled, "I think it was the most general and stupendous spree I ever witnessed. There was not a dozen sober men on board the ship except the prisoners, and had these not been ironed it might have proved a dearly bought frolic."

One sailor became so drunk that, upon returning to the *Shenandoah*, he was ordered overboard and placed in one of the raider's boats. And, once in the boat, he jumped into the frigid Okhotsk. "The water was below the freezing point and the cold bath did him much good," Chew recalled. "After hauling him in[to] the boat I had him lashed down to prevent him going overboard again." Making matters worse, when the *Abigail*'s remaining liquor did reach the *Shenandoah*, the libations during the next few days wreaked havoc on the ship's good order and discipline. "We found it impossible to prevent our men from getting it," Francis Chew recalled. Midshipman John Mason was equally outraged: "Had it been merely the men who became intoxicated it would not have been so bad, but I regret to say that some few of the officers committed themselves."

Naval ordinances prohibited drunkenness on duty, and Captain Waddell—mindful of the legal sword of Damocles hanging over the operations of the cruiser—believed that only a by-the-book enforcement of international laws governing commerce raiding separated the *Shenandoah*'s enterprise from what the Confederacy's enemies called it: outright piracy. The captain thus felt dutybound to enforce, and to make a display of enforcing, all ordinances concerning both drunken behavior and the disposition of properties from prizes.

Waddell had been willing to turn a blind eye to international laws concerning the recruitment of neutrals to his crew. He was also willing to overlook the appropriation by his men of small items from prizes—say the additions to Francis Chew's private library filched from the whaling vessels at Ascension Island. But if such infractions became blatant, widely known throughout the ship and, moreover, contributed to an erosion of order on the raider, that was another matter. Beyond that, the captain no doubt also perceived in such freelance looting and drinking the specter of potential mutiny. In a May 29 order to William Whittle, Waddell made clear his concerns:

> Sir: Private appropriation of prize property is prohibited. All articles sent from prizes to the ship must be sent to you, to be transferred to the paymaster's department. You will be pleased to call the attention of the officers to this order, and require a rigid adherence to it. Any violation of it coming under your observation must be brought to my knowledge.
>
> Respectfully,
> James I. Waddell

Whittle, for his part, hardly required a letter from the captain to stoke his own outrage over the episode. "I never had such a time," he recalled. "Our men have heretofore been so clear of any such that it comes, as something new, still harder but I am determined that they shall not repeat it." During the next few days, as the identity of the culprits in the spree became clear, Whittle fashioned a variety of punishments for them: suspensions from duties, confinement to quarters, confinement in irons, even being gagged and triced up. Second Lieutenant Dabney Scales, who had brought over a stash of whiskey from the prize and hid it in John Blacker's cabin, was temporarily relieved of his officer's duties. For his complicity in Scales's scheme, Blacker—the former Irish sea captain recruited in Melbourne who served as the captain's clerk—was banned from the wardroom. Other culprits included Assistant Surgeon Fred J. McNulty, Acting Second Carpenter John Lynch, and Boatswain George Harwood.

The punishments meted out to both officers and men damaged shipboard morale. More insidiously, the episode expanded existing fissures among the ship's officers and widened the already yawning distance between Captain Waddell and the ship's entire crew. Feeling a need to tighten discipline among the crew, Waddell, in the days ahead, reaffirmed existing ordinances and promulgated new ones—including, to the men's great annoyance, a ban on smoking in the *Shenandoah*'s engine room.

Beyond that, Waddell may have asked at least one officer to snitch on the others. John Blacker made that charge against the captain one evening by way of explaining to other officers his removal from the officers' quarters to steerage; more specifically, Blacker claimed to have rebuffed the captain's entreaty, telling him "he did not want to act as spy of the Captain on the other officers."

Upon hearing of Blacker's accusation William Whittle reported it to Waddell, who labeled it "a deliberate falsehood." Afterward, Waddell summoned Blacker to his cabin and, with Lining and Whittle as witnesses, confronted him. As Lining recalled the exchange, Blacker, pressed by Waddell, did not deny that he had told the other officers that Waddell had asked him to act as a spy. But, Blacker added, he had drawn that "<u>inference</u>" from a conversation he had a night earlier with the captain.

According to Waddell, the conversation to which Blacker alluded took place in Waddell's cabin. The captain had called the meeting after realizing that Blacker had earlier lied to him when asked whether he knew the whereabouts of any unaccounted-for whiskey. Blacker had assured the captain that he didn't. But Waddell subsequently learned that Blacker was in fact hiding in his own cabin a beaker—a small cask—of whiskey for Lieutenant Scales. It was only after learning of that deception by Blacker that Waddell put Scales "under suspension" for several days and banned Blacker from the wardroom.

Blacker's suggestion that Waddell had asked him to spy may have been truthful, or it may have been a stratagem fashioned by an embarrassed officer seeking to save face among his colleagues. Regardless, the incident no doubt intensified an ever thickening stew of acrimony aboard the *Shenandoah*.

At noon on Sunday, May 28, the Confederates set fire to the *Abigail* and, by two o'clock, were sailing away from her burning hulk. During the next few days, the *Shenandoah* resumed her northwestern course along Kamchatka's west coast. Now, however, a refinement attended Waddell's hunting. From the ship's brand-new corporal, Thomas Manning, Waddell and Whittle had heard a great deal about St. Jonas Island—today's Iony Island—an icy speck of land in the Sea of Okhotsk one hundred miles due north of Sakhalin Island. This time of year, Manning had assured the ship's officers, "all the whalers" gather at St. Jonas, waiting for the late spring melting of the sea's ice. And once those surrounding waters were clear, the vessels entered a whale-rich bay—today's Zaliv Shelekhava—four hundred miles northeast of the island. The Confederates' proper strategy seemed obvious. "We will remain here," Whittle recorded, "until they come up to enter the NE bay, and pick them up there."

Late May and the first few days of June brought the *Shenandoah* cool, bracing weather, and, for purposes of reading, in that pre-electric era, endless illuminated days. On May 30, as the Confederates—at latitude 57°48' N, longitude 152°24' E— sailed just outside the entrance to the northeast bay, William Whittle savored the view from the raider's quarterdeck. "Kamshatska [*sic*] on starbd bow & Siberia on port bow," he noted. "All covered with snow and distant about 80 miles. This is a droll part of the world. It is never dark as you can read on deck all night. The sun rises at 3 a.m. & sets at 9 p.m."

June 1 found the Confederates in a similarly agreeable repose: becalmed on what Chew called a "smooth, glassy sea," feeding bread to flocks of gulls, savoring "magnificent" sunsets and otherwise in no hurry to go anywhere. They were, after all, determined to wait out the melting of the ice and the passage of whaleships across their position. "There was not a cup full of wind as the sailors say and we lay in the water like a painted ship on a painted ocean," Chew wrote.

But, as they had learned in the wake of their carefree days on Ascension, all idylls are destined to end, and the wee hours of June 3 found the *Shenandoah* being lashed by cold, windy rains. By the following afternoon, the winds had stiffened into a moderate gale and the rains to snow. Seasoned Arctic mariners would instantly have appreciated the operationally dangerous, even deadly, perils of that afternoon's meterological drama. But most of the *Shenandoah*'s Southern officers had no experience in these climes. "I have never seen such weather at sea in my life," Whittle recalled. "The ship had the appearance of being made of glass." At least initially, the officers reveled in this ship-board scene of sublime beauty. "The rigging is entirely covered in ice," Chew noted. "Icicles hanging down from the braces, yards &c present quite a beautiful appearance. This is the first time I have seen a ship clothed in ice; what little canvas we have spread looks like solid ice."

They soon realized, however, that the beauty posed equally sublime dangers. The ship's running rigging was frozen in place and her crew utterly unable to trim her sails. "The braces, blocks, yards, sails and all the running rigging was perfectly coated with ice from a half to two inches thick," Waddell recalled. As the ship's officers pondered their predicament, their concerns grew still more acute as they realized that, with no time to raise steam, the raider's prow was headed straight into an ice field.

Beyond the icy crust that coated the ship's sails and rigging, dangerous icicles clung from her masts and yards. Of particular worry to Waddell was the ice that coated the *Shenandoah*'s braces—the ropes by which the yards, the spars upon which sails hang, are turned horizontally about the ship's mast. This icy coating risked damage to the blocks, the pulley systems used to haul the ropes and sails. In other words, until the Confederates cleared the braces and rigging of ice, they would remain—no less than would a crewless ghost ship afloat on an uncharted sea—hostage to the vagaries of Arctic winds and currents.

"The crew was sent aloft with billets of wood to dislodge the ice and free the running gear," Waddell recalled. "The large icicles falling from aloft rendered the deck dangerous to move upon, and it soon became covered with clear, beautiful ice." Afterward, the resourceful Waddell ordered the men to scurry about the deck, gathering the ice into "tanks, casks, and every vessel capable of receiving it." In short order, they had collected several thousand gallons of fresh water.

By noon that day, June 4, the sun had burned away the morning's cloud cover, and the *Shenandoah*'s rigging hung free of ice. But as the mallet-swinging crew, working aloft that morning, had been freeing the rigging, the cruiser had continued her course straight toward the dreaded ice fields. Yes, the Confederates could now trim their sails, but they faced another problem. "On every side of us, as far as the eye could reach, extended the field ice," recalled Hunt. "And as the ponderous floes came together, the crushed and mangled débris rose up into huge mounds of crystal blocks, seemingly as immovable and imperishable as the bluff's [*sic*] on shore. Indeed, it was impossible while gazing off over the scene of wildness and desolation by which we were surrounded, to conceive the possibility of an avenue of escape opening through such barriers."

A team led by Lieutenant Sidney Smith Lee, Jr., the deck officer on that watch, began tossing ropes and grapnels over the *Shenandoah*'s bulwarks, hooking them onto blocks of ice and nudging the ship away from the cakes that trapped her. By eight o'clock that evening, their efforts had moved the steamer out of immediate danger. Even more fortuitous, the weather warmed and a passage out of the floe soon beckoned. Seizing the opportunity, the Confederates backtracked, sailing out of the ice field by the same route by which they had entered it.

Later that evening, however, dense fogs again enveloped the ship and snow began to fall. Initially, the snow—still a novelty for the ship's Southern-born officers—inspired a playful atmosphere. Francis Chew recalled several officers, in the sallow light of the sub-Arctic summer night, "engaged in a regular schoolboy 'snow-balling.'" By midnight, however, the fog had thickened to the point that the raider's lookouts were unable to see what, an hour later, had become clearly visible to all: once again, the *Shenandoah* was heading straight into an ice floe.

Belowdecks, as the cruiser experienced her second grinding

encounter with an Okhotsk ice field, Cornelius Hunt's imagination inventoried the possible damage to the ship: "As I lay
in my berth, I could hear the huge blocks thundering and
chafing against the side of the ship as though it would dash her
in pieces. It was an anxious night to all on board. None of us
were familiar with Arctic cruising, and consequently were to a
great extent incompetent to judge of the imminence of the
danger." This time, however, the ship's rigging remained free,
and during the next few hours the officers on the successive
watches, lieutenants Dabney Scales and John Grimball, successfully managed again to "wear" the ship—to sail it on a circular
course and thus leave the ice by the same route they had entered
it.

The Confederates inspected as best they could the raider's
hull and concluded that the icy scrapes had done the *Shenandoah* no serious damage. During the first encounter, Chew recalled, "fortunately we were not making but about three knots
and the ice was well broken up so the shock was not great."
Similarly, Hunt recalled of the second encounter, "the hours of
darkness wore away at last, without leaving us to mourn any
serious accident. In a few places the copper had been chafed
through, but this was about the greatest injury we had sus-
tained." Moreover, in both instances the *Shenandoah* had encountered the ice in relatively smooth waters. As Chew put it,
"Had there been a sea on[,] we would have been in great danger: our thin sides could not have resisted those large pieces
which would necessarily have been thrown against them by
the waves."

Since entering this forlorn arm of the northwest Pacific two
weeks earlier, Waddell had successively set courses for the Gulf
of Tauysk on the sea's northern shore, and for Shantarskie

Island, off its western shore. In both cases, however, icy waters had forced him to make other plans. And, days earlier, after abandoning hopes of reaching Shantarskie Island, he had settled on St. Jonas Island as his new intended destination.

From the Confederates' June 4 position of latitude 57°51' N, longitude 150°18' E, St. Jonas lay about two hundred miles distant. The island served as a meeting place for gams among masters and mates of various vessels, a place to exchange the latest intelligence on the constantly shifting migratory patterns of the whales. If the Confederates could touch at St. Jonas Island, some of them believed, the odds of finding and capturing—without firing a shot—fifteen to thirty whaling vessels would be ten to one.

But Captain Waddell's and the other officers' bleak imaginings of the fate they could have met in the ice floes left all of them with grave reservations about the wisdom of trying to get to St. Jonas and, more generally, of remaining in the Sea of Okhotsk.

As Waddell and the *Shenandoah*'s other officers pondered their chances with the ice, William Whittle revived his perennial idea of seizing an enemy vessel and outfitting her as a subsidiary Confederate raider. "My idea is to catch one vessel, put a crew on her and let her go into the ice, fitted as she will be for the purpose," he confided to his diary on June 5. "If this vessel be fitted out as I most earnestly do and will recommend, I will try and command her."

Whittle's diary gives no hint of Waddell's reaction to his executive officer's most recent invocation of an old idea. The captain's recent behavior had reinforced Whittle's perception of him as a man whose incessant contemplation of legal conse-

quences continued to erode his self-confidence as a naval commander. Though none of the officers believed it prudent to remain in the Sea of Okhotsk and go to St. Jonas Island, Waddell
nonetheless felt compelled, as he had on Las Desertas and in
Melbourne, to gather them and discuss the matter. From Whittle's perspective, the convocation, on the morning of June 5,
had but one purpose: through a group ratification of his decision, the captain intended to "arm & secure himself against any
future censure."

That morning, weighing the pros and cons of touching at
St. Jonas, several officers noted that "the greater part of the
fishing is done in the Gulfs and Bays." But, as Chew recalled the
exchange, "according to the Laws of Nations we have no right
to interfere with them there." Acknowledging that restriction,
Waddell countered that a visit to St. Jonas Island, however now
diminished of whaling vessels, would at least give them strong
odds of capturing a few more Yankee whaleships. But, then
again, their course to and away from the island risked another
passage through perilous ice. "The captain explained the case &
asked if in our opinion it was safe to put the ship in ice," Chew
recalled. To no one's surprise, "the vote was taken & the majority said not [to] put her in the ice." Only Lieutenant John
Grimball and Sailing Master Irvine Bulloch voted to sail for
St. Jonas Island.

Waddell concurred with the officers. Beyond its unpre-
dictable ice and fog, the Okhotsk posed a dog's breakfast of
other problems for the steamer—including, as Waddell pointed
out, powerful, navigation-confounding currents. "It was evident from the quantity of drift ice in view that the floe was westward, and to continue the ship in that direction would be
useless and dangerous," he later wrote.

At the conclave's conclusion, Waddell, typically opaque,

announced no decision; indeed, three days later, after many of the officers suspected a change in course, the captain had still announced no change of plans. However, even with no formal announcement from him it became apparent the day after the meeting, judging from the *Shenandoah*'s new northeastern course, that Waddell now had other strategic priorities. "It is generally supposed," Chew noted on June 8, "that we are going to leave the Okhotsk Sea for Behring [*sic*] Sea and Straits."[2]

FIFTEEN

Bering Sea

After Captain James Waddell had abandoned all hopes of more conquests in the Sea of Okhotsk, a new optimism, along with crisp Arctic breezes, propelled the *Shenandoah*. As the raider sailed southwesterly, back toward the Kuril Strait and the North Pacific Ocean, even Captain Ebenezer Nye, the Confederates' prisoner from the *Abigail*, had to admit that he'd never seen such fine spring weather in this part of the world. On June 11, two small whales played around the raider; while the Confederates delighted in the sight, hoping it was a harbinger of approaching triumphs, the whalemen aboard the ship—old habits dying hard—reflexively wanted to reach for their now long-gone whaling gear.

Spirits rose still higher the next day as Whittle reported that, apparently succumbing to Thomas Manning's blandishments, twelve more men from the *Abigail*—more than from any previous prize—had signed shipping papers with the Confederates. Most of the new men were Kanakas, Whittle recalled, noting, "Such names I never read—among them were Jim California, John Boy &c., one's name was from his being so tall was 'Long Joe'—but some one suggested that he had better reverse it, so he just put himself down as Joe Long—They are a poor looking set but they can haul in the ropes."

The next morning, June 13, the *Shenandoah*, once again passing through the Kuril Strait back into the Pacific, shaped a northeastward course toward the Bering Sea. By then the Confederates' optimism had so ripened that they found themselves fretting about how to relieve themselves of all the new prisoners they were certain would soon be crowding the ship. As the morning fog burned away and the raider, now with a fine breeze behind her, glided northward at a respectable six knots, the Sea of Okhotsk faded like a barely recalled dream. Contemplating Kamchatka's eastern coast, off the *Shenandoah*'s port bow that afternoon, Lieutenant Chew even indulged a wisp of nostalgia for the past two weeks' adventures, including the foul weather and the close calls when ice obstructed the raider: "No doubt that when sitting by a good fire, enjoying all the comforts of the land, the remembrance of that day will give great pleasure."

A new dilemma, however, now confronted the *Shenandoah*. The shallow Bering Sea to which the Confederates were bound lay north of two groups of islands: the Aleutians, which stretched southwesterly from the Alaskan peninsula of the same name, and the Komandorskies, two tiny islands that lay to the east of the Kamchatka Peninsula. Because of the summer fogs that shroud the deep Pacific waters south of these two archipelagoes and the strong northerly Kuroshio—the Japan Current—that pushes through the northern Pacific, these waters, even under the best of circumstances, demanded careful navigation.

Upon leaving the Sea of Okhotsk and reentering the North Pacific, Captain Waddell sought to run a course west of the Aleutians and between two of the Komandorskies: Bering Island to the east, and Copper Island to the west. The twin dangers of the currents and the myriad islands in this swath of sea meant that any navigational error risked running the ship aground on one of the treeless specks of land that lay scattered throughout this northern fringe of the Pacific Ocean.

On June 16, the Confederates, by now well beyond latitude 50° north, found themselves in a boreal realm where the sun in early summer remained above the horizon for some eighteen hours each day. But because of the North Pacific's fog, visibility from the ship rarely exceeded more than a hundred yards in any direction. For the *Shenandoah*'s officers, that impaired vision created yet another, potentially more dangerous problem. Because the sun remained all but invisible, they found themselves unable to take the customary noon reading on their sextants to determine their position. They could thus make only educated guesses. Whittle that day summed up their problem: "Not having had an observation for three days we had run by dead"—as in the old logbook abbreviation "ded.," from deduced—"reckoning and estimated that we were about 34 miles to the S & E of Copper island and about 60 from Behring Island—we did not know where we were and which of the two we saw." Moreover, a falling-off of winds that afternoon left them even more vulnerable to the strong ocean current running to the northwest.

In the end, the Confederates had little choice but to assume that they were, in fact, looking upon Copper Island and that the ocean's currents would put them on a direct course for Bering Island. Operating on that assumption, Whittle ordered up steam, had the propeller lowered, and put the ship on a precautionary east-northeast course. By his and Captain Waddell's deduction, that course would, regardless of the island's correct identity, allow them to clear Bering Island.

Their course correction proved astute. That afternoon, as the fog burned off, the Confederates cleared both Bering and Copper Islands. And, by the day's end, the officers' navigational hunch had led them out of the deep Pacific and safely into the Bering Sea. But the two men also knew that luck, or some higher force, had played no small role in their delivery from the day's drama. As Whittle recalled with due humility, "The fog is very dense and had it not lifted when it did this fore noon, our ship's ribs would most certainly have been in an uninhabited island—Surely God is with us."

Two days later, Saturday, June 18, as the skies cleared, the Confederates caught a fresh breeze and lifted their propeller from the water. And, at the hour of the meridian—after four foggy days of nervous dead reckoning—they were finally able to "shoot" the sun again with their sextant and determine their position: latitude 55°47' N, longitude 171°28' E.

Sailing northeasterly over the next few days, pleasant weather and sturdy winds welcomed the Confederates to the Bering Sea's higher climes. But the *Shenandoah*'s officers also remained ever wary of the dangers ice posed to their ship. On June 19 Whittle watched nervously as the raider's speed increased from nine to eleven and a half knots. With a new appreciation for the fragility of their ship relative to the bulky, reinforced whaleships that regularly plied these waters, he soon ordered the *Shenandoah*'s canvas shortened to single-reefed topsails. "We are now in a region which will not allow us to run too fast as we might be roused up at midnight by striking floe ice. This ship should never go into ice—she is to[o] frail."

———

As the Confederates sailed northeasterly through the Bering Sea, they prepared to begin the phase of their mission that by now everyone on board knew constituted the cruise's raison d'être: the destruction of the Yankees' western Arctic whaling fleet. For the past few weeks Waddell and Whittle had spent hours poring over the whaling charts they had gathered at Ascension Island. They had also spent hours with Thomas Manning, debriefing the *Abigail*'s former second mate on whatever latest information he could recall about these whaling grounds. Beyond that, the *Shenandoah*'s master's mate, Cornelius Hunt, ever since Captain Ebenezer Nye had come aboard, had spent hours flattering the old mariner, slyly trying to tap the New England sea captain's vast knowledge of western Arctic whaling grounds.

Each spring, New England whaleships edged their way through the fog and ice along the Bering Sea's Asian—Siberian—shore, toward the Bering Strait. Eventually they found their way northeasterly to three principal areas where, however briefly, bowhead whales gathered during their northern migration: Cape Navarin, Cape Thaddeus, and Indian Point. And, by June 21, the Confederates knew that they were approaching those very points.

By 11:00 a.m. that morning, they realized that they were close to Cape Navarin. Hungry for a fresh capture, the Confederates came in for a closer look. Fifteen miles off the cape, however, dangerous soupy fogs forced them to check their approach. But shortly thereafter, as the mist cleared and visibility returned, the raider suddenly rang with the report all had been waiting to hear—a "sail" had been spotted ahead of the *Shenandoah*'s bows. As the raider approached her newest quarry, Captain Waddell ordered a boarding party readied and all hands rushed to their assigned tasks. In the end, however, the report proved a false alarm. Anticlimactically, the "sail" turned out to be a rocky headland known to more experienced mariners in these waters as Sail Rock.

But that disappointment failed to dampen spirits for long. The raider was now sailing on a northeastward course and, soon enough, Cape Thaddeus appeared off her port bow. The Confederates had finally arrived exactly where James Bulloch, ten months earlier, had instructed Captain Waddell to go.

Lieutenant Francis Chew, gazing upon Cape Thaddeus that day—the longest day of the year—experienced a particularly poignant satisfaction. It was, after all, through Chew that the captain, the previous March, had intimated to the rest of the crew that he intended to take the raider north to hunt the Yankees' "polar fleet." And now, three months later, marking the *Shenandoah*'s arrival off Cape Thaddeus, Chew could barely contain himself: "From this cape all along the Siberian shore, up to Behring straits, is a great whaling ground at this season. The vessel[s] fish here until the ice breaks up in the straits so as to allow them to go into the Arctic. Now, we propose to <u>fish</u> on this ground also."

Raising their martial ardor to fever pitch, that evening the Confederates noticed that pieces of meat and blubber increasingly littered the waters of their northeastward course. Though most of the *Shenandoah*'s crew were new to the Arctic, they knew enough about whaling to recognize that the floating chunks of meat were evidence that a whaling vessel, or vessels, were somewhere close, "cutting in"—butchering a recently killed whale. Determining that the waters' currents were running northeasterly and thus concluding that their quarry must lie somewhere to their southwest, the officers set off in pursuit.

Hours later, just past midnight, the Confederates spotted a distant plume of smoke lying across the lingering Arctic summer twilight. They were confident that it came from a fire in some vessel's tryworks, the brick oven aboard whaleships in which caldrons of whale blubber are heated to render their contents into oil. The Confederates kept their course during the night; and confirming their initial hunch, at 9:00 a.m., they spotted two sails off their port quarter. An hour later, by now close enough to smell the smoke, they realized that the larger of the two was hove to with a whale alongside her. At 11:00, Waddell dispatched a boarding crew to capture this vessel, the *William Thompson*, of New Bedford, and an hour later another detail seized the second ship, the *Euphrates*, also of New Bedford.

Both vessels had only recently arrived on the whaling ground, so each had only a few hundred barrels of whale oil. Commencing the day's scavenging aboard the *Euphrates*, the Confederates soon came up with a worthy load of goods, including several navigational instruments, clothes, beef, sugar, coffee, potatoes, and a few hogs. At 3:00 p.m., after removing the *Euphrates*' crew and setting the ship afire, the Confederates began transferring booty from the *William Thompson*. Waddell—always glad to conserve coal that otherwise would be burned to condense salt- into fresh water—particularly welcomed the discovery aboard the ship of five large tanks containing a thousand gallons of fresh water. The two vessels were brought alongside each other, and blocks and tackles were put into position to hoist the casks onto the *Shenandoah*.[1]

However, before that transfer had barely begun, the *Shenandoah*'s lookouts spotted yet another sail. Preparing for their third chase of the day, Waddell ordered the master and mates of the *Euphrates* and the *William Thompson* to remain aboard the *Shenandoah* and instructed the boarding party on the *William Thompson* to remain there to guard the ship and her crew.

At 5:45, the *Shenandoah*, again flying a Russian flag, commenced the chase for her latest quarry. As the raider approached the ship, however, Waddell, somehow deducing that it was a neutral vessel, held off dispatching a boarding crew to the ship. Instead, he passed close enough for him and his officers to "speak" the ship, a common practice, in those pre-telegraph days, of stopping long enough to exchange the latest on weather conditions, their vessels' respective recorded position, and other vital mariners' information—including, in this case, the ship's nationality.

Frederick A. Barker, the captain of this whaleship, the *Robert L. Towns*, was, as it turned out, a Nantucket Yankee. Even so, his ship was out of Sydney, Australia. And, as the two vessels came close enough to exchange greetings, Waddell recalled, "her master was anxious to learn the name of our ship, and I gave to him Petropauluski."

Waddell longed to conceal his ship's true identity. For, while international law forbade the *Shenandoah* to capture a neutral, no law forbade Captain Barker from spreading the word to other vessels that a Confederate raider was loose in the Arctic mist. Even so, the *Shenandoah*'s officers surely understood that Barker was unlikely to be fooled by Waddell's effort to pass the raider off as a Russian man-of-war. As John Mason later recalled, "I doubt wheather [*sic*] he believed it, for we had one ship then burning; & yard tackles up, taking on board stores from the other. The prizes were some distances off, it is true, but I think John Bull was up to snuff."

Actually, Barker was even more "up to snuff" than the Confederates gave him credit for. In fact, the *Robert L. Towns'* captain had been in Australia during the *Shenandoah*'s Melbourne stopover and, if only through newspaper accounts, he knew of the raider's predations. In the days following his own encounter with Waddell, Captain Barker headed north toward Cape Bering and Indian Point, determined to warn any vessels there of the raider's presence.

Even more discomfiting for the Confederates than their worries about Captain Barker was the news that had been passed along to them by the captured officers and crew of the *William Thompson*. The New Bedford whaling vessel, en route to the Arctic, had been in port in California as recently as April 22, and her men told the Confederates of President Lincoln's assassination and of a simultaneous attempt on the life of Secretary of State Seward. "But the worst," Mason recalled, "is the capture of Richmond & Charleston, the surrender of Lee with 20 thousand men & the capture of some twenty thousand more; it is difficult to believe this, but the accounts are so minute that there must be some truth in it." In his own recollections, Waddell makes no reference to this latest intelligence. Mason, for his part, reverted to his usual strategy in such moments: "I put the best face on the matter possible & try not to believe it."

After Waddell's exchange with Captain Barker, the *Shenandoah*—passing by the still-burning wreck of the *Euphrates*—returned to the *William Thompson*, where the Confederates resumed their work. By 3:00 a.m., they had transferred to the *Shenandoah* the crews and provisions of both whaleships. Afterward, the *William Thompson* was fired, and the *Shenandoah* resumed steaming northeast toward the Bering Strait to hunt more whaleships.

During the next nine hours, the Confederates passed, with increasingly intimidating frequency, countless ice floes. By noon, these ice fields had become so extensive that the Confederates were frequently forced to stop steaming in order to scan the water for openings in the ice ahead of them.

"On the starboard beam," Hunt recalled, "stretching as far as the eye could reach, was a seemingly unbroken sea of ice, while on the port beam rose up the cold, dreary shores of Northern Asia, as sterile and inhospitable a region as my eyes ever looked upon." The region's desolation notwithstanding, the men found themselves charmed by the Bering Sea's wildlife. Among other curiosities, according to Hunt, "seals in vast numbers were swimming in the water, or composedly floating on the drifting ice, and notwithstanding their cold bed, seem to enjoy vastly the ray's of the sun that for so small a portion of the year makes its heat felt in these high latitudes."

Just after 12:00 that afternoon, as they steamed deeper into the Bering Sea's whaling grounds, the Confederates spotted nine vessels, five of them clustered around a nearby ice floe. To Waddell's dismay, foreign flags flew from the peaks of two of the five. The foreign colors could be a protective ruse raised by Yankee whaleships. But, then again, Old Glory waved from the other three vessels. Raising their own U.S. flag, the Confederates moved in to capture the three vessels that were of obvious Yankee origin. The first ship, the *Milo* of New Bedford, was, Hunt recalled, "a staunch, but slow-sailing craft, evidently built expressly for this hazardous cruising."

Rather than send a boarding party to the *Milo*, Waddell steamed close enough to the whaleship's stern to summon her captain to board the raider with his ship's papers. The *Milo*'s master, Jonathan C. Hawes—"a fine looking old veteran, standing over six feet two, and straight as an arrow," by Hunt's lights—complied with Waddell's entreaty. Afterward, realizing that he had just set foot on the infamous *Shenandoah*, Hawes told Waddell that he knew all about the Confederate raider; he had been in Australia when the *Shenandoah* visited Melbourne. But, he added, he certainly didn't expect, under any circumstances, to find a Confederate ship in the Arctic. What was more, Hawes said, he had recently heard that the war had ended.

In his memoirs Waddell recalled that he had heard similar reports of the war's end from the men aboard the *William Thompson*. But, lacking definitive information, he had ignored them. This time, however, he pressed for proof. "I then asked for documentary evidence," he recalled in his memoirs. "He had none, but 'believed the war was over.' I replied that was not satisfactory, but that if he could produce any reliable evidence, I would receive it. He answered 'that he could not produce any reliable evidence.'"

Hawes told Waddell that, upon spotting the *Shenandoah* that afternoon, he had mistaken the raider for a steamer expected in these seas any day now to conduct a survey for a cable to be laid across the Bering Strait, connecting Alaska and Siberia. But as Hawes recalled the circumstances of the *Milo*'s capture, Waddell's mind was soon far away, wrestling with a nagging question: how was he to accommodate and care for his growing roster of prisoners? Soon enough, if he didn't find a way to dispose of them, the *Shenandoah*'s captive passengers would include not only the men of the *Milo*, but the former crews of the *Abigail*, the *Euphrates*, and the *William Thompson*. Beyond that, the *Shenandoah*'s captain felt a twinge of personal sympathy for the likable Yankee captain, whose wife and daughter were aboard the *Milo*.

Eventually, Waddell proposed a deal: if Hawes would agree to take all of the *Shenandoah*'s prisoners aboard the *Milo* and sail directly to San Francisco and, before setting out, sign a bond for $40,000—payable to the Confederate government at the war's end—Waddell would not burn the vessel. The Yankee skipper thought for a moment and answered, "I will give bond and receive all prisoners you may put on board."

As the two men concluded their agreement, Waddell was pining to capture the other nearby whaling vessels. To prevent the *Milo*'s premature departure, he ordered Captain Hawes to return to his own ship and trim his foretopsail aback. He also ordered the whaleship's master to send his entire crew and all of his boats over to the *Shenandoah*. And, as a final guarantee of the *Milo*'s compliance with the bargain the two men had just struck, Waddell posted a Confederate detail aboard the vessel. Earlier that afternoon, the Confederates had confiscated the *Milo*'s register book. Confident that—without a crew, boats, or his register, and guarded by Confederates—Hawes would make no escape attempt, Waddell and the *Shenandoah*'s mates then shaped a course for the other nearby whaleships.

By now a freshening breeze had arisen and two of those nearby vessels, after observing the interactions between the *Shenandoah* and the *Milo* and deducing that they lay in dangerous proximity to a Confederate raider, had already begun to make full sail toward a nearby ice field. In short order, after firing two warning shots, the Confederates overhauled and captured the slower of the two vessels, the ship *Sophia Thornton*, of New Bedford. Eager to safeguard this latest addition to his growing fleet of prizes before commencing the day's next chase, Waddell ordered the *Sophia Thornton*'s captain and mates aboard the *Shenandoah*. He also ordered Lieutenant Dabney Scales, who had led the boarding crew that captured the ship, to remain aboard that prize and communicate with the *Milo*. The Confederate officers now in charge of the *Milo*, meanwhile, were to trim her sails and bring her around to join the *Sophia Thornton*. Afterward, both vessels were to follow the *Shenandoah*.

It quickly became clear that the second fleeing bark was far more sprightly than other Confederate captures. In the quickening breeze, the *Shenandoah*—under steam and fore-and-aft sail, and soon reaching eleven knots—spent an exciting two hours chasing the ship. The raider's quarry was fleet. But, running for the Siberian coast, the sailing vessel eventually proved no match for the Confederate steamer. At 5:45 p.m., as the *Shenandoah* drew within artillery range of her quarry, Hunt recalled, "We brought her to with a shot from our thirty-two pounder Whitworth rifle, which whistled past her stern. She had crowded on all the sail she could carry, but it availed her little in her laudable efforts to avoid capture."

When a boarding crew led by Lieutenant Sidney Smith Lee, Jr., reached this latest prize, the aptly named bark *Jireh Swift*, they found her officers and crew already packed, dunnage in hand, and prepared to disembark. Twenty minutes later, this swift bark that had almost eluded the Confederates was in flames.

Upon the *Shenandoah*'s reunion later that day with the *Milo* and the *Sophia Thornton*, the ongoing transfer of provisions and prisoners among those vessels resumed. But even as the prisoners from the *Jireh Swift* were being transferred to the *Milo*, Waddell set out in pursuit of the other whaling vessels. This time, however, the effort proved fruitless. As Hunt recalled, "Several of the vessels which we had first seen engaged in trying out blubber, we now discovered were surrounded by such extensive fields of ice, that we dared not venture after them." Put another way, the lessons learned by the Confederates amid the ice floes of the Sea of Okhotsk remained ever vivid in their minds.

That night, Hunt recalled, the *Shenandoah* hove to alongside the *Milo* and the *Sophia Thornton*. Captain Waddell had allowed the officers and crew of the *Sophia Thornton*—soon to leave for California aboard the paroled *Milo*—to revisit their ship, affording them one last chance to remove any "provisions and other necessaries to make them comfortable on their passage from San Francisco." The prisoners greeted Waddell's gesture with "general satisfaction." But, as Hunt recalled, they had less enthusiasm for the other half of his command: "It was to fire the ship, when they had finished taking whatever they wanted away from her." Because the next morning the *Shenandoah* would be returning to her errand of destruction, Waddell wanted the men of the *Sophia Thornton*, before boarding the *Milo* for their voyage to San Francisco, to burn their own ship. "This," Hunt remembered, "they reluctantly promised to do."

Wary of the prisoners' fealty to that incendiary promise, Waddell decided to remove any temptations they might feel, should a robust breeze pick up, to commandeer the *Sophia Thornton* and sail away. He ordered her masts cut down. The *Shenandoah*'s officers, Hunt recalled, also reminded the prisoners that, during their last visit to their old ship, they "would be within range of our eight-inch shells which would certainly be dropping down among them, if our instructions were not implicitly obeyed."

In their more lighthearted moments during late June, the *Shenandoah*'s officers found amusement in the navigational curiosity that their Arctic passage crossed and recrossed the International Date Line several times. Lieutenant Grimball, marking in the logbook what might otherwise be an ordinary June 22, reveled in the opportunity to escape the everyday tyranny of calendars and meridians; it was as if—once again, as on Ascension Island—they had become characters created by Jules Verne, as he later recalled: "This day we made additionally eventful by crossing the 180th meridian of longitude, making that week eight instead of seven days." Indeed, in the *Shenandoah*'s logbook for that week, Thursday, June 22, repeating itself, sprawls over two successive pages. As Grimball recalled, "We made this addition [in our logbook] to avoid being twenty-four hours ahead of time when we got home, as it happened to Phineas [*sic*] Fogg in his trip 'Around the World in Eighty Days'!"

At 6:30 on the morning of June 23, the *Shenandoah*'s lookouts spotted two sails against the southwest horizon. A half hour later, as the raider steamed toward this newest prey, the Confederates, looking back at their former position, witnessed fiery confirmation that the crew of the *Sophia Thornton*, now safely aboard the *Milo*, had fulfilled their grim end of the bargain with Waddell. As Hunt recalled the scene, "A bright tongue of flame shot heavenward, telling us the prisoners had performed their distasteful task."

Over the previous two days, as flames had successively consumed the *Jireh Swift* and the *Sophia Thornton*, the depredations of the *Shenandoah*, unbeknownst to the Confederates, had been observed by other vessels. Two miles away from the scene of that morning's fires were the *William Gifford* of New Bedford and the *Gustave* of Le Havre. "Warped," or tied together by ropes, and painted gray, the two vessels looked like a single ship. After the *Shenandoah* had steamed away that morning, the two went their separate ways to warn other vessels of the raider's presence: the *William Gifford* sailed south, and the *Gustave* headed north. The latter, a French ship, was commanded by a Captain Valupré. During the Crimean War, an American whaleship had alerted him that a Russian ship was pursuing him and, ever since, he had hungered for an opportunity to return the favor.

Inflicting still more damage on the *Shenandoah*'s prospects, the raider's June 23 actions against the *Jireh Swift* and the *Sophia Thornton* had also been observed by two nearby Hawaiian vessels. And the captains of the *Kohola* and the *Hae Hawaii*, too, in the days and miles ahead, took it upon themselves to warn other vessels of the raider's presence.

But the bravest and most dramatic effort to stem the *Shenandoah*'s destruction had come from two of the Confederates' former prisoners. Prior to the *Milo*'s departure for California earlier that same day, on the morning of June 23, the prisoners crowded aboard her from the captured *Sophia Thornton* had been required to torch their own ship. Once that blaze, witnessed by the men aboard the *Shenandoah*, had been set, the *Milo* sailed away toward San Francisco, her captain thus fulfilling his promise to Waddell.

Once the *Milo* was out of sight of the *Shenandoah*, however, the whaleship's crew and passengers witnessed one of the most singular acts of defiance ever committed against the raider. From the start, Ebenezer Nye, captain of the *Abigail*, which was captured by the *Shenandoah* on May 27 in the Okhotsk Sea, had resented the Confederates' taking and burning of his ship. So that morning he, the *Abigail*'s first mate, and other men from that vessel lowered two of the *Milo*'s whaleboats onto the water and set out for Cape Bering, two hundred miles away, to alert the gaggle of whalers likely gathered there.

A trip over that many miles of ice-clogged open waters was dangerous enough. But because Nye had signed Waddell's parole papers, if caught by the Confederates he could face harsh punishment. As it turned out, however, a mere two days after Nye and the other men had bid adieu to the *Milo*, the New Bedford bark *Mercury* picked up the party. Nye told his rescuers of his own ship's destruction and, according to the *Mercury*'s logbook, "stated that the ship was within a few miles of us and said if we went any further East we should be in danger." Shortly thereafter, the *Mercury* spoke another vessel, the *Florida*, relayed the warning, and "we all put to the westward hoping to keep out of sight."[2]

By 8:10 a.m. on June 23, the *Shenandoah* had captured yet another prize, the *Susan Abigail*, a trading brigantine from California. Because the ship's master, Captain R. R. Redfield, planned to trade with local tribes of "Esquimaux"—Inuit—for furs, the ship carried an assortment of trade goods that the Confederates were glad to acquire, including guns, pistols, calico, twine, needles, and other handy notions.

But of all the items found aboard the *Susan Abigail* none arrested Captain Waddell's attention more than recent newspapers from the ship's home port of San Francisco. Within those papers, Waddell later claimed to have read a report that, rather than surrendering his forces, as in fact he had on April 9, General Robert E. Lee had eluded Federal troops attempting to pin him down in Virginia, and had fled to North Carolina with most of his army intact. There, according to this erroneous report, Lee's forces, vowing to fight on, had joined with those of General Joseph E. Johnston. Moreover, Waddell recalled, the newspapers carried "the announcement that the Southern Government had been removed to Danville [Virginia]." Of even greater moment to Waddell, "They also stated that at Danville a proclamation was issued by President Davis, announcing that the war would be carried on with renewed vigor, and exhorting the people of the South to bear up heroically."

In his memoirs, Waddell claimed that on reading those reports he immediately questioned Captain Redfield "as to the general opinion in San Francisco about the condition of American affairs." To that question, Waddell claimed, Redfield could only answer, "Opinion is divided as to the ultimate result of the war. For the present the North has the advantage, but how it will all end no one can know, and as to the newspapers they are not reliable." Moreover, Waddell added, soon after the trading brig's capture three of her men joined the *Shenandoah*, "which was good evidence that they did not believe that the war had ended. They were not pressed to ship, but sought service under our flag."

No records have confirmed the circumstances in which those three enlistees shipped aboard the raider. And among the extant *Shenandoah*'s diaries, Whittle's alone makes reference to any news gleaned from the Confederates' encounter with the *Susan Abigail*. And his recollections of what was learned comport far more truthfully with what newspapers by that season were accurately, and widely, reporting. On June 23, the executive officer noted, "The vessel which we captured today is one of the latest arrivals from San Francisco and brings the confirmation of the assassination of Lincoln, fall of Charleston, Savannah, Wilmington, Richmond and the surrender of Genl Lee with 16000 men." Even so, after noting this "confirmation" of the Confederacy's destruction, Whittle in his next sentence finds reason, or at least faith, for continued hope: "The news is, if true, very bad, but 'there's life in the old land yet,' 'Let us live with a hope.' 'The God of Jacob is our refuge.' Oh let us trust in him."

Increasingly dire and frequent reports of a faltering Confederacy had been reaching the ship throughout that spring
and into June. And though Whittle and other officers strove
mightily to find reasons to hope for the best, the reports of the
Confederacy's collapse and the war's end had become increasingly difficult to dismiss. It thus seems unlikely, given the de-
pressing battlefront reports that had haunted them before and
since they left Liverpool—including those that reached them
at Melbourne and on Ascension Island—that, by late June, the
news of General Lee's surrender would have been seriously
doubted.

Regarding Waddell's state of mind on June 23, 1865, more
revealing perhaps than his memoirs—set down two decades after the war—is what he did, and did not, write that week. To
wit, in the *Shenandoah*'s logbook entry for that day, Waddell
recorded no war news that had reached him. Nor did he record
anything on his purported exchange with the *Susan Abigail*'s
master. However, the matter apparently weighed on him in the
following days, and he felt obliged to write a shipboard letter,
dated June 27, that was included in the documents that were
eventually removed from the cruiser:

> The brig "Susan Abigail" sailed from San Francisco about
> the 19th of April, bringing [local newspapers] to the
> 17th of April. I read from one of the April papers dis-
> patches for surrender by Gen'l Lee to Gen'l Grant and
> an announcement of a proclamation issued by President
> Davis at Danville to the people of the South declaring
> the war would be carried on with renewed vigor.
>
> J. G. Waddell,
Lieut. Commanding
Jun. 27, 1865

Casting immediate doubt on Waddell's version of events in his shipboard letter is his assertion that the *Susan Abigail* had sailed from San Francisco "about the 19th of April," carrying local newspapers current to the "17th of April." In fact, the brigantine likely carried papers far more current than that. For in truth she had left San Francisco on April 27, eight days later than Waddell's estimate. By then eighteen days had elapsed since the Army of Northern Virginia had surrendered, thirteen days since Lincoln had been assassinated, and news of the widespread acceptance of the war's end, speedily spread by the transcontinental telegraph completed in 1863, filled California newspapers.

It is also of no small significance that Waddell penned his June 27 letter four days after his exchange with the *Susan Abigail*'s master. The timing suggests that even if the conversation with Captain Redfield did take place along the lines described by Waddell—in itself, a doubtful proposition—Waddell nonetheless entertained sufficient personal doubts about the Confederacy's survival to feel obliged to protect himself against possible later criminal charges for peacetime destruction of U.S. vessels—hence his reference to Davis's proclamation urging a continuation of armed struggle.

The *Susan Abigail*'s captain pleaded with Waddell to spare his ship. Clad in a majestic fur coat, a souvenir of his last sojourn in these climes, Captain Redfield told Waddell that this was to be his final Arctic trading journey—and that he expected, through his own personal bartering, to clear about $30,000. But Waddell was unmoved; as Hunt recalled, the *Shenandoah*'s captain rarely gave personal sympathies a veto over perceived military duties. Furthermore, Hunt recalled, "Captain Waddell seldom took much notice of what prisoners said, so long as his own conscience approved."

On June 24, the day after the *Susan Abigail*'s officers and crew were transferred to the *Shenandoah* and the Confederates had taken their fill of booty, Waddell ordered the trader burned. The rest of that day found the *Shenandoah* alternately sailing and steaming, much of the time in a dense fog, on a westerly course toward St. Lawrence Island. The haze soon became so thick that, fearing collision with ice floes, the Confederates were occasionally forced to heave to and await clearer skies. The next morning, however, when the sunlight did break through, the men had a welcome view: off their starboard bow lay the northern tip of St. Lawrence Island, a popular spot for mariners trading with local Inuit.

That morning of June 25 the men of the *Shenandoah* reveled in the splendid weather and "light airs"—force 1 breezes on Admiral Beaufort's wind scale. Having reached a northern latitude of 63°50', Captain Waddell, otherwise always eager to conserve coal by unfurling canvas to the wind, was ready to implicitly acknowledge the distance he and his Southern warriors had put between themselves and the windier environs whence they had just come. As Hunt recalled, "On the 25th we commenced steaming, and from that time till we finally left the Arctic Seas, we made comparatively little use of our sails."

That morning the *Shenandoah* stuck to her westward course toward St. Lawrence Island. But to avoid an ice field looming before the raider, Waddell steamed on to a track northeast of the island. En route, at 10:00 a.m. the Confederates spotted two sails. They immediately gave chase but the pursuit proved fruitless, turning up a French and a Hawaiian vessel. Both soon sailed north, no doubt warning other mariners of the *Shenandoah*'s presence.

Another chase that day at around 5:00 p.m. proved more

fruitful; spotting a sailing ship flying Old Glory off their starboard bow and giving chase, the Confederates soon came within hailing distance of the ship *General Williams*, of New London, Connecticut. At that moment, the bark was hove to, cutting in a whale near an ice floe off St. Lawrence Island's northern shore. Passing under her stern, the Confederates ordered her master to gather his papers and board the raider.

Once aboard, the *General Williams*'s master, William Benjamin, demanded justification for the raider's interference with his vessel. When the Confederates explained to him their purposes and informed him that his ship would be burned, Mason recalled, Benjamin wept. "The pith of the joke was that when we hoisted our colours he did not know what it meant & didn't suspect any thing until we told him how matters stood, when he commenced to plead that <u>he never done us no harm</u> &c."

Once again, however, appeals to Captain Waddell's sympathies proved unavailing. After taking the bark's thirty-four officers and crew as prisoners, the Confederates thoroughly ransacked Captain Benjamin's bark. She yielded a rich haul. The vessel, Hunt recalled, seemed to be carrying more money than any other *Shenandoah* prize. Waddell noted that the ship's master alone had $405 in cash. Other seized booty included three chronometers, a sextant and various nautical instruments, and three hogs. At 7:00 p.m., Waddell ordered the bark fired.

As the Confederates ransacked and later burned the *General Williams*, they were visited by numerous Eskimos, who had paddled over from St. Lawrence Island's northern shore in their walrus-skin kayaks. Most of the Confederates seemed to admire the natives' watercraft. Hunt described the kayaks as "ingeniously constructed affairs." But, just as Lieutenant Whittle had shown scant interest in knowing the names of any of the Kanakas aboard the raider, so he was similarly dismissive of the

Inuits. To him they were "a miserable looking race of people of a light copper color, with straight black hair, but well formed and muscular. They were dressed from head to foot in skins of the thickest kinds. They live on fish & whale blubber, and are believed to be no more choice in their diet than buzzards." Prejudices aside, however, the Confederates delighted in the opportunity to trade tobacco for various Eskimo goods. "I got some furs and some walrus tusk," Chew recalled, and for two plugs of tobacco Lining picked up a dogskin hide.

That evening—as the *Shenandoah* lay hove to off St. Lawrence Island—the Confederates spotted three sails to the north.[3]

Sixteen

The Hardest Blow
Against Yankee Commerce

In the hours after midnight on Monday, June 26, the raider pursued in quickening light the three vessels she had spotted the previous evening. "It was a clear beautiful morning, the northern sky richly crimsoned by the rising sun," Lieutenant Francis Chew recalled. The Confederates captured all three vessels: the ships *William C. Nye*, of San Francisco, and *Catharine*, of New London; and the bark *Nimrod*, of New Bedford. The three provided a haul that included, in addition to quantities of beef, flour, molasses, sugar, and pork, six chronometers and two sextants.

For the master of the *Nimrod*—not to be confused with the British vessel of the same name that the Confederates had overhauled and released the previous January—the capture seemed a recurring nightmare. Earlier in the war, James M. Clark had been master of another New England whaling vessel, the bark *Ocean Rover*, which the raider *Alabama* sank in the Atlantic on October 8, 1862. Now, three years later, as Clark was brought aboard the *Shenandoah* the first man he saw was the same young lieutenant—in all likelihood, Irvine Bulloch—who had led the *Alabama* party that had boarded the *Ocean Rover*. According to an account of the reunion later published by the New Bedford *Republican Standard*, the Confederate officer, upon recognizing Clark, extended his hand and greeted the Yankee captain "as an old acquaintance, and seemed to regard the whole affair as an excellent joke." But, the paper remarked, Captain Clark found himself "utterly unable to see it in that light" and "was not half so glad" to see the Confederate "as the latter was to see him."[1]

Later that morning, a *Shenandoah* lookout spotted five more sails to their north. But before chasing any more prizes Waddell had to confront the problem of the *Shenandoah*'s growing prison population. Following the raider's most recent prizes, it had swollen to about 250 men. As Cornelius Hunt noted, this was "a much larger delegation of Yankees than we cared to have on board the *Shenandoah* at a time, with nothing to do but plot mischief."

To allay fears of a mutiny, Waddell, after putting the *Nimrod*, *William C. Nye*, and *Catharine* to flame, ordered twelve whaleboats that had been confiscated from the three, now burning, barks lowered on to the water; the boats were then roped together and loaded with prisoners. With the lead boat secured to the *Shenandoah*, the raider set off on her next chase. To avoid capsizing the whaleboats in tow, the raider kept her speed no higher than six knots. Adding to the caution, the raider's nervous officers had to negotiate a difficult passage, "winding among the ice floes like the trail of a serpent," Hunt recalled. "It was a singular scene upon which we now looked out. Behind us were three blazing vessels, wildly drifting amid gigantic fragments of ice; close astern were the twelve whaleboats with their living freight; and ahead of us the five other vessels, now evidently aware of their danger, but seeing no avenue of escape."

Of the five vessels spotted that morning, Waddell refrained from capturing the one that lay closest to the *Shenandoah*—the bark *Benjamin Cummings*. Having heard rumors of a smallpox infestation aboard the vessel, he decided that her capture would pose too great a risk. Another ship spotted that morning managed to escape on her own; the remaining three were not so lucky. In short order the Confederates captured the *General Pike*, the *Isabella*, and the *Gypsy*.

Since the recent death at sea of the *General Pike*'s captain, the bark had been commanded by her first mate, who, upon boarding the *Shenandoah*, proposed a deal: "If you ransom the Pike her owner will think me so fortunate in saving her that it will give me a claim on them for the command," Waddell recalled the whaleman's offer. As the *Shenandoah*'s commander pondered the proposal, however, it seems likely that the raider's teeming prison population weighed on Waddell's mind more than any sympathy for the *General Pike*'s first mate.

Regardless, the deal was struck, and the first mate signed a bond for $30,000, agreeing to sail his ship directly to San Francisco. As part of the agreement, all of the officers and crew captured that morning from the *General Pike*, the *Isabella*, and the *Gypsy* were paroled by the Confederates and placed aboard the *General Pike*. Though the bark's first mate later claimed that he had agreed to take only 160 prisoners, Waddell placed 222 men on board, "making with my own crew, 252 all told, all crowded into this small ship." He also reported that Waddell sarcastically dismissed concerns about crowded conditions on the bark, and whether they even had enough food for their return voyage: "He said if I did not have provisions enough on board to reach San Francisco, I should cook [the] Kanakas, as I had plenty of them."

After the *Gypsy*'s paroled officers and crew had boarded the *General Pike*, the Confederates fired the *Gypsy*. An hour later, they captured the *Isabella*, paroled her officers and crew, and transferred all of them to the *General Pike*. That evening—after taking on nine thousand gallons of water and other provisions from their most recent prize—the *Shenandoah* steamed a safe distance away from the *Isabella*. A destruction party was dispatched and the old bark was set afire. As flames from the *Isabella* rose against the Arctic sky, the *Shenandoah* steamed northward toward the Bering Strait.

The *Shenandoah*'s polar hunting seemed to be getting better and better. On the forenoon watch the next day, June 27, Lieutenant Dabney Scales spotted five more sails to their north. And, like the *Shenandoah*, all of them were headed north, deeper into the Bering Strait and toward the Arctic Ocean. However, a moderate headwind from the north—"the first little puff we have had up here," Mason recalled—was now obstructing the vessels' shared course.

The *Shenandoah*'s steam engine generally gave the raider a distinct advantage under such circumstances. But had the Confederates sought to overcome the headwinds by using steam power, the smoke from their smokestack—a sure giveaway in this realm where steamships rarely ventured—would likely alert the Yankees to their approach. Even if the Confederates managed to capture one or two whaleships, the others would certainly escape. Waddell had no choice but to let the *Shenandoah*'s steam go down and, for now, place his faith in canvas.

By the next morning, June 28, the previous day's breeze had given way to weaker, lighter winds, and the Confederates got up steam. None then knew it, but they were about to commence what would be the single most predatory day of the *Shenandoah*'s career. More significantly, the raider's actions that day would also be the final offensive hostilities carried forward in the name of the Confederate States of America.

At 6:30 a.m., twelve miles southwest of the Diomede Islands, the Confederates spotted ten sails to the north and one to the south. But because that one vessel was in their lee, they decided to make her the object of the morning's first chase. The fleet to their north, after all, was going nowhere soon, "as," in Whittle's words, "the wind is too light." The capture of the leeward vessel, the bark *Waverly* of New Bedford, came at 10:00. After ransacking the bark and taking her crew of thirty-three as prisoners, the Confederates immediately torched her. Then, at 11:00, while gingerly avoiding the ice floes crowding the surrounding waters, they set out toward East Cape and the other ten whaling vessels.

Two hours later, the *Shenandoah* approached an area just south of East Cape. Also known as Cape Dezhnev, East Cape marks the Bering Strait's northwestern edge. Then and now, this eastern tip of Siberia's Chukchi Peninsula is celebrated for being, as Francis Chew noted, the "most eastern point of Asia." Arriving at 1:00 p.m. just south of that hallowed point, the Confederates again spotted the ten vessels. As the *Shenandoah* drew closer, the Confederates could now see that the configuration actually consisted of a cluster of nine vessels—all gathered around a listing, apparently crippled, bark.

It had been a day since an ice floe punched a hole in the hull of the bark *Brunswick*. The distress signal that Alden Potter, the vessel's master, had raised the day before—an upside-down U.S. flag—had, within hours, drawn a fleet of nine New England whaleships.

Twenty-four hours later, all nine vessels remained clustered around the *Brunswick*, most swinging at anchor in these shallow, ice-littered waters. But apart from buying his ship's whaleboats, cargo, and gear, which Potter had auctioned off in an effort to reduce costs for the vessel's owner, his would-be rescuers had been unable to offer any real help. Thousands of miles from any shipyard and having abandoned hopes of returning his ship to port, what Potter needed now was a way to get himself and his crew out of the Arctic. So, the plume of smoke rising outside East Cape Bay that afternoon came, initially, as a welcome sign.

By 1:00 the steamer had entered the bay, and the spirits of the men aboard the *Brunswick* rose still higher. Yes, this could be the Confederate raider that, months earlier, had stopped at Melbourne, and otherwise had wreaked havoc against American merchant and whaling vessels. But it was now June 28, and the Civil War had ended more than two months ago. Given the latter fact, Captain Potter and others standing on the *Brunswick*'s deck surmised that the stark black ship flying the U.S. flag belonged to the Western Union Telegraph Expedition, which had been expected there for weeks. As the steamer came closer, Potter dispatched a whaleboat to ask if the steamer would be willing to provide his officers and crew with passage to the nearest port. Leading the whaleboat delegation on Potter's behalf was Jeremiah Ludlow, master of the *Isaac Howland*, one of the whaling vessels circled around the *Brunswick*.

Once the *Shenandoah* had arrived within artillery range of the ten whaleships, Waddell and the raider's officers, like men anticipating a huge feast, eagerly prepared to launch the boarding parties. They double-checked to make sure that all their arms were ready and loaded; however, their work was interrupted. Ruffling the otherwise calm water beneath their rail, the whale-boat carrying Captain Ludlow of the *Isaac Howland* had just come alongside the *Shenandoah*. Taking the U.S. flag flying over the raider at face value, Ludlow remained ignorant of her mission, even after boarding her. As Waddell recalled the ex-change between the two captains, he gave Ludlow's entreaty a curt evasive reply. "We are very busy now," he said, when asked if they could assist the *Brunswick*. "But in a little time we will at-tend to you."

Ludlow thanked the abrupt Waddell, said goodbye, and re-turned in the whaleboat to the *Brunswick* to give her master the encouraging news. Once he was gone, the Confederates has-tened their preparations for their own work. Boarding parties were soon lowered on the water, and the *Shenandoah*'s guns were positioned to provide any artillery support that might be needed. There were ten Yankee whaling vessels in the bay to capture, and the Confederates had only five boats. The element of surprise, all agreed, would be critical to their success and, to fully exploit that advantage, the boarding parties would need to maximize stealth, coordination, and efficiency. Each boarding party had orders to capture specific vessels and to bring their masters, first mates, and papers back to the *Shenandoah*.

The boarding crews of the five whaleboats began thread-ing through the day's windless waters toward their helpless, becalmed quarries. Not until too late did the men aboard the whaleships realize that their cable-laying steamer was, in fact, the infamous *Shenandoah*; not until the five boats had come close enough for the whaling seamen to recognize the gray uni-forms of the officers leading each of the boarding crews did any of them truly appreciate the depth of their troubles. By then, Lieutenant John Grimball had fired a warning shot over the whaling vessels, producing a thunderous noise on this otherwise tranquil day. Almost simultaneously, the Confederates still aboard the *Shenandoah* lowered Old Glory and raised in its place the Confederate navy ensign. With such bombast as preamble, the boarding parties' officers, with one glaring exception, had no trouble winning compliance with the orders they shouted upon reaching each of the ten vessels—declaiming in succession that the officers and men of each craft were now prisoners of war, and all their vessels and cargoes prizes of the CSS *Shenandoah*. Each ship's master and his mates were ordered to report, with their vessel's documents, to the *Shenandoah*.

In short order, the ships *Brunswick*, *James Maury*, *Isaac Howland*, and *Nassau*; and the barks *Congress*, *Hillman*, *Covington*, *Favorite*, *Martha*, and *Nile* were captured. As Chew recalled, "This day we gave the hardest blow that Yankee commerce has yet received."

Only the *Favorite*, from Fairhaven, Massachusetts, offered any resistance. That day, as the Confederates were seizing the other nine whaling vessels, the *Favorite*'s seasoned master, Captain Thomas G. Young, then in his early fifties, took to the roof of his cabin. There he loaded firearms and bomb guns, the latter being the bulky shoulder-fired, muzzle-loaded guns used to fire rope-trailing harpoons into whales.

As a boarding party rowed alongside the *Favorite*, Young commanded them to "stand off." Apparently unnerved by his defiance, the Confederate boarding party began rowing back to the *Shenandoah*. Observing from the raider the boarding party's interactions with the salty master of the *Favorite*, Captain Waddell inferred what was transpiring. Thus, even as the boarding party was returning to the raider, he instructed the deck officer to shift the *Shenandoah*'s position so as to be able to train one of her guns on the *Favorite*. And, in a departure from usual practice, he instructed the gunner, if ordered to fire, to fire low. This time Waddell would waste no gunpowder on warning shots.

In the meantime, the *Favorite*'s other officers were working to persuade Young of the futility of his defiance. Why sacrifice your life, they asked, in such a useless gesture? But Young was in no mood for such counsel. Yes, he answered, he would likely die, but, if nothing else, he might have the satisfaction of taking with him the infamous Captain Waddell of the Rebel pirate ship *Shenandoah*. Unbeknownst to Young, the *Favorite*'s officers had quietly removed the percussion caps from his bomb-guns, as well as his additional ammunition. Then, leaving Young alone to make his stand, the officers took to the bark's boats.

The *Shenandoah*, meanwhile, had been brought alongside the *Favorite* and the deck officer on that watch ordered Young to lower his colors.

"I'll see you d— first," Young reputedly answered.

If you don't, the Confederate officer replied, "I'll shoot you."

"Shoot and be d—d," Young retorted.

Done with talking, Waddell ordered his men to board the *Favorite*. At that moment, Young tried to fire one of his bomb-guns, but—click—to no effect. Now realizing the futility of further resistance, he finally surrendered to the Confederates and, complying with orders, boarded the *Shenandoah*. The ferocity of Young's devotion to the *Favorite*, it was said, arose from his reputed part ownership in the vessel. But, according to Hunt, as the *Shenandoah*'s officers talked with him that day it became clear to them that liquor had contributed to his recalcitrance: "When he came on board, it was evident he had been seeking spirituous consolation, indeed to be plain about it, he was at least three sheets in the wind, but by general consent he was voted to be the bravest and most resolute man we captured during our cruise."

That afternoon, Captain Young languished in irons in the *Shenandoah*'s cramped topgallant forecastle. Waddell, meanwhile, was once again wrestling with his old problem of having too many prisoners. In the end, he bonded the *Nile* for $41,000, loaded her with 190 men in addition to her own crew, and dispatched her to San Francisco. Upon boarding the *James Maury* that afternoon, the Confederates—confirming a story that Waddell had heard on Ascension Island—learned that her captain, Slumon L. Gray, had died in Guam the previous March and had left behind, aboard the ship, his widow and their two small children. Because of the duration of whaling voyages, often years away from home port, it was not uncommon for whaleship masters to bring their families along.

Waddell had been touched by the plight of the widow and her children. Earlier in the day, he had even asked Captain Ludlow, during his brief visit aboard the raider, to point out the *James Maury*. In light of the widow and her children's sad fortunes, Waddell decided to ransom the *James Maury*. Bonded for $37,000, she was loaded with prisoners, bringing her numbers to 222 souls. With Captain Gray's remains preserved in a cask of whiskey, the ship was sent off to San Francisco.

By four o'clock, the Confederates began burning the other eight vessels they had captured that afternoon at East Cape: the *Hillman, Nassau, Brunswick, Isaac Howland, Martha, Favorite, Covington,* and *Congress.* But even as the vessels burned, the *Shenandoah*'s officers, eager for more prizes, began preparing to head north through the Bering Strait into the Arctic Ocean. Anticipating such a northward advance, the ship's officers had taken advantage of a noontime break in the day's blanket of fog to take out a sextant and determine their position. However, before the Confederates could weigh anchor, another fog settled over the Bering Strait. Nervous about the ice that also certainly lay ahead of them, Waddell decided that it was best to remain in place until the fog lifted. He ordered an anchor, dropped into the shallow twenty-three fathoms of water that surrounded them.

Swinging at anchor just south of East Cape, but at a safe distance from their condemned prizes, most of the Confederates spent the next few hours watching as flames consumed the eight vessels. But Cornelius Hunt, as he recalled, turned his gaze toward the *Nile* and the *James Maury*, the two vessels that had been spared; to him they possessed a singular grace. "In the distance, but where the light fell strong and red upon them, bringing out into bold relief each spar and line, were the two ransomed vessels, the Noah's Arks that were to bear away the human life which in a few hours would be all that was left of the gallant whaling fleet."

In the hours after the prize crews had returned to the *Shenandoah*, Waddell sat down with those who had led each party and conducted a detailed inventory of the day's destruction. Among the officers who participated in that meeting, one finds a bravado running through their recollections, a gush of triumph that no doubt helped the men distance themselves from the more baleful news that had been reaching them of the Confederacy's withered fortunes. "This day we have destroyed property to the amount of $400,563 and bonded property to the amount of $78,600," Whittle boasted. "This will create an excitement. I trust it will do our hearts good by encouraging our noble people." Midshipman John Mason, who personally played a role in boarding four of that day's captured vessels, similarly crowed: "We captured more ships to [*sic*] day than the 'Georgia' in her whole cruise."[2]

Around midnight, the fog lifted enough to allay Captain Waddell's safety concerns, and the Confederates began carefully steaming northward. At only a few knots, they nonetheless passed rapidly through the Bering Strait. By 1:00 a.m. on June 29, though a dense fog again obstructed their vision, "we felt sure that we were through Berhing Straits [*sic*] and fairly in the Arctic Ocean," Whittle recalled.

Five hours later, at around 6:00 a.m., "the fog cleared away, giving us a most beautiful day with a pure bracing atmosphere," Chew noted. "The sun was high above the horizon & was warm and pleasant." Looking south, the Confederates could clearly see, as expected, East Cape and the Diomede Islands. It was a heady moment—they could "see two Continents at the same time, what very few have seen," Lining recalled. According to Whittle, sometime after 10:00 a.m. "we went inside of the Arctic Circle"—north of latitude 66°34'—"as was shown by our bearings. I suppose Yankeedom will be astonished at our coming away here after them."

The Confederates pined to begin their hunting north of the Bering Strait, in the Arctic Ocean, whose waters, Waddell believed, teemed with Yankee whaling vessels. The captain based that expectation on a tip he had gotten from Thomas Manning, the otherwise widely disliked recruit from the *Abigail*. Perhaps a bit overwhelmed with their recent success, the Confederates allowed dreams of even grander glories to flit through their minds. "From some source best known to himself," Cornelius Hunt recalled, Manning had "learned that a fleet comprising about sixty sail, had passed up through Bering's Straits into the Arctic Ocean, but a short time previous."

But by 10:00, intimidating fields of ice had begun to slide into view before both of the raider's bows, and Waddell ordered her engine halted. Before plunging any farther north, he wanted to study what lay ahead. "We looked in vain for a clear space beyond the ice," Chew recalled, "and as far ahead as our glasses would reach there was one continuous line." More ominously, the ice toward which the raider's prow was pointed seemed thicker than any they had yet encountered, in some instances rising up to twenty feet above the water. Though the *Shenandoah*'s officers hungered for more prizes, as their gaze fell across the ice fields stretching toward the horizon they concluded that to penetrate farther north risked their ship's destruction. At 10:30 a.m., Waddell ordered the *Shenandoah*'s prow swung southward, back toward the Bering Strait.[3]

SEVENTEEN

"A Sort of Choking Sensation"

L ate in the day, on June 29, 1865, as the *Shenandoah* steamed south somewhere near East Cape, the Bering Strait's fog lifted enough for the Confederates to make out the still-burning hulk of one of the previous day's prizes. Since the day previous, the fire-gutted wreck had gone adrift and was now being swept by Arctic currents into the same icy realms that, the Confederates cautiously hoped, lay safely behind the *Shenandoah*'s stern. For the Confederates, the burning whaleship's icebound fate offered yet another cautionary tale of the dangers portended by these climes. The Confederates, after all, had hardly escaped the Bering Strait's seemingly endless repertoire of ice and fog.

The next day, as a moderate breeze rose from the north, another fog fell over the strait, reducing visibility to a hundred yards. At 5:30 p.m., to conserve coal, the Confederates lifted the propeller and made sail with topgallants and the outer jib. The evening's hampered visibility and the fact that they were still in the Bering Strait gave First Lieutenant William Whittle pause. "I went to bed feeling very uneasy for fear of ice," he recalled. At around 1:00 a.m.—now July 1—a dream that the raider had gone into the ice interrupted the lieutenant's sleep.

Whittle returned topside, where he found Lieutenant Sidney Smith Lee on the quarterdeck. They were due west of St. Lawrence Island and a fog still lay across the sea. But otherwise everything seemed fine, "the ship going very nicely [at] 6 knots."

One thing, though, did trouble Whittle: the sea's smooth waters. He asked Lee how long the waters had been so calm.

Ever since he had come on deck an hour earlier, at midnight, Lee answered. He also told Whittle that the waters had been smooth for the final two hours of John Grimball's evening watch—the 10:00 p.m. to midnight shift.

That information only made Whittle more nervous. Standing on the quarterdeck and contemplating the waters around them, Whittle told Lee, "My dream said that we were very near ice."

To young Lee, the water's calmness portended nothing in particular and he accorded no significance to Whittle's dream or fears. Mostly, he just wanted 4:00 a.m. to roll around so that he could go below and warm himself around the wardroom stove. Besides, First Lieutenant Whittle had earned a reputation for skittishness in these northern waters. "The 1st Luff," as John Mason put it, "has a wholesale terror of ice." Whittle needed some sleep, there really was nothing for him to see on the quarterdeck given the morning's fog, and he had no particular reason to doubt Lieutenant Lee's attentiveness. Even so, the first lieutenant remained anxious. Besides, he probably couldn't sleep anyway. Deciding to linger on the quarterdeck a while longer, he went below to get his overcoat.

As Whittle reached his cabin, however, a lookout's cry of "Land dead ahead"—quickly amended to "Ice ahead"—pierced the foggy morning's silence. Moments later, the rumble of the raider as she plowed into an ice floe reverberated through the ship. Whittle managed to return topside in time to witness the collision. "The shock was very heavy and those below thought that she had knocked a hole in her bow," he noted.

As Whittle went forward to supervise the lowering, once again, of protective mats over the ship's bow sections, Lee gave orders for all sails to be taken in. By then the raider was well into the ice and, having been bounced backward, was being violently pushed astern by the concussion of the collision. "I feared the loss of the rudder," Whittle recalled. Like worries of a hole in the ship's bow after earlier mishaps, Whittle's fear of the broken rudder proved unfounded. But the ship was hardly out of danger.

"She lay cosily blocked in on all sides by ice 20 to 30 feet in thickness," Waddell recalled. Further complicating matters, "in the meantime the current was sweeping the ice around and enclosing us in," Lieutenant Chew recorded. "It soon became evident we would have to force our way through the whole mass extending as far as the eye could reach." To save the ship, the Confederates needed to find a way out of the entire ice field. "All sail was furled, steam was raised," Chew recalled. "A boat was lowered and sent ahead with a grapnel to make fast to the ice, a line leading onboard."

Men in hats and overcoats, ropes and grapnels in their gloved hands, soon began scurrying across the cakes of ice. To Surgeon Lining, their efforts, appearing at once heroic and desperate, recalled scenes from Arctic painter Elisha Kent Kane's canvases. After a path through the ice had been cleared, men in a boat rowed toward the raider's stern and, as her steam engine began to churn, used poles and oars to keep her propeller clear of the ice. The Confederates soon succeeded in reversing the ship's course and extricating her from this latest close call. Equally gratifying, they later concluded that the mishap had done no apparent damage to her hull's copper skin. And a break in one of the three chains linking the tiller to the rudder was quickly repaired.

Working their way south over the next five hours, the Confederates spent the rest of the morning negotiating what seemed an endless maze of ice floes. At 4:30 a.m., having apparently reached the end of the ice field, the Confederates again lowered the propeller and began steaming. But at 6:00 loose pieces of ice began to appear before the bow. As the floes thickened, the Confederates slowed down and again hung mats over the bows to soften the impact of any collision with the ice. Toward 9:00 a.m., the Confederates could see the southern limits of the ice field. However, as they steamed toward that boundary they found themselves racing against time and nature. "Just as we were getting out all the passages were closed up," Chew recalled. "We had to force our way frequently striking but going along very slowly."

While passing through the icy labyrinth, the raider spotted in succession two hove-to northbound vessels. Upon closer inspection, they proved to be non-U.S. vessels: the *Robert Towns*, a French whaling vessel, and the *Kohola*, the very same Hawaiian brig that a week earlier had, unbeknownst to the Confederates, set out to warn other ships of the raider's presence. From the latter, the *Shenandoah*'s men once again heard the news that for the past few weeks they had sought to deny. Lee, they were told, had surrendered and Lincoln had been killed.

The next day, July 2, found the *Shenandoah* under steam and still in fog. The Bering Strait and its ice, however, soon lay behind them. Steaming under stay sails that afternoon, the Confederates thought they spotted a sail, but it disappeared quickly in the dense fog. With no prize to chase, and this being the first Sunday of the month, the crew mustered and the Articles of War was read for the benefit of new enlistees.

For Captain Waddell, weary of the cold, ice, and fog, "It was now time to run the steamer out of these waters, into more open seas," as he later recalled. The dangers posed by the waters in and around the Bering Strait, conditions that on June 27 had destroyed the whaleship *Brunswick* and, two days later, imperiled the *Shenandoah*, remained fresh in his mind. Chastened by his ship's near-imprisonment in Bering Strait ice, Waddell knew all too well that the raider's design and construction, compared with those of more durable whaling ships, only compounded such dangers.

Beyond those perils, Waddell also knew that the *Shenandoah*'s successes had eroded her element of surprise. The *Milo*, captured and bonded on June 23, was now en route to San Francisco. Following her were the bonded *Nile* and *James Maury*. Upon their arrival, the U.S. Navy would certainly dispatch ships to hunt down the raider. Indeed, the U.S. naval stations that ringed the Pacific had long ago been informed of the *Shenandoah*'s predations. Too many other vessels, U.S. and foreign, had seen and smelled the fires and smoke from the burning hulks of prizes or had learned of the destruction from other ships. Moreover, Waddell knew that the *Shenandoah*'s battery of guns and cannons would be no match for those of any U.S. Navy man-of-war.

A week after the Confederates had crossed the Arctic Circle, reaching their voyage's northern apogee, the *Shenandoah*, though southbound, remained in the Bering Sea, north of the Aleutians—on July 4, at latitude 53°52' N, longitude 173°00' W.

It was the Fourth of July, but Whittle plaintively asked his diary, "Who can celebrate it?" Many Southerners throughout the war had continued to celebrate an Independence Day whose heroes—Washington, Jefferson, and others—most still revered. But with the Union's capture, on July 4 two years earlier, of the Mississippi River stronghold of Vicksburg, the day's annual passage had become irrevocably linked in the minds of many Southerners with a major Confederate defeat. For the *Shenandoah's* first lieutenant, however, it still held powerful, if emotionally twisted, meanings:

> If any people can celebrate the day the Southerners are the ones, for they now are battling [for] the same rights, aggravated by causes ten times as strong, as those for which in 1775 they fought, but if such a thing be possible and those wicked men be successful, I for one would regret from the depth of my heart that we ever knew a 4th of July[,] for tomorrow I would rather be ruled over by the President of Liberia than the Yankees. Yes I would rather see the most worthless negro in the whole world rule over us than the Yankees.

The executive officer's inner turmoil notwithstanding, the Fourth of July otherwise brought the Confederates waters calm enough for steaming. But fog still blanketed the surrounding area. In the Amukta Pass, a break in the Aleutian Islands chain just south of their position, Waddell intended to cross from the Bering Sea into the North Pacific.

The Aleutians sweep from the Alaskan Peninsula first in a southwesterly arc, then northwesterly, for about 1,100 miles to their western terminus at Attu Island. The chain consists of fourteen large islands, fifty-five smaller ones, and countless islets.

Only a few miles of water lay between many of the archipelago's islands, and, for mariners, the narrow passages between them spelled grave danger. Thus the Amukta Pass—at latitude 52° N, longitude 172° W—served as a choke point for ships passing between the Bering Sea and the North Pacific. But it was also a juncture that demanded exacting navigation.

That latter weighed heavily on Captain Waddell on the morning of July 5 as he approached the Amukta Pass. Or, to be more precise, as Waddell *assumed* he was approaching the Amukta Pass. Two days earlier, a ghostly fog had fallen over the *Shenandoah*'s southern course, rendering it impossible for the Confederates to take their usual noon astronomical readings. As a consequence, the raider's officers had been forced to rely on dead reckoning, which was only moderately safe in those island-dotted waters.

As the *Shenandoah* approached the position that Waddell deduced to be the Amukta Pass, he had to make a choice: wait for the fog to lift to confirm his hunch, or plow blindly through and hope for the best. In the end, as he recalled, he chose the latter, concluding that "the drift of the ship would perhaps prove more fatal than running on a direct course from [our] last observation."

Then the Confederates enjoyed a bit of luck. That morning, as the raider moved through the fog and across the waters that Waddell assumed to be the Amukta Pass, the mists lifted, confirming their dead reckoning. "When the ship was believed to be [in] about the centre of the pass, land was seen from both beams." Bringing still more pleasure to the Confederates, they soon spotted off their port beam the active volcanic island of Amatignak. "No flames could be seen," Lieutenant Chew recalled. "But a dark dense mass of smoke rose to a great height." The *Shenandoah* had left the Arctic.[1]

Bulloch, in his orders to Waddell the previous fall, had provided a copious enumeration of targets, course suggestions, and references to nautical charts to assist the *Shenandoah*'s captain. In the section meant to guide Waddell's activities *after* he left the Arctic, however, Bulloch's advice had been maddeningly vague.

> If she is in sufficiently sound and staunch condition to justify further cruising, you might run to the southward through the Marquesas and Society Islands, where it is likely you may find some whalemen; from whence you might proceed to Valparaiso, get the latest news, and make arrangements to sell the ship or to bring her into the Atlantic, as her condition or the political state of affairs might render desirable. You should at all times exercise a large discretion, and you would be perfectly justified in selling the ship and sending the crew to their homes, if they desire it, whenever her failing powers would seem to indicate that she was no longer fit for service.

If Waddell brought the ship to a port in England or France, Bulloch warned, it was unlikely that he would be allowed to take her out again. Likewise, he warned, Confederate ships had of late suffered great difficulties in gaining entry to the ports of countries such as Spain, Portugal, and Brazil: "In view of these circumstances and the great distance between the North Pacific and Atlantic ports wherein you might find shelter, I am inclined to think that when you have performed the work assigned you[,] the best disposition you could make of the Shenandoah would be to sell her, either somewhere on the west coast of

South America or to adventurous speculators in the Eastern seas." Such a sale, Bulloch suggested, had two advantages: the Confederacy would earn a partial return on the cost of the ship and, by selling her, the raider's officers would avoid returning in the ship to Europe, "where, as Confederate States property, her presence might give rise to harassing questions and complications."

What Bulloch's orders left unsaid was precisely what, for reasons of morale and decorum, he could not bring himself to say. And that is this: if the *Shenandoah*'s captain ever found himself contemplating the more desperate contingencies contained in Bulloch's orders—if Waddell ever found himself thinking of selling the ship to any available taker—the raider's cruise, so far as Bulloch was concerned, would be over. Having attacked the Union's western Arctic whaling fleet, the *Shenandoah* would have accomplished her mission and, for all practical considerations, have no further military purpose. Indeed, the fatalistic tone of Bulloch's orders even carried an unspoken suggestion that if Waddell ever found himself contemplating their dire contingencies, the war could well be over—and the Confederacy a lost cause. In short, as Waddell understood, these final passages of Bulloch's orders were addressed to a captain who, for whatever reasons, would by then—much as if the biblical Job had taken up sailing—be very much on his own.

As it turned out, however, as the biblical voice in the whirlwind eventually guided hapless Job out of his woes, so Captain Waddell, weeks earlier, had stumbled on an idea—a daring nocturnal strike on the city of San Francisco—that seemed destined to impart fresh, even startling, purpose to the raider's cruise. In one masterful stroke, Waddell would at once rebuke Bulloch's endgame fatalism and inscribe his own name among the Confederacy's pantheon of heroes. And now that the *Shenandoah* had completed her Arctic mission and was back in the Pacific, the timing seemed propitious for bringing this plan to fruition. "It was the 5th of July when the Aleutian Islands were lost to view and the craft made for the parallel where west winds would hasten her over to the coast of California, for I had matured plans for entering the harbor of San Francisco and laying that city under contribution." Beyond that, Waddell might even be able to capture one or more of the "treasure steamers"—the gold-laden steamships that occasionally sailed from San Francisco with gold bound for the Atlantic seaboard.

Waddell later claimed that the idea of such an assault came to him after perusing the San Francisco newspapers that the *Shenandoah* had taken the previous June from the *Susan Abigail*—and his account of the scheme warrants quoting in full:

The newspapers which were captured gave intelligence of the disposition of the American naval vessels and I was not unfamiliar with their commanding officers or their sagacity. In the harbor of San Francisco was an ironclad commanded by Charles McDougal, an old and familiar shipmate of mine. We had been together in the Saginaw and McDougal was fond of his ease. I did not feel that he would be in our way, any officer of the Shenandoah was more than a match for Mc[Dougal] in activity and will. There was no other vessel of war there, as I concluded from San Francisco newspaper reports, and to enter the port after night and collide with the iron ram was easy enough, and with our force thrown upon the ironclad's deck and in possession of her hatches, no life need have been lost. Mc could have been with the officers secured, and e'er daylight came, both batteries could have been sprung on the city and my demands enforced.

The ironclad that Waddell had read about in the San Francisco paper was the USS *Camanche*, a two hundred-foot-long, single-turret "monitor" delivered unassembled to that port by the USS *Aquila* earlier in the war. The *Aquila* later sank in the harbor, but the ironclad's pieces were raised and reassembled. The *Camanche* was commissioned in May 1865 and, as Waddell correctly assumed, remained in San Francisco Harbor that summer as the *Shenandoah* was sweeping down the Pacific toward what he hoped would be the raider's, and his, greatest triumph.

July 6, the day after the Confederates cleared the Amukta Pass, found Captain Waddell cheered to be under sail again in open seas. More than that, his recent escape from the Arctic's perils and heady thoughts of his contemplated strike on San Francisco further swelled his spirits. Capturing the moment in his memoirs, he wrote, "Again in the North Pacific Ocean, with fine weather, and the Aleutian Islands astern, I felt an unbounded sense of freedom."

Soon under sail again and reaching speeds of up to nine and a half knots, the Confederates over the next week delighted in their return to pleasant weather and less demanding work conditions. Many of the officers caught up on their reading. Others simply welcomed the chance to again take naps in the light breezes and benign sun whose rays, with temperatures reaching into the mid-sixties, warmed the ship's decks.

Not that the crew fell into complete idleness during those days. To Executive Officer Whittle, the good weather provided an opportunity for neglected ship maintenance. On the morning of July 11, for instance, the ship rang with the sound of sawing as sailors cut planks to use as scaffolds to hang over the raider's sides, so that the hands could paint the ship. By

4:00 p.m. that same day, the raider's black hull glistened with a newfound boldness.

On July 13, to celebrate their revived spirits, as well as the captain's forty-first birthday, the ship's commissioned officers invited Waddell to a special dinner in their wardroom. None of the officers could remember when they had last dined on anything but their usual bare wooden table, but for this occasion Lieutenant John Grimball, caterer for the occasion, had spread a bright white tablecloth before them, thus creating, Chew recalled, "quite a home-like appearance." He noted, "We had a very fine dinner, fresh meats and vegetables, great luxuries at sea. Two or three different kinds of wine, &c." The festivities, however, were disrupted, if not entirely deflated, by an unexpected gale that had begun to lash the ship.

By mid-July, the heavy woolen clothes the Confederates had bundled in weeks earlier to stave off the Arctic cold had long since been abandoned. And, according to Hunt, doubtless speaking for the entire crew, "a watch on the deck instead of an irksome duty had become a pleasant pastime." The raider's crew also welcomed the return of distinct periods of night and day, and visible evening stars—natural phenomena of which they had been deprived in the cold, foggy Arctic.

However, as the raider plowed ever southward, at least one soul aboard her, First Lieutenant William Whittle, was thinking less about the Arctic conditions they had just escaped—more about something that lay ahead of them. Somewhere not too far in front of the *Shenandoah*, Whittle believed, no doubt lay the *Milo*, the whaleship they had captured and bonded off Cape Navarin on June 23, with orders to sail directly to San Francisco.

In theory the Confederates' brief excursion into the Arctic

Ocean had given the *Milo* a nice head start on the *Shenandoah*. But Whittle also assumed that the advantage the raider enjoyed as a steam-propelled vessel had allowed them to more than make up for the *Milo*'s lead. By his calculations, the whaleship would not have reached San Francisco yet. But she soon would: "I think that about a week from now, she will arrive in San Francisco," he confided to his diary on July 17. The *Milo*, he predicted, will "report us in the Arctic when we will be booming along some 800 miles [from] where their whole fleet will be looking for us." In short, Whittle gleefully concluded, the *Milo*'s arrival in San Francisco will "spread a panic."[2]

As it turned out, Whittle's estimate of the date of the *Milo*'s arrival off the Golden Gate proved astute. On July 20, three days after he confided his prediction to his diary, the whaleship sailed into San Francisco Harbor. And, as Whittle had also predicted, the *Milo*'s arrival did spread a panic. For months the entire West Coast of the United States had been abuzz with speculations about potential strikes by the *Shenandoah* and other Confederate cruisers. That spring, in the wake of the raider's departure from Melbourne, rumors circulated that she was California-bound, for the purpose of capturing one of the treasure steamers that sailed from San Francisco.

Fears of the cruiser along the Pacific, however, were not wholly focused on attacks at sea. Residents of San Francisco and other Pacific Coast locales spent much of the war bracing for a sea-to-land assault. One rumor suggested that San Francisco lay so vulnerable to the Confederates that a ship dispatched by the *Shenandoah* had actually slipped into the port to procure provisions for the raider. Another correspondent, faulting the U.S. Navy's failure to dispatch a man-of-war anchored in San

Francisco to pursue the *Shenandoah* on the open sea, noted, "If she waits long enough she will not be troubled to hunt up the pirate, as the latter may come and look after her." Indeed, fears of such attacks reached north all the way to Puget Sound. There, one local resident recalled, "we were occasionally stirred up with reports that the Shenandoah, which had been destroying our whale vessels in the Arctic, was coming to destroy the government buildings at Cape Flattery and Neah Bay, and burn up the mills and towns of Puget Sound."

With such speculation rampant up and down the Pacific Coast, as the *Milo* passed through the headlands of the Golden Gate on July 20 she was greeted by a flotilla of small boats. Later, when she reached the port and dropped anchor, newspaper reporters scurried aboard to hear what had brought her back to San Francisco so soon, before the end of the whaling season. And over the next few days, local newspapers carried sensational stories of the fate suffered by the *Milo* and other hapless whaling vessels in the waters in and around the Bering Strait. Meanwhile, calls by the *Milo*'s owners and insurers for retaliation against the Confederates were soon joined by parties connected to other San Francisco vessels known to have been sunk by the *Shenandoah*—including the *Susan Abigail* and the *William C. Nye*, destroyed in the Bering Strait, and the *Edward Cary*, burned on Ascension Island.

David McDougal, commander of the U.S. Navy's Mare Island shipyard in San Francisco Bay, was called on to send out at least one man-of-war to hunt down and destroy the raider before she could sink any more ships. McDougal knew the Navy had no ships in port that were suitable for the job. On July 23, he wired Navy secretary Gideon Welles, requesting permission to fit out as a man-of-war the privately owned mail steamer *Colorado*, then in port, and dispatch her to hunt down the *Shenandoah*. But inexplicably—and typifying the lackluster response the Navy accorded the hunt for the *Shenandoah*—the telegram failed to reach Welles until August 18.[3]

Aboard the *Shenandoah*, meanwhile, by mid-July, though it apparently stirred little conversation, word of Waddell's hopes of striking San Francisco and her treasure steamers had apparently leaked among the raider's officers. Throughout that month, as they sailed southeast through the Pacific, the Confederates watched to see if and when the captain would make an eastward course adjustment to send them toward the Golden Gate. By July 17, however, it had become obvious that Waddell had no such intention. The *Shenandoah* that day reached latitude 37°16' N, longitude 147°38' W, a position roughly parallel with San Francisco but over a thousand miles to the west.

In retrospect—the bravado of his memoir's professed San Francisco plans notwithstanding—it seems doubtful that Waddell, in July 1865 and ever more aware of the Confederacy's faltering fortunes if not of its actual defeat, would have seriously contemplated such a bold action—particularly without coordination with other Confederate forces. Navy secretary Stephen Mallory and other Confederate strategists had throughout the war, in general terms, discussed attacking San Francisco. But plans for such an attack crop up in no contemporary *Shenandoah* journals, logs, letters, and the like.

Indeed, the sole allusion to some sort of raider action off the California coast in any of those papers appears in John Thomson Mason's diary entry for July 17—the very day that the raider's course was taking the Confederates south of San

Francisco. "Our skipper seems determined to get back 'round the horn as quickly as possible," he noted. Indeed, Mason then chastises Waddell precisely for his eagerness to pass along the California coast "without trying to make more captures."

> We are avoiding the California coast where we might take our chances of capturing one of the mail steamers. The skipper of course must know best, but I think we might make the attempt.
>   My humble opinion is that we will go home as hard as we can stave it & any more prizes we may capture will come in our way.

Oddly enough, on July 19, two days after Mason lamented Waddell's apparent indifference to capturing more prizes, the captain decided to take advantage of the continuing clear weather to order the first, all-out "general quarters" drill of the *Shenandoah*'s entire battery. Summoned by the boatswain's whistle, all hands rushed to their battle stations, just as if the ship was under attack. The drill gave the ship's senior officers a chance to see how the crew would perform if confronted by an enemy man-of-war.

On the face of it, the order to run the general-quarters drill presumed a wildly optimistic reading of events transpiring thousands of miles to the east. In light of the reports Waddell had already read in newspapers from captured vessels, it also constituted, to say the least, a curious gesture: By ordering the exercise, was the captain trying to convince the crew, and himself, that, even if their captain had forsaken the idea of a strike on San Francisco, the war had not ended? Was he merely trying to rekindle a sense of purpose to bolster the men's flagging morale? Or through the drill—a cynic might call it a charade—

was he laying one more brick in the foundation of an eventual defense against possible later charges of piracy? For a captain who would order general quarter drills was clearly one who believed he still commanded a man-of-war on active duty.

Perhaps all three motivations drove Waddell that day. His memoirs make no allusion to the drills, and, with one exception, those of other *Shenandoah* officers venture no speculation about any undisclosed motives. Lieutenant Francis Chew records that the day's drills, which included the firing of two blank cartridges from each of the raider's starboard guns, left the captain "not pleased with the exercise":

> I suppose he wished to . . . see that order, that quickness, attained on a man-of-war after long practice[,] forgetting that he has never ordered this exercise before, and that we have to labor under great disadvantage in working our guns. The guns' crew have been drilled very little; for months after getting to sea we had no men to put at the guns, and of late, dispensing of captured vessels, has occupied all our attentions and time.

First Lieutenant Whittle and other officers that day, Chew recorded, "were of the opinion that the men did remarkably well for the first exercise, and expressed surprise that they should have done as well." Captain Waddell, however, was left crestfallen. Undeterred, the following morning he ordered an encore of the general-quarters drill, only this time without even gunpowder. To Chew, the crew showed "improvement" over their previous day's performance. But, then again, the lieutenant also implied that the exercise might, in the end, be intended to serve another purpose. If nothing else, it distracted the crew from other matters. "I suppose now that great guns

drill will be the new 'hobby' for the future; at least for a time."
Chew also observed that Waddell began these drills "energeti-
cally at first, gives orders in an abandon but in a short time his
ardor will cool."

At still another general-quarters drill four days later, Whittle
reported, "The men did pretty well." But, likely reflecting the
views of others aboard the raider, Whittle found it difficult to
draw much satisfaction from the men's preparations for a war
that, increasingly, he had come to believe was all but ended.
"All day I have been thinking of my dear ones at home, and
thinking the reports about the occupation of Virginia as true.
My thoughts are sad! sad! sad!!!"

By July 31—at latitude 17°52' N, longitude 122°33' W—
the Confederates were well within the breezy realm of the northeast trades. But though they had, for days, stood squarely across
the tracks of ships bound for the Sandwich Islands, China, and
Japan, they spotted no sails. For Lieutenant Whittle, it wasn't
necessarily prizes for which he hungered. "I wish we could see
a vessel if but to get some news," he wrote. "We have none
since we heard of the death of President Lincoln. I trust that
none of our people had any thing to do with it. If he had been
killed in battle 'twould have been the fate of war; but not to be
assassinated." As soldiers commanding a commerce raider, the
Shenandoah's officers already lived with the sting of having their
personal honor brought into question by their participation in a
method of warfare that many regarded as no better than piracy.
Now, with this latest news of an act that even they considered
beyond the pale of morally respectable tactics, they could only
hope that its taint would not further darken their own honor
and that of their cause.

———

By late July, Captain Waddell had abandoned whatever idea of raiding San Francisco he had ever entertained. Even so, as the raider's southeasterly course brought the Confederates increasingly closer to the coasts of southern California and then Mexico, San Francisco's treasure steamers and other possible prizes remained very much on the captain's mind. Such vessels, after all, routinely made voyages from San Francisco and other Western ports to Panama, and toward Cape Horn bound for New York.

On July 24, he recalled, on reaching longitude 129° N, the raider's course off Mexico's coast "was parallel with the land and we kept a sharp lookout, for we were then in waters frequented by the enemy's vessels." A week later, on August 2, they reached latitude 16°20' N, longitude 121°11' W—a position about a thousand miles west of Mexico's southern coast. At 12:30 that afternoon, after the raider's lookout spotted a sail moving on a northwesterly course, the Confederates got up steam, made chase, and soon overhauled the vessel. The bark *Barracouta* flew English colors, and upon boarding her a prize crew led by Sailing Master Irvine Bulloch quickly ascertained that those colors reflected the bark's true registry. That their afternoon's quarry proved to be anything other than a Yankee ship disappointed the Confederates. But still more disappointing—indeed shattering—was the news conveyed by the recent San Francisco newspapers that she carried.[4]

The *Shenandoah*'s captain had no way of knowing it, but four days before the Confederates had captured the *Susan Abigail*, on June 23—and ten weeks after General Robert E. Lee had surrendered his Army of Northern Virginia—Commander James Bulloch, CSN, had sat down at his desk in Liverpool and penned a letter; addressed to Captain Waddell, it commenced with a recitation of the downward spiral of surrenders of the Confederacy's various armies and the captures of Jefferson Davis and his vice president, Alexander Stephens.

It noted that the new U.S. president, Andrew Johnson, had, since then, declared the war to be at an end, and that the various European powers, having withdrawn the rights of belligerents formally accorded to the Confederacy, had now banned the entry of Confederate ships into their ports, for both repairs and fresh supplies. "I hereby direct you to desist from any further destruction of United States property upon the high seas and from all offensive operations against the citizens of that country," Bulloch wrote.

Beyond that admonition, however, Bulloch provided little guidance to what Waddell should do next. He simply referred the *Shenandoah*'s captain to his earlier, October 1864, orders, now rendered obsolete by recent developments, and struck an exculpatory note: "Ignorance of the present condition of the *Shenandoah* and of the point at which this letter may reach you renders it impossible to give specific instructions to the disposal of the ship." Bulloch's orders boiled down to encouraging Waddell to do his best: to take care of and, if possible, pay off, his crew; and, given current political circumstances, "to come to Europe, or to await elsewhere the further development of events in the United States before venturing to go to any part of that country or the Confederate States."

Lacking any other means of getting a letter to the *Shenandoah* and Waddell, the Confederacy's representative in England, John Murray Mason, also the adoptive father of the *Shenandoah*'s Midshipman Mason, had asked Great Britain's foreign secretary, Earl Russell, if he would allow Bulloch's letter to be copied and dispatched to the British consuls at three ports—

Nagasaki, Shanghai, and the Sandwich Islands—where, Bulloch suspected, the *Shenandoah* might land. With the foreign secretary's blessings, copies of Bulloch's dispatch to Waddell soon found their way not only to the consuls designated by Bulloch but to British consuls all over the world.

When the *Shenandoah* encountered the *Barracouta* on August 2, Captain Waddell of course knew nothing of Bulloch's letter to him. Its contents, however, could not have shocked the Confederates more than the news they received that afternoon from the *Barracouta*. Lieutenant Dabney Scales's log entry for that day grimly encapsulated the revelation:

> Having received by the Br. Barque Barracouta the sad intelligence of the overthrow of the Confederate Government, all attempts to destroy the shipping or property of the United States will cease from this date, in accordance with which the 1st Lieu, W. C. Whittle, Jr., received the order from the commander to strike below the battery and disarm the ship and crew.

Moreover, the Confederates learned from the newspapers aboard the *Barracouta*—which had left San Francisco on July 20, the day after the *Milo*'s return there—that the former Confederacy's President Jefferson Davis and Vice President Alexander Stephens were both being held as prisoners by the United States government.

For four months, the Confederates had seen and heard about newspaper stories that carried similar reports of the South's demise. But this time was different. Not only did the reports aboard the *Barracouta* offer fuller accounts of the Confederacy's collapse but they came via the maritime officers of a nation not party to the war.

After months of wearying efforts to deny those reports— and, more recently, days of pointless general-quarters drills— the raider's crew members, like men rolling a boulder up an increasingly steep hill, had exhausted the will required for such exertions. Within moments, columns of ink marching across the pages of faded newspapers had vanquished all their lingering hopes that the Confederacy had somehow survived. Men who, days earlier, had practiced firing cannons from their decks at imaginary Union vessels now prepared to busy themselves stowing those same armaments belowdecks.

Suddenly, the Confederates' cherished list of destroyed prizes, once such a source of pride, now read like a bill of criminal indictments. Similarly, the splendidly expansive camaraderie that had once united them soon gave way to an ornery inward despair.

"The sadness still continues, deepened rather by a better appreciation of our difficulties & after a night's thought," Lining confided to his diary the next day. "I began thinking of the old & young ones at home this morning, & I had the first heart cry I have had for many a day." That same day found Midshipman Mason in a similar brown study:

What will they say when they know that we have destroyed, captured twenty five vessels, whalers. I am afraid we would stand but a small chance after this Arctic Exploit; and for this reason we are not anxious to be captured. Que Dieu nous guide—If the worst comes to the worst however, I think I could hang as gracefully as any other man, though I must confess the idea is unpleasant, & when I think of it, I feel a sort of choking sensation.

Even if they escaped the hangman's noose, Lieutenant Whittle figured, the *Shenandoah*'s men faced lives of diminished expectations: "To know how I feel would give any one the blues. How my position is altered; no country, no home; no profession, and alas; to think the fondest wish of my heart, i.e., to marry, must be abandoned. Oh! my darling Pattie; how can I give thee up?!! GOD grant me support."

Francis Chew similarly despaired: "Our situation now is very peculiar, and very dangerous. The Powers which extended to us the 'Rights of Belligerents' have withdrawn them and excluded us from their ports. We are in the broad Pacific, the nation we represent over run, are now called 'Pirates' and will be picked up by any man-of-war that happens to see us."

Cornelius Hunt later claimed that the *Barracouta*'s officers "deeply sympathized with us in our unpleasant dilemma" and warned the Confederates that several U.S. cruisers and a British man-of-war had been sent to search for them. To Hunt, the lurking presence of such ships meant that the *Shenandoah*'s plight had become "like running a very gauntlet of life to hope to escape all these dangers unscathed."

Waddell, upon receiving what he finally accepted as credible confirmation of the Confederacy's surrender, felt obliged to disarm the raider. Reversing the process they had performed at Las Desertas, the Confederates began the sullen task of reconverting the raider into a merchant ship. Legal and practical considerations propelled Waddell's disarming of the ship. The captain was certainly thinking about his defense against charges of piracy that he expected to face. Of more immediate concern, however, was his desire to avoid attracting the attention of any passing man-of-war they might stumble upon. He assumed that many of those men-of-war—of the United States and Great Britain but also of other nationalities—would consider themselves legally justified in seizing the *Shenandoah*, taking her crew prisoner, or even sinking the steamer with all of them still aboard.

Eager to avoid both of those eventualities, Waddell, beyond stowing weapons and ammunition in the ship's holds, also ordered the men to restore the *Shenandoah* to her earlier merchantman appearance. Thus, over the next few days, gunports were filled in, and the steamer's black smokestack whitewashed. Having gone from hunter to hunted, the *Shenandoah* needed more than the ability to fly false colors; she needed, chameleon-like, a new skin.[5]

EIGHTEEN

"Long Gauntlet to Run"

T hree decades after the Civil War, Captain Waddell, in recollecting the days following the *Shenandoah*'s August 2, 1865, mission-altering encounter with the *Barracouta*, presented himself as a man of steely resolve:

> My life had been checkered, and I was tutored to disappointment; the intelligence of the issue of the fearful struggle cast a deep stillness over the ship's company and would have occupied all my reflection had not a responsibility of the highest order rested upon me in the course I should pursue, which involved not only my personal honor, but the honor of the flag intrusted to me, which had been thus far triumphant. I first thought that a port in the South Atlantic would answer all my purposes for taking the ship, but upon reflection I saw the propriety of avoiding those ports, and determined to run the ship for a European port, which involved a distance of 17,000 miles—a long gantlet to run and escape. But why should I not succeed in baffling observation or pursuit? There was everything to gain and only imaginary dangers. The ship had up to that time traversed over 40,000 miles without accident.

But Waddell's plainspoken account of his behavior during the cruise concealed a train of vacillations, dissembling, and ill judgments that had, over the past eight months, unraveled shipboard morale on his now suddenly stateless vessel. In the days after the ship's encounter with the *Barracouta*, the captain's aloofness evaporated. In discussing their new situation with the ship's other officers—an exchange in which he showed far more solicitousness than he had in similar past encounters—Waddell finally acceded to what Charles Lining recalled as the "majority" view of the ship's officers: they would return to Australia. Recalling the dinners and balls of past months, they assumed that a friendlier reception would await them there than in other ports. Waddell's decision also comported with his own expressed view that the likely presence of Union gunboats in the North Atlantic rendered a return to Europe too dangerous. Thus, after bidding adieu to the *Barracouta*, Waddell ordered a course shaped for Sydney. There, he told several officers, they would surrender the *Shenandoah* to British or U.S. officials. Afterward, he and the other Confederates would find another ship and leave for England.

The captain retired that evening apparently content with his decision. But he soon had other plans. "During the night," Chew recorded, "he concluded not to go to Australia to abandon the ship there[,] throwing a lot of young officers on shore without money in a port thousands of miles from home, but to make his way to some other English port on the Atlantic side & the course was changed accordingly—as yet we do not know to what port he intends to go." And when Irvine Bulloch and Sidney Smith Lee, on August 3, implored the captain to re-embrace his original decision to take the ship to Sydney, Waddell told them that "he had made up his mind to go to Liverpool," telling the officers that "he would be -d-d- if he did not take her there." In truth, however, Waddell's professed steely resolve possessed a hollow core. Later that same day, he told Lining that "he was in honor bound to carry this ship into some Yankee port and there deliver her up." And, according to Lining, those weren't the only ideas considered by Waddell: "Another is that he will carry her into some English port & there deliver her to the Yankee Consul."[1]

Nervously summoning their courage, several officers soon presented Waddell with a petition asking him to clarify the *Shenandoah*'s final destination. In response, he chose to speak to the entire crew. To Waddell, the crisis demanded more than that the officers rally to his side, as they had done in similar impasses in Melbourne and on the Sea of Okhotsk. He also needed—as when he sought their support at Las Desertas—to rally the full complement of crewmen. And so, two full days after they had spoke the *Barracouta*, the captain went before the ship's officers and crew. At 1:00 on the afternoon of August 4, standing on the quarterdeck and looking down into the anxious young faces below him, Waddell began by thanking the men for their service and saying that he bore no resentment toward the officers for their petition, which by Midshipman John Mason's account, the captain noted, was appropriately "subordinate" in tone. Then, addressing himself specifically to the seamen, he told them that, as leaders facing difficult choices, he and the ship's officers faced a situation that "is far worst than that of any of you." Unlike the raider's seamen, Waddell and his commissioned officers, after all, could face thorny criminal charges when the cruise concluded—some punishable by long stretches in prison, some even by hanging.

Such future worries aside, Waddell continued, he and the other officers had made their decision. "I shall take the ship into the <u>nearest</u> English port and all I have to ask of you men, is to stand by me to the last," he said. "As for our cruise, it is a record which stands for itself & all you have to do is be proud of it."

Cries of, "We are," "We will be," and "We'll stand by you" greeted the oration. "The Captain's little speech [*sic*]," Mason later noted, "was delivered with much feeling & several of the officers & some of the men did in reality shed tears." Even so, undertones of Waddell's—and all of the officers'—suddenly odd standing with the men permeated the oration. The legitimacy of their command, after all, had vanished with the end of the Confederate state, which made the captain's closing caveat all the more odd: if Waddell and his officers later decided on a different course, all were expected to accept that new decision. As Lining recorded the oration, the captain said "that if he thought [it] proper to go elsewhere they [the crew] would continue to obey [Waddell's orders] as they had always done."

Despite its verve, a baffling vagueness attended Waddell's speech. For instance, when referring to the closest English port and his intention to sail for it, why did he not specify the name of that port? As Mason reflected the next day, "The minds of many of the men & officers are considerably exercised to know which is 'the nearest English port.'" After all, the steamer's officers knew how to read charts and logs, and knew that, by that day, August 5, their southern path had taken them to latitude 12°44' N, longitude 121°03' W—a position distant from both Australia and England, but on a course that suggested the latter, or perhaps the British port of Cape Town, as their destination. As Mason noted, "From the course we are steering, it is not probable that we will go to Australia. I think the Captain still intends to go to England, or he may go to Cape Town."

The day after Waddell's speech, the Confederates completed the task of stowing the raider's armaments and filling in her gunports. "In appearance our ship was a quiet merchantman, peacefully pursuing her way, with naught to apprehend from any vessel she might encounter on the high seas," master's mate Cornelius Hunt recalled. Or, as Midshipman Mason wryly put it, "Our old ship is now as harmless as a woman without finger nails or teeth."

Even so, the ship's new look could not stave off Mason's growing weariness of the tedium of life at sea:

> All day long you hear nothing but the old cry: "Royal clewlines!" "Flying jib downhaul or Royal sheets!" "Flying jib halliards!["] &c &c. I am horribly tired & sick of the sound of blocks & ropes; of being knocked about when lying or sitting, & when walking, it is always on an inclined plane which is continually changing its position . . . I never want to hear a Boatswain's whistle again; it is about the only <u>music</u> we have, except perhaps some wretched accordion, horribly performed on by some amateur artist; of all musical or rather discordant instruments, can any thing be more unmusical, more detestable than an accordion? I think the man who invented such an abortion should have been hung for murder in the first degree."

By Cornelius Hunt's lights, the romantic verve that had once animated the ship's decks, cabins, and wardroom had given way to anxious faces fearful of all encounters with other ships. "The lookouts, it was true, still mounted aloft, but it was not to scan the seas for ships that might be captured, but to maintain a faithful watch and ward over any suspicious sail that might make its appearance above the horizon."

The next day, August 6, a southwestern breeze arose and the Confederates raised the raider's propeller and collapsed her smokestack. It was the first Sunday of the month, but the Confederates dispensed with their usual muster. Ostensibly, the drill was canceled because of rain. But, then again, it would have been a dispirited exercise. Four days after their encounter with the *Barracouta*, no one on the ship—probably not even Waddell—knew for certain just where their captain planned to take them. In his journal entry that day, Francis Chew, echoing a common assumption, reported, "It is generally supposed that we are going to the Cape of Good Hope, from the fact that Cape Town offers more advantages for getting to Europe than any other port in the Atlantic." By contrast, midshipman John Mason feared that same prospect. "I should dislike exceedingly to be put ashore in Cape Town, for I would not have money enough to take the steamer to England; and sailing vessels rarely come there; one would not get away for months." In truth, however, none of the men knew where Waddell was taking them. As Chew put it, "As yet we do not know to what port he intends to go."

In the void left by a more concrete pronouncement from Waddell, rumors and speculation spread through the ship like a tropical fever. And with both came questions: Under international law, were the Confederates obligated to surrender their ship? Or would their captain be justified in taking her into a port and blowing her up? And, if they did surrender the *Shenandoah*, which would be the best port in which to give her up?

Proponents of particular approaches coalesced into camps, each with its own perspective on the law marshaled to advance their self-interests. Those, for instance, who favored blowing up the ship based their advocacy on the assumption that, though there had been an "annihilation" of the Confederacy, "no treaty of peace" had been signed. Yet another group argued that, even in the absence of a formal armistice, the Confederacy's destruction entailed that all property of the vanquished government now belonged to the United States. Thus the *Shenandoah* must be surrendered to U.S. authorities at the nearest U.S. port. Yet another group, one that included John Mason, advocated surrendering the ship, but at a third-party port, in England or perhaps France. There, he suggested, the ship, as "public property," could be surrendered to the national officials of whatever port they decided to land in, who would then adjudicate her ultimate fate. "But our persons not belonging to [any] government, we are not bound to surrender them."

To Mason, the captain's actions seemed increasingly perplexing: "Our captain's position is indeed a most difficult & embarrassing one, & I do not envy him, he has decided the matter on his own responsibility without calling any regular council." Even more acidly, the midshipman asserted, "It is a melancholy fact that our captain is not the firmest, or most decided man alive, for as I have just shown—he vascilates [*sic*], never being positive about any thing."

On August 17, the Confederates, sailing down the western meridian of 116°, crossed the equator for the third time in ten months. Finding their way that day through the South Pacific, toward Cape Horn, they dutifully noted the return of the Southern Cross and other familiar astronomical fixtures. "Again we are in the Southern Hemisphere, and its numerous stars are brightly lighting our weary way," Whittle noted. But the sense of adventure that had enlivened their outward voyage the previous year was long since exhausted. Adding to the men's despondency, complaints arose that Waddell, in his ongoing efforts not to attract attention to the steamer, had reverted to his perennial habit of sailing on short canvas, a practice that revived fresh expressions of an old criticism. "Merchant ships," Lining noted, "carry [more] sail, as compared with ourselves."

Indicative of shipboard morale, the growing despondency of Midshipman Mason, who had once fancied the *Shenandoah* as the commencement of a romantic life at sea, was becoming a bottomless well: "I must say that twelve months experience at sea has destroyed all the romance of a sailor's life for me; the constant confinement within the narrow limits of the ship; this total deprivation of the society of females, which has so softening an influence on all men; the many other privations, among which the miserable diet is not the least important. All these produce a sum total which can only be properly appreciated by those who have experienced them—What must this life, so unbearable to me, be to a common sailor, who has ten times the privations that an officer would have?"

Throughout the cruise, to distract them from their cares and to combat boredom, Mason and his fellow officers welcomed any and all diversions. Early on, chess had been a wardroom favorite. But by early summer, Lining recalled, "dumb bells & gymnastics have taken the place of chess" in that same room. In time "good hard, exercise" would give way to another diversion: "Hammocks are now all the rage." Finding a new use for the ship's ample supply of ropes and canvas, the sailors began stretching hammocks across all manner of spaces. And after the hammock craze had blown over would come yet another shipboard craze. "Sewing is now the mania on board," Lining observed. "If any enter our ward-room he might think himself in a tailor's shop. I counted five officers who were making pan-taloons, & I am engaged on a night-shirt."

Amid such obvious efforts by the officers to provide distractions from their problems, Francis Chew, for one, found himself grateful that the polyglot seamen who made up the rest of the crew had not yet resorted to mutiny. "The Government being overthrown, we proscribed, and entrance into foreign ports prohibited, one would suppose that insubordination & disrespect would manifest themselves, but nothing of the sort; the crew to a man felt great sympathy," he wrote in his journal. Chew's gratitude was reinforced by his awareness that those enlistees had shipped aboard the *Shenandoah* not out of any love for the Confederacy but for the "good pay" promised them. But all, Chew grimly noted, had since realized "that it is now idle to entertain any idea of getting their pay."

The men's sense of having burned, eaten, drunk, or worn out most of the ship's supplies reinforced the tedium. On August 19, two days after the ship crossed the equator for the third time, First Lieutenant Whittle noticed that the depletion of stores in the ship's holds had begun to deprive the *Shenandoah* of needed ballast. "Our ship is getting light and we have to watch her carefully," he wrote. "Having been out so long it stands to reason that her weight is greatly decreased." Unlike past periods, however, when the ship's officers had noted the depletion of their resources—everything from food to canvas— this time it was different: their withdrawal from commerce raiding meant that there would be no more prizes to replenish their supplies. Nor, given their situation, would they be putting into any other ports before reaching their final destination— wherever that turned out to be. Put more simply, though they could not know how long their cruise would take, it fell to the officers to make sure their limited supplies lasted until they reached its end.

Though stowing the ship's armaments had helped restore some of her trim and stability, as the crew went through coal and other provisions ballast continued to dwindle. And, as the steamer plowed through Cape Horn's treacherous waters, her officers became obsessed with restoring some of the lost weight. On August 22, John Mason noted that "the beef is being used & as fast as the barrels are emptied, they have to be put down in the ground tier & filled with salt water for ballast."

As anxieties and shortages grew more acute a festering incivility fell over the officer's mess: "Words pass at the Supper Table between Bulloch & Mason from some little arguments," Lining lamented. "How foolish these arguments are—they never convince any one, & so often lead to ill feelings." Lining's patients and their ailments reflected the mounting toll. The surgeon found himself treating Waddell for a stiff neck, and when the chloroform liniment he prescribed to the captain failed to remedy the soreness, Lining had him sit up all the next day, and came around that night with a hot toddy to help him sleep. When that also failed to solve the problem, Lining returned the third night with a still more potent medicine, "a strong punch to put him to sleep."[2]

As shipboard irritableness mounted, so did infractions of rules and regulations, ranging from drunkenness to tardiness for drills. While these violations tended to be small-caliber, Waddell's insistence on punishing each one widened the growing breach between him and the crew, and exposed his steadily diminishing authority. Indeed, the captain's increasingly uncertain sense of his command further widened that breach.

Three weeks after the Confederates' encounter with the *Barracouta*, Waddell learned that Lieutenant Dabney Scales had shown up late for quarters. But when Waddell summoned Scales to the captain's quarters he—implicitly acknowledging the *Shenandoah*'s tacit decommission as a military vessel—departed from standard naval procedure. As recounted by Lining, Waddell admitted that he "was only Master of the ship & therefore had no right to punish him." Instead, Waddell told Scales that henceforth he was relieved "of all duty" and should "consider himself as a passenger at large on board this vessel until he got into port."

Waddell's action only exacerbated the situation. "Not content [with] this to stir up the bees," Lining recorded, "he must go & kick over the hive, by doing the most impolitic thing he possibly could do by asking 'Blacker,' his clerk to keep the watch. Thereupon 'Hunt' refused to do duty under Bulloch with whom he was at dagger points, & he also was told to consider himself as a passenger!" Yet when Blacker heard about the row he, too, refused to take the watch, whereupon Waddell himself stepped in and took the turn on the deck.

These developments only sowed more discord and intrigue. "Great whispering going on all about, I can't go to talk to any one without stumbling upon a private confab. and withdraw to my room," Lining recalled. "The result of all the talking amounted to Bulloch's going to Waddell & offering to take the watch, as he did not think it looked well to see the Captain of a ship keeping watch when there was so many officers on board." As for Scales, relieved of duties and told to consider himself a mere passenger on the ship, he vowed to avoid any appearance of obligation to Waddell and determined to go into the ship's forward section and "pull off his coat & work with the men for his passage." The two men eventually resolved their differences, and Scales was restored to duty. "How, or why, I never asked,"

Lining commented. But the armistice came too late to repair ill feelings.

A similarly revelatory incident occurred seven days after Scales's initial infraction, when Lieutenant Whittle caught Smith Lee sneaking a smoke from his pipe during his morning watch. The men exchanged words, and Lee vowed that Whittle could not stop him from smoking. Informed of the incident, Captain Waddell called Lee to his quarters and demanded that he promise never to smoke on duty again. Long-standing naval tradition prohibited smoking while on duty. The rule had never formally applied to officers, but in recent days Waddell, resolving that officers should set an example for seamen, had extended it to the entire crew.

To Waddell's chagrin, however, Lee refused to make that promise. Thereupon the captain promptly stripped the young officer of his watch. That afternoon, Waddell summoned the other watch officers to his quarters. Recounting the action he had taken against Lee, Waddell said that, regretfully, all of them would have to take longer watches. But rather than simply nodding, the officers professed sympathy for Lee. Moreover, Grimball "spoke up" and told the captain that he did not think anyone had a right to demand such a promise—and that "he himself had smoked on watch & if he had been caught he expected to be punished for it, & when the punishment was over to be restored to duty." Scales then told the captain that he, too, had smoked on duty.

"The Captain" Lining recalled, "seemed thunderstruck & said that he had nothing more to say. Afterwards, he issued a formal order banning officers from smoking on their watches, or leaving the deck until regularly relieved." But, simultaneously eroding his authority even as he imposed new rules, Waddell also restored Lee to his watch. As Lining put it, "So ended the 'fencion,' in which like so many others the Captain has come out to leeward."

During most of August strong breezes had graced the *Shenandoah*'s South Pacific passage. But by early September the ship was still west of Cape Horn, in the doldrums, and averaging, as she did on September 3, as few as five miles a day on her southeastward course. Any day now, as they drew closer to Cape Horn, the men expected to find what Whittle called the "brave westerlys" that blow through that legendary domain of storms and ice. But, for now, the light variable winds that greeted them barely sufficed to counteract the strong northerly currents challenging their southeastern course.

The *Shenandoah*'s slow progress proved agonizing. It also gave the Confederates more time to ponder their general condition and to wonder if their weary sea legs would ever again step on dry land. It had been eleven months since the men left England and almost five months since they sailed from Ascension Island.

Adding to their frustration was the need to rely on canvas. Waddell, always eager to conserve coal, was now even more determined to preserve it as ballast, which the ship would need in its confrontation with Cape Horn's famous winds.

On September 6, the westerlies that torment Cape Horn mariners finally struck—and the Confederates made the most of them. "We have," Whittle noted, "carried all plain sail—unbent all our studding sails." Indeed, on that single day the *Shenandoah* logged 190 miles on her southeastern course. During the next few days, as the west winds grew in power, blowing the ship along at speeds reaching 15 knots, the Confederates continued to log impressive distances. On September 9 alone, they logged 262 miles, their best single run since commencing their voyage.

By the twelfth, they had made steady progress but still remained in the South Pacific. That afternoon the Confederates spotted a sail about ten miles off their lee beam. Like the *Shenandoah*, the English merchantman *West Australian* was sailing on an eastbound course around the Horn. She was the first ship the Confederates had seen since the *Barracouta* and, still in sight the next day, she raised English colors and signaled. But, Chew recalled, "we paid no attention to her signal, nor even showed a flag; for we have none and did not wish to make use of that of any nation." The Confederates, though hungry for fresh news, were desperate not to spread any about themselves. Still later that same day, the steamer silently passed three more sails, all bound to the west.

On September 14, the *Shenandoah* passed some fifty miles to the south of Diego Ramírez, a handful of naked rocks about sixty miles southwest of Cape Horn. The next day, though the skies remained clear, the Confederates felt a fresh motion in the air. "Beautifully clear weather, but blowing like scissors—with a heavy sea," Whittle noted. The *Shenandoah* was now sailing into a fresh gale rising from the north. "So the cape," Chew concluded, "would not let us pass without giving us a specimen of the heavy weather for which it is so famous."

During the next two days, gales, rain, and heavy seas slapped the *Shenandoah*. On September 16, the Confederates lay due south of the western edge of the Falkland Islands. As razor winds battered the ship with "unabated fury," Chew, checking his copy of Matthew Maury's 1855 *Physical Geography of the Sea*—a bible to that generation of navigators—noted that Cape Horn was "the most stormy quarter of the globe." Even so, he recorded, "the gale we now have, although very severe, is spoken of as 'Nothing' by the old 'Cape Horners' on board, some of whom have doubled the Cape ten or more times in all seasons of the year."

The winds having blown the cruiser east of her intended course, the following day the Confederates faced the challenge of finding a safe passage between the Shag Rocks and the Georgian Islands east of Cape Horn. Further complicating matters were the icebergs that soon began crowding the waters around them. Adding to their difficulties, Waddell complained, "We were without a moon to shed her cheerful light upon our desolate path and the wind was so fierce that the ship's speed could not be reduced below five knots per hour." With clouds obstructing navigational observations and formidable currents pulling the cruiser easterly, Waddell—concluding it imprudent to heave to—resolved to stay under sail and do his best to avoid collision with the floating islands of ice looming ahead.

During the day, as the cruiser threaded her way between the frozen towers, the Confederates crowded about her rails, gawking like tourists at the sublime spectacles. "Passing a large number of icebergs, entirely too thick to make navigation through them either safe or comfortable," Lining noted. "One that we passed was about 180 feet high & a little broader perhaps than it was high." The surgeon noted that, though barren, the iceberg seemed, like some miniature continent, to have its own self-contained landscape: "It has a cliff in it, extending nearly to the water's edge. The breakers dashed up against it to immense heights. It was a very strange sight." And when night fell the icebergs gained an even more mysterious aura, appearing to Waddell to be sprung from the imagination of a military architect: "Some of the icebergs were castellated and resembled fortifications with sentinels on guard."[3]

On September 22, the ship, having reached latitude 49°11' S, longitude 36°00' E, Lieutenant Whittle noted, "Smooth sea,

pleasant weather." Even better, the thermometer's mercury column now hovered in the mid-forties; "I trust we are out of all
ice." Clear of Cape Horn's storms and ice, the Confederates
now refocused their attentions on the still unresolved matter of
where they were bound. Almost two months earlier, Captain
Waddell had promised to deliver the *Shenandoah* "to the nearest English port." Many, if not most, of the men had interpreted that to mean Sydney. But the captain had instead sailed
southeastward, dropping through the Pacific and doubling
Cape Horn. And, in the ensuing days, he had done or said
nothing to clarify just where he was taking them.

Beyond that, he had compounded confusion with various
contradictory declarations. In exchanges with individual officers, Waddell had hinted variously that he might go to Cape
Town, or perhaps Liverpool, and surrender the ship to British
officials. He had even talked of going to another foreign, possibly French, port and surrendering to U.S. officials. Many crew
members equated that option with certain imprisonment and
even death. By late September, then, the sphinxlike vagueness
of Waddell's declaration to take them to the closest English port
was fueling ever more fervent conjecture and debate among the
crew. As the *Shenandoah* plowed steadily northeasterly, away
from Cape Horn, most of the ship's officers came to belong to
one of two competing schools of thought. As Lining put it,
"Those who wish to go to Cape Town or some other port in the
North Atlantic going in for Longitude, those who are for England for Latitude, & so we designate each other."

By September 27, the *Shenandoah* had reached latitude 43°14' S,
longitude 23°20' W, a position a few degrees south of Cape
Town. There, in the mid-Atlantic, a *Shenandoah* crewman, wa-
gering on either Liverpool or Cape Town, could still conjure

ample reasons to bet either way. But as the ship plowed steadily onward, one of those bets took increasingly worse odds. During the next few days the *Shenandoah*'s course would irrevocably eliminate one of those possibilities.

Bantering in the wardroom that evening, Lining, favoring Cape Town, sensed imminent triumph for his side. "Opinions as to where we ought to go running very high," he noted; even so, "still going on a good course for the Longitudes." But Lieutenant John Grimball—favoring Liverpool, a Latitude man—rejected any argument for Cape Town, declaring that "he would rather be Captured & kept in prison twenty years than go into Cape Town." Not to be outdone by Grimball's hyperbole, the engineer, Matthew O'Brien, a firm Cape Town man, asserted that if the captain did steer toward Liverpool he "hopes that we might be Captured if we go into the North Atlantic."

The next day, as a south wind swept the *Shenandoah* ever closer to Liverpool, the Longitudes resolved to make a final stand. That day and the next, a group of the steamer's senior officers—Francis Chew, Irvine Bulloch, Charles Lining, Matthew O'Brien, W. Breedlove Smith, and O. A. Browne—quietly met and drafted a petition asking Captain Waddell to reconsider his apparent decision to surrender the *Shenandoah* in Liverpool.

Determined to avoid any taint of mutiny, the officers couched their entreaty in deferential language: "In consideration of the present unparalleled state of affairs, we have taken the liberty of respectfully laying this communication before you, to convey to yourself the anxiety and regret with which we regard the prospect of a passage in this ship, under the altered circumstances in which she is placed, to a country so distant as England." So long as the men could claim a nation and government for which to fight, the petition stated, they had fought "cheerfully and with alacrity."

Now, we respectfully submit, all these motives for exertion are gone. Our country and Government have by the sad fortunes of war ceased to exist; our cruise, as such, has long since come to a conclusion; our battery and small arms struck below; we are entirely without means of defense—in point of fact, without even the right to defend ourselves if attacked—and are consequently at the mercy of any passing cruiser.

Any course they took, the officers argued, exposed the Confederates to capture, imprisonment, and possibly death. Even going to Cape Town required the *Shenandoah* "to run the gauntlet some 2,000 miles." But, "in going to England we would be exposed and the risks certainly doubled for about three times that distance." Those dangers, they added, were daily compounded by the ship's increasingly unsafe condition, which rendered her vulnerable "against the terrible weather we must expect in the North Atlantic and on the English coast. We see that she is already quite light, and would, if chased by a United States cruiser, hardly be able to carry on the requisite amount of canvas to enable us to escape." Closing their petition, the officers once again disclaimed "any intention or desire to trammel upon your judgement or interfere with your functions."

The officers delivered their petition to Waddell on September 28, and before the day's end the captain received yet another pro–Cape Town petition from ten of the ship's noncommissioned officers. To the earlier list of the dangers of going to Liverpool, this petition noted the ship's dwindling supply of coal. It also pointedly referred to Waddell's earlier vow to deliver them to the "<u>nearest</u> English port," and declared that the time had come to deliver on that promise. "We are now near one, viz, Cape Town, which for many reasons holds out more inducements than any other port to make us wish to be taken there."

Throughout the controversy, Midshipman Mason, who opposed going to Cape Town, insisted that the majority of the *Shenandoah*'s men, officers and seamen alike, welcomed the idea of going to England. Liverpool, in particular, was a familiar place, and with James Bulloch and other Confederate operatives there they stood a better chance of getting paid and of getting back home. Moreover, Mason regarded both petitions as barely veiled flirtations with mutiny. Neither, he noted, referred to the "C.S.S. Shenandoah" but to the "Steamship Shenandoah." And the signatories on both documents, dispensing with titles of rank, simply used their first and last names—"thus," Mason recalled, "seeming to assume a position of 'independence,' which is as mild an expression as I can use." By Mason's reading, the second petition, compared to the first, was even "less respectful & very dictatorial."

Making the case for Cape Town, the second petition noted that the African port was a stopover for homeward-bound ships of the East India Company and other merchant vessels bound for England. And, the petitioners noted, Cape Town lay but ten to fourteen days away from their current position, whereas England was about forty. In closing, the petition asked the captain, if he must insist on passing Cape Town and sailing to Liverpool, to at least sail close enough to the African coast to give those crewmen who wished to leave there the opportunity to land "at some one of the bays to the northward [of Cape Town], which we would infinitely prefer to the chances of capture or shipwreck."

Given Cape Town's distance from the far-flung homes of these sailors, the Longitude men's drastic request, which included no solicitation for funds to get them home, was tantamount to asking to be abandoned in what was, for them, a remote corner of the world—hardly an encouraging index for the state of shipboard morale.[4]

At 3:00 p.m. on the afternoon of the twenty-eighth, the senior officers on both sides of the debate gathered in the *Shenandoah*'s wardroom at Waddell's request. There the captain, leaning on his familiar tack, joined them for a "council of the Lts." According to Lieutenant Chew, Waddell began the meeting by telling the officers that he had earlier planned to take the ship to Cape Town. But recently, he told them, he had decided to take her "to Europe." Waddell declined to say which European port he had in mind, but most of the men in the wardroom assumed that he meant Liverpool. Even so, while ostensibly clarifying his intentions, the captain had once again clothed his declaration in a veil of ambiguity.

Then Waddell surprised the men. Though he had his own ideas about the best course for the ship, he said that he was willing to be "governed by the opinion of the council." He then left the wardroom, and for the next hour the five lieutenants— Whittle, Chew, Grimball, Lee, and Scales—read aloud the petitions and discussed, often angrily, their relative merits. The pro–Cape Town Chew smelled defeat for his side: "Before the discussion began we knew the vote would go in favor of Europe, from having had so many expressions of opinion. In private, however, the 1st Lieut. [Whittle] and myself strove hard for our course, but the other side stubbornly held on to their opinions."

The Latitudes defeated the Longitudes three to two. But the captain's council of lieutenants, as Francis Chew and William Whittle had suspected, turned out to be as much a stacked deck as a democracy. Recounting a conversation with Whittle that offered a vista on the Machiavellian machinations of their ostensibly open-minded captain, Lining wrote, "Besides knowing what officers did not sign the petition, Whittle told me that the Captain was the first person who told him what the opinion[s] of the different officers were." The council meeting, Whittle said, only confirmed Waddell's already accurate knowledge of how each of the men would vote, and not until he was certain of that knowledge had the captain proposed his latest exercise in shipboard democracy.

When the sun rose the next morning, the weeks of debate were over. Even so, wounded feelings among those who favored Cape Town persisted. "I am sorry to see how high party feeling runs, & I fear it may yet bring me some trouble," Lining wrote. Indeed, he had come to regret his entire participation in the affair.

Young Midshipman Mason, "a Liverpoolite to the backbone," confessed that his side was unable to resist a bit of gloating over its triumph over "the Cape Town crowd" and displayed "anything but a Christian spirit." Or, as his compatriot Lieutenant John Grimball put it, "We 'hogged' them after all." To further ratify their win, five pro-Liverpool officers—Grimball, Lee, Scales, McNulty, and Mason—soon sent Waddell their own "address," expressing "unqualified approbation" of his stated course. And, if that missive failed to buoy Waddell's spirits, by the day's end he had received a similarly laudatory letter from members of the ship's crew—this one bearing seventy-one signatures.

Two names, however, never appeared on any of the petitions and cross-petitions that circulated through the *Shenandoah* during those three days: those of Lieutenant Sidney Smith Lee and Executive Officer William C. Whittle, Jr. According to Mason, Lee, "always so cool" and regarded on the ship as an "oracle" for his keen legal judgment, personally favored going to Cape Town. But out of loyalty to Waddell, who often consulted with him on legal matters, Lee not only refused to sign any petitions but also lobbied hard for the captain's position.

Similarly, and again according to Mason, Whittle also favored going to Cape Town. But, like Lee, he steadfastly avoided activity subversive of the ship's chain of command. "Papers, petitions, &c &c are not my fort[e]," he confided to his journal. "As Executive officer I will have nothing [to] do with them." Nonetheless, Whittle did have strong feelings about those who challenged Waddell's intention. "There is a feeling approaching a panic among them which I consider very disgraceful," he noted. "A large majority of the officers are vehemently opposed to running the unnecessary risk of going to England. All are in favor of going to Cape Town." As for his own feeling toward Waddell's plans, Whittle noted, "He has my support in anything except one, & that would be any attempt to go to a Yankee port."

By the end of the imbroglio, Francis Chew had concluded that Waddell was less Machiavelli, more Hamlet: "I see now why the capt. did not wish to let his destination be known while we were in the Pacific; he did not know himself." Surgeon Charles Lining, meanwhile, concluded that, at least partially, a lust for historical posterity animated Waddell's insistence on sailing all the way back to England. "He wanted it said that this ship had gone around the World, & that she was the only Confederate vessel that ever did it."[5]

———

On the evening of September 29, the *Shenandoah*'s northern course through the mid-Atlantic crossed the path of her outbound track the previous November. "Last night we completed the circumnavigation of the globe," Chew noted, marking the moment. "It was about 10 p.m. that our ship occupied the same position that she did last year." Whittle wrote, "In that time we have travelled over 45,000 statute miles of water; we have been around the world—the first to carry our downtrodden flag around."

But a moment that by all rights should have been cause for celebration did little to dispel the Confederates' painful circumstances. "We have done our work nobly, and honorably," Whittle recorded, but "in the eyes of our prejudiced enemies" the men were "placed in the same category with Captain Kidd."

More immediate problems, however, were at hand. That night, as the *Shenandoah* approached the previous year's position in the mid-Atlantic, Captain Waddell dispatched a bottle of champagne to the wardroom, along with a congratulatory note. Right away, a toast was raised to the captain's health. But, as Lining recalled, the mess had already divided into "cliques." Of the five Cape Town men present at the table, three walked out; only Chew and Lining, among their numbers, remained. "I thought this public display was in exceedingly bad taste & showed rather a contemptible spirit," Mason recalled, "for the Captain I am sure was actuated by the best motives, having saved this bottle for the occasion, little dreaming what unpleasant circumstances would attend the event." Though Lining also had favored Cape Town, he nonetheless regretted the display of contempt: "I do think a point might have been strained under the circumstances, as I think it was kindly & politely meant."

Further evidence of the ill feelings permeating the ship, a rumor soon circulated that accused master's mate Cornelius Hunt of squirreling away several hundred dollars taken from one of the prizes. Hunt, though a Liverpool partisan, had nonetheless become hostile toward the man whom he later called the "ungentlemanly" Waddell. The story, Lining and others believed, had originated with master's mate John F. Minor, likewise a Liverpool man but also a confidant of Captain Waddell. Upon learning of the rumor, Hunt asked Lieutenant Whittle to investigate its veracity and origins. Whittle's subsequent investigation exonerated Hunt but failed to ascertain the rumor's origins. Lining's diary entry on the incident, however, perfectly captures its larger context and ramifications. It was, the surgeon wrote, "another wretched scandal flying around [the] ship."[6]

NINETEEN

"A Perfect Hell Afloat"

By early October 1865, now retracing the North Atlantic tracks of her outward voyage a year earlier, the *Shenandoah* was finding her way back to England. As the Confederates plowed ever northward—each day standing on the steamer's deck anxiously scanning the horizon for any signs of a man-of-war—they lived in fear of the consequences of any such encounter.

Indeed, with each passing day the *Shenandoah*'s world was growing ever more constricted—perpetually shrinking in food and fuel, geography and time. The Confederates thus had ample reasons to fear the worst. In the case of British warships, however, the more draconian of their worries had less basis in reality than they realized. A month earlier, belatedly responding to official U.S. outrage over the steamer's post-Appomattox raiding, Her Majesty's government, on September 17, had issued a circular to her officials around the world, instructing them, if the *Shenandoah* arrived in any British harbor, to immediately seize the ship.

More recently, on October 6, orders had been issued to the commanders of the Queen's vast and far-flung fleet of warships, telling them to keep an eye out for the *Shenandoah*. But that order also explicitly stated that the steamer should only be detained if "she be found to be sailing as a vessel of war," vindicating Waddell's stowing of the ship's armaments in early August. And neither set of British orders—those to port officials or to men-of-war commanders—called for detaining the raider's crew. The orders to Her Majesty's warships, in fact, explicitly stated that if the *Shenandoah* was detained, the ship itself should be turned over to the U.S. Navy. However, her "crew—including officers—should not be given up to the United States authorities, but allowed to go free."

Of course, that October of 1865 as they sailed through the Atlantic Ocean, the officers and crew of the *Shenandoah* knew nothing of such official letters passing aboard far-flung ships to other ships and harbors around the world. On the fourth, once again crossing the Tropic of Capricorn, the Confederates had marked their reentry into the tropics, a transit that, as they soon discovered, also inaugurated a debilitating period for them. As the Confederates glided along on their northeasterly course, waiting for the freshening southeast trades to hasten their passage, they endured the uncomfortably warm temperatures they had expected in these climes. But they also confronted an unexpected throat-parching drought.

As temperatures soared to 110° on deck and even hotter below, the drought gave new impetus to Waddell's ongoing anxieties about the ship's perilously low supply of fresh water. In days past, the captain might have used the steam engine to condense seawater into potable water for the men. But with coal in short supply for both ballast and fuel, that option had scant appeal. As Waddell ordered water rations reduced, the men, hoping for rain, soon placed pots, vases, and all other available containers on the ship's deck.

The reduction in water rations proved punishing. Even

officers were allocated no water for washing. For the seamen aboard the ship, the drought constituted a far worse hardship. "The men, who work about decks all day, feel this more than the officers by far," Midshipman John Mason had to admit. "They have no coffee in the morning watch, another privation, [though] they get grog three times a day which is a kind of substitute for water."

Underscoring the dwindling of supplies, several cases of scurvy broke out. According to Mason, the cases were "not serious," though the young sailor confessed, "I have a wholesome terror of the horrible disease, indeed much more than I expected."

As the *Shenandoah* headed back to England from her global circumnavigation, the ship's officers indulged a heightened self-consciousness about that achievement and a newfound fascination with nautical maps. As Surgeon Lining put it, "Chart making mania now on the Tapis." The men created the charts by consulting their various copies of the ship's log. Early on, after all, Waddell had instructed each of the commissioned officers to maintain during the cruise his own copy of the ship's deck log. Not that chartmaking had no competition in its claims on the men's attention—far from it. In inspiring sheer exuberance among the men, no nautical event could compete with the dance spectacles that took place with increasing frequency.

One evening, Lining recalled, the Confederates "had three of the Kanakas to sing and dance for us, some of the songs were very sweet, but the dancing was excellent." Two evenings later, he recalled, the crew, aided by a little liquid encouragement, were ready to try out some of their own steps. "At night, 'Lee' got all the dancers among the men by the main hatch & by a little whiskey set them dancing until after nine o'clock."

Typically, on U.S. and Confederate naval ships, the absence

of female partners would be solved by some of the men affixing aprons or handkerchiefs around their waists to indicate their role as the designated "ladies" for that dance. The attendant efforts of the men so adorned to move with ladylike grace and speak in high voices only prodded more guffaws from spectators on the sidelines.

On October 9 and 11, the Confederates marked two milestones in their voyage: the first anniversary of their sailing from Liverpool aboard the *Laurel,* and their fourth crossing of the equator, respectively. But whatever inclination the crew felt to celebrate, both events were overshadowed by the worsening conditions aboard the ship. For, as the officers slowly realized, the *Shenandoah,* and most especially her hull, had not escaped from her polar adventures unscathed. Specifically, the copper sheathing that protected the ship's bottom had been torn or rubbed off in many places, thus exposing the teak planking beneath it to barnacles and sea grass, which slowed the ship's movement. "We do not sail near as well as we would have done with a smooth bottom & proper trim," Mason wrote. "Our copper was much rumpled amongst the ice in the Arctic & Okhotsk seas & we are by no means in good trim."[1]

Far more distracting, if not outright ominous, on October 9, the day the Confederates marked their year afloat, Lining diagnosed the *Shenandoah*'s third and most recent case of scurvy. Moreover, given their water shortage and the fact that, since leaving the Arctic, the crew's diet had increasingly consisted exclusively of salted beef and pork, with no vegetables or fruit, the doctor felt powerless to combat the disease. "I hope that [it] will not spread too much" was the most optimistic prognosis he could offer.

Concurrent with the scurvy cases, shipboard tempers flared with increasing frequency. As Lining soon complained, "Our ship is fast become a perfect Hell afloat, & only wants a few more quarrels in the ward room to become entirely so." Indeed, on the same day that Lining diagnosed the Confederates' third scurvy case, the ship's assistant surgeon Fred J. McNulty and Captain Waddell's clerk John Blacker got into a row.

Things became serious after McNulty, an Irish Catholic, called Blacker, an Irish Protestant, "an English-Irish Orangeman." Allegedly, McNulty had been drunk, and Lieutenant Whittle claimed that by the time he intervened to stop the fight McNulty was brandishing a pistol. Upon learning of the disturbance, Captain Waddell sent McNulty to his cabin, with orders to stay there until further notice.

The following morning, however, in a conversation in Waddell's stateroom, McNulty insisted that he had not been drunk during the confrontation. Indeed, he said, any intemperate language on his part had been prompted by Blacker's own "abusive language"—about the captain. What was more, McNulty insisted that, far from brandishing the pistol confiscated during the contretemps, he had merely taken the weapon out to show and, presumably, to surrender to Whittle.

Waddell ordered McNulty released from confinement. Whittle complied with the order but was hardly done with the matter. He immediately sought out two witnesses who could corroborate his own account of the incident. Moreover, one of those witnesses told Whittle that it was McNulty, not Blacker, who had used language critical of the captain. Then and there, Whittle recalled, he resolved that his future orders must be accorded more respect by Captain Waddell. "I made up my mind that my reports should not be so treated or considered—for his [McNulty's] every ground was false."

Immediately, Whittle summoned McNulty, and with Lieutenant Dabney Scales—one of Whittle's two witnesses, present— "I asked him if he intended to deny my report." But even in the presence of Scales and Whittle, McNulty insisted on the version of events he had given Waddell that morning. As Whittle recalled, the assistant surgeon answered, "All I say, sir, is that I was not drunk."

Pressed, McNulty did acknowledge that he had been "intoxicated" during the fight. But he stood by his claim that he had pulled out his pistol only to show it to Whittle. As Whittle grew increasingly exasperated, McNulty had a suggestion. "Well, sir," he said, "when we get on shore, there is a way to settle this thing."

The proposal, Whittle recalled, stunned him. But, without hesitation, he recounted, "I said yes, and that at any time or place I would be ready to do so."

The following day, October 12, Lieutenant Smith Lee, conscripted as McNulty's second, delivered a letter to Whittle. McNulty, formalizing his challenge, demanded that the first lieutenant retract his accusation that the assistant surgeon had lied in his original report to the captain. Failing that, McNulty concluded, "Such other satisfaction as is looked for between gentlemen is expected at your earliest convenience."

Waddell, who still limped from a youthful duel, left no record of his own thoughts concerning the prospects of *une affaire d'honneur* on *his* ship, between *his* executive officer and the perennial reprobate McNulty. Whittle, however, did, and in it he expressed an explicit disapproval of the practice. Nonetheless, he also believed that he could hardly retract his accusations. More to the point, he longed for a quick way out of this quandary. Dabney Scales, as a witness to the original Blacker-McNulty exchange, was by now uncomfortably enmeshed in the nasty affair. So Whittle asked him if he could imagine any way that the two men could settle the issue on the ship. When Scales answered no, Whittle then asked his own designated second, Surgeon Charles Lining, to confer with Smith Lee on the matter. After Lining and Lee agreed that no duel could take place on the ship, Whittle, still later that day, wrote, and sent via Lining, his own letter to McNulty.

In his letter Whittle declined to retract his offending language and reaffirmed his acceptance of McNulty's challenge. But he closed by asserting that any resolution of the matter would, by necessity, have to be postponed: "As the ship is not a place where such things can be settled, as soon as we get ashore, full satisfaction will be given you." No record exists of the two men's ever consummating their duel, and the odds are that they never did. But though ostensibly buried with courtly aplomb, the dispute between the two men had only created more ill will and tensions aboard a ship already afflicted with scurvy and shortages of water, food, and fuel, with crew morale as battered as the copper sheet that once protected the ship's wooden hull.

In early October, the *Shenandoah* had breezed along on the northeast trade winds. On October 11, she had, for the last time, crossed the equator. Still later that day, the Confederates found themselves within a half mile of a southwest-bound sailing ship. One of the *Shenandoah*'s officers, drawing on his days on other ships, deduced that the bark was a merchantman on an England–Bombay run. Upon spotting the *Shenandoah*, the bark began heading straight toward the cruiser, apparently intending to speak the Confederates.

Indeed, it came so close that the men of the *Shenandoah* were able to revel in the sight of two women passengers standing on her decks—the first females they had seen in months. But as the bark came closer, apparently making preparations to signal the Confederates, Captain Waddell gave orders to maintain all speed with no course change. "The captain does not intend to communicate with any vessel," Chew complained. However prudent the captain's reticence under the circumstances, many of the *Shenandoah*'s officers regretted his precaution—if only for the missed opportunity to bring themselves up-to-date on currents events. "I dare say," Lining lamented, those on the passing bark must have left "thinking us a very ill-mannered set of beings. I only wish I knew all the news that she ought to have on board."

Two days later, the Confederates, ever longing for fresh water, had cause for exaltation when gathering clouds suddenly burst in an afternoon shower. Within minutes, raincoat-clad officers and seamen crowded the *Shenandoah*'s decks, each man running toward the various casks, pots, and other vessels that they had put in place for just this sort of downpour. "What a change in the circumstances about decks," Chew commented. "For once Jack had enough water to wash down [his] salt horse." The following morning—at 2:00 a.m., October 14—an even heavier downpour lashed the ship's decks. Lieutenant John Grimball, who had the mid-watch that morning, began waking the rest of the crew "by making," Lining recalled, "the biggest row on deck that was ever heard & swearing worse than the army in flanders."[2]

As the washed and rehydrated Confederates, meanwhile, made their way higher and higher into the North Atlantic, the frequency of their sightings of other ships increased. On October 14, having reached a position of latitude 6°07' N, longitude 24°36' W, the Confederates had arrived at a crossroads of east–west and north–south shipping lanes. Whittle spotted so much canvas that afternoon that he couldn't help wistfully re-calling bolder days. "A great many sails in sight," he noted. "If we were as we used to be, we would have been running every which way to catch a prize."

On October 24, Lieutenant Francis Chew, spreading a chart be-fore him, found the *Shenandoah*'s current position: latitude 29°16' N, longitude 35°06' W. Then, running a finger across the map, he found Cape Clear, a renowned landmark on Ire-land's far southwestern coast. By now it had become clear to all on board that Captain Waddell intended to steam toward Cape Clear, thence into St. George's Channel, the strait linking the Atlantic Ocean to the Irish Sea, and, finally, to Liverpool.

For the steamer's sea-weary crew, the countdown of miles until their return to England was well under way, and estimat-ing the sailing time to Cape Clear had become a shipboard pastime. The *Shenandoah* had done some good sailing during the past few days, covering about, or even exceeding, two hun-dred miles every twenty-four hours. Even so, as the steamer approached the 30° Parallel, Lieutenant Chew noted that the strong northeast trade winds of the past few days seemed to be dying. Taking all factors into consideration, he estimated that Cape Clear lay only 1,920 miles distant—"12 days more!"

The next day, October 25, as the *Shenandoah*'s northern course reached latitude 31° N, longitude 35° W—a position parallel with the commencement point of her cruise at Las Desertas—a growing nervousness greeted each sighting of other ships. "If a Federal cruiser was to be found anywhere she would be in that region of ocean," Waddell recalled. Thus, at about 4:00 that afternoon, a cry of "Sail ho!" immediately brought a gaggle of officers to the ship's rail. "Glasses swept the northern horizon in search of the sail, but she was visible only from aloft."

When the lookout first alerted the Confederates to the presence of a westbound ship off the *Shenandoah*'s port bow, she remained too distant for him to make out her rigging. But by the time Waddell sent a second lookout aloft, the Confederates' distance from the vessel, he recalled, had narrowed; she seemed to have shifted to a tack that was headed straight toward the Confederates. "From the spread of her canvas and masts she looked like a steamer . . . she was standing a little more to the east of north than the Shenandoah was heading."

Waddell faced a dilemma: this mystery vessel might be a U.S. Navy man-of-war. And, if so, the present course of the two ships would in due time leave the *Shenandoah* vulnerable to the approaching ship's guns. But if the approaching ship was indeed a Federal cruiser, certainly she had already spotted the vessel to her south and was now studying this unknown ship's sails and rigging, and pondering whether she might be the infamous *Shenandoah*. Thus, while Waddell's first impulse might have been to change direction and speed away to elude the approaching ship, such a precipitous move entailed yet another risk. "We could make no change in the course of the ship or the quantity of sail she carried, for to arouse the suspicions of the sail might expose the Shenandoah to investigation. Whatever she was she had seen our ship and might be waiting to speak her."

Ultimately, Waddell kept the *Shenandoah* on her present course, hoping that darkness would fall over the North Atlantic before she came too close to the approaching ship. Once night fell, the Confederates could raise steam, furl their sails, and put a safer distance between themselves and the other ship.

In the meantime, lest a chase ensue, Waddell ordered the

men to be prepared to raise steam, before nightfall if necessary. And, to slow their progress toward the other ship, he immediately ordered the *Shenandoah*'s propeller lowered into the water to create drag. But otherwise he made it clear that, for now, they should do nothing to visibly alter the steamer's appearance or course. "The situation was one of intense suspense, for our security, if any remained, depended on a strict adherence to the course we were pursuing," Waddell recalled. "Any deviation from that would probably be noticed from the sail. We could not reduce sail to lessen her progress through the water."

The tension increased as the two ships drew closer, and a *Shenandoah* lookout reported that the mystery vessel was indeed a steamer—thus convincing almost the entire crew that she was a man-of-war. When darkness finally fell, the two ships were but three miles apart. Only then did Waddell order the *Shenandoah*'s prow turned to an eastward course—all lights doused, more sails furled, and steam raised. As the Confederates headed eastward, their passage concealed by the night and the white smoke from the coal they had received in Melbourne from the *John Fraser*, Waddell delighted in the ship's performance: "We had all the advantages to be expected." It was the first time since the Confederates had crossed the equator in the Pacific—a distance of more than 13,000 miles—that they had used the steam engine.

The *Shenandoah* continued eastward for another fifteen miles. Then, that night and well into the following morning, she steamed north for one hundred miles. At which time the raider lay within seven hundred miles of Liverpool, other sails dotted the Confederates' horizon. But, to Waddell's relief, all of them lay at a safe distance from the steamer—and, more important, there was no sign of the ship they had seen the previous day, a vessel that everyone assumed had been a man-of-war.

Having braved the past twelve months, the *Shenandoah*'s men should have enjoyed an easy confidence in completing the cruise's final days. But as the Confederates approached Cape Clear another, darker drama was playing out on board the cruiser. The health of several crewmen was failing. On October 24, the same day that Chew estimated the ever dwindling number of miles to Cape Clear, Midshipman John T. Mason grimly reflected in his journal, "I hope they may all live until we get into port." Noting for the record that he was "not at all superstitious," he nevertheless wrote, "I should like to see the cruise finishing without our losing a man." Like soldiers, who as their tour of duty draws to its close become ever more fearful of death, so the Confederates were increasingly put on edge by the plight of their ailing shipmates.

Several crewmen were ill, two of them gravely: Sergeant George Canning, a Southern-born member of the ship's Marines; and a seaman known as William Bill, from the Sandwich Islands. Of the two, Canning had been ailing the longest. Accompanied by his black servant and slave, Edward Weeks, Canning had shipped with the Confederates the previous January as the *Shenandoah* lay docked at Sandridge outside Melbourne. He fell ill, however, even before the Confederates reached the Arctic. Indeed—convinced that he had a better chance of surviving a trans-Siberian journey than the duration of the *Shenandoah*'s voyage—Canning had requested that he be put ashore on Kamchatka while the raider was in the Sea of Okhotsk. Captain Waddell declined the request, and for most of Canning's term on the *Shenandoah* he had been bedridden in his cabin.

Despite his invalidities, Canning had become, if not a popular crew member, certainly one of the most provocative. More to the point, he became an enigma: Canning claimed to have been an aide-de-camp to the Reverend Major General Leonidas Polk; and that he had been mustered out of the Confederate army after being wounded at the Battle of Shiloh. Beyond that, he seemed deliberately vague about his war record—as he was about his birthplace, his family, and his friends. Even Edward Weeks, Canning's servant, was something of a mystery. Presumably a slave in the South for most of his life, he had gained his freedom by setting foot in Australia, in the British Empire. Yet somehow, for reasons now lost to us, he had remained with Canning.

Since October 24, as Canning's condition worsened, Surgeon Lining had acceded to his patient's request to be allowed to sleep on the ship's deck. Concluding that it was "better to let him sleep on deck, than let him fret himself to death down in his bed," Lining arranged to have a canvas cot stretched beneath one of the whaleboats suspended on the ship's deck.

As the *Shenandoah*'s men passed by Canning each day, few gave him more than days to live. But, as it turned out, he was not the first crew member to meet his maker. The Sandwich islander William Bill, who breathed his last on October 26, would claim that sad distinction. Called that afternoon to examine the seaman's body shortly after his death, Lining took solace in the fact that those who were at William Bill's side at the end said he had died peacefully. "Poor fellow!" Lining later lamented. "He had been suffering Venerial [*sic*] for a long time & was covered with ulcers, all about the throat & chest. It must have attacked his internal organs as well."

Preparatory to a burial at sea the following day, Bill's body, along with two eight-inch shell casings to weight it down, was sewn up tightly inside the sheet of canvas that had served as his cot. Typically, for burials at sea, the deceased was sewn up by the ship's sailmaker in the canvas that had been his hammock, with the final stitch, by established tradition as a final check that he was indeed dead, going through the corpse's nose.

That night, covered with a Confederate flag, the canvas-enshrouded corpse of the Sandwich Islander lay in state atop a plank on the lee side of the *Shenandoah*'s poop deck. Completing the scene, shifts of honor guards stood watch over the body through the night.

The Confederates held the funeral service for the Maui-born sailor on the ship's poop deck rather than on the main deck, the customary setting for such services, in deference to Sergeant Canning, who remained in his cot on the main deck. Anxious to avoid upsetting the ailing Canning, the *Shenandoah*'s officers did their best to keep him from learning of Bill's death. The poop deck not being visible from Canning's cot, it seemed the natural place for the service.

At 9:30 that morning just after quarters, Captain Waddell read some biblical verses. Then, Chew recalled, "the end of the plank was lifted and the body went down into its watery grave; a mournful splash, a few bubbles and ripples on the water and he disappeared forever."

Despite the efforts of those who officiated, the service left Surgeon Lining singularly unimpressed. In retrospect, he believed, the decision to hold the funeral on the poop deck—aft but about ten feet above the surrounding water—to hide it from Sergeant Canning had exacted, literally, a steep price in ceremonial decorum: "It was very badly managed, I think, as the body was thrown into the sea from the 'poop.'"

The Confederates had hoped to prolong Sergeant George Canning's life by concealing from him William Bill's death. And on October 28, the day after Bill's funeral, Canning did indeed seem to feel a little better. Two days later, however, he, too, was dead, having expired at 5:45 p.m. on October 30. With his servant, Edward Weeks, beside him and Lining holding his wrist, the patient quietly passed away. "He died very easily, had been conscious but a few moments before, & even recognized & attempted to speak to me after I came down," Lining recalled. "He only gave four or five gasps & all was over. His disease was 'Phthisis,' brought on by a gun shot wound through the right lung, which, he said, was received at the battle of 'Shiloh' while he was serving on Genl Polk's staff."

Canning's burial at sea occurred the following day. But this time—with the ship's crew now somewhat familiar with the drill, and not obliged to hold the rite on the poop deck—the ceremony came off without a hitch. Because Canning had been a Roman Catholic, the service was read by his co-religionist, Assistant Surgeon Fred J. McNulty. Afterward, the body was slid, with requisite pomp, off its plank, over the rail of the main deck, into the briny deep.

In the days and hours after Canning's death, most of the men spoke well of the dead. Even so, the solemnity of death did not quiet the ship's discords. Lieutenant Whittle's estimation of Canning's character burned with particular heat. He found the late sergeant's treatment of Edward Weeks damning. "The poor old negro [Weeks] who waited on him, was by him terribly abused and he cursed him most terribly up to the very last," Whittle wrote. "Oh! it is a terrible sight when you see a man die, who up to the last breath is a sinner." Similarly, Lining concluded, Canning "was an ungrateful man, never thinking that any one did him a favor by doing any thing for him, but rather that all things should be done for him, no matter what it might cost others."

Mostly, however, Canning had departed an enduring puzzle. "There is something in the history of this man that none of us knows," Lining reflected. Supposedly, he had had a Southern-born wife. And after Shiloh he had emigrated to England, and then to Australia, where he came aboard the *Shenandoah*. But beyond those events, to say nothing of their veracity, none of the crew could claim to know much more about Canning. He had, Lining wrote, a "great reticence on all subjects that related to his past life."

Midshipman John Mason had been as close as anyone to Canning. Two months before Canning died, he asked Mason—should he not live to see the *Shenandoah* reach her final port—to pack up his journal and other belongings and send them to an address that Mason would find in a notebook of his. But only about ten days before his death did the Confederate Marine sergeant get around to writing in that book, and, as it turned out, he stopped before completing the promised address.

In the days after Canning's death, Mason, hoping to find a lead to go on, began going through the deceased sailor's personal effects. But that, too, yielded no avenues. "Upon examining his journal, papers &c. I find nothing that gives any clue to his family & friends or their whereabouts," Mason recorded. Upon recalling that Canning once alluded to his wife's living in Paris's Saint Germain neighborhood, Mason made a resolution: a Francophile anyway, he determined that, once his seafaring days had ended, he would see for himself if the streets and wide sidewalks of Paris revealed the answer to *l'énigme* of the late Sergeant George Canning, CSMC—and, if they did, to return his friend's journal to Mrs. Canning. In the meantime, one of the last—probably the very last—men to die in service to the Confederate cause had ended his days, much as he lived them, as an unknown soldier.[3]

By November 1, the *Shenandoah* lay within a thousand miles of Liverpool, her final destination. Having reached a position west of France in the Atlantic Ocean, at latitude 46°16' N, longitude 22°04' W, the Confederates were now headed northward toward Ireland's Cape Clear. But, as the ship's officers began counting down the days to their final port, the mood on board became anything but jubilant. A nervousness reinforced by fresh memories of the two recent shipboard deaths took hold.

Since August, the Confederacy's defeat had cast a pall over the ship. But now, as the officers carefully marked off on their charts and logs the cruise's final degrees and minutes, they seemed unnerved by every shift in the weather, every ship that passed them—in short by every occurrence, regardless of how banal, that might by any stretch of the imagination be interpreted as a harbinger of dark tidings.

Captain Waddell seemed particularly ill at ease. For as long as anyone could remember, it had been a quarterdeck pastime, when the captain was out of earshot, for the ship's younger officers to criticize him for what they considered the endemic timidity of his handling of the vessel. At the first sign of a freshening or shifting wind, they complained, Waddell immediately gave orders to reduce sails. For the past few days, however, that tendency had seemed all the more pronounced. As they drew closer to port, the captain seemed all the more compelled to slow their homeward progress. As Francis Chew, on November 1, complained, "Of late the captain's timidity in carrying sails is more marked than ever, he fears that every squall will capsize the ship."

A similar nervousness also coursed through Waddell's executive officer. "Some how or other I look forward to our safe arrival in an English port with very little hope," Whittle lamented on November 1. "I feel somehow or other as tho' some great calamity was hanging over me—why, I can't divine—or what I can't imagine, as it really seems to me that our cup of grief is already full." The next day, Whittle painted his doubts in even darker colors. "We are," he wrote, "men with something awful hanging over us."

Spirits lifted later on that afternoon, November 2, as the *Shenandoah*, now 400 miles south of Cape Clear and facing baffling northeast winds, began steaming once again. By noon the next day, the Confederates had covered 164 miles during the past twenty-four hours and were just 280 miles from Cape Clear, a distance that was reduced to 210 miles in the next eight hours. Now mere days from Liverpool, the ship's paymaster began settling accounts with officers and crew. Overseeing that process, Waddell, Whittle, and the ship's paymaster, Breedlove Smith, knew that they faced a dispiriting task. To pay in full what was owed to all of the ship's officers and men would require $30,000. But after adding up their depleted treasury and deducting the likely cost of the pilot who would be needed to guide them into Liverpool's port, the ship's funds came to but $4,000. In the end, though the men were eventually paid in British and American coin, a decision was reached to pay each man $1 for every $7.10 owed him.

By that discount, ordinary seamen concluded the cruise with paltry sums; William Temple recalled receiving £5. Lieutenant Whittle received $45.90 for the total $326 due him. Similarly, Surgeon Charles Lining, who was due $547.19, received only $77.06. After being paid, Lining made some bleak calculations to determine how the discount had affected his prorated daily pay. "If I had to stay aboard much longer I would get still less," he recorded. "It reverses the old saying of more days more money, for now it is more days less money."

By nightfall the following day, November 3, the *Shenandoah* was approaching Cape Clear, on Ireland's southeastern coast, toward which the Confederates had originally set a direct course. But rather than steaming close enough to spot the famous cast-iron lighthouse on the tiny island of Fastnet in those waters, Captain Waddell had now shaped a course straight into St. George's Channel toward Liverpool. That evening and following early morning the Confederates sprinted an impressive 207 miles, and when the sun rose on the fourth they gazed from their port bow on the Irish coast—their first landfall since passing by the Aleutian Islands 122 days and 23,000 miles earlier. Sweetening the moment was a prideful confirmation of their navigational prowess. "We could not have made a more beautiful land fall," Waddell recalled. "The beacon in St. George's Channel was where and at the time looked for." As the steamer edged closer to the ports of the British Isles, her course soon teemed with other ships, still a source of anxiety for the Confederates. In this case, however, they found that at least one of those passing vessels, a passenger ship, offered a sight that ameliorated some of those concerns: her deck offered the welcome sight of various ladies. As Lining recalled, the "first petticoats I have seen for many a day."

But even petticoats and the Confederates' satisfaction at entering St. George's Channel could not dispel their growing worries. Though mere hours lay between them and Liverpool, anxieties about their fate continued to multiply with each of those passing hours. They did, however, find some consolation in their belief that, by entering St. George's Channel, they had eluded at least one possible calamity. As Whittle put it, "Unless a gross violation of neutral waters be submitted to, we will be safe from capture even if we were to fall in with an American man-of-war." Though uncertain of his legal scholarship, Whittle assumed that because England and Ireland shared a common government, the entire Irish Sea that lay between them constituted British waters. This seemed, by his lights, sound theory. "But I would rather not have the experiment tried."

On November 5, the day that the Confederates entered St. George's Channel, Paymaster Breedlove Smith paid off the ship's seamen. Of those payments, discounted by the same terms as those for the officers' pay, Lining, straining credulity, recalled that "none seem dissatisfied, except some, who were drunk." Waddell, addressing the entire crew, promised that upon reaching Liverpool he would try to obtain more money for them. But Lining's own journal entry goes on to suggest that perhaps he had overstated the sailors' alleged complacency about their reduced compensation: "This evening I hear that there is a report that they intend to˙come aft this evening & see if they cannot get some to make up their one—but all this is bosh! the men are too near England[,] if nothing else to attempt such a thing—besides they know the officers too well to attempt it."

Doing their best to stave off worries of an eleventh-hour mutiny, both officers and men were kept busy packing their various belongings. In addition to his own possessions, John Mason took special care to pack the late George Canning's journal and other items, which he had promised to deliver to their rightful owner, whoever that might be. He also gave special care to packing a cherished souvenir of the voyage: "Scales has made me a beautiful scale drawing of our good ship 'Shenandoah.' It is exactly like her & the execution of it is admirable." Like everyone on board, Mason feared what might happen to them when they reached Liverpool. Would they face prosecution and imprisonment in England or the United States? Would the letters, if any, that awaited them bring bad news from the South of family and other loved ones? And, if forced to remain in England, what sort of prospects would they face? As sons of a defeated nation, would they even be able to make a living?

But though such fears haunted them, the Confederates also relished the prospect of being back on land. After all, unless they were imprisoned they would be able to see many of the friends they had made in England. Even simpler pleasures beckoned. "I never longed so much for something 'nice' to eat," Mason noted. "It is not that I attach much important to such matters, but it is now so long since we have had any thing to eat but 'salt horse' & salt pork, that every one hankers after 'a good feed of fresh grub.' "

Just before midnight in the waning minutes of November 5, Captain Waddell, after firing rockets and burning blue lights, managed to hail a Liverpool pilot boat just outside the port. Though it was late, even officers who were normally asleep at this hour had gotten up to witness this moment and, more important, to hear from the pilot what news he might bring to their deck. Fearful of the reaction of an Englishman upon hearing the word *Shenandoah*, Waddell, when he originally hailed the pilot, had identified the steamer as the *America*, ninety days out of Calcutta.

Once the pilot had scrambled up the companion ladder, the Confederates revealed the ship's true identify. His reaction, however, proved disappointingly anticlimactic. Neither shocked nor impressed, he seemed, if anything, blasé. Cornelius Hunt's re-creation of the subsequent exchange accords with the gist of contemporary accounts: "As he came over the side he was met by our first lieutenant who bade him 'Good morning.'

"'Good morning,' the pilot responded; 'what ship is that?'

"'The late confederate steamer *Shenandoah.*'

"'The duece it is! Where have you fellows come from last?'

"'From the Arctic Ocean.'

"'Haven't you stopped at any port since you left there?'

"'No; nor been in sight of land, either. What news from the war in America?'

"'It has been over so long people have got through talking about it. Jeff Davis is in Fortress Monroe, and the Yankees have had a lot of cruisers out looking for you. Haven't you seen any of them?'

"'Not unless a suspicious looking craft we sighted off the Western Islands was one.'"

As the pilot entered the pilothouse and took the wheel, a wistful Hunt pondered the reception they might have received had the Confederacy been triumphant: "In that event we should have been the heroes of the hour, sought after and feted as we had been in Melbourne, and crowds of visitors would have besieged us from morning till night." But as they all well knew that would not be the case here; indeed, whether the rest of the crew knew it or not, Captain Waddell had spent many of his final hours aboard the *Shenandoah* polishing a letter to Earl Russell, Britain's foreign minister, surrendering the steamer to Her Majesty's government.

By midnight the tides were rolling out of the River Mersey. Waddell asked the pilot whether he thought he could get the steamer in the now shallower waters across the bar that limned the bay. When the pilot answered no, Waddell—his eagerness to conclude this voyage trumping his usual apprehension—told him to try anyway. The pilot complied and by 4:00 a.m. the *Shenandoah* was caught on the sandbar. The Confederates would have to wait for the tides to turn and lift the steamer off. To Whittle, that delay augured yet another possible danger. Thinking of all those sea-weary sailors crowded into the ship's forward section, unhappy about the reductions in their promised pay, the executive officer feared that the intervening hours might yield a mutiny. As a consequence, Hunt recalled, "during the night, the First Lieutenant came around and warned the officers to keep their revolvers about them, as he had seen enough to make him apprehensive that a plot was on foot among the crew to secure what valuables there were on board."

No mutiny arose that evening, and after waiting several hours for the tides to turn at 7:00 a.m. the pilot instructed the officer in the wheelhouse to signal the engineers below to start the steam engine and propel the ship forward, off the bar. "Soon after daylight," Hunt recalled, "we got clear of the bar, and steamed up the river toward the city, with the flag that had accompanied us round the world flying at our peak for the last time. The fog shut out the town from our view, and we were not sorry for it, for we did not care to have the gaping crowd on shore witness the humiliation that was soon to befall our ship."[4]

Twenty

"The Old Ship Became Fainter and Fainter"

On the morning of November 6, as the *Shenandoah* anchored in the River Mersey astern the HMS ship of the line *Donegal*, Whittle was standing on the steamer's poop deck. As Cornelius Hunt recalled the scene, looking up at the Confederate ensign that was still waving from the steamer's stern, Whittle turned away lest anyone see the tears rolling down his face. Moments before the ship was to be surrendered to waiting British authorities, the quartermaster hauled down the Confederate ensign for the last time. Afterward, he presented the folded banner to Whittle, who, in turn, immediately offered it to Captain Waddell.

Meanwhile, Captain James A. Paynter of the *Donegal* had boarded the *Shenandoah*. Greeting the Royal Navy commander, Waddell formally surrendered the ship to him, and handed him a bag of cash, for which the *Donegal*'s paymaster later issued the following receipt: "Received of Captain James I. Waddell a bag said to contain $820.38, consisting of mixed gold and silver, as per papers annexed to the bag." Waddell also gave Paynter the letter of surrender he had written to Foreign Minister Russell during the *Shenandoah*'s final hours at sea:

MY LORD: I have the honor to announce to your lordship my arrival in the waters of the Mersey with this vessel, lately a ship of war, under my command, belonging to the Confederate States of America.

The singular position in which I find myself placed and the absence of all precedents on the subject will, I trust, induce your lordship to pardon a hasty reference to a few facts connected with the cruise lately made by this ship.

After detailing the ship's mission, and her activities through the previous summer, Waddell told of his subsequent "surprise" that August upon learning from the *Barracouta* that the war had ended. Curiously, however, Waddell also stated that, even after his encounter with the British ship, he remained not completely convinced that the war was over. Even so, after that meeting "I desisted instantly from further acts of war, and determined to suspend further action until I had communicated with a European port, where I would learn if that intelligence were true." Credulous or not, this depiction of events in Waddell's letter of surrender certainly casts the captain in a more flattering, forbearing role than that of the stubbornly recalcitrant commander of a commerce cruiser.

In attempting to characterize the final leg of the *Shenandoah*'s cruise, and his present situation, Waddell was at a loss. "History is, I believe, without a parallel," he wrote in his letter. As for the ship's disposition now that it was in a British port,

I do not consider that I have any right to destroy her or any further right to command her. On the contrary, I think that as all the property of [the Confederate] Government has reverted by the fortunes of war to the

Government of the United States of North America, therefore this vessel, inasmuch as it was the property of the Confederate States, should accompany the other property already reverted. I therefore sought this port as a suitable one wherein to "learn the news," and, if I am without a Government, to surrender the ship with her battery, small arms, machinery, stores, tackle, and apparel, complete, to her Majesty's Government for such disposition as in its wisdom should be deemed proper.

Dispensing with his military title, he signed the letter simply "James I. Waddell."

After the *Shenandoah* had anchored, a customs officer who boarded the steamer informed the Confederates that they would be allowed to go ashore. But because the offer came with the restriction that none of the crew could take their belongings off the ship, none took up the invitation. Still later that day, the same British officer returned and formally took possession of the ship. But this time he gave instructions that no one was to leave the ship until Liverpool's officials had heard from their superiors in London's Whitehall. Reinforcing that order, that evening a detachment of Royal Marines boarded the ship, "with orders," as Charles Lining recalled, "to render any assistance that might be necessary. All hands were then relieved of duty."

The *Shenandoah*'s arrival in the Mersey sparked sharp protests. U.S. consul Thomas Dudley, U.S. minister Charles Francis Adams and other U.S. officials called for her crew's arrest and the ship's confiscation. And the reaction of much of the British public and press carried a similar tone. The *Times* of London called the steamer's return to England "an untoward and unwelcome event." For his part, Foreign Minister Lord Russell, upon receiving Waddell's letter of surrender, promptly turned all questions concerning the raider over to lawyers in his ministry.

That evening and the next day, British naval officials brought provisions aboard, and the crew, officers and hands alike, dined for the first time in months on eggs, milk, and other fresh foods. The officers, Lining recalled, also got such "little luxuries as whiskey[,] tea, with sugar, pipes, tobacco &c." As a consequence, November 7, the *Shenandoah*'s second day in port, found the former raider's crew now well-fed prisoners aboard their own ship, relieved of all former duties, and awaiting a telegram from London that would decide their fate. To amuse themselves, Lining recalled, they "spent the day in looking at the steam-boat loads of people who came by to have a gaze at us, as if we were wild beasts." The Confederates were even more amused, the surgeon recalled, when the English gunboat HMS *Goshawk* "came along side & made fast to us, to keep us from going to sea—the ridiculous idea, as if we had not just come off such a sea voyage as to wish to get to sea again."

British marines notwithstanding, that night several officers, slipping over the ship's rail into an awaiting dingy, "took French leave & spent the night on shore." Among that group, Lieutenant Irvine Bulloch returned at daybreak the next morning, and Lieutenant Sidney Smith Lee, Jr., returned a few hours later, at 10:00 a.m. The third officer, master's mate Cornelius Hunt, never returned. To prevent a repetition of such free-wheeling liberties, the posted guard was doubled, and the dingy used the previous evening was hoisted onto the *Shenandoah*'s deck. As a further guarantee, the captain of the *Goshawk*, which remained lashed to the *Shenandoah*, issued orders that no boats should come alongside the steamer. Anyone wishing to leave or board the *Shenandoah* would have to cross the British gunboat's decks.

At 7:00 that same evening, November 8, the *Shenandoah*'s officers were dining in the wardroom when a British steamer edged alongside them and Captain Paynter of the *Donegal* boarded with the news they had been awaiting: a telegram had arrived from London, stating that law officers of the Crown had ruled that except for British subjects in the *Shenandoah*'s crew, the Confederates—officers and seamen—were free to leave the raider. To sort out the crew members' nationalities, First Lieutenant Whittle, at Paynter's behest, soon called the entire crew on deck. "We were all mustered [on] one side of the vessel," Seaman William Temple, a British subject, recalled. "Lieutenant Whittle called our names and number, and as each man was called he passed in front of Captain Paynter, who addressed to each, 'What countryman are you?' All the Englishmen, Scotch, or Irish answered that they were southerners." The others in the polyglot crew, those who were not British subjects, Temple recalled, "answered according to their nation." Ignoring the obvious fact that many of those seamen who now claimed to be Confederates—or, more to the point, not to be British subjects—were lying, Paynter, apparently weary of the entire matter, allowed everyone to leave.[1]

By 8:30 p.m. everyone had packed, and after a customs agent inspected their luggage the entire crew boarded a ferry waiting alongside. As the ferry took the Confederates to Prince Albert's landing, Waddell thanked the men and said his final goodbyes. During her thirteen-month cruise, the *Shenandoah* covered

58,000 miles and became the only Confederate ship to circum- navigate the globe. She had destroyed 32 vessels, ransomed 6 others, and taken 1,053 prisoners. In all, the value of the vessels and cargoes destroyed by the raider, according to her officers' calculations, came to $1.4 million. Moreover, Waddell later boasted, "The last gun in defense of the South was fired from her deck."

As the ferry moved through Liverpool's harbor, the Confeder- ates took in their final view of the *Shenandoah*. "I grew sadder & sadder as the outline of the old ship became fainter and fainter in the increasing distance," Lieutenant Chew recalled. "Farewell dear old ship, farewell! I have seen you for the last time! I shall never again trod your deck!"

But, sentimentality aside, Chew, then and there, also re- solved never again to perform naval service:

> Man has adapted to many strange and unnatural habits, and this going to sea is one of them; henceforth, ships, sea gales, squalls, cabins, long, weary four-hour watches, royal clewlines &c farewell!!! And you "Salt Horse and Hard tack" may I never be forced to eat you again! At present I am resolved to earn my bread onshore if pos- sible; should it come to the worst and I am reduced to stealing or starving I will think of again following the sea, but until that necessity is fully realized I will engage in some shore employment, however laborious it may be.

Two days after the ruling by the Queen's law officers had freed the steamer's crew, the *Shenandoah* itself was officially turned over to the Confederates' durable Liverpool nemesis, U.S.

consul Thomas Dudley. In the wake of that transfer of title, as arrangements went forward to sail the ship to New York, a correspondent working for *The New York Times* accompanied Dudley on an initial inspection of the steamer. Reflecting the vessel's thirteen months at sea and, no doubt, his own paper's pro-Union bias, the reporter found the ship's general state nothing short of deplorable: "The whole vessel above and below was in the most filthy condition. It would seem almost impossible for humanity to have degraded itself to such a state of absolute neglect." He also noted that Captain Thomas F. Freeman, the American mariner handpicked by Consul Dudley to command the *Shenandoah*'s cruise to New York, after inspecting the vessel, preparatory to her sailing, had asked "for chloride of lime and men for cleansing, as it would be impossible for any one to remain on board without immediate and thorough cleaning and purification."

Equally revealing, as the *Times* correspondent prowled the ship's holds and cabins he recorded an inventory of goods that, however random and incomplete, nonetheless seemed, like some misbegotten ballad, to recapitulate the raider's entire twisted saga of triumphs, deceptions, and star-crossed misadventures:

> In the after saloon, on the starboard side, were fifty-one chronometers, five empty cases for chronometers, ten sextants and quadrants in the locker, thirteen of same outside, (twenty-three in all); three compasses, seven marine clocks and two barometers, a small case twenty inches long, thirteen inches wide, eight inches deep, sewed up in fine canvas, unopened; another one of nearly [the] same size, in a newspaper wrapper apparently of Japanese make; sixty or seventy volumes of different

books, four large quartos (WEBSTER's "Illustrated Dictionary," &c.), an old sabre, double-barrelled fowling-piece, dismounted rifle, a blunderbuss, some charts, hair sofa, tables, chairs, and a crimson plush divan around the saloon, it being evidently the Captain's room. In the safe was a bag of specie containing $828[.]38 in gold and silver coin, most of the latter being Mexican, Southern American and other foreign coins, with some American halves and quarters, five-franc pieces, and a few English shillings. Below were three tons of powder, fifteen hundred pounds of tobacco, two hundred and fifty pounds of tea, a quantity of sperm oil, six casks of spirits, fifty live shells, short supply of stores, except salt beef and pork, two Whitworth guns, four smooth bores or broadside guns, (two ordinary guns on deck,) and in her store-room between decks, two large iron bread tanks, empty; old sails, &c. The vessel had a full set of MARRYATT's signals (twelve [flags] in number,) a large quantity of flags of different nations, (although Mr. LLOYD [of Lloyd's of London] stated that he was told by the men that many others had been torn up for cleaning brass, &c.) and in different rooms a number of charts.[2]

As for the money still due the *Shenandoah*'s Confederate crew, Waddell apparently did try, with mixed success over the coming weeks, to get the men fully paid. Seaman William Temple, for instance, learned that on November 11 a clerk from the ship came by Liverpool's Sailor's Home, met there with a group of his fellow seamen and paid each "in full in English gold." But, two days later, when Temple and another group of seamen met with the same clerk at the same lodging, he told them that he lacked enough money to pay all of them in full. Though due £49, Temple recalled, "I got only £22."

Over the coming weeks, the non-British members of the crew dispersed into local lodgings and the households of English friends, then into other realms increasingly distant from Liverpool. Little is known of the postwar fates of the polyglot seamen of the *Shenandoah*'s crew, including those of the four African-American seamen who had sailed on the raider: John Williams, who had left the steamer in Melbourne; and Edward Weeks, Charles Hopkins, and Joseph Stevenson, who apparently were still aboard the raider when she reached Liverpool. Suffice it to say that, whether in Australia or England, the plight of these four men—far from home, close to broke, and facing racial and class prejudices—could not have been an easy one.

Far more is known of the postwar paths of the *Shenandoah*'s senior officers. The amnesty conditions offered at the end of the Civil War were set by Abraham Lincoln's successor, President Andrew Johnson. Those who had fought against the United States as seamen aboard Confederate naval ships were generally entitled to an automatic amnesty and thus free to return to the United States. Senior officers, however, tended to fall into one or more categories of those for which amnesty could be won only through direct application to the president. Officers who had been educated at West Point or Annapolis, those who had left the country during the war to assist the rebellion, and those who, as U.S. Army or Navy officers, had resigned their commissions in order to assist the Confederacy all required supplication to the president.

Thus, though all of the *Shenandoah*'s officers hoped to return to the United States to get on with their lives, obstacles blocked their road home. Beyond President Johnson's publicly promulgated amnesty requirements, the Confederates heard reports that, domestically and abroad, U.S. officials remained committed to punishing, even by hanging, the *Shenandoah*'s officers. In April 1866, William Whittle, from exile in Argentina, wrote to Commodore Samuel Barron, who was still in Paris, relating discouraging news from another *Shenandoah* veteran, Midshipman Orris Browne, also living in exile in Argentina. Browne's father in Virginia had written his son to say he recently "had an interview with the President and many leading men in Washington." The news that came out of that meeting, Whittle wrote, "plunged us to a depth of misery." In his letter to Barron, Whittle related what Browne's father had heard in the meeting:

> They did not hesitate to say that you were pirates—and that you would be hung within a week after falling into their hands. They say that after many years some of the junior officers might be allowed to return in safety, but as to the Capt. and his principal officers, they can never come back. They contend that sworn affidavits are on file from more than fifty of the crews of the vessels destroyed, [and] that complete and satisfactory information had been furnished the Capt. of the downfall of the C.S.A. government. Do not come back. "Dismiss any such idea forever from your mind." These are in the main the very words used, but any how the sense was as is here conveyed. Thus we are as, God knows, most cruelly & unjustly banished from all we hold dearer than life itself.

In the weeks and months after the raider's return to England, the *Shenandoah*'s senior officers struck out on different paths. Lieutenant Irvine Bulloch remained in Liverpool, and through his half brother James Bulloch found work as a cotton broker in the city's port. The senior Bulloch, who had almost single-handedly acquired the Confederacy's fleet of British-built ships, would remain in Liverpool for the rest of his life, becoming an active member of the port's maritime business community. During the early stretches of those years, Bulloch's young nephew Teddy Roosevelt made extended trips to England gathering research for his book *The Naval War of 1812*, published in 1882. On his visits, he often stayed with his Uncle Jimmy. And it was during those visits that Roosevelt encouraged Bulloch to write his own two-volume Civil War memoir, *The Secret Service of the Confederate States in Europe*, published in 1883. Bulloch always regretted that he had been unable to build a more formidable Confederate navy; and in his conversations and correspondence with his nephew Teddy, he played a major role in convincing the future U.S. president of the priority of attaining global naval superiority for America, and of beating other countries to the task of building and controlling a canal across Panama's isthmus. Ironically, the other major figure in bringing T.R. to that perspective was the historian and retired U.S. Navy officer Alfred Thayer Mahan, who had served on Union blockade duty during the Civil War and detested commerce raiding. Never pardoned for his Civil War activities, Bulloch made but one postwar trip to America, a clandestine journey in 1877 to visit friends and family. He died in 1901.

Unlike James and Irvine Bulloch, however, most of the officers associated with the *Shenandoah* were forced to look beyond England to rebuild their lives; in most cases, their gazes turned toward Latin America, where they hoped to make fortunes in mining or in agriculture: Dabney Scales, Francis Chew, and John Grimball found their way to the Confederate colony of Carlota, built near the city of Vera Cruz, Mexico, as part of a 500,000-acre land grant established by Emperor Maximilian in September 1865 to encourage Confederate immigration to Mexico. William Whittle, Sidney Smith Lee, Jr., Orris Browne, and John Mason, together in the winter of 1866, went to Argentina. There in Rosario—Argentina's second-largest city, fast becoming a popular enclave for former Confederates—the four ex-Confederates bought fifty acres and established a cattle, chicken, and vegetable farm.

Before leaving Europe, however, Mason did try to fulfill the shipboard promise made in the fall of 1865 to the dying George Canning, and to himself, to find in Paris that enigmatic sailor's wife, other family members, or anyone close to him, and return his dead friend's sea journal and personal effects. Mason placed ads in the *Times* of London and in *Le Siècle*. Two Englishmen eventually came forward—one claimed that the late seaman owed him money; the other purported to be Canning's brother—but Mason found both unconvincing and soon abandoned his search.[3]

As federal amnesty policies for Confederates moderated, the *Shenandoah*'s officers, one by one, returned to America. Pardoned as a group in 1867, Orris Browne, Sidney Smith Lee, Jr., John Mason, and William Whittle, after selling their farm in Rosario, embarked on divergent roads. Browne and Smith Lee returned to Virginia to run their own farms. Mason studied law at the University of Virginia, established a legal practice in Baltimore, then later returned to Virginia to farm. Whittle settled in Norfolk, Virginia, where he resumed sailing as captain of several passenger steamers for a line that ran between Norfolk and Baltimore. After 1890, when the line was sold, he became a founder and vice president of a Norfolk bank. Retiring in 1917, he died three years later. During his later years, Whittle was an officer in the Confederate Veterans organization, through which he kept up with his old shipmates. As a coda to his *Shenandoah* diary, it should be noted that, as he had predicted after the Confederates spoke the *Barracouta*, he never married his beloved Pattie.

Instead, in 1872 he wed Elizabeth Calvert Page, a prominent Norfolk resident and the daughter of general and Confederate navy commander Richard Lucien Page. However incongruous with the executive officer's years of rough persuasion, the two-story Federal-style house in Norfolk that the couple shared—Elizabeth's childhood home, now called the Taylor-Whittle house—is today the headquarters of the city's chapter of the Junior League.

After his pardon, Dabney Scales, whose efforts with Francis Chew and John Grimball to establish a plantation in Carlota had foundered, settled in Memphis. There he opened a law practice, served in the state legislature, and lived long enough to return to service in the U.S. Navy as a lieutenant in the Spanish-American War. Grimball, for his part, returned to Charleston, studied law, and ran a legal practice in New York for sixteen years before returning to South Carolina and becoming a rice planter. Less is known about the later years of Francis Chew, except that he left Mexico in 1866 to return to Missouri, where he had a job waiting for him.

Among the raider's officers, Charles Lining seems to have remained in Latin America the longest. Having left England for Argentina in 1867, he soon won a post as a government-appointed surgeon in Santiago del Estero, a position that he retained until 1874. Afterward, he left for Paducah, Kentucky, where he practiced medicine until his death in 1897.

By slipping over the raider's rails in Liverpool, on November 7, 1865—thus taking "French leave" from the *Shenandoah*—master's mate Cornelius Hunt had been among the first crewmembers to depart the ship. But with the appearance in 1867 of his vivid Civil War recollections, he became among the first to publish an account of the raider's cruise.

Hunt's taste for military adventure, however, remained unsated. In 1869, he joined a group of Civil War veterans recruited for the fledgling army of Ismail Pasha, Khedive of Egypt. The recruits, recommended to Egypt's modernizing ruler by General William Tecumseh Sherman and other U.S. Army officers, enlisted for hire to fight in an anticipated war against Egypt's Ottoman Empire overlords. The Khedive's ambitions for independence had been swollen by the completion in 1869 of the Suez Canal and a boom in Egyptian cotton ironically nourished by Britain's growing reliance on the staple after the American Civil War interrupted cotton shipments from the American South. The anticipated war with the Ottomans did come but went badly for Egypt: the Khedive abdicated in 1879 and his movement collapsed during the next decade. By then, Cornelius Hunt—killed in 1873 in a fall from a horse—had secured the sad distinction of becoming the first American soldier to die in Egyptian military service.

Of those *Shenandoah* officers, however, who returned to America and civilian life, James Waddell seems to have traveled the most tortured road home. As Whittle later informed Commodore Samuel Barron, within a week after the steamer's return to England in November 1865, Waddell suffered "three or four hemorrhages of blood [*sic*] from the lungs and for a long time was at the point of death." His medical emergency had coincided with equally bleak news from home: thirteen months earlier, the day after her husband's departure from England aboard the *Laurel*, Ann Waddell had sailed from Liverpool for America. But upon Ann's return to the couple's home in Maryland, Federal authorities had imposed restrictions on her liberty.

At one point she was even imprisoned. Mrs. Waddell was later required to sign a bond stipulating that during the conflict she would neither see nor communicate with her husband.

Upon regaining his health, Waddell, joined by Ann, moved to the town of Waterloo, close to Liverpool, where, presumably with James Bulloch's help, he found work in Britain's shipping industry. Pardoned by the U.S. government in 1875, he returned to America and found work with the Pacific Mail Line as captain of a steamer operating between San Francisco and Yokohama. On one of those trips, however, his ship, the 4,000-ton *San Francisco*, struck an uncharted reef off the Mexican coast.

Though most considered the accident unavoidable and Waddell did manage to get the ship to shore and evacuate all of her passengers, questions persisted about his conduct in the incident. Within a few years, he had retired from the line, moved to Annapolis, Maryland, and taken a job with the Maryland State Fishing Force as captain of vessels guarding the state's fisheries. During the 1880s, in his final sea war, the captain won headlines for a series of raids that vanquished a group of notorious "oyster pirates" who had been poaching on Maryland's Chesapeake Bay. In his final years, Waddell also found time to pen a memoir of his career aboard the *Shenandoah*. The old captain died at age sixty-one on March 15, 1886, in Annapolis, where today he lies buried in St. Anne's Cemetery, just outside the U.S. Navy Academy.

In December 1865, shortly after the *Shenandoah*'s return to England, Waddell, in a letter widely published in U.S. newspapers, recalled the turmoil aboard the cruiser after she spoke the *Barracouta*. In the letter, specifically recalling the petition urging him to clarify his destination, he accused the officers who signed the document of setting "a bad example to the crew" and engaging in "conduct [that] was nothing less than mutiny."

Waddell's memoirs, however, were not published until 1960, seven decades after his death. In them, putting aside bitterness, he lavishly praised all of the *Shenandoah*'s officers. Laying aside his differences with Whittle, he particularly thanked his executive officer "for his faithful and watchful discharge of duty." Of his own alleged culpability for destruction of Union ships after the "cessation of hostilities," however, Waddell remained steadfastly defiant: "There is no reason to believe that I ever received or did receive any credible news even of General Lee's surrender til the second day of August, when I instantly put the guns in the hold and sailed for Liverpool." Similarly, Waddell also remained stubbornly unbowed on the subjects of the Confederate cause for which he had fought and his side's commerce raiding.

> If privateering, as they still will have it, was the vice of the Confederates, then the Federals are responsible for having sanctioned it. If it was the one engine of war which harassed them most, then they reaped the penalty of having fabricated it. It is well known that when Europe conspired to put down the system, America refused to divest warfare of one of its most cruel accessories.

That notwithstanding, in 1964, in a spirit of Civil War centennial sectional–reconciliation, the U.S. Navy commissioned the USS *Waddell*, a destroyer named in honor of the former U.S. Navy officer who had resigned that commission to command the CSS *Shenandoah*.[5]

During the Civil War, Secretary of State William Seward argued that the British government should be held liable for the destruction of American shipping by Confederate commerce raiders obtained in Great Britain or otherwise assisted in British ports. In 1869 Massachusetts senator Charles Sumner, chairman of the Senate Committee on Foreign Relations, estimated British liability for Confederate commerce raiding at $15 million for destroyed ships and cargo. However, because Sumner believed that British complicity in both commerce raiding and blockade running had greatly prolonged the war, he also sought to hold Britain liable for a total of $2.5 billion—for half the cost, he said, of the entire war. But, at least initially, he did not seek a cash settlement. Instead, with a large Irish-American constituency, he proposed that the claim be liquidated by Britain's agreeing to abandon its dominion over "all parts of the Western Hemisphere including all provinces and islands." Such a cession would have included Canada, Newfoundland (yet to join the Dominion of Canada created in 1867), Bermuda, and the British West Indies. Britain, not surprisingly, ignored the request.

In 1871, with the Treaty of Washington, the United States and Great Britain, along with Italy, Switzerland, and Brazil, established a tribunal at Geneva to settle the two nations' dispute. And in September 1872 the "Alabama Claims Commission," named for the Confederacy's most infamous raider, after collecting thousands of pages of testimony, awarded the United States $15.5 million from Britain's treasury as compensation for damages done by Confederate raiders. Neither before nor afterward—despite vigorous efforts by her owner and Kingdom of Hawaii diplomats—did Britain, or the United States, provide from those rewarded damages a requested $75,000 compensation for the *Harvest*, the duly registered Hawaiian whaleship mistakenly claimed by Waddell to have been a U.S. vessel and burned at Ascension Island.

As for the *Shenandoah*, the Alabama Claims tribunal ruled that the British government was not liable for the *Sea King*'s conversion into a raider or for any of the ship's acts prior to reaching Australia. But the panel did hold that during the raider's stopover in Melbourne the British government had failed to enforce its neutrality obligations and was therefore liable for all the raider's destruction to American shipping after her departure from Hobson's Bay on February 18, 1865. In the wake of that settlement, the United States, drawing on those funds, established its own domestic court to hear raider claims by individual shipowners and others; and that court eventually paid out $6 million in damages. But neither the Alabama Claims Commission nor the U.S. government's payments to individual shipowners could undo the damage done to the American merchant marine by Confederate raiders.

In putting commerce raiders to sea, Confederate navy secretary Stephen Mallory had three key objectives: to bolster the Confederacy's international image as a formidable power; to drive up marine insurance costs for Northern shipowners, thus increasing domestic political pressure for the Union to make an early peace with the South; and to draw U.S. Navy ships away from the Federal blockade of the South's coast. In the end, the Confederacy did accrue propaganda dividends from the raiders. And the raiders did damage the Union merchant marine and thus drive up insurance costs. But the commerce raiders utterly failed in creating pressure to end the war and in drawing U.S. Navy gunboats away from the Union's blockade of the Confederate coast.

As for the *Shenandoah*'s additional, more specific objective, the destruction of the U.S. whaling fleet, Secretary Mallory could claim a measure of success. That destruction fell particularly hard on New Bedford, Massachusetts. The town's *Republican Standard*, in a November 1865 story headlined "Whalers Destroyed by the Pirates," grimly tallied the destruction: twenty-seven whaling vessels lost to Confederate raiding. Nearby Provincetown, having lost six whaleships to the Confederates, was the closest runner-up in the same tally of depredations.

"This is a more severe blow than New Bedford has experienced since the British invasion of the shipping and business part of the town in 1788," the *Republican Standard* that August had inveighed, recalling a British attack on the port during the American Revolution. A week later—lest anyone overlook the widespread conviction in New England of just which country across the Atlantic should be held responsible for the *Shenandoah*'s rampage—the *Republican Standard* reprinted an editorial from the Boston *Commercial Bulletin* that likened the raider to a celebrated British commercial steamship of that day: "To call her a Confederate vessel of war, is a downright falsehood. She is to this day as much a British vessel as the Great Eastern; and we believe this is the light in which she is viewed by our own Government."

The U.S. whaling fleet, from a total of 186 vessels in 1861, had been reduced to a hundred vessels by the war's end. But that statistic distorts the impact of Confederate raiding. While Confederate raiders destroyed forty-six whaling vessels, another forty or so New England whaling vessels had been purchased during the war by the Federal government for its "stone fleet," the aging and granite-filled vessels it soon escorted into Confederate waters and scuttled to block the entrances to various Southern ports, principally Charleston's. The *Shenandoah*'s raiding activities and the scuttling of the stone-fleet vessels certainly damaged America's whaling industry. But, from a long-range perspective, both phenomena only hastened the demise of a dying U.S. and international industry. For by the 1860s, oil-derived fuels and lubricants were already crippling international demand for whale-derived products. Moreover, the U.S. whaling fleet was further reduced by a series of Arctic disasters during the 1870s, and by the growing adoption by foreign competitors, principally Norwegian, of technological innovations.

But though the Confederate raiders failed to accomplish all the strategic hopes their Confederate sponsors had assigned to them, they did do lasting damage to the American merchant marine. Moreover, Confederate commerce raiding had the effect of tamping down what had become, by 1861, an increasingly robust American challenge to Great Britain's global supremacy in commercial maritime shipping. Even as the war raged, the New York *World*, in July 1864, had decried, "More than 1,000 of our ships we have been compelled to sell to foreigners because our flag furnished no protection but on the contrary is but an incentive to the pirate's torch." During the Civil War, the United States lost more than half the tonnage of its merchant fleet: some 800,000 tons to foreign flags; another 110,000 tons to Confederate raiders. It was a loss from which, the American merchant marine suffered well into the twentieth century.[6]

Following the transfer of her registry to the United States government, the *Shenandoah* sailed from Liverpool on November 21, 1865, bound for New York. Two days later, John Mason, in his diary, contemplated the former raider as she found her way through St. George's Channel into the Atlantic. "There has been a dreadful gale in the channel & I hope sincerely she has gone to the bottom," he wrote. "I don't want to see her again as a yankee."

As it turned out, Captain Thomas F. Freeman and the *Shenandoah*'s new crew of fifty-five, battered by that very gale, were forced to return to Liverpool on December 6, "short of coal and [with a] loss of sails." After the aborted voyage, U.S. consul Thomas Dudley, on March 22, auctioned off the ship at Liverpool. Her purchaser, Nathaniel Wilson, paid £15,650 for the steamer. He then immediately resold her at a profit of £1,000 to an agent for the sultan of Zanzibar. The sultan planned to refit her as a personal yacht. But when that proved to be more expensive than anticipated, he rechristened the steamer as the *El Majidi* and put her into service as a merchant freighter. In 1879, after striking an uncharted reef, the old steamer, along with her motley ghosts, disappeared beneath the waters of the Indian Ocean.[7]

Appendix A

The *Shenandoah*'s Prizes

Date of Capture	Name and Type of Vessel	Home Port	Location When Captured	Fate of Vessel	Declared Value of Vessel and Cargo
1864					
Oct 29	*Alina*, bark	Searsport, Maine	lat 15°25' N long 26°44' W	scuttled	$95,000
Nov 5	*Charter Oak*, schooner	San Francisco	lat 7°38' N long 27°49' W	burned	$15,000
Nov 7	*D. Godfrey*, bark	Boston	lat 40°42' N long 28°24' W	burned	$36,000
Nov 10	*Susan*, brigantine	New York	lat 4°24' N long 26°39' W	scuttled	$5,436
Nov 12	*Adelaide*, bark	Baltimore	lat 1°45' N long 29°22' N	bonded	$24,000
	Kate Prince, ship	Portsmouth	lat 1°45' N long 29°22' W	bonded	$40,000
Nov 13	*Lizzie M. Stacey*, schooner	Boston	lat 1°40' N long 28°24' W	burned	$15,000
Dec 4	*Edward*, bark	New Bedford	lat 37°47' S long 12°30' E	burned	$20,000

Date of Capture	Name and Type of Vessel	Home Port	Location When Captured	Fate of Vessel	Declared Value of Vessel and Cargo
Dec 29	*Delphine*, bark	Bangor, Maine	lat 39°13' S, long 68°33' E	burned	$25,000
1865					
April 1	*Edward Carey*, ship	San Francisco	Pohnpei (Ascension Island)	burned	$15,000
April 1	*Pearl*, bark	New London	Pohnpei	burned	$10,000
April 1	*Hector*, ship	New Bedford	Pohnpei	burned	$58,000
April 1	*Harvest*, bark	Honolulu	Pohnpei	burned	$34,759
May 27	*Abigail*, bark	New Bedford	Sea of Okhotsk	burned	$16,705
June 22	*William Thompson*, ship	New Bedford	off Cape Thaddeus	burned	$40,925
June 22	*Euphrates*, ship	New Bedford	off Cape Thaddeus	burned	$42,320
June 22	*Sophia Thornton*, ship	New Bedford	Bering Strait	burned	$70,000
June 22	*Milo*, ship	New Bedford	Bering Strait	bonded	$46,000
	Jireh Swift, bark	New Bedford	Bering Strait	burned	$61,960
June 23	*Susan Abigail*, brigantine	San Francisco	Bering Strait	burned	$6,500
June 25	*General Williams*, ship	New London	Bering Strait	burned	$44,740

Date of Capture	Name and Type of Vessel	Home Port	Location When Captured	Fate of Vessel	Declared Value of Vessel and Cargo
June 26	*William C. Nye*, ship	San Francisco	Bering Strait	burned	$31,512
	Nimrod, bark	New Bedford	Bering Strait	burned	$29,260
	Catharine, ship	New London	Bering Strait	burned	$26,175
	General Pike, bark	New Bedford	Bering Strait	bonded	$30,000
	Isabella, bark	New Bedford	Bering Strait	burned	$38,000
	Gypsy, bark	New Bedford	Bering Strait	burned	$34,369
June 28	*Waverly*, bark	New Bedford	Bering Strait	burned	$62,376
	Martha, bark	New Bedford	Bering Strait	burned	$30,307
	Hillman, bark	New Bedford	Bering Strait	burned	$33,000
	Brunswick, ship	New Bedford	Bering Strait	burned	$16,272
	James Maury, ship	New Bedford	Bering Strait	bonded	$40,550
	Nassau, ship	New Bedford	Bering Strait	burned	$40,000
	Isaac Howland, ship	New Bedford	Bering Strait	burned	$75,112
	Congress, bark	New Bedford	Bering Strait	burned	$55,300
	Nile, bark	New London	Bering Strait	bonded	$25,550

Date of Capture	Name and Type of Vessel	Home Port	Location When Captured	Fate of Vessel	Declared Value of Vessel and Cargo
June 28	*Favorite*, bark	Fairhaven	Bering Strait	burned	$57,896
June 28	*Covington*, bark	New Bedford	Bering Strait	burned	$30,000

Discrepancies abound in assessments by *Shenandoah* officers of the individual and aggregate values of their thirty-eight prizes—thirty-two vessels destroyed, six bonded. Monetary figures above—which, like similar tabulations, cumulatively amount to about $1.4 million—derive from a table published in master's mate Cornelius Hunt's 1867 memoirs, as well as the ship's logbook and other contemporary documents. Hunt's figures, however, generally comport with those from other documents. Hunt, in the same table, also asserted that the *Shenandoah* captured a total of 1,053 prisoners during her thirteen-month voyage.

Appendix B

Schedule of Deck Watches
Mid-watch   0000–0400
Morning Watch   0400–0800
Forenoon Watch   0800–1200
Afternoon Watch   1200–1600
Dogwatches   1600–1800, 1800–2000
Evening Watch   2000–2400

Explanation of knots: unit used to measure a ship's speed—one knot equals about 1.15 miles per hour.

Notes

1. Of Ice Floes and Arctic Fires

1. Kirschbaum, William G., "Captured in the Arctic by a Confederate Cruiser," circa 1890s profile of Alden Potter from undated, unidentified New England newspaper, in Scrapbook 2, 270, New Bedford Whaling Museum; *Republican Standard*, Aug. 31, 1865; Cornelius Hunt, *Cruiser*, 85, 100—paginations for Hunt's memoirs in endnotes reflect those given at top of page in their republication in *Magazine of History*, which replicate page numbers in work's original publication; Waddell, "Extracts from Notes," in *Official Records of the Union and Confederate Navies in the War of the Rebellion* [hereafter *ORN*], Series 1, vol. 3, 800, 801; Mason Journal 4, June 27, 1865 [no reliable pagination].

2. Davis, *Rise and Fall*, vol. 2, 700; for an excellent study of Civil War's denouement, see Winik, *April 1865*.

3. Merli, *Great Britain*, 5; MacGregor, *Fast Sailing Ships*, 221–25.

4. Luraghi, *Navy*, 32.

5. Fowler, *Two Flags*, 51–52.

6. Fowler, *Two Flags*, 35–37; Merli, *Great Britain*, 9.

7. Fowler, *Two Flags*, 42; Luraghi, *Navy*, 7.

8. Durkin, *Mallory*, 3–156; Merli, *Great Britain*, 10–14; Mallory to C. M. Conrad, May 10, 1861, in *ORN*, Series 2, vol. 2, 69.

9. Semmes, *Afloat*, 92.

10. Fowler, *Two Flags*, 275.

11. Vandiver, *Rebel Brass*, 71–74; Curry, "Echoes," 67–68.

2. "A Good, Capital Ship in Every Respect"

1. Bulloch, *Service*, vol. 2, 46–47; Merli, *Great Britain*, 14–18; Mallory, "Report," April 26, 1861, *ORN*, Series 2, vol. 2, 51.

2. Spencer, *Navy*, 4.

3. Bulloch, *Service*, vol. 1, 32, 33, 45, 47, 65.

4. Mallory to Bulloch, July 18, 1864, in Bulloch, *Service*, vol. 2, 112.

5. Bulloch to Mallory, Feb. 18, 1864, in *ORN*, Series 2, vol. 2, 589; and Merli, *Great Britain*, 54.

6. Mallory to Bulloch, March 21, 1864, in *ORN*, Series 2, vol. 2, 613.

7. Whittle, "Cruise," 239; Mason Journal 3, Oct. 30, 1864; Mallory to Bulloch, March 21, Aug. 10, 1864, *ORN* Series 2, vol. 2, 613, 701; Mallory to Bulloch, Aug. 19, 1864, *ORN*, Series 2, vol. 2, 707–8; Brooke memo, Aug. 19, 1864, in *ORN*, Series 2, vol. 2, 708, 709; Bulloch, *Service*, vol. 2, 125, 130–31.

8. Bulloch, *Service*, vol. 2, 131–36; Bulloch to Mallory, Sept. 16, 1864, in *ORN*, Series 2, vol. 2, 723–25.

9. Bulloch, *Service*, vol. 2, 127–28.

10. Merli, *Great Britain*, 230, 327 n. 23.

11. Mason Journal 3, Oct. 30, 1864; for Whittle birth date, see Whittle Diary, Jan. 16, 1865: 112; Bulloch, *Service*, vol. 2, 144–45; Waddell, *Shenandoah*, 76–77, 90, 91. Bulloch to Mallory, Sept. 29, 1864, in *ORN*, Series 2, vol. 2, 729–30; Hunt, *Cruiser*, 8, 9.

12. Bulloch to Mallory, Oct. 20, 1864, in *ORN*, Series 2, vol. 2, 736–37; Bulloch, *Service*, vol. 2, 128–32; William A. Temple affidavit, Dec. 6, 1865, in *The Case of Great Britain as laid before the Tribunal of Arbitration Convened at Geneva* [hereafter *CGB*], vol. 3, 968.

3. Black Cruiser on a Thames Night

1. Bulloch to Whittle, Oct. 6, 1864, in *ORN*, Series 2, vol. 2, 731–32; Whittle, "Cruise," 241.

2. Bulloch to Whittle, Oct. 6, 1864, in *ORN*, Series 2, vol. 2, 731–32; *Times* of London, Oct. 7, 1865.

3. Merli, *Great Britain*, 56–57; for further background, see study of Dudley's activities in Liverpool, Milton, *Lincoln's Spymaster*.

4. Merli, *Navy*, 61–62.

5. Dudley to Adams, Dec. 11, 1861, in U.S. State Department Records, National Archives, Consular Dispatches, Liverpool, vol. 20; Merli, *Great Britain*, 57 n. 16.

6. Merli, *Great Britain*, 61.

7. Adams to Russell, Nov. 10, 1864, in *CGB*, vol. 3, 563–64; and Seward-Adams, Dec. 3, 1864, in *Foreign Affairs*, 367; Merli, *Great Britain*, 228, 327 n. 21.

8. Collins to Welles, enclosure, April 11, 1864, in *ORN*, Series 1, vol. 3, 10–11.

9. Moran, *Journal*, vol. 2, 1337; ibid., 1142n.1; Moran to Craven, Oct. 11, 1864, in *ORN*, Series 1, vol. 3, 343–44; Whittle, "Cruise," 242.

10. Hunt, *Cruiser*, 9-11; Mason, "Last," 601.

11. Moran, *Journal*, vol. 2, 1338; Moran to Craven, Oct. 11, 1864, in *ORN*, Series 1, vol. 3, 344.

12. Hearn, *Raider*, 255.

13. Dudley to Adams (Nov. 16, 1864), John Hercus (Nov. 12, 1864), and John Wilson (Nov. 14, 1864) affidavits, in *CGB*, vol. 1, 750–54.

4. Las Desertas

1. Waddell, *Shenandoah*, 90–93; Mason Journal 3, Oct. 30, 1864; Bulloch to Waddell, Oct. 5, 1864, *ORN*, Series 1, vol. 3, 749–55. Waddell misstates the date of the *Sea King*'s initial appearance off Funchal as Oct. 18; Lining, in Diary, Oct. 12, 1864, 2, offers correct date: Oct. 17.

2. Curry, "Echoes," 94–95; Mason Journal 3, Oct. 30, 1864. Background on Mason, born in 1844—Whittle, Mason tribute, in Scales, "Cruise," 489–90.

3. MacGregor, *Fast Sailing Ships*, 220–25; Shenandoah Plans, Maritime Division, Smithsonian Institution; *The New York Times*, Nov. 24, 1865.

4. Lining Diary, Oct. 18, 1864: 3; Lining birth date, Jan. 6, 1834, in Lining Diary, Jan. 6, 1865: 52.

5. Waddell, *Shenandoah*, 84–87; Lining Diary, Oct. 19, 4–5; Chew Diary, Nov. 2, 1864 [no pagination]; Mason Journal 3, Oct. 24, 1864; Whittle Diary, Oct. 26, 1864, [7], 8; Whittle, "Cruise," 243.

5. A Bucket of Sovereigns

1. Waddell, *Shenandoah*, 90, 94; Grimball to John Berkley Grimball, hereafter "father," Dec. 23, 1864, JBG Papers; Hunt, *Cruiser*, 13; Whittle, "Cruise," 243–44; Bulloch, *Service*, vol. 2, 143, 144; Waddell, "Extracts," *ORN*, Series 1, vol. 3, 794–95; Bennett, *Union Jacks*, 8–9, 54, 57–59, 62–64, 183.

2. Mason Journal 3, Oct. 30, 1864; Mason, "Last," 601–2; Bulloch, *Service*, vol. 2, 39, [139] 143; Temple affidavit, Dec. 6, 1865, *CGB*, vol. 1, 968; Waddell, "Extracts," in *ORN*, Series 1, vol. 3, 793–94; Bulloch to Mallory, Nov. 17, 1864, *ORN*, Series 1, vol. 3, 758; Chew Diary, Nov. 2, 1864; Whittle Diary, Oct. 26, 1864, [7], 8.

3. Grimball to father, Dec. 23, 1864, in John Berkley Grimball [hereafter JBG] Papers; Bulloch to Waddell, Oct. 5, 1864; Mallory to Bulloch, Nov. 17, 1864, in *ORN*, Series 1, vol. 3, 752, 757; John Wilson affidavit, *CGB*, vol. 1, 753; Temple affidavit, Dec. 6, 1865, in ibid., 968; Thomas Jackson affidavit, Jan. 27, 1865, ibid., 875–76; John Hercus affidavit, Nov. 12, 1865, in ibid., 750–51.

4. Whittle, "Cruise," 244; Bulloch, *Service*, vol. 2, 143; for an account of the scene by British seaman John Wilson, see *Republican Standard*, Aug. 10, 1865; Grimball to father, Dec. 23, 1864, JBG Papers.

5. Whittle, "Cruise," 244; Chew, "Reminiscences," 1, 2, in Francis Thorton Chew Papers, 1–2; Mason Journal 4, April 16, 1865: 61. Chew birth date, Sept. 24, 1841, in Chew Diary, Sept. 25, 1865.

6. Lining, Oct. 19, 1864, 4; Melville, *White–Jacket*, 371; Whittle Diary, Oct. 26, 1864: 8–9; Semmes, *Afloat*, 411–13; Chew Diary, Nov. 2, 1864: 4, 5; Waddell, *Shenandoah*, 94–97.

7. Bulloch, *Service*, vol. 2, 139–40, 146, 147; Waddell, *Shenandoah*, 91–102; Waddell, "Extracts," in *ORN*, Series 1, vol. 3, 798.

8. Whittle, "Cruise," 244; Waddell, *Shenandoah*, 85, 86, 94, 100; Bulloch, *Service*, vol. 2, 39–40; Hearn, *Gray Raiders*, 260; Waddell, "Extracts," in *ORN*, Series 1, vol. 3, 796, 798, 804; Waddell, "Notes," in *ORN*, Series 1, vol. 3, 796–97; Lining Diary, Oct. 19, 1864: 4; Whittle Diary, Oct. 26, 1864: 8, 9; Chew Diary, Nov. 2, 1864; Waddell, *Shenandoah*, 94–97.

6. Crossing the Royal Yards

1. Whittle Diary, Oct. 26, Nov. 14, 1864: [7,] 8, 9, 44; Hunt, *Cruiser*, 15; Still, *Confederate Navy*, 115; Curry, "Echoes," 28, 29, 39, 40; Waddell, *Shenandoah*, 95–97; Hunt's prior service, see *CGB*, vol. 1, 964.

2. Whittle Diary, Oct. 26, 1864, Nov. 14, 1864: 8, 9, 44; Whittle, "Cruise," 44; Hunt, *Cruiser*, 15; Waddell article, in Malone, *Dictionary of American Biography*, vol. 10, 302–3; Curry, "Echoes," 28–30; Lining Diary, Oct. 20, 1864: 6; Barron to Waddell, Sept. 5, 1864, Bulloch to Waddell, Oct. 5, 1864, both in *ORN*, Series 1, vol. 3, 749; Waddell, *Shenandoah*, 96.

3. MacGregor, *Fast Sailing Ships*, 220–25; "Pirate Shenandoah," *The New York Times*, Nov. 24, 1865; Wells, *Confederate Navy*, 19–25; Still, *Confederate Navy*, 180–83; Shenandoah Plans, Maritime Division, Smithsonian Institution. In pinpointing dates, nautical positions, and other key information for this narrative, author has generaally relied on Lieutenant John Grimball's copy of the *Shenandoah*'s logbook. (See

Note on Sources 393–96) However, to avoid excessive repetition, these consultations, except in rare cases, generally go uncited in endnotes. Likewise, in instances where specific logbook entries are indicated in text or notes, unless stated otherwise, the reference derives from Grimball's copy of the logbook.

4. Hunt, *Cruiser*, 16–17; Waddell, *Shenandoah*, 100, 104. Lining Diary, Oct. 27, 1864; Whittle Diary, Oct. 26, 27, 1864: 8, 9; Hunt inaccurately wrote that the Oct. 27 encounter with the *Mogul* took place a day later.

5. Bauer, *Maritime History*, 246–49; Dalzell, *Flight*, 247; Hunt, *Cruiser*, 17.

7. King Neptune's Court

1. Whittle Diary, Oct. 28, 29, 1864: 9–12; Lining Diary, Oct. 28, 29, 1864: 9–10; Mason Journal 3, Oct. 30, 1864; Hunt, *Cruiser*, 18, 19; Mason, "Last," 603.

2. Whittle Diary, Oct. 29, 30, 1864: 12, 15–16; Waddell, *Shenandoah*, 85–106, 145; Bulloch to Waddell, Oct. 5, 1864, *ORN*, Series 1, vol. 3, 753–54; Hunt, *Cruiser*, 15–20; Whittle, "Cruise," 244–45; Mason, "Last," 603; Herman Wicke affidavit, Feb. 14, 1865, *CGB*, vol. 1, 877–78; affidavits for F. C. Behucke, Feb. 14, 1865, ibid., 878–79; and William Bruce, Feb. 7, 1865, ibid., 862–64; Shipping Articles of the *Shenandoah*, Museum of the Confederacy.

3. Whittle Diary, Nov. 2, 5, 1864: 20, 23–27; Still, *Confederate Navy*, 184; Ashe, "Shenandoah," 322–23; Melville, *White-Jacket*, 657; Curry, "Echoes," 129 n. 6; Wells, *Confederate Navy*, 41–43; Valle, *Rocks and Shoals*, 38–45, 71–72; for text of original 1800 U.S. Navy Articles of War, see ibid., 285–96.

4. Lining Diary, Nov. 6, 7, 1864: 15, 16; Waddell, *Shenandoah*, 109; Whittle Diary, Nov. 7, 1864: 29–30; Bulloch, *Service*, vol. 2, 148; Lonn, *Foreigners*, 286; Grimball to John Berkley Grimball, Dec. 23, 1864, in JBG Papers; Lining Diary, Nov. 7, 1864: 16.

5. Reidy, "Black Men in Navy Blue," *Prologue*, vol. 33, no. 3, online access; Ramold, *Slaves, Sailors, Citizens*, 19–24, 55–58, 61–62, 65, 145–47; *Union Jacks*, 156–158; Whittle Diary, Dec. 8, 1864: 78. Walter James Madden affidavit, Feb. 9, 1865, *CGB*, vol. 1, 875; John Williams affidavits, Feb. 16, 10, 1865, in ibid., 809, 874; George Brackett affidavit, Feb. 3, 1865, in ibid., 869–70; Whittle Diary, Dec. 8, 1864: 78. Midshipman Mason, in Mason Journal 4, Feb. 9, 1865 (out of sequence entry follows that for March 18, 1865), denied that tricing took place aboard the raider. Testimony of such practices, he ar-

gued, came from men who had freely shipped aboard the *Shenandoah* but who, upon deserting in Melbourne, had been "induced to swear to all sorts of atrocious things by anti-Confederate partisans." The presence of such a denial in a diary full of candid, often critical comments about the ship's senior officers is puzzling. Numerous seamen testified to tricings, and even the diary of William Whittle, who ordered and in many cases administered them, teems with accounts of the practice. Mason's denial then, however puzzling, seems best explained by a genuine, even willful, ignorance of the practice. Tricings, after all, tended to take place in the topgallant forecastle and other parts of the ship, away from Mason's usual haunts—the weather deck and the wardroom. Moreover, as Mason later established when he refused to read newspaper stories about the Confederacy's faltering fortunes, the young midshipman often sought to avoid disturbing information.

6. Lining Diary, Nov. 10, 12, 1864: 17, 18–21; Whittle Diary, Nov. 10, 12, 13, 20, 1864: 34, 35, 37–38, 43, 52; Still, *Confederate Navy*, 126; "who had ever heard of a gray sailor" quote in ibid., 126; James Ford, captured seaman from *Susan*, affidavit, Feb. 2, 1865, in *CGB*, vol. 1, 869.

7. Whittle Diary, Nov. 13, 14, 15, 20, 1864: 43–45, 47, 52; bond figure for *Adelaide* from *Shenandoah* logbook, Nov. 12, 1864; Lining Diary, Nov. 13, 1864: 21; Hunt, *Cruiser*, 26.

8. Breezing Up

1. Grimball to John Berkley Grimball, Dec. 23, 1864, in JBG Papers; Lining Diary, Nov. 23, 1864: 25; Chew Diary, Jan. 20, 1865, list of crew in *CGB*, vol. 1, 974–97; Whittle, "Cruise," 247; Melville, *White-Jacket*, 372; Whittle Diary, Nov. 10, 1865: 35.

2. Whittle Diary, Nov. 24, 27, Dec. 11, 1864, Jan. 8, 1865: 56, 59–60, 81, 107. Whittle diary reference to having been with Pattie on "one single occasion" (Jan. 8, 107 in ms.) is omitted in published version of Whittle diary—Whittle, *Memorable*, 101.

3. Whittle Diary, Nov. 18, 25, 27, Dec. 4, 1864: 50, 57, 68; Lining Diary, Oct. 19, Nov. 17, 18, 19, Dec. 4, 1864: 5, 23, 29–30, 68; Hunt, *Cruiser*, 29.

4. Hunt, *Cruiser*, 30–31; Lining Diary, Dec. 4, 1864: 29–30; Whittle Diary, Dec. 4, 1864: 68–70.

5. *Edward*'s capture in *Republican Standard*, Oct. 31, 1864, March 9, 1865; *Lizzie M. Stacey* capture, in ibid., March 9, 1865; Whittle Diary,

Dec. 6, 7, 1865: 72–73, 77; Hunt, *Cruiser*, 31–33; Lining Diary, Dec. 6, 7, 1864: 31–34; Waddell, *Shenandoah*, 121.

6. Rodgers to Welles, Jan. 5, 1865, with enclosure; and Rodgers to Welles, Jan. 9 and 9, 1865 (two letters on same day) in *ORN*, Series 1, vol. 3, 403–6; Clark to Welles, Feb. 14, 1865, in ibid., 424–25. For more on USS *Iroquois*, *Wachusett*, and *Onward*'s hunt for *Shenandoah*, see Rodgers to Welles, Sept. 29, 1864; Welles to Robert Townsend, captain of USS *Wachusett*, March 3, 1865, in ibid., 228–29, 444–45.

7. Bulloch to Waddell, Oct. 5, 1864, *ORN* Series 1, vol. 3, 753; Whittle Diary, Dec. 8, 15, 25, 1864: 78, 84; Hunt, *Cruiser*, 34–37; Waddell, *Shenandoah*, 116–17; *Shenandoah* logbook, Dec. 25, 1864; William West identified, *CGB*, vol. 1, 975; Lining Diary, Dec. 25, 1864: 41–42.

8. Whittle Diary, Dec. 13, 16, 17, 1864: 83, 85–88, 90; Robinson, *Shark*, 15; Waddell, *Shenandoah*, 58–59; Harris, et al., intro to Whittle, *Memorable*, 3–5, 13–14; Curry, "Echoes"; Lining Diary, Dec. 13, 15, 16, 18, 1864: 37, 38, 39. For astute discussion of the raider's officer corps, see "Chapter One: The Officers of the *Shenandoah*," in Curry, "Echoes," 25–56.

9. Chew Diary, Dec. 29; Hunt, *Cruiser*, 42–43; Lining Diary, Dec. 29, 30, 31, 1864: 45–47, Jan. 1–2, 1865: 48–49; Waddell, *Shenandoah*, 119–22; Whittle Diary, Jan. 1, 1865: 102.

10. Mason Journal 3, Dec. 21, 1864; Chew Diary, Jan. 13, 1865; Lining Diary, Jan. 16, 18, 1865: 55–56; Hunt, *Cruiser*, 70–71; Whittle Diary, Jan. 17, 18, 1865: 113–14.

11. Whittle Diary, Jan. 19, 21, 22, 1865: 114–15, 117–118; Lining Diary, Jan. 22, 23, 25, 1865: 57–58; Chew Diary, Jan. 25, 1865; Melbourne *Age*, "Supplement," Jan. 19, 1865; Waddell to Barron, Jan. 25, 1865, *ORN*, Series 1, vol. 3, 759.

9. "A Decidedly *Recherché* Affair"

1. Lining Diary, Jan. 25, 1865: 57; Whittle Diary, Jan. 25, 26, 1865: 119–21; Waddell to Darling, Jan. 25, 1865, in Waddell, *Shenandoah*, 124; Waddell to Barron, Jan. 25, 1865, in *ORN*, Series 1, vol 3, 759; Waddell to Mallory, Jan. 25, 1865, in ibid., 759–61; Grimball to John Berkley Grimball, Dec. 23, 1864, JBG Papers; Chew Diary, "Melbourne," March 12, 1865; King to Sir W. Wiseman, Jan. 26, 1865, in *CGB*, vol. 1, 764; Payne to Col. Henderson, Feb. 10, 1865, in ibid., 821–22.

2. William Nichols affidavit, Jan. 26, 1865, in *CGB*, vol. 1, 857–58; Blanchard to Adams, Jan. 26, 1865, in ibid., 856–57, Francis to Blanchard, Jan. 25, in ibid., 858. Blanchard to Darling, Jan. 26, 1865, in ibid., 858.

3. Francis to Waddell, Jan. 26, 1865, *ORN*, Series 1, vol. 3, 761; Lining Diary, Jan. 26, 1865: 59–60; Whittle, Jan. 26, 1865: 121; Mason Journal 4, Jan. 29, March 18, 1865; Hughes, *Fatal Shore*, 562–66; 1860 Melbourne pop. from Mitchell, *International Historical Statistics: Africa, Asia & Oceania, 1750–2000*, 44; Mason Journal 4, Jan. 18, 29, 1865; Potts, *Young America*, 56–57, 146; Curry, "Echoes," 165; quote from miner who joined *Shenandoah* in Michael Cashmore affidavit, Feb. 16, 1865, *CGB*, vol. 1, 881; Ballarat *Star*, Jan. 27, 1865.

4. Whittle Diary, Jan. 26–29, 1865: 121–26; Blanchard to Seward, Feb. 23, 1865, *CGB* vol. 1, 851–56; Still, *Confederate Navy*, 186; and Curry, "Echoes," 155–56, 156 n. 32; Melbourne *Age*, Jan. 27–Feb. 1, 1865; Lining Diary, Jan. 29, 31, 1865: 61, 62; Mason Journal 4, Feb. 3, 1865.

5. Hunt, *Cruiser*, 54–55; Lining Diary, Feb. 4, 8–10, 1865: 64, 66–70; Ballarat *Evening Post*, Feb. 10, 1865; Mason Journal 4, March 18, 1865; Curry, "Echoes," 157, 186 nn. 11, 12, 13; Whittle Diary, Jan. 27, 1865: 122; Waddell to Francis, Jan. 28, 1865, and Francis to Waddell, Jan. 30, 1865, in *CGB*, vol. 1, 905–7; Waddell, *Shenandoah*, 125; Temple deposition, Dec. 6, 1865, in *CGB*, vol. 1, 970.

10. "The Old Sea Dogs Chuckled"

1. Hunt, *Cruiser*, 51; Melbourne *Argus*, Jan. 25, 1865; San Francisco *Daily Alta Californian*, July 22, 1865; Lyttleton to Waddell, Feb. 8, 1865, in Waddell, *Shenandoah*, 126–27; Mason Journal 4, March 18, 1865; Lining Diary, Feb. 3, 17, 1865: 63, 76; Curry, "Echoes," 191; Standish to Waddell, Feb. 1, 1865, in *ORN*, Series 1, vol. 3, 766; Francis to Waddell, Feb. 7, 1865, in *CGB*, vol. 1, 907–8; Waddell to Francis, Feb. 7, and Francis to Waddell, Feb. 14, 1865, in ibid., 907–8; Waddell, *Shenandoah*, 140.

2. Potts, *Young America*, 14; Whittle Diary, Jan. 12, 1865: 110–11; *Shenandoah* logbook, Jan. 29, 1865; Williams affidavits, Feb. 10, 11, in *CGB*, vol. 1, 873–74; partial list of former *Shenandoah* prisoners from Victoria Public Records Office, in Curry, "Echoes," 192; Wicke affidavit, Feb. 14, 1865, in *CGB*, vol. 1, 877–78; Curry, "Echoes," 194; Waddell, *Shenandoah*, 132, 136–38; Lining Diary, Feb. 13–14, 1865: 74.

3. Lining Diary, Feb. 14, 18, 1865: 72–74, 76; Waddell to Francis, Feb. 14, 1865, *ORN*, Series 1, vol. 3, 770–71; Waddell, *Shenandoah*,

134–35; Melbourne *Argus*, Feb. 15, 18, 1865; Mason Journal 4, March 18, 1865: 39, 41; Chew Diary, "Melbourne," March 12, 1865; Lining Diary, Feb. 18, 1865: 76; Melbourne *Argus*, Feb. 15, 1865.

4. Hunt, *Cruiser*, 56–58; Lining Diary, Feb. 18, 1865: 76; Waddell, *Shenandoah*, 132–34, 140–41, 180–81; Waddell to Darling, Jan. 25, 1865, in Waddell, *Shenandoah*, 124; Ballarat *Star*, Feb. 17, 1865; Waddell, "Extracts," in *ORN*, Series 1, vol. 3, 812; Hearn, *Gray Raiders*, 158–60, 179–82, 186, 189, 193; Nepveux, *Trenholm*, 24, 26, 56; Temple affidavit, *CGB*, vol. 1, 970.

5. Waddell, *Shenandoah*, 137; Lining Diary, Jan. 27, 1865: 60; for date of Whittle appointment with Darling, see also Whittle Diary, Jan. 27, 1865: 122; Stern, *When the Guns Roared*, 106–7, 294–95; Marvel, *Alabama and the Kearsarge*, 202–3.

11. "Doubtful Shoals"

1. Still, *Confederate Navy*, 145–74; Curry, "Echoes," 217–18; Waddell, *Shenandoah*, 140; Whittle Diary, Feb. 20, 23, 24, 26, 28, March 1, 1865: 127, 130, 132, 134–36; Lining Diary, Feb. 26, 1865: 78.

2. Lining Diary, Feb. 28, March 5, 1865: 78, 80; Chew Diary, "Melbourne," March 10, 13, 17, 22, 1865; Waddell, *Shenandoah*, 142–43; Whittle Diary, March 5, 1865: 138; Mason Journal 4, March 18, 1865.

3. Chew Diary, March 2, 14, 1865; Whittle Diary, Feb. 26, 28, March 1, 2, 12, 15, 1865: 132–37, 143, 148–49; Lining Diary, March 9, 1865: 81.

4. Whittle Diary, March 15, 1865: 149; Chew Diary, March 22, 23, 24, 25, 26, 1865; Lining Diary, March 23, 24, 26, 29, 1865: 83, 84, 85, 86; Gibson, *Yankees*, 168; Waddell, *Shenandoah*, 143; Maude, *Cruze*, vii–ix.

12. Ascension Island

1. Hanlon, *Stone Altar*, 40–41, 60–61, 74, 89–92, 108–11, 204; identification of mission, Hanlon, e-mail to author, March 2, 2005; Gibson, *Yankees*, 114, 118, 268–78; Mason Journal 4, April 2, 14, 1865; Waddell, *Shenandoah*, 143–49; Hunt, *Cruiser*, 61–64; Whittle Diary, April 1, 1865: 163–64; Chew Diary, April 1, 1865; Lining Diary, April 1, 1865: 87.

2. Hunt, *Cruiser*, 63–69; Mason Journal 4, April 2, 1865; Hanlon, *Stone Altar*, 40–41, 204; Lining Diary, April 2, 1865: 89; Whittle Diary, April 2, 3, 1865: 166, 169; title of chief from Hanlon, e-mail to author,

March 2, 2005; Waddell, *Shenandoah*, 148, 150, 154-55; Waddell, "Extracts," in *ORN*, Series 1, vol. 3, 819.

3. Whittle Diary, April 1, 2, 3, 1865: 165, 167, 169; *Republican Standard*, Aug. 24, 1865; Hunt, *Cruiser*, 64, 68; Waddell, *Shenandoah*, 145, 151, 155; Mason Journal 4, April 2, April 14, 1865; Chew Diary, April 2, 5, 11, 12, 1865; Lining Diary, April 6, 9, 12, 1865: 91, 93, 94; Hanlon, *Stone Altar*, 3.

4. Mason Journal 4, April 2, 14, 1865; Hanlon, *Stone Altar*, 78-80; Chew Diary, April 2, 5, 6, 10, 11, 1865; Hunt, *Cruiser*, 68-69; Whittle Diary, April 9, 1865: 171; Sturges's identification, Hanlon, e-mail to author, March 2, 2005; Lining Diary, April 13, 1865: 94; Finney, *Site Identification*, 19 [and in same volume, "Preservation Plan" appendix 2].

13. Pacific Spring

1. Whittle Diary, April 1, 2, 14, 23, May 1, 1865: 165, 167, 168, 175, 180, 184, 187, 188; Mason Journal 4, April 15, 29, 30, 1865; Chew Diary, April 5, May 5, 6, 7, 9-11, 1865; *Winik*, April 1865, 195; Waddell, *Shenandoah*, 156; Hunt, *Cruiser*, 74-77.

14. Sea of Okhotsk

1. Chew Diary, May 18, 20, 21, 22, 23, 26, 27, 1865: 129; Lining Diary, May 20, 21, 1865: 104; Hunt, *Cruiser*, 74-76, 80-81; *Republican Standard*, Aug. 17, 24, 1865; Whittle Diary, May 27-June 12, 1865: 196-211; Waddell, *Shenandoah*, 157-58; Temple affidavit, Dec. 6, 1865, *CGB*, vol. 1, 972. For background on mid-1840s origins of European and U.S. whaling in Sea of Okhotsk, see Webb, *On the Northwest*, 110, 317 n. 168, 327 n. 14.

2. Waddell, *Shenandoah*, 158-62; Temple affidavit, Dec. 6, 1865, in *CGB*, vol. 1, 968; Chew Diary, May 27, 28, June 1, 3, 4, 5, 7, 8, 1865; Mason Journal 4, May 28, 1865; Waddell to Whittle, May 29, 1865, in *ORN*, Series 1, vol. 3, 775; Whittle Diary, May 28, 29, 30, June 3, 4, 5, 1865: 197, 198, 199-204; Hunt, *Cruiser*, 76-79; Lining Diary, May 27-31: 106-8.

15. Bering Sea

1. Chew Diary, June 11, 12, 13, 16, 19, 21, 1865; Whittle Diary, June 12, 16, 19, 21, 1865: 211, 214, 216, 217, 218. Bockstoce, *Whales, Ice and Men*, 112; Waddell ("Extracts," in *ORN*, Series 1, vol. 3, 825) assessed

aggregate value of vessels *Euphrates* and *William Thompson* as $83,000 and claimed that combined they had on board 800 casks of whale oil.

2. Waddell, *Shenandoah*, 164–66; Mason Journal 4, June 22, 1865; Hunt, *Cruiser*, 83–88; *Republican Standard*, Aug. 3, 17, 24, Dec. 21, 1865; Whittle Diary, June 12–13, 1865: 210–23; Williams, "Jireh Swift," in *Neptune*, 27 (1967): 263; *Mercury* logbook, June 25, 1865, in Old Dartmouth Historical Society, New Bedford Whaling Museum; Grimball, "Career," 123, misstates date repeated, in *Shenandoah* logbook. Correct repeated date was Thursday, June 22, 1865.

3. Hare, *Salted Tories*, 9; Waddell, *Shenandoah*, 164–67; *Republican Standard*, Aug. 31, 1865; Waddell letter, Jan. 27, 1865, in DuBose Family Civil War Collection, Atlanta History Center; for *Susan Abigail*'s departure from San Francisco, see San Francisco *Daily Alta Californian*, April 28, 1865; Mason Journal 4, June 23, [24, 1865]; Whittle Diary, June 13–25, 1865: 212–25; Chew Diary, June 25, 1865; Lining Diary, June 25, 1865: 110; Hunt, *Cruiser*, 89–93.

16. The Hardest Blow Against Yankee Commerce

1. Kirschbaum, "Captured," New Beford Whaling Museum; *Shenandoah* logbook, June 26, 1865; *Republican Standard*, Aug. 31, 1865; William C. Nye affidavit, *CGB*, vol. 1, 850–51; background on Clark, Lund, *Whaling Masters and Whaling Voyage*, 68; for background on William C. Nye, see ibid., 713; logbook for the bark *Mercury* of New Bedford, July 20, 1863, to May 25, 1867, George S. Tooker master, New Bedford Whaling Museum. In the Aug. 31, 1865, *Republic Standard* story, Captain Clark of the *Ocean Plover* and *Nimrod* identifies his Confederate interlocutor as Lieutenant Sidney Smith Lee—an impossibility, as Lee never served aboard the *Alabama*. In all likelihood, the story confuses Lee with another young lieutenant—in fact, the *Shenandoah*'s only lieutenant who had also served aboard the *Alabama*, and who, moreover, bore a famous Confederate surname: Irvine Bulloch.

2. Kirschbaum, "Captured," New Beford Whaling Museum; Waddell, *Shenandoah*, 168–71; Whittle Diary, June 27–28, 1865: 226–30; Hunt, *Cruiser*, 94–102; *Republican Standard*, Aug. 24, 31, 1865; Mason Journal 4, June 28–29, 1865; Chew Diary, June 27–28, 1865; Young's age from *Ship Registers of New Bedford*, 2; U.S. Census 1860; more on Young in Lund, *Whaling Masters and Voyages*, 362; Gray's death in ibid., 153; Starbuck, *American Whale Fishery*, 102–3.

3. Kirschbaum, "Captured," New Bedford Whaling Museum; Whittle Diary,

June 29, 30: 230–31; Hunt, *Cruiser*, 102; Waddell, *Shenandoah*, 171; Lining Diary, June 28–29, 1865: 120–21; Chew Diary, June 28–29, 1865.

17. "A Sort of Choking Sensation"

1. Whittle Diary, June 29–July 4, 1865: 230–35; Mason Journal 4, July 1, 1865; Waddell, "Extracts," in *ORN*, Series 1, vol. 3, 830; Waddell, *Shenandoah*, 172–73; Lining Diary, June 29–July 5, 1865: 120–22; Chew Diary, July 1, 2, 5; Hunt, *Cruiser*, 102–6; Waddell, *Shenandoah*, 172–75.

2. Bulloch to Waddell, Oct. 5, 1864, in *ORN*, Series 1, vol. 3, 754–55; Waddell, *Shenandoah*, 174–75; "U.S.S. Camanche," in *ORN*, Series 2, vol. 1, 50; Whittle Diary, July 6, 11, 14, 17, 1865: 236, 237, 242–43; Lining Diary, July 6–13, 1865: 123–24; Chew Diary, July 13, 14, 1865; Hunt, *Cruiser*, 105.

3. McDougal to Welles, July 20, 23, 1865, in *ORN* Series 1, vol. 3, 569, 571, and 571 n.; *Republican Standard*, May 4, Aug. 13, Oct. 5, 1865; "Address of James G. Swan," Washington Pioneer Association, 107; Hare, *Salted Tories*, 38.

4. Chew Diary, July 19, 20, 1865; Whittle Diary, July 19, 20, 25, 31, 1865: 244–47, 249–50; Mason Journal 4, Aug. 3, 1865.

5. Bulloch to Waddell, June 19, 1865, in *ORN*, Series 1, vol. 3, 776–77; Bulloch to Mason, June 19, 1865, in ibid., 775–76; Mason to Russell, June 20, 1865, in ibid., 777; E. Hammond, British secretary of state, to Mason, June 22, 1865, in ibid., 778; *Shenandoah* logbook, Aug. 2, 1865; Lining Diary, Aug. 3, 1864: 130; Whittle Diary, Aug. 9, 1865: 254; Mason Journal 4, Aug. 3, 1865; Chew Diary, Aug. 6, 1865; Hunt, *Cruiser*, 107–8.

18. "Long Gauntlet to Run"

1. Waddell, "Extract," *ORN*, Series 1, vol. 3, 832; Waddell, *Shenandoah*, 176–77; Chew Diary, Aug. 3, 6, 1865; Mason Journal 4, Aug. 3, 1865; Lining Diary, Aug. 2, 3, 1865: 129–30.

2. Chew Diary, Aug. 4, 6, 18, 1865: 130–31; Mason Journal 5, Aug. 4, 5, 7, 8, 9, 22, 1865; Waddell, *Shenandoah*, 177–79; Whittle Diary, Aug. 3–22, 1865: 252–59; Lining Diary, June 15, Aug. 4, 13, 19, 23, Sept. 6–8, 11, 23, 1865: 131, 114, 134–35, [139], 140, 141, 145, 182; Hunt, *Cruiser*, 109.

3. Lining Diary, Aug. 24–27, 31, Sept. 1, 21, 1865: 135–37, 138–[39],

144; Chew Diary, Aug. 26–Sept. 21, 1865; Whittle Diary, Aug. 23–Sept. 21, 1865: 259–69; Waddell, *Shenandoah*, 178–79; Mason Journal 5, Aug. 22, Sept. 28, 1865.

4. Whittle Diary, Sept. 12, 1865: 269; Lining Diary, Sept. 26, 1865: 145–46; Chew et al. to Waddell, Sept. 28, 1865, in *ORN*, Series 1, vol. 3, 779–80; Codd et al. to Waddell, Sept. 28, 1865 in *ORN*, Series 1, vol. 3, 781–82.

5. Chew Diary, Sept. 27, 30, 1865; Lining Diary, Sept. 27–30, Oct. 2, 1865: 146–49; Grimball et al. to Waddell, Sept. 29, 1865, and Morton et al. to Waddell [Sept. 29, 1865], in *ORN*, Series 1, vol. 3, 782–83; Waddell, *Shenandoah*, 179; Whittle Diary, Sept. 27–30, 1865: 271–74; Mason Journal 5, Sept. 29, 1865; Grimball quoted in ibid., Sept. 29, 1865.

6. Whittle Diary, Sept. 29, 1865: 272–73; Chew Diary, Sept. 30, 1865; Lining Diary, Oct. 2, 1865: 148.

19. "A Perfect Hell Afloat"

1. Whittle Diary, Oct. 4, 1865: 276; Chew Diary, Oct. 10, 13, 17, 19, 21, 1865; Mason Journal 5, Oct. 9, 10, 21, 1865; Lining Diary, Oct. 10, 19, 21, 1865: 152, 159, 160; Circular to colonial officials of British ports, Sept. 7, 1865, in *CGB*, vol. 1, 923; Russell to lord commissioners of the admiralty, Oct. 6, 1865, in ibid., 923–24; Still, *Confederate Navy*, 185.

2. Chew Diary, Oct. 11, 13, 14, 1865: 215–16; Lining Diary, Oct. 10, 11, 13, 14, 19, 1865: 152–54, 156–59; Whittle Diary, Oct. 10–12, 1865: 280–83.

3. Whittle Diary, Oct. 14, 24, 25, 26, 30, 31, 1865: 284, 290–92, 295–96; Waddell, *Shenandoah*, 179–81; Chew Diary, Oct. 24, 26, 1865; Mason Journal 4, June 18, 1865; Mason Journal 5, Oct. 20, 24, 27, 1865; Lining Diary, Oct. 24, 27, 30, 31, 1865: 161–64. Waddell, *Shenandoah*, 181, asserted that he was later told that the mystery ship the *Shenandoah* encountered on October 14 was "probably" the USS *Saranac*. That, however, seems unlikely in that the side-wheel steam sloop spent the entire Civil War on patrol duties in the Pacific and remained there until sinking in 1875—from "Saranac," *Dictionary of American Naval Fighting Ships*, electronic access.

4. Chew Diary, Nov. 1, 3, 5, 1865; Whittle Diary, Nov. 1–3, 1865: 296–300; Lining Diary, Nov. 1–3, 5, 1865: 165–66; Waddell, *Shenandoah*, 181–82; Mason Journal 5, Nov. 2, 1865; Hunt, *Cruiser*, 117–19; Temple affidavit, Dec. 6, 1865, in *CGB*, vol. 1, 973.

20. "The Old Ship Became Fainter and Fainter"

1. Robert W. Warwick to H. Lloyd, Nov. 8, 1865, *ORN* Series 1, vol. 3, 782; Waddell to Russell, Nov. 6, 1865, ibid., 783–84; Hunt, *Cruiser*, 118–28; Lining Diary, Nov. 6–8, 1865: 167–70; *Times of London*, Nov. 8, 1865: Temple deposition, Dec. 6, 1865, *CGB*, vol. 1, 974; Paynter to secretary of admiralty, Nov. 8, 1865, in ibid., 949; W. G. Stewart, acting collector, and J. W. Lilley, inspector general, to commissioner of customs, Nov. 6, 1865, in ibid., 933; Paynter to the secretary to the admiralty, Nov. 10, 1865, in ibid., 950–51; *The New York Times*—two stories, both Nov. 24, 1865—"The Shenandoah, The Release of Her Crew" and "The Pirate Shenandoah as She Appeared when Turned Over to the American Consul." The *Shenandoah*'s flag and other artifacts from the raider now belong to the Museum of the Confederacy, in Richmond, Virginia.

2. Waddell, *Shenandoah*, 184; Chew Diary, Nov. 1, 4, 1865; Horan, intro, in Waddell, *Shenandoah*, 43; *The New York Times*, "Pirate Shenandoah," Nov. 24, 1865.

3. Temple deposition, Dec. 6, 1865, *CGB*, vol. 1, 973; Whittle to Samuel Barron, April 13, 1866: 2, in Barron Family Papers, Virginia Historical Society; Dalton, *Roosevelt*, 84, 548–49 n. 23; Curry, "Echoes," 318, 319, 322; Harris et. al., intro, in Whittle, *Memorable*, 41, 42; Lining Diary, Oct. 31, 1865; 164, 166; Mason Journal 5, Nov. 12, 13, 17, 19.

4. Curry, "Echoes," 319–28; 367–68; Harris et. al., intro., in Whittle, *Memorable*, 40–44; Hunt's memoirs contained doubtful, unsubstantiated accusations that Waddell absconded with funds from the ship's treasury—Hunt, *Cruiser*, 129–30. For background on Civil War veterans in Egyptian Army, see Morgan, *Recollections of a Rebel Reefer*, 266–314, and Hesseltine and Wolf, *Blue and Gray on the Nile*; for references to Hunt, see Hesseltine and Wolf, *Blue and Gray on the Nile*, 21, 75, 83, 112–13, 117, 236, 255, 271.

5. Curry, "Echoes," 315; various documents and newspaper clips, Waddell Papers, North Carolina Archives; Whittle to Samuel Barron, April 13, 1866: 3 (inverse), in Barron Family Papers; Horan, intro, in Waddell, *Shenandoah*, 42–45; Waddell letter, Dec. 27, 1865, in Hunt, *Cruiser*, 130–32; Waddell, *Shenandoah*, 184–87, 193; *Dictionary of American Naval Fighting Ships*, electronic access.

6. Dalzell, *Flight*, 229–36, 247; Waddell, *Shenandoah*, 47; Hearn, *Gray Raiders of the Sea*, 304–9; *Republican Standard*, Aug. 3, 10, Nov. 23, 1865; Bauer, *Maritime History*, 246–49; New York *World*, July 7, 1864.

7. Waddell, *Shenandoah*, 43, 50, 51; Dalzell, *Flight*, 228–29; Mason Journal 5, Nov. 23, 1865.

Note on Sources

For almost a century, historians studying the *Shenandoah* and other Civil War vessels have pored over the copious materials, mostly official letters and other government documents, collected in the magisterial thirty-one-volume *Official Records of the Union and Confederate Navies in the War of the Rebellion*, published by the federal government between 1894 and 1922.

Published accounts of the cruise written by at least eight *Shenandoah* officers shed further light. Those memoirs include the two slightly different versions of Captain James I. Waddell's recollections—one, titled "Extract from Notes," in the *Official Records*; the other, edited by James David Horan, separately published. Still other background on the raider may be gleaned from crew members' letters found in several repositories. (For specific information on these and other sources mentioned herein, see Bibliography, pages 397–404.)

But what truly sets the *Shenandoah*'s records apart from those of other Confederate vessels are the contemporary writings that survived her cruise. Begin with the six duplicates of her logbook, copied by officers aboard the raider that are now held by various archives—those of Midshipman John Thomson Mason (the Museum of the Confederacy); Acting Master Irvine Bulloch (Chicago Historical Society); Lieutenant John Grimball

(Charleston Library Society); Lieutenant Francis Chew (University of North Carolina); and Captain James I. Waddell (North Carolina State Archives). Finally, there is the raider's so-called clean log, the official logbook copied at the cruise's end for official purposes and now owned by the Atlanta Historical Society.

Recorded by the ship's deck officers who stood each of the day's successive seven watches, the *Shenandoah*'s logbook, in all of its faithfully copied incarnations, presents sparely inscribed but essential, often hour-to-hour, information on the ship's location, course, and speed, as well as wind, weather, and sea conditions. Each deck officer also recorded anything notable that transpired on his watch—an observational dog's breakfast that included landfalls, unusual sightings, captures of ships, cargoes and crews, and infractions of shipboard rules. Providing still more—but in the end limited—insight into the cruise is Captain Waddell's "Abstract Log of CSS Shenandoah," which appears in the *Official Records*. In truth, however, its title is a misnomer. For this document is less a log than, ostensibly, the captain's day-to-day barebones notes from the cruise. But, apparently reconstructed from an earlier document, its value is diminished by chronological gaps and errors.

In the end, for the historian, the most prized jewels in the *Shenandoah*'s archival treasure chest are the four shipboard officers' diaries that survived her cruise and that animate *Sea of Gray*—those of Surgeon Charles Lining, Midshipman Mason, First Lieutenant William Whittle, Jr. (those three held by the Museum of the Confederacy); and Lieutenant Francis Chew (held by the University of North Carolina, Chapel Hill). Individually and collectively, this quartet of journals conveys a rare and intimate picture of day-to-day life aboard a Confederate raider.

Recollections written after the fact by participants in historical episodes are on occasion reliable. More often, however, such memoirs—such as some of those authored by the *Shen-*

andoah officers, penned decades after the war and scantly re-searched—can be notoriously unreliable.

Why do such memoirs written after the passage of years of-ten lack the authority—and passion and fluidity—of writings produced closer to the events they chronicle? The reasons are myriad: memories fade; in other cases, memoirists, nursing old grudges, omit personally embarrassing episodes or hurl un-founded charges at rivals; in still other cases, aspiring to magna-nimity, they deliberately downplay or omit past disputes.

In both factual detail and emotional content, these postwar *Shenandoah* memoirs tend to be far less vivid than the four di-aries penned in the heat, or the ennui, of shipboard life. To be sure, the shortcomings of bias and other human frailties that blunt any written sources limit the officers' diaries. At the very least, however, these diaries—even allowing for biases and omis-sions—tend to be more reliable in transmitting the core facts of chronicled incidents. And when a discrepancy surfaces in one diary's account of a jointly described incident, the other diaries tend to provide a check on accuracy. Beyond that, the diaries tend to present a naked version of the officers' state of mind—with raw biases abundantly on display.

In many ways, this was—at least for officers—the ideal di-arist's ship. As the only Confederate vessel to complete a cir-cumnavigation of the globe, the *Shenandoah* took thirteen months to complete her cruise. During that time, weeks often passed between encounters with enemy ships. Such intervals left officers, once they had completed their daily duties and watches, with little to do except read books and write in their journals, an impulse compounded by their growing self-consciousness of their cruise's historical importance.

Still other *Shenandoah* documents offer glimpses of life at sea for common sailors in the Confederate navy. We have no sea-men's diaries from the cruise. But after peace returned, wartime

assaults on Union shipping by the *Shenandoah* and other raiders
sparked legal actions by the United States against Great Britain.
U.S. prosecutors sought to hold Great Britain liable for attacks
by Confederate ships upon Union vessels. And the thousands of
documents generated by that litigation, by both U.S. and British
officials, offer yet another bountiful vein for historians of Confederate commerce raiding.

To strengthen the American case, during and after the war
U.S. diplomats posted to England and Australia took scores of
affidavits from people whose wartime experiences might but-
tress Uncle Sam's case. In the case of the *Shenandoah*, those
deposed included seamen held as prisoners aboard the raider.
Still other affidavits came from sailors who had voluntarily, or
through coercion, elected to "ship" with the Confederates—to
join the raider's crew. Beyond offering a glimpse into the daily
lives of these seamen, these affidavits—particularly in their
wrenching depictions of shipboard physical torture—counter-
claims by *Shenandoah* officers' sources that the Confederates
never employed coercion to win enlistments.

Together, these voices from the *Shenandoah*—in tone variously formal and chatty, sentimental and boyish, generous and
rueful, exuberant and despairing—not only yield fresh insights
into the raider's military and sailing operations; in their depictions of interactions among the raider's crew and other fellow
shipmates—including women, Pacific islanders, and African
Americans—these voices reveal the dynamics of Confederate
ideology on matters of race, class, nationalism, and gender. Beyond that, just as Winslow Homer's illustrations of camp scenes
capture unguarded moments in the lives of Civil War infantry,
so these *Shenandoah* documents grant us entrée into the
everyday life of Confederates at sea, an intimate portrait of
young men at war.

Bibliography

Manuscripts and Papers

Francis Thornton Chew Diary, in Francis Thornton Chew Papers, University of North Carolina, Chapel Hill, N.C.

DuBose Family Civil War Collection, Atlanta History Center, Atlanta, Ga.

Charles Edward Lining Diary, Museum of the Confederacy, Richmond, Va.

Thomas H. Dudley Collection, Huntington Library, San Marino, Cal.

Logbook of the *Shenandoah*, Chicago Historical Society, Chicago, Ill.

Logbook of the *Shenandoah*, Charleston Library Society, Charleston, S.C.

Logbook of the *Shenandoah*, Atlanta History Center, Atlanta, Ga.

John Berkley Grimball Papers, Duke University Library, Durham, N.C.

John Thomson Mason Journal [in five parts], Museum of the Confederacy, Richmond, Va.

Logbooks and miscellaneous documents, Dartmouth Historical Society, New Bedford Whaling Museum, New Bedford, Mass.

Shipping Articles of the *Shenandoah*, Museum of the Confederacy, Richmond, Va.

James Iredell Waddell Papers, North Carolina Division of Historical Resources, Archives and Records Section, Raleigh, N.C.

William C. Whittle, Jr. Diary [photocopy], Virginia Historical Society, Richmond, Va.

Government Documents and Publications

Atlas to Accompany the Official Records of the Union and Confederate Armies. Washington: Government Printing Office, 1880–1901.

Case of Great Britain as Laid Before the Tribunal of Arbitration Convened at Geneva . . . 3 vols. Washington, D.C.: U.S. Government Printing Office, 1872.

Case of United States to Be Laid Before the Tribunal of Arbitration to be Convened at Geneva . . . London: Richard Bentley & Sons, 1872.

Civil War Naval Chronology, 1861–1865. Washington, D.C.: U.S. Government Printing Office, Naval History Division, 1971.

Dictionary of American Naval Fighting Ships. 8 vols. Washington, D.C.: U.S. Supt. of Docs, U.S. Naval History Division, 1859–81, and electronic access.

Official Records of the Union and Confederate Navies in the War of the Rebellion. 31 vols. Washington, D.C.: U.S. Government Printing Office, 1894–1922.

Papers Relating to the Treaty of Washington. 6 vols. Washington, D.C.: U.S. Government Printing Office, 1872–74.

War of the Rebellion: A Compilation of the Official Records of the Union and Confederate Armies. 128 vols. Washington, D.C.: U.S. Government Printing Office, 1880–1901.

Savage, Carlton, ed. *Policy of the United States Toward Maritime Commerce in War.* Washington, D.C.: U.S. Government Printing Office, 1934.

Published Memoirs and Correspondences

Adams, Charles Francis, et al. *A Cycle of Adams Letters.* 2 vols. Boston: Houghton Mifflin, 1920.

Bigelow, John. *France and the Confederate Navy.* 1888. Reprint, New York: Bergman Publishers, 1968.

Bulloch, James D. *Secret Service of the Confederate States in Europe.* 2 vols. New York: G. P. Putnam's Sons, 1884.

Dana, Richard Henry. *Two Years Before the Mast.* 1840. Reprint, New York: Harper & Row, 1965.

Grimball, John. "Career of the Shenandoah" Feb. 3, 1863. Originally published in *Sunday News,* Charleston, S.C., *Southern Historical Society Papers,* vol. 25 (1897): 116–30.

———. "The Photograph Album of Lt. John Grimball, CSN." Commentary by John Mills Bigham. *Military Images* 15 (May–June 1994): 6–8.

Davis, Jefferson. *Rise and Fall of the Confederate Nation.* 2 vols. 1881. Reprint, New York: Thomas Yoseloff, 1958.

Hunt, Cornelius E. *The Shenandoah: or, the Last Confederate Cruiser.* New

York: Carleton & Co. 1867; Reprint, New York: William Abbatt, 1910, as Extra No. 12 of *The Magazine of History with Notes and Queries.*

Lumpkin, Martha Neville, ed. *"Dear Darling Loulie": Letters of Cordelia Lewis Scales to Loulie W. Irby During and After the War Between the States.* Boulder, Colo.: Ben Gray Lumpkin, 1955.

McNulty, Dr. F. J. "The Shenandoah: Her Exploits in the Pacific Ocean, After the Struggle of 1861–65 Had Closed." *Southern Historical Society Papers* 21 (1893): 165–76.

Mahan, Captain A. T. *The Influence of Sea Power Upon History.* 1890. Reprint, Boston: Little, Brown, 1916.

Mason, John Thomson. "Last of the Confederate Cruisers." *Century Illustrated Magazine* 56 (1898): 600–11.

Melville, Herman. *White-Jacket: or, the World in a Man-of-War* [1850], in Melville, *Redburn, White-Jacket, Moby Dick.* Reprint of works, New York: Library of America, 1983.

Moran, Benjamin. *The Journal of Benjamin Moran, 1857–1865.* 2 vols. Chicago: University of Chicago Press, 1948–49.

Morgan, James Morris. *Recollections of a Rebel Reefer.* Boston: Houghton Mifflin, 1917.

Scales, Dabney. "Cruise of the Shenandoah." With tribute to John Thomson Mason by William C. Whittle. *The Confederate Veteran,* 12 (1904): 489–90.

Semmes, Raphael. *Memoirs of Service Afloat.* Baltimore: Kelly, Piet & Co., 1869.

Swan, James G. "Address of James G. Swan delivered at the fourth annual reunion of the Washington Pioneer Association at Port Townsend, June 1887." Transactions of the Washington Pioneer Association, 1883–1889.

Waddell, James I. *C.S.S. Shenandoah: The Memoirs of Lieutenant Commanding James I. Waddell.* Edited by James David Horan. New York: Crown Publishers, 1960.

Welles, Gideon. *Diary of Gideon Welles.* 3 vols. New York: Norton, 1960.

Whitman, Walt. *Leaves of Grass.* 1855. Reprint, New York: Library of America, 1982.

Whittle, William C. "Cruise of the Shenandoah." *Southern Historical Society Papers* 35 (1907): 235-58. Originally published in Whittle, "Cruises of the Confederate States Steamers *Shenandoah* and *Nashville*" (n.p., 1910).

Whittle, William C., Jr. *Voyage of the Shenandoah.* Edited by D. Alan Harris and Anne B. Harris. Tuscaloosa: University of Alabama, 2005.

Contemporary Newspapers, Magazines, and Serials
Ballarat (Australia) *Evening Post*
Ballarat *Star*
Century Illustrated Magazine
Charleston *Sunday News*
Confederate Veteran
Illustrated News of London
Lloyd's List (London)
Lloyd's Register of British and Foreign Shipping (London)
Melbourne *Age*
Melbourne *Argus*
New Bedford (Massachusetts) *Republican Standard*
The New York Times
New York *World*
San Francisco *Daily Alta Californian*

Secondary Sources
Adams, Epraim Douglass. *Great Britain and the American Civil War.* 2 vols. New York: Longmans, Green & Co., 1925.

Ashe, S. A. "Shenandoah: A Sketch of the Eventful Life of the Confederate Cruiser." *Southern Historical Society Papers* 32 (1904): 320–28.

Bauer, K. Jack. *A Maritime History of the United States.* Columbia: University of South Carolina Press, 1988.

Baynham, Henry. *Naval Ratings of the Nineteenth Century.* London: Hutchinson, 1971.

Bennett, Michael J. *Union Jacks: Yankee Sailors in the Civil War.* Chapel Hill: University of North Carolina Press, 2004.

Bockstoce, John R. *Whales, Ice, and Men: The History of Whaling in the Western Arctic.* Seattle: University of Washington Press with New Bedford Whaling Museum, Massachusetts, 1986.

Brooke, George M., Jr. *John M. Brooke: Naval Scientist and Educator.* Charlottesville: University Press of Virginia, 1980.

Busch, Briton Cooper. *Whaling Will Never Do for Me: The American Whaleman in the Nineteenth Century.* Lexington: University of Kentucky, 1994.

Curry, Angus. "Echoes of a Civil War: The CSS *Shenandoah* and Its Officers." Diss.: La Trobe University, Bundoora, Australia, 2002.

Dalton, Kathleen. *Theodore Roosevelt: A Strenuous Life.* New York: Random House, 2002.

Dalzell, George W. *The Flight from the Flag: The Continuing Effect of the Civil War upon the American Carrying Trade*. Chapel Hill: University of North Carolina Press, 1940.

Davis, William C. *Jefferson Davis: The Man and His Hour*. New York: HarperCollins, 1991.

deKay, James Tertius. *The Rebel Raiders*. New York: Ballantine, 2002.

Duberman, Martin. *Charles Francis Adams, 1807–1886*. Stanford: Stanford University Press, 1960.

Durkin, Joseph T. *Stephen R. Mallory: Confederate Navy Chief*. Chapel Hill: University of North Carolina Press, 1954.

Finney, Suzanne, and Michael Graves. *Site Identification of a Civil War Shipwreck Thought to Be Sunk by the C.S.S. Shenandoah in April 1865*. Washington, D.C.: National Park Service, 2002.

Foster, Kevin J. "The Diplomats Who Sank a Fleet." Parts 1 and 2. *Prologue* 33 (fall 2001). Electronic access.

Fowler. *Under Two Flags: The American Navy in the Civil War*. New York: Norton, 1990.

Gilbert, Benjamin Franklin. "The *Shenandoah* Down Under: Her Sojourn at Melbourne." *Journal of the West* 5 (1996): 321–35.

Gibson, Arrell Morgan. *Yankees in Paradise: The Pacific Basin Frontier*. Albuquerque: University of New Mexico Press, 1993.

Hanlon, David. *Upon a Stone Altar: A History of the Island of Pohnpei to 1890*. Honolulu: University of Hawaii Press, 1988.

Hare, Lloyd C. M. *Salted Tories: The Story of the Whaling Fleets of San Francisco*. Mystic, Conn.: Marine Historical Association, 1960.

Harland, John. *Seamanship in the Age of Sail*. Washington, D.C.: Naval Institute Press, 1984.

Hearn, Chester G. Gray. *Raiders of the Sea: How Eight Confederate Warships Destroyed the Union's High Seas Commerce*. Camden, Me.: International Marine Publishing, 1992.

Herman, Arthur. *To Rule the Waves: How the British Navy Shaped the Modern World*. New York: HarperCollins, 2004.

Hesseltine, William B., and Hazel C. Wolf. *The Blue and Gray on the Nile*. Chicago: University of Chicago Press, 1961.

Hill, Jim Dan. *Sea Dogs of the Sixties*. Minneapolis: University of Minnesota Press, 1935.

Hohman, Elmo P. *American Whaleman: A Study of Life and Labor in the Whaling Industry*. 1928. Reprint, Clifton, N.J.: Augustus M. Kelley, 1972.

Horn, Stanley F. *Gallant Rebel: The Fabulous Cruise of the C.S.S. Shenandoah*. New Brunswick, N.J.: Rutgers University Press, 1947.

Hughes, Robert. *Fatal Shore*. New York: Vintage, 1986.

Jones, Robert E. "Rebel Without a War." *Military History Quarterly* 9 (1996): 72–79.

Jordan, Donaldson, and Edwin J. Pratt. *Europe and the American Civil War*. Boston: Houghton Mifflin, 1931.

Karsten, Peter. *The Naval Aristocracy*. New York: Free Press, 1972.

Lavery, Brian. *Ship*. Washington, D.C.: Smithsonian Institution, 2004.

Lonn, Ella. *Foreigners in the Confederacy*. Gloucester, Mass.: Peter Smith, 1965.

Luraghi, Raimondo. *A History of the Confederate Navy*. Translated by Paolo E. Coletta. 1993. Reprint, Annapolis, Md.: Naval Institute Press, 1996.

McPherson, James M. *Battle Cry of Freedom*. New York: Oxford University Press, 1988.

MacGregor, David R. *Fast Sailing Ships: Their Design and Construction, 1775–1875*. London: Naval Institute Press, 1973.

Marvel, William. *The Alabama and the Kearsarge: The Sailor's Civil War*. Chapel Hill, N.C.: University of North Carolina Press, 1996.

Maude, F. W. Foreword in Giles, W. E. A. *Cruize in a Queensland Labour Vessel to the South Seas*. Edited by Deryck Scarr. Pacific History Series, no. 1. Canberra: Australian National University Press, 1968.

Merli, Frank. *Great Britain and the Confederate Navy, 1861–1865*. Bloomington: Indiana University Press, 1970.

Milton, David Hepburn. *Lincoln's Spymaster: Thomas Haines Dudley and the Liverpool Network*. Mechanicsburg, Penn.: Stackpole Books, 2003.

Morgan, Murray. *Confederate Raider in the North Pacific: The Saga of the C.S.S. Shenandoah, 1864–65*. Pullman, Wash.: Washington State University Press, 1995 (originally published as *Dixie Raider*, New York: E. P. Dutton, 1948).

Nepveux, Ethel Trenholm Seabrook. *George Alfred Trenholm*. Charleston, S.C.: Comprint, 1973.

Nordhoff, Charles. *Man-of-War Life*. 1855. Reprint, Annapolis, Md.: Naval Institute Press, 1985.

Owsley, Frank Lawrence. *King Cotton Diplomacy: Foreign Relations of the Confederate States of America*. 2nd ed. Revised by Harriet Chappell Owsley. 1931. Reprint, Chicago: University of Chicago Press, 1959.

Pearl, Cyril. *Rebel Down Under: When the 'Shenandoah' Shook Melbourne, 1865*. Melbourne: Heinemann, 1970.

Philbrick, Nathaniel. *In the Heart of the Sea: The Tragedy of the Whaleship Essex*. New York: Viking, 2000.

——. *Sea of Glory: America's Voyage of Discovery, The U.S. Exploring Expedition, 1838–1842*. New York: Viking, 2003.

Potts, E. Daniel, and Annette Potts. *Young America and Australian Gold: Americans and the Gold Rush of the 1850s*. St. Lucia, Australia: University of Queensland Press, 1974.

Ramold, Steven J. *Slaves, Sailors, Citizens: African Americans in the Union Navy*. DeKalb, Ill.: Northern Illinois University Press, 2002.

Reidy, Joseph P. "Black Men in Navy Blue During the Civil War." *Prologue* 33 (fall 2001).

Robinson, Charles M., III. *Shark of the Confederacy: The Story of the CSS Alabama*. Annapolis, Md.: Naval Institute Press, 1995.

Scharf, Thomas J. *History of the Confederate States Navy*. New York: Rogers & Sherwood, 1887.

Schooler, Lynn. *The Last Shot*. New York: HarperCollins, 2005.

Spencer, Warren E. *The Confederate Navy in Europe*. University: University of Alabama Press, 1983.

Stern, Philip Van Doren. *When the Guns Roared*. New York: Doubleday & Co., 1965.

Still, William N., ed. *The Confederate Navy: The Ships, Men and Organization, 1861–65*. Annapolis, Md.: Naval Institute Press, 1997.

Thomas, Evan. *John Paul Jones: Sailor, Hero, Father of the American Navy*. New York: Simon and Schuster, 2003.

Valle, James E. *Rocks and Shoals: Order and Discipline in the Old Navy, 1800–1861*. Annapolis, Md.: Naval Institute Press, 1980.

Vandiver, Frank. *Rebel Brass: The Confederate Command System*. Baton Rouge: Louisiana State University Press, 1956.

Wayland, John W. *Pathfinder of the Seas: The Life of Matthew Fontaine Maury*. Richmond, Va.: Garrett & Massie, 1930.

Webb, Robert Lloyd. *On the Northwest: Commercial Whaling in the Pacific Northwest 1790–1967*. Vancouver, Canada: University of British Columbia Press, 1988.

Wells, Tom Henderson. *The Confederate Navy: A Study in Organization*. University: University of Alabama Press, 1971.

Williams, Frances Leigh. *Matthew Fontaine Maury: Scientist of the Sea*. New Brunswick, N.J.: Rutgers University Press, 1963.

Williams, Harold. "Yankee Whaling Fleets Raided by Confederate Cruisers: The Story of the Bark *Jireh Swift*, Captain Thomas Williams." *American Neptune* 27 (October 1967): 263–78.

Woodworth, Celia. "The Confederate Raider Shenandoah at Melbourne." *U.S. Naval Institute Proceedings* (June 1973): 67–75.

Reference Sources

Benét, William Rose. *The Reader's Encyclopedia.* New York: Harper & Row, 1965.

Bowditch, Nathaniel. *American Practical Navigator.* 1802. Rev. ed., Washington, D.C.: U.S. Government Printing Office, 1943.

Central Intelligence Agency. *World Factbook.* Electronic access.

Cochran, Thomas C., and Wayne Andrews, eds. *Concise Dictionary of American History.* New York: Charles Scribner's Sons, 1962.

Garraty, John A., and Jerome L. Sternstein. *Encyclopedia of American Biography.* 2nd ed. New York: HarperCollins, 1995.

Geoghegan, W. E. "Reconstructed Plans for the *Shenandoah*, CSN." Collection of Warship Plans, Smithsonian Institution.

Lund, Judith Navas. *Whaling Masters and Whaling Voyages Sailing from American Ports.* New Bedford, Mass.: New Bedford Whaling Museum, 2001.

Malone, Dumas, ed. *Dictionary of American Biography,* 22 vols. New York: Charles Scribner's Sons. 1928–58; revision in 10 volumes, 1958.

Mitchell, B. R. *International Historical Statistics: Africa, Asia & Oceania, 1750–2000.* New York: Palgrave, Macmillan, 2003.

Morris, Richard B., ed. *Encyclopedia of American History.* Rev. and enl. New York: Harper & Row, 1961.

Raines, O. L. *Model of Shenandoah* [scale model of ship]. Museum of the Confederacy, Richmond, Va., 2004.

Websites

Bishop Museum of Cultural and Natural History, Honolulu, Hawaii: www.bishopmuseum.org

Mystic Seaport Museum and Library, Mystic, Conn.: mysticseaport.org

New Bedford Whaling Museum, New Bedford, Mass.: www.whalingmuseum.org

Naval Historical Center, Washington, D.C.: www.history.navy.mil

Acknowledgments

In writing about the *Shenandoah*, I sail in the wake of a full complement of able historians—among them John Bockstoce, George W. Dalzell, Chester G. Hearn, James D. Horan, Murray Morgan, Frank J. Merli, Cyril Pearl, Warren F. Spencer, and Philip Van Doren Stern. More recently, new light has been shed on the commerce raider by D. Alan Harris and Anne B. Harris, editors of a fine annotated edition of the diary of William C. Whittle, Jr., the ship's executive officer; and by Angus Curry, author of an excellent dissertation on the *Shenandoah*'s officers, completed at La Trobe University in Bundoora, Australia. The works of scholars focused more broadly on the Civil War's naval theater and maritime history in general, and various regional specialists also inform this work, among them: William M. Fowler, Arrell Morgan Gibson, Gary W. Gallagher, Raimondo Luraghi, William Marvel, William N. Still, Jr., and Tom Henderson Wells.

Still other historians assisted not only through their writings; they also kindly agreed to read and comment on various chapters of this manuscript. Those generous souls include Suzanne Finney of the University of Hawai'i at Manoa; Stuart Frank of the New Bedford Whaling Museum in New Bedford,

Massachusetts; David Hanlon, Director of the Center for Pacific Islands Studies at the University of Hawai'i at Manoa; Steve Haycox of the University of Alaska in Anchorage; and whaling historian Bob Webb. As much as Blanche DuBois, the historian often depends on the kindness of strangers, and I thank all these fine scholars for taking the time to share their expertise with me.

Still other research professionals—consulting logbooks, ship registries, diaries, letters, and the like—fielded various questions, providing the oakum to plug factual holes in the narrative. Those good Samaritans include Toni Carr of the Virginia Historical Society in Richmond, Virginia; Cara Griggs of the Museum of the Confederacy in Richmond, Virginia; Bob Holcombe and Bruce Smith of the National Civil War Naval Museum in Columbus, Georgia; Gale Munro of the Naval Historical Center in Washington, D.C.; Becky Livingston of the National Archives in Washington, D.C.; and Laura Pereira and Michael Dyer of the New Bedford Whaling Museum. Thanks as well to numerous other staff members at the aforementioned institutions who provided help.

Gratitude is also due the following individuals and research institutions: the Adams National Historical Park in Quincy, Massachusetts; the American Philosophical Society in Philadelphia, Pennsylvania; Susan Lebo of the Bishop Museum in Honolulu; Michael Butzgy; Debbie Vaughan of the Chicago Historical Society; the Library of Congress in Washington; John Coski of the Museum of the Confederacy; Bernard Cox; Teddy Roosevelt biographer Kathleen Dalton; Janie C. Morris of Special Collections at Duke University in Durham, North Carolina; the FDR Library in Hyde Park, New York; Olga Sapina of the Huntington Library in San Marino, California; Steve Burrows of the Commissioners of Irish Lights in Dublin; Robert B. Hitchings and Charlene H. Loope of the Kirn

Memorial Library in Norfolk, Virginia; the La Trobe University Library in Bundoora, Australia; Nick Smith of the National Maritime Museum in Greenwich, England; Anne Gleave of the Merseyside Maritime Museum in Liverpool, England; Paul Cyr of the New Bedford Free Library in New Bedford, Massachusetts; the New York Public Library in Manhattan; the North Carolina State Archives in Raleigh, North Carolina; Ozzie Raines; Ethel Trenholm Seabrook; Father Tom Smith, S.J.; Loli Bann of the Smithsonian Institution in Washington; John Mills Bigham of the South Carolina Confederate Relic Room and Museum in Columbia; the Southern Historical Collection at the University of North Carolina, Chapel Hill; Ann Morgan of the Taylor-Whittle House in Norfolk, Virginia; Mike McKinley of the National Park Service's Tredegar Iron Works Site, Richmond, Virginia; the Library of Virginia in Richmond; Gerard Hayes of the State Library of Victoria in Melbourne, Australia; and Joy Werlink of the Washington State Historical Society Research Center in Tacoma.

For their support, advice, and bonhomie, I thank my friends Dan Carter at the University of South Carolina, Ernie Freeberg of the University of Tennessee, and Jim Ronda of the University of Tulsa. Closer to home, at Emory University, gratitude is due to friends and colleagues Wally Adamson, Teresa Burk, Steve Enniss, Fraser Harbutt, John Juricek, Jana Lonberger, Linda Matthews, Jim Roark, and Susan Socolow. Particular thanks are due my friend Marie Hansen of Woodruff Library's Interlibrary Loan Department, who doggedly tracked down myriad and often obscure documents from all over the world. I'm likewise grateful to the entire staff of Emory's wonderful Woodruff Library—particularly its Circulation, Reference, and Interlibrary Loan departments, and its Manuscript, Archives, and Rare Book Library.

Finally, allow me to express profound gratitude to Kevin

Foster for his essential help on this book. Based in Washington, D.C., Kevin—a superb naval historian—serves as chief of the National Parks Service's National Maritime Heritage Program. As I learned over these past months, Kevin possesses a robust passion for and broad knowledge of all things maritime. Kevin not only encouraged the writing of this book, he shared with me his vast knowledge of seafaring in general and the Civil War's naval theater in particular. Kevin also read and commented on the complete manuscript, doing his best to keep the narrative seaworthy and to warn me away from the often hidden reefs of lubberly diction and assumptions.

At Hill and Wang, I thank assistant editor Kristy McGowan, June Kim, and JoAnna Kremer. In a thousand different ways they kept this project on track, including coordinating the book's illustrations and charts, all the while maintaining their unflappable professionalism and good cheer. I also thank Carol Anderson, who copyedited the manuscript; illustrator Joe LeMonnier, who produced the book's lovely line drawings and charts; Laura Shaw, who designed the elegant book jacket; and the talented Jonathan D. Lippincott, who is responsible for the book's overall design. Gratitude is also due to my agent, Susan Rabiner, for her sage counsel and enthusiastic support of this book.

As a historian, my turf is nineteenth-century America. I'm also the lineal descendant of two Confederate soldiers, one a mere three generations removed from me. Beyond that, I'm the son of a merchant marine midshipman who, during World War II, after a German U-boat sank the SS *Fort Lee*, the tanker on which he was serving, spent two weeks in a lifeboat in the Indian Ocean before being rescued.

Given all that, you'd think that a book on a Confederate Navy cruiser that preyed on her enemy's civilian ships would've been right across the plate for me—an obvious choice of book topic. Alas, this one nearly passed me by.

But, then again, that's one of the things that smart editors do—match up authors with the right book topics. Three years ago, while talking about book ideas with my editor, Thomas LeBien, who also wears the hat of publisher at Hill and Wang, I made a passing reference to the *Shenandoah*.

Never having heard of this ship, he asked me to tell him more. I did, and then we moved on to other topics.

What I didn't see that day was the lightbulb going off in Thomas's head.

He called the next day to ask what I thought about writing a book on the *Shenandoah*—a short book, he suggested, that would precede the longer Civil War book we had already been discussing. I immediately liked the idea and, within weeks, had plunged into the research. But what neither of us knew that day was how rich the sources available for research were.

So I thank Thomas for suggesting this idea. I also thank him for bringing his considerable editorial talents and passion for history to the resultant manuscript—one longer and, I hope, richer than the book we originally imagined. He is, in short, the sort of editor with whom an author gets to work only if he or she is very lucky. More to the point, now that this book, our second together, is finished, I'm counting on that beer that Thomas has been promising me at the Old Town Tavern—one of his favorite watering holes and a sentimental favorite of mine from my own Manhattan days.

On the home front, thanks to Bob Dylan, the Rolling Stones, and Joni Mitchell for perking up the hours of writing. I also thank my canine friend Zoie, not just for the companionship but for reminding me of the joy, from time to time, of straying from the computer and into the clear light of day.

To my wife and best friend Meta Larsson: words cannot convey my gratitude for your encouragement, sound judgment, patience, and the thousand other ways your love has nurtured this book.

Finally, my parents James and Martha Chaffin provided—among their other generosities during my childhood—the books, the love of reading, and the trips to historical sites that stirred my early love of history. More than that, they gave me the encouragement and freedom to dream of becoming a writer. While conducting research for this book, detouring off course into another century, I looked into the sinking of my father's tanker, the SS *Fort Lee* by the German submarine *U-181* on the evening of November 2, 1944. My research was not extensive. But, as I soon learned on visiting my parents, some of what I gleaned was news to my father—and, sadly, not all of it was good: of the four lifeboat parties that escaped the burning tanker, one of them apparently was never heard from again.

The news was sad. But it occasioned one of the best conversations my father and I ever shared. And before I left my parents' house that day, he gave me a cherished possession—his 1943 edition of Nathaniel Bowditch's *American Practical Navigator*, a bible to him and to generations of navigators, reaching back to the presidency of Thomas Jefferson. That volume now occupies an honored place in the bibliography of this work. And it is to both my parents that their decidedly landlubber son, with love and gratitude, dedicates this book.

Index

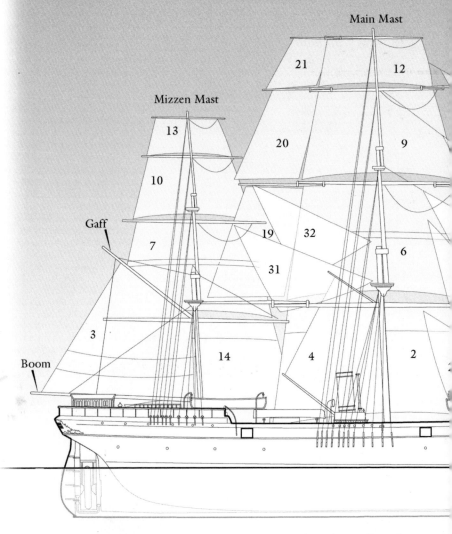

SAIL PLAN OF THE CSS *SHENANDOAH*

Main Mast

Mizzen Mast

Gaff

Boom

21
12
13
20
9
10
19
32
7
6
31
3
14
4
2

1	Foresail	9	Main topgallant sail
2	Mainsail	10	Mizzen topgallant sail
3	Spanker	11	Fore royal
4	Gaff mainsail	12	Main royal
5	Fore topsail	13	Mizzen royal
6	Main topsail	14	Mizzen (square)sail
7	Mizzen topsail	15	Fore studdingsail
8	Fore topgallant sail	16	Fore top stunsail